The
Ministry
in
Historical
Perspectives

The Ministry in Historical Perspectives

Edited by H. RICHARD NIEBUHR and
DANIEL D. WILLIAMS

1817

HARPER & ROW, PUBLISHERS, San Francisco
Cambridge, Hagerstown, New York, Philadelphia
London, Mexico City, São Paulo, Sydney

Chapter X is added for the papercover edition of this book; otherwise
the content is unchanged from the original edition.

THE MINISTRY IN HISTORICAL PERSPECTIVES. Copyright © 1956,
1983 by Harper & Row, Publishers, Inc. All rights reserved. Printed in
the United States of America. No part of this book may be used or
reproduced in any manner whatsoever without written permission
except in the case of brief quotations embodied in critical articles and
reviews. For information address Harper & Row, Publishers, Inc., 10
East 53rd Street, New York, NY 10022. Published simultaneously in
Canada by Fitzhenry & Whiteside, Limited, Toronto.

FIRST HARPER & ROW PAPERBACK EDITION

Library of Congress Cataloging in Publication Data
Main entry under title:

THE MINISTRY IN HISTORICAL PERSPECTIVES.

    (Harper's ministers paperback library)
    1. Clergy—History—Addresses, essays, lectures.   I. Niebuhr,
H. Richard (Helmut Richard), 1894-1962.   II. Williams, Daniel Day,
1910-1973.   III. Ahlstrom, Sydney E.   IV. Series.
BV660.2.M535   1981   262'.1'09   80-8899
ISBN 0-06-066232-8   AACR2

83 84 85 86 87 10 9 8 7 6 5 4 3 2 1

Contents

CONTRIBUTORS

SYDNEY E. AHLSTROM, *Professor of American Religious History, Yale University*

ROLAND H. BAINTON, *Professor of Church History, Yale Divinity School*

EDWARD ROCHIE HARDY, *Professor of Church History, Berkeley Divinity School*

WINTHROP S. HUDSON, *Professor of Church History, Colgate-Rochester Divinity School*

JOHN KNOX, *Professor of New Testament, Union Theological Seminary, New York*

SIDNEY E. MEAD, *Professor of American Church History, Federated Theological Faculty, University of Chicago*

ROBERT S. MICHAELSEN, *Dean, School of Religion, Iowa University*

WILHELM PAUCK, *Professor of Church History and Historical Theology, Union Theological Seminary, New York*

GEORGE H. WILLIAMS, *Professor of Church History, Harvard Divinity School*

Introduction

The authors of this study of the Christian ministry in its historical development were enlisted for the project by the directors of the survey of theological education in the United States and Canada which was undertaken in 1954 under the sponsorship of the American Association of Theological Schools.* In the effort to appraise the present needs of the church and its ministry, and to understand what new demands are made today upon theological education, our attention was inevitably drawn toward a review of what the ministry has been, the forces which have shaped its forms and practice, and to the asking of some new questions which present experience raises concerning the ways in which the church and its ministry can cope with their fundamental task in the world. Very little has been done to give an overall account of the functions of the ministry, seen in the context of the forces which shape the church and which in turn are challenged and modified by the church's life. There are innumerable studies of the *doctrine* of the ministry; but few if any of the kind here undertaken in modest scope.

It was therefore a source of especial satisfaction to the survey team when these church historians agreed to write the book here presented as an integral part of the report of the survey.

The aim of the writers was not simply a chronological account of the ministry in various periods, but a symposium in which a variety of viewpoints on the meaning of the historical development would be presented. In pursuit of this goal the book was planned in group discussion, outlines were reviewed, and first drafts of the chapters circulated for criticism. Each author was of course free to develop his own material and state his own conclusions, and each is alone responsible for the statements in his contribution. Since the writers represent several Christian communions their judgments reflect both a command of the historical data and the enrichment which comes from somewhat different perspectives upon the nature of the ministry. Thus Dr. Pauck's interpretation of the significance of preaching in the Protestant Reformation

* Members of the survey staff are H. Richard Niebuhr, director; Daniel D. Williams, associate director; and James M. Gustafson, assistant director.

arises from an inner appreciation analogous to that with which Dr. Hardy views the significance of the priesthood in the Anglican tradition. Dr. Hardy and Dr. Hudson examine the church in the Puritan period from somewhat different though in the end remarkably congenial attitudes. Dr. Mead and Dr. Michaelsen give their accounts of the American development from points of view which have been developed through their own close attention to the special features of American church life.

The phrase "historical perspectives" serves further to acknowledge the necessarily restricted scope of this study. Not only would each writer plead the limitations of space in dealing with his topic; but the volume as a whole becomes more selective in its attention as it moves from the ancient church to the present. After the study of the biblical and patristic periods attention is given primarily to the churches in the West. The Protestant Reformation on the Continent and in Great Britain is dealt with along with some attention to Catholic ministries in the modern period. The last two chapters consider only the churches in the United States and are concerned largely with Protestantism. Thus the account obviously neglects the Eastern Churches, modern Roman Catholicism, and Protestant as well as other communions outside the United States in the modern period. The stimulation of further attention to the history of these ministries is hoped for as one result of what has been done here.

In the discussions preceding the writing it became clear that certain fundamental themes concerning the ministry would challenge each writer's attention. Without presuming to summarize the many insights reached in the following chapters we may briefly anticipate some of these dominant themes.

First, there is the astonishing adaptability and variety of the ministerial office along with the maintenance of its unity of purpose and dedication. The very word "minister" poses the problem of the variety while it affirms the underlying unity. As the New Testament word for "servant" it has its origin in Jesus' mission as expressed in the statement "The Son of Man came not to be ministered unto but to minister." Yet the word "minister" is only one among the many which designate the church's ordained and appointed leadership. "Minister" belongs peculiarly to the Reformed tradition in contrast to "priest" in the Catholic and Anglican traditions, and "pastor" in the Lutheran and many other protestant churches. Yet all these names pass back and forth through the traditions and become useful in many ecclesiastical vocabularies.

The orders of ministry display an intricate variety and complexity of titles from subdeacon to bishop. To these must be added the ministerial functions: teacher, chaplain, missionary, evangelist, counselor, and, in our day of complex church organizations, secretaries and directors of councils of churches, social action commissions and countless others. The plethora of offices exhibits the capacity of the church to adjust to new demands, and yet to hold to the core of universal loyalty and function implied in all ministry whatever the differences in interpretation of the significance of the office.

Certain functions upon which the church depends have always been laid upon the ministry: responsibility for the church's liturgical and sacramental life, the preaching of the gospel to the church and to the world, teaching, being a pastor to the flock, and responsibility for administering the church's affairs. Though there are different interpretations of ordination and radically diverse views of the nature of the ministry, we cannot fail to recognize authentic accents of ministerial authority and service in the many types of ministry here described. Universal elements in Christian experience stand forth in the bishop's sermon referred to by Dr. Williams which encourages an ancient congregation with the image of the church as the ship which bears life to a safe haven, or in Thomas Fuller's tribute to William Perkins quoted by Dr. Hudson, "an excellent surgeon at the jointing of a broken soul and at stating of a doubtful conscience," or in Frank Weston's address to the Anglo-Catholic congress quoted by Dr. Hardy: "You cannot claim to worship Jesus in the tabernacle if you do not pity Jesus in the slum." Human frailties, the variety of human talents, social and economic forces, considerations of status and prestige, heroism and devotion all have played their part; but the history would be unintelligible without the realization that the spirit of the "Servant" has been remembered and honored, and that it lends a thread of unity to the whole.

A second theme arises from the distinction between clergy and laity which has been a source of creative tension and of conflict. Inevitably the ministers appear as the guardians of the church's order and tradition who must instruct, persuade, rebuke, and convert a sometimes unruly and religiously illiterate laity. Even where the theory of a particular communion has been strongly against special privilege or status for the clergy, in practice the ministers have often retained primary responsibility and initiative as the "speaking aristocracy in the face of a silent democracy" which calls the church back to its mission in the time of reformation and decision.

A third theme counterbalances the one just stated, for the history shows how the church as a whole and the laity in particular have sought to provide checks upon ministerial power. Just because that power is so greatly reinforced by the sanctity of the office, the common sense of the church has often asserted the necessity for safeguards against its abuse. There are of course the charlatans who exploit or counterfeit the gifts of the spirit; and the church has had to devise protections against them. But even the most responsible ministries may find themselves confronting the distrust or wariness of citizenry and laity. In Calvin's Geneva, for example, we see the suspicion of too much political power in clerical hands, and at the same time the insistence of ministers and church alike upon the precious freedom of the pulpit.

In the fourth place, light is thrown upon present issues in theological education by the discovery that the drawing of too sharp a line between the preaching, priestly, and teaching offices does violence to what the ministry has actually been. Where preaching has sometimes been exalted as the central act in which the preacher becomes "ambassador to God and destiny" in John Donne's phrase, pastoral care and the approach to God in prayer and sacrament have yet been acknowledged as essential to the service for which the minister is called. And though in some times and places the sacramental office of the priest has seemed to be his sole service, yet the church in that same time has been awakened by the preaching which summons whole generations to repentance and faith. In our day theological schools have as a major concern their responsibility for a ministry which recognizes the full dimensions of the Christian community. It is dangerous to think of the church's life in the narrow terms of any one function however meritorious in itself it may be.

We have suggested some of the broad conclusions which are elaborated and supported in these chapters. It was neither intended nor expected that the history here written should lead to prophecy. Specific directives for answering present-day problems may rarely be derived from the past alone; but it may be more important to realize the power of the church to preserve its worship and witness while it discovers new forms through which it can cope with a shifting and perplexing world. The church must not be passive to the forces which play upon it, nor can it afford to live by the sheer inertia of traditional conceptions of the ministerial office. In the search today for a more adequate theological education a discernment of the richness, originality, and flexibility of the church's provision for its leadership may prove of especial significance.

In the last chapter Dr. Michaelsen describes some recent developments in the kind of demands which the minister in the American churches finds himself having to meet. He must be administrator, preacher, priest, and pastor in the complex life of a community, and perform the original and sacred duties of his calling in a setting which requires of him new strategies, skills, and insights. As he goes about his work he and his congregation will share a deeper understanding of the church's task through knowledge of the history of the ministry in its strength and weakness; and they will take courage in this splendid heritage of spiritual power and devotion.

This volume and the survey of theological education were made possible by a generous grant from the Carnegie Corporation. It should be said that the Carnegie Corporation is not the author, owner, publisher, or proprietor of this or other publications issued by the staff of the *Study of Theological Education in the United States and Canada,* and is not to be understood as approving by virtue of its grant any of the statements made or views expressed therein.

The thanks of the editors must be given to their colleague, James Gustafson, for invaluable assistance and to Mrs. Fleur Ferm, Mrs. Miriam Smith, and Mrs. June Gerrish for efficient service in the preparation of the manuscript.

It remains only for the editors to express to the writers their gratitude for loyal co-operation, and their sense of personal reward in the learning which came from the discussions we had together.

THE EDITORS

July 29, 1956

The
Ministry
in
Historical
Perspectives

I

The Ministry in the Primitive Church

JOHN KNOX

The Greek word for "ministry" is *diakonia;* and it is significant that this term was in New Testament times, as it is still, the most favored way of referring inclusively to the church's workers and their work. When Paul gives us the first account we possess of the various functions being performed by individuals in the primitive church (I Cor. 12:4-30), he speaks of them as "varieties of ministry." He can refer to himself and to other workers as "ministers" of the new covenant, or of Christ, or of God, or of the church, or of the gospel, or simply as "ministers," and to their work as a "ministry of reconciliation." (II Cor. 3:6, 11:23; Col. 1:7, 25, 4:7; II Cor. 5:18; etc.) The letter to the Ephesians, probably a generation later, in summing up the significance of "apostles," "prophets," "evangelists," "pastors and teachers," uses the same word: "for the work of the ministry." In Acts the apostolate itself is referred to as a *diakonia* (Acts 1:17; cf. Eph. 4:11-12). The word, whether in Greek or English, means simply "service;" and although it soon came to stand for a particular ecclesiastical office, the office of the deacon, its original more inclusive sense was never completely lost. Thus "Timothy" is enjoined to appoint "ministers" (in the sense of deacons) and to fulfill his own "ministry" in the other, more general, sense; and the same writer, the author of the Pastoral Epistles, can both describe the qualifications of the "deacons" and allude to the *diakonia* of Paul (I Tim. 1:12, 3:8, 12, 4:6; II Tim. 4:5). Thus also, even today, if we wish a term which includes the archbishop as well as the pastor of the humblest congregation, we speak of "the ministry." And so, in word at least, we obey Jesus' injunction: "Whoever would be great among you must be your servant [*diakonos*], and whoever would be first among you must be the slave of all" (Mark 10:43-44).

In ancient usage *diakonos* primarily meant "waiter," and there are those who find the origins of the Christian ministry in the exigencies of the common meal. The "deacons" were waiters, and since there would have needed to be a "head-waiter," [1] the office of the bishop would always have existed, by whatever name it was called. This is only one of many possible theories about the beginnings of the orders of the early ministry—a matter to be discussed later—but the basic meaning of the term will remind us of how realistically the idea of service was taken in the primitive church and how humble and unpretentious were its first ministers. The Christian worker is also often described in the New Testament as a "slave" (*doulos*). Paul and others can call themselves "slaves" of Christ. But the emphasis of this term is primarily upon a status or relationship—the slave is the property of his master, belongs utterly to him—whereas *diakonos* denotes not primarily a status (although this may be implied), but a function, the function of useful service. A minister (*diakonos*) of Christ is useful to Christ, assisting in the fulfillment of Christ's purposes in the world. A minister of the church is useful to the church, serving its members in all possible ways and contributing to the growth and effective functioning of the church itself. A minister of the gospel is useful to the gospel, making known the good news of what God had done in Christ so that the gospel may reach those for whom it is intended and may have its true fruits.

In the course of this book we shall be dealing with many kinds of ministry and with many divergent, and often conflicting, conceptions of its nature and significance. We shall better keep our bearings among all the diversities and changes of this history if we remember that the word "ministry" serves, not only to designate the full number of the church's leaders, but also to designate the true meaning of Christian leadership, the essential character which both qualifies and unites all true leaders of the church—unites them with one another and with Christ, who "came not to be ministered unto, but to minister, and to give his life a ransom for many" (Mark 10:45).

I

Anyone who attempts to give an account of the organization of the ministry in the primitive church and of the various functions it performed must almost necessarily begin with an acknowledgment of the difficulties which beset his undertaking. These difficulties are so grave, and with our present resources so definitely insurmountable, that a clear picture of the early ministry is simply beyond our reach. This is true partly because of the meagerness of our sources. If by the "primitive church" we mean the church of the first century and the first quarter, say, of the second—and such a period represents the approximate range of this chapter—we have at most only the New Testament documents and some of the Apostolic Fathers; and none of these documents is concerned to set forth in any full or systematic way the constitution of the church or the methods of its work. Later writings, particularly manuals of church order, undoubtedly have something to tell us about earlier practices, but they do not throw any strong or steady light into the shadows of the Apostolic Age. Any reconstruction of the primitive church's ministry—as indeed of any other phase of its outward life—must rest upon what are regarded as the implications of a very few scattered passages in a very meager literature. The New Testament documents are rich indeed in indications of the concrete nature, the quality, the "feel" of the early Christian life itself, but are, for the most part, silent concerning the forms of organization and procedure which prevailed. One may account for this virtual silence by saying either that the writers did not regard such forms as important or that they took them for granted; but the silence itself is undeniable.

The problem is further complicated by the fact that even where an early writer speaks of the ministry, one often cannot be sure what part of the church he speaks for or what period in its development he represents. Paul gives us in I Cor. 12 what is undoubtedly one of our earliest glimpses of the kinds of ministry being exercised in the primitive church. But how representative is this picture? We can certainly rely on it as being, as far as it goes, a true picture of what was happening in the church at Corinth, and his formula, "God has appointed in the church," at least suggests that the same general picture applies to other Pauline communities. But to what extent does it apply to the rest of the primitive church, and were there not, in all probability, significant differences even among the Pauline churches? As for Acts, the Gospels, the Pastorals, the *Didache,* and other later sources, considerations chronological as well as geographical, must enter into our evaluation of the hints about early church order which they contain. The book of Acts, for example, because it was written late in the first century or early in the second, has much to tell us about the Christianity of that period; but because it is undoubtedly partly based on much older sources, it also tells us much about the most primitive church. But can we surely discriminate one element from the other? Even if we could, the question would remain how widely prevalent any given feature of the church may have been, whether in the earlier or the later period. The fact of the matter is not only that the church of the New Testament period was in a state of rapid development, but also that the lines or directions of this development were not the same in every part of the church; and even where the general pattern was identical, the growth was not proceeding everywhere at the same rate.

The fact that both chronological and geographical considerations are involved at almost every point in the study of the early ministry poses a problem as to method. Shall we center our attention primarily upon geographical areas or upon chronological periods? There are advantages—and the constant danger of overfacile generalization—in each method; and we can hardly follow either consistently. We shall be moving, in a general way, from the earlier to the later part of our period, but we must remember constantly to distinguish between what we can know about one church at one time and what we can only guess about another church at the same time or even about the same church at an earlier or later stage in its development.

II

Fortunately we can begin with some assurance. There may be some doubt about the origins of the apostolate, but there can be none that the apostles were the spiritual leaders of the primitive church. The apostles were the church's first ministers—"first" both in the sense of earliest and in the sense of most responsible and most revered. This is obviously the view of the author of Luke-Acts; it is clearly implied in many sayings in the Gospels; and Paul, our earliest source, puts it beyond question. Not only does he take for granted the authority of the apostle and vigorously defend his own apostleship, but he quite explicitly affirms the primacy of the apostle among the servants of the church: "And God has appointed in the church first apostles . . ." (I Cor. 12:28). It is perhaps too obvious to need pointing out, but these evidences of the status of the apostle only confirm what on more general grounds would have been expected in any case. If by "apostle" is meant one who was called to his work by Jesus Christ himself (either during the human career or immediately after the resurrection), it was inevitable that such persons should have come to hold positions of largest responsibility and authority among the primitive churches.

To be sure, there are those who challenge this definition of the term "apostle." The word, of course, means "one sent out," usually as an ambassador, the authorized messenger, of an individual or group. So it was used among both Jews and Greeks. It could, then, have the simple meaning of "missionary" and apply to most, if not all, of the traveling evangelists of the early church. That meaning of the term is found in the *Didache*, once in Acts, and several times in Paul (*Didache* 11:3-6; Acts 14:4, 14; II Cor. 8:23; Phil. 2:25, and, possibly I Thess. 2:6 and Rom. 16:7). It is often said that this was the earlier meaning of the term, and that the more restricted use to designate persons standing in a unique relation to the original event in Palestine was a later development. But the evidence for this view is unconvincing. It is true that Acts, one of the later books, ordinarily uses the word in the narrower sense; but this same document can, as we have just seen, employ it with the other meaning also. On the other hand, the *Didache*, which adopts the broader sense and seems to use the terms "apostle" and "prophet" interchangeably, can scarcely be regarded as a primitive document. The use of the term by Paul is, in this respect, very much like Luke's later usage. He occasionally may employ it in the broad common sense of messenger; but he normally ascribes to it a sense as exalted and particular as Luke does, although he would certainly not identify the apostles in just the same way. Luke identifies them with the twelve, or perhaps with the twelve and James the brother of Jesus. Paul only once (if indeed then)[2] refers to the twelve and it is quite impossible to say just whom he thought of as apostles except that he and Peter and probably James were among them. But for Paul, no less than for Luke, the apostolic group was both definite and closed. In a word, there may have been differences of opinion among the early Christians as to just who the apostles were; but there are many indications that from the very beginning the term designated a special and restricted class—eyewitnesses of the event itself, commissioned as his ambassadors by Jesus Christ in a unique sense. If this was not true, there ceases to be any discoverable ground for the primacy of the apostle.

If we cannot know how many apostles there were, we certainly cannot speak with any assurance of the areas in which they severally served. A few centuries later we find accounts of a primitive division of the world among the apostles—Thomas going to India or Parthia and others of the twelve to other districts, very much in the manner in which in the third or fourth century bishops might be appointed for various unevangelized territories. Such stories are late and obviously legendary, but it is noteworthy that in one of our most primitive and most authentic sources, the letter to the Galatians, there is also an account of a division of responsibility among the apostles. Paul tells us that when the leaders of the church at Jerusalem (the "pillars") saw that he "had been en-

trusted with the gospel to the uncircumcised, just as Peter had been
entrusted with the gospel to the circumcised (for he who worked through
Peter for the mission to the circumcised worked through [him] also for
the Gentiles)," they gave him and his associate Barnabas "the right hand
of fellowship," that he (with Barnabas) "should go to the Gentiles and
they to the circumcised" (Gal. 2:7-9). How this passage should be
interpreted in detail is far from clear. Are Paul and Peter the only
apostles—or are they at least "apostles" in a quite special sense—and is
the entire "world" being divided between them? Other passages in Paul
can be cited as indicating that he thought of himself as *the* apostle to the
Gentiles. On the other hand, Paul can speak of "those who were apostles
before me," indicating that he knew of a number of other "apostles," at
least to the Jews (Gal. 1:17). He tells how, on the occasion of his first
visit to Jerusalem after his conversion, he visited Cephas but "saw none
of the other apostles except James the Lord's brother" (Gal. 1:8-19).
This phrase, while it does not require, strongly suggests, that he thought
of James as an apostle; but it clearly requires the presupposition that he
knew of other apostles besides himself, Peter, and James. Did he fail to
see "other apostles" because it happened so or because he made an effort
not to see them, or was it because they were carrying on the work of
evangelists outside of Jerusalem? If so, where? And among Jews or
Gentiles? Was the "John" who is named as one of the "pillars" also an
"apostle"? If there was a grand division of leadership in the church's
mission as between Paul and Peter, was the division defined on racial
or geographical lines? And in what relation do James and John, the
other "pillars," and especially James, stand to Peter's mission? These are
questions to which no certain answers can be given; but division of
responsibility of some kind is clearly indicated.

This indication of the pregnant but perplexing passage in Galatians
is confirmed by the many signs that Paul was aware of himself as having,
under Christ, the highest responsibility and authority in a definite section of the church. This section is not clearly defined and was probably
not definable in strictly geographical terms. It clearly included many
churches which had been established by him and his associates around
the Aegean and eastward as far as Galatia. Are we to interpret the letter
to the Romans as an effort to make contact with a Gentile church which
properly belonged to his jurisdiction but which he had not founded or
yet had an opportunity to visit?[3] This is not unlikely, but whether Paul
thought of all predominantly Gentile churches as belonging to his
"diocese" or not, one cannot doubt the existence of the "diocese" itself

(although it is clear that some apostles or professed apostles did not acknowledge his jurisdiction). He tells of his resolution not to "build on another man's foundation," thus not only intimating his sense of a certain authority among his own churches, but also clearly indicating the fact that others also were laying "foundations"—though just who they were and where they were working we are not told. It is not improbable that some of these "foundations" lay within the geographical area where Paul chiefly worked.

The book of Acts seems to associate the "apostles" particularly with Judea, and one gets the impression that, instead of severally exercising authority in various areas, they constituted a kind of council located in Jerusalem, an apostolate which corporately ruled the church in its totality. Although this picture must be suspected as being in part the product of the interest of the author of Acts in promoting the unity of the church in his own period, nevertheless Paul's words in Gal. 1:17-19 in a measure confirm it, at least as regards the concentration of apostles in Jerusalem. He tells us that after his conversion and call he did not "go up to Jerusalem" to see those who had been "apostles before [him]," thus implying that one went especially to Jerusalem to see "apostles"; and though on a later visit to that city he saw only Peter and James, his very denial that he saw "any other apostle" suggests that he might have been expected to meet more than a few of them there.

As for the work of the apostle and the relationship he sustained with the churches, we must depend almost entirely on the letters of Paul—and this mean that we can know very little except about Paul's own apostleship. The very term suggests—what all our data confirm—that the apostle was an itinerant evangelist. Paul not only gives such a picture of himself, but he seems to imply it of "the other apostles" also (I Cor. 9:5). Their primary function was the preaching of the gospel, the proclamation of the event in Palestine with which God was bringing history to a close, the bearing witness to the new creation in Christ, the calling of men to repentance; but this meant the establishing of churches, and implied the duty and authority of supervision. We can see Paul in his letters performing this duty and exercising this prerogative. Hans von Campenhausen in his recent book [4] makes much of the respect Paul shows for the integrity and freedom of his churches, pointing out that his directions to them are more likely to be exhortations than commands. This is true; and in a measure this attitude reflects a fundamental conception of Paul—namely, that the church is greater than any apostle or than all the apostles together. These are servants of the church, not its masters. They belong to the church; not the church to them. But the recognition of such facts as these must not obscure Paul's sense of apostolic authority: "God has appointed in the church first apostles." Paul may, as he says in Philemon (vvs. 8-10), "prefer to appeal" in the name of love; but he does not fail to make clear that in doing so he is voluntarily relinquishing a right "to command" of which as an apostle he is deeply conscious and which he expects his churches to acknowledge.

Paul lets us see in his letters not a little of what was involved in this supervisory role of the apostle. It meant, at least for him, a good deal of anxiety and activity. The final and climactic item in a long catalogue of his sufferings as an apostle is his "care of all the churches" (II Cor. 11:28). He sought to keep in constant, or at least frequent, touch with them. He visited them as often as he was able (and there is no way of reconstructing, even approximately, the itinerary of his movements back and forth, to and fro, among his churches). More often perhaps he sent one of his assistants, men like Timothy, Titus, Silvanus, Epaphras, and others. And frequently, as we have even better reason to know, he wrote letters. Such communication moved in both directions: Epaphroditus, Stephanas, Fortunatus, and Achaicus, who visited Paul as representatives of congregations, figure as prominently in Paul's correspondence as some of his own assistants and agents; and he received letters as well as sending them (I Cor. 7:1). Merely to name the matters on which he was called upon to express an opinion or pass a judgment is to be reminded of the complexity and the difficulty of this administrative or pastoral phase of the apostle's task. He might be called on—at any rate, *Paul* was called on—to settle a moral question, as about sexual relations, or divorce, or the propriety of a marriage between a Christian and a pagan, or to give counsel about the disciplining of a member; to compose a quarrel between two Christians; to ward off a threatened schism; to correct disorders in worship; to clarify, or confirm, or apply some tradition he had already transmitted; to deal with differences of opinion among the members of a church about the eating of food consecrated by pagan rites or with similar scruples; to handle the delicate matter of master-slave relations within a church; to supervise the raising of a large sum of money among a number of churches; to pacify a congregation morbidly excited by apocalyptic expectations—in a word, to apply Christian conscience and common sense to a wide range of practical problems, great and small.

It would be a mistake to suppose that Paul's situation was exactly matched by that of any other apostle. Paul lets us know very emphatically of one difference between him and others. The apostles generally were supported by the churches—we have no way of knowing whether through some regular arrangement or through occasional gifts —whereas he supported himself by his trade. He informs us, too, that some of the apostles were married and that their wives often accompanied them on their travels, whereas this was certainly not true of Paul. Although full allowance must be made for such differences and for the unique genius and convictions of Paul, nevertheless in the absence of other evidence we are justified in assuming that the general pattern of the relations of other apostles with other churches and of the functions they performed was basically the same. The itinerant character of other apostleships we have already had occasion to notice, and the reference to those who "came from James" in Gal. 2:12 suggests that others besides Paul made use of traveling representatives. Although there were undoubtedly important differences of opinion among them— in Gal. 2:11-14 we can actually see some of these differences among Paul, Peter, and James—there were also large areas of agreement; and these traveling evangelists and chief pastors, accepted as standing uniquely close to the revealing event and therefore as having a unique personal authority, constituted a very important binding element among the churches of the first century, geographically so widely scattered and culturally so diverse.

III

We began our consideration of the "apostle" with Paul's affirmation that "God has appointed in the church first apostles," and we may appropriately begin our discussion of other ministries in the early church by reminding ourselves of the rest of his statement: ". . . second prophets, third teachers, then workers of miracles, then healers, helpers, administrators, speakers in various kinds of tongues" (I Cor. 12:28). With this passage should be placed the allusion in Phil. 1:1 to "bishops and deacons" and also what we find in Rom. 12:6-8: "Having gifts that differ according to the grace given to us, let us use them: if prophecy, in proportion to our faith; if service, in our serving; he who teaches, in his teaching; he who exhorts, in his exhortation; he who contributes, in liberality; he who presides, with zeal; he who does acts of mercy, with cheerfulness." [5] If we may take these statements as indicating the way the ministry was composed in the churches with which Paul was familiar, what are we to make of them?

Sometimes a distinction is drawn between the "charismatic" ("Spirit-given") ministry in the early church and the "institutional" ministry. But if such a distinction was made by others in the primitive period—which seems rather dubious—it certainly was not made by Paul. The ministry was in every part charismatic; and if by "institutional" one can mean "contributing to the growth and orderly functioning of the church," it was also in every part institutional. To be sure, Paul refers to the "bishops and deacons" at Philippi—and these terms suggest an "institutional" ministry—but one must not make the mistake of identifying these with the formally elected or appointed, the ordained, officials of a later period. The "bishops and deacons" are those members of the Philippian church who have proved to have administrative gifts—gifts of wisdom, efficiency, and tact, some in planning and oversight (the "bishops" or rulers), others in actually performing the various particular tasks belonging to what may be called the "business" of the congregation (the "deacons" or helpers). It is altogether probable, as has frequently been pointed out, that they are specifically addressed in this particular letter because Paul has just received the gift of money from the Philippian church which these administrators and workers have been largely responsible for raising and sending. It is quite possible that Paul is not making here a distinction between two classes of persons at all, but between two functions which the same persons may perform. The "overseers" serve, and the "servers" oversee. In I Cor. 16:15-16 Paul directs the Corinthian church to "be subject" to "the household of Stephanas" who have "devoted themselves to the service [diakonia] of the saints" and to those who work with them. Was Stephanas one of the "bishops" or one of the "deacons"? Perhaps both; or both at different times. We are not dealing with formal offices, but with functions for which persons were as certainly spiritually endowed as for prophecy or healing. Indeed, the "deacons" and "bishops" of Philippians are almost certainly to be identified with the "helpers" and the "administrators" of I Cor. 12:28 and with the helpers of several kinds and the "presidents" who are mentioned in Rom. 12:6-8; and it is scarcely open to question that Paul thinks of these persons as being "gifted" as certainly, and in the same sense, as the "prophets" and "teachers," not to speak of the workers of miracles and the speakers with tongues. In I Cor. 12:28 they are mentioned, indeed, between the healers and the ecstatics. What could more clearly indicate that Paul thinks of them as exercising a "charismatic" function? The same meaning is no doubt to be seen in the fact that the administrators (or bishops) are mentioned only after the helpers (or deacons) in the same passage, and that in Rom. 12:6-8 the "presidents" are placed between two classes of helpers—those who contribute and those who show mercy. There are no distinctions of "inferior" and "superior" among these workers in the churches. They are all recipients and agents of the same Spirit; and whether some of them always exercised the one kind of function or the other (that is, superintending or helping), or whether all of them at certain times exercised both functions, they were equally members of the body of Christ, equally indispensable to its proper and effective functioning, and therefore equally significant.

As to the kind of "business" which needed to be planned and carried through, our sources tell us little in detail; but what we know about organized social life of any kind in any period, as well as what knowledge we have of the situation of the primitive churches, will enable us to fill out the picture to some extent. It is obvious that a local congregation, meeting often for worship and the common meal, would meet for other purposes as well. The question of whether the service of "the Word" and the *agape* (and Eucharist) were two services or one, or whether different usages in this respect prevailed in different churches can be left open. We can also leave unanswered the question whether meetings for "other purposes" were held in connection with meetings for worship and fellowship, or were specially called; probably both patterns were followed. But there can be no doubt that such meetings took place and that their purposes were manifold. Decisions had to be made from time to time as to where or when services of the church would be held; the church needed to be told of the impending visit of an apostle, or of some prophet or teacher from abroad; a question has been raised as to the good faith of one of these visitors, and there must be some discussion of the point and a decision on it; a fellow Christian from another church is on a journey and needs hospitality; a member of the local congregation planning to visit a church abroad needs a letter of introduction to that church, which someone must be authorized to provide; a serious dispute about property rights or some other legal matter has arisen between two of the brothers and the church must name someone to help them settle the issue or must in some other way deal with it; a new local magistrate has begun to prosecute Christians for violating the law against unlicensed assembly, and consideration must be given to ways and means of meeting this crisis; charges have been brought against one of the members by another member, and these must be investigated and perhaps some disciplinary action taken; one of the members has died, and the church is called on for some special action in behalf of his family in the emergency; differences of opinion exist in the church on certain questions of morals or belief (such as marriage and divorce, or the resurrection), differences which local prophets and teachers are apparently unable to compose, and a letter must be written to the apostle—who will write this letter and what exactly will it say?

These are special or occasional concerns, and it is obvious that the list might go on almost indefinitely. There were also more regular administrative operations. Sick persons needed to be visited and the bread and wine of the Eucharist brought to them, along with what financial help they might need. The poor generally, especially the aged and the widows and the orphans, must be assisted. Certain persons who were giving full time to the work of the church and who had no other means of support—perhaps an apostle or one of his associates, perhaps a local prophet, teacher, administrator, or other worker—must be sustained. Such dispensations of help to the needy of various kinds required congregational funds, and such funds involved planning, soliciting, collecting. As individuals demonstrated their ability to administer such matters, they would more and more be relied on; but the congregation as a whole would be expected to determine policy at every point and often, no doubt, would be called on to make *ad hoc* decisions in questionable cases.

We are likely to suppose that the administrative work required in a first-century church was much more simple than in a modern congregation of the same size. But this supposition is probably mistaken. When a first-century Jew or pagan decided to become a Christian, he became dependent upon a new community for the supplying of all his needs in a way which the modern Christian, at any rate within the West, can scarcely imagine. The church had to assume almost total responsibility for the whole person of its members and for every aspect of their relations with one another. In even the smallest congregation in even the earliest period every one of the concerns we have mentioned (and obviously we have not begun to exhaust the possibilities) would arise; and as congregations grew larger, as they rapidly did, the "business" of the church would become correspondingly more difficult and complex. When we remember that congregational meetings had to be planned, called, and conducted, and that their actions must be recorded, communicated to those concerned, and actually implemented and carried out, we shall hardly wonder either that there should have been from the very beginning, and in great variety, "helps" and "governments," as the King James Version translates the terms in I Cor. 12:28, or that the offices of "bishop" and "deacon" became so important in the church of a somewhat later period.

IV

But for all the importance of this core of workers in the primitive local church, they did not hold first place in its regard. Paul, although he apparently refuses to make a distinction of rank between the "helpers" and the "overseers," specifically says (after mentioning the apostles), ". . . second prophets, third teachers" (I Cor. 12:28). The priority of prophecy in Paul's estimation is also indicated in I Cor. 14:1, where he urges his readers earnestly to desire the spiritual gifts, "especially" that of prophecy. Fifty years or so later, the *Didache,* the earliest manual of church order that we have, also clearly ascribes first place among the servants of the church to the prophets and teachers, although the writer knows the offices of bishops and deacons as well (15:1-2). And the writer of Acts tells us that it was "prophets and teachers" of Antioch who determined that Paul and Barnabas should undertake a mission to Cyprus and who "laid hands on them and sent them off" (13:1-3). This account of the origin of Paul's apostleship must, in the light of Gal. 1:1-2:10, be rejected, but the reference to the presence and authority of "prophets and teachers" at Antioch is in line with Paul's own words and with the much later testimony of the *Didache.*

Who, or what, were these "prophets" and "teachers"? Again, as in the case of the early "bishops" and "deacons," we may ask whether the terms always designate two distinct classes of person, or whether a distinction in function is primarily indicated. The term "prophet" suggests the "numinous"—visions, revelations, being in "the Spirit," initiation into divine secrets, and the like. The prophet, endowed with this ecstatic character and given access to these sacred mysteries, reports his experiences and interprets their meaning, as far as he is able, to the congregation. But most important in his message, as in that of the teacher also, would always be the good news of God's action in Christ, the event of Christ's advent, life, death, and resurrection, which had so recently occurred—which indeed was still occurring, for the coming of the Spirit was a part of the event and Christ was soon to come again to bring to fulfillment what had been begun. The prophet would not only be fully persuaded of the event and acutely aware of its implications, but he would be an unusually sensitive participant in the new common life which had issued from it. He would also be extraordinarily capable of communicating the concrete meaning of the new life, the life of the Spirit, to others and of making articulate for them their inmost and deepest yearnings and satisfactions. The prophet was able to speak in such a way as that the believer would want to say "Amen"; and the unbeliever would find himself "convicted," "called to account," the "secrets of his heart . . . disclosed" so that "falling on his face" he would "worship God" and "declare that God was really present" (I Cor. 14:16, 25). The *Didache* calls the prophet the "high priest" of the church; and it is altogether likely that the conduct of worship and the presiding at the Eucharist were from the beginning committed to one or another of the prophets.

The word "teacher" suggests instruction in the more ordinary sense, a setting forth, perhaps in somewhat more objective fashion, of the facts of the tradition and the truth of the gospel, the inculcation of true beliefs, the encouraging of appropriate ethical impulses and conduct. The epistles of the New Testament show us the teacher at work. In them, for the most part, the good news is taken for granted, and instruction is being given in some of its implications—theological and ethical. The fact that Jesus is characteristically known as a teacher must reflect, not only the original facts, but also, in some degree, the importance of the teacher's role in primitive Christianity; and indeed the preservation and development of the gospel tradition of Jesus' words must have been largely the work of the early teachers.

But the line between prophet and teacher in the primitive church is not easy to draw: the prophet would often have been—indeed, how could he have helped being?—also the teacher; and the teacher would often have been the prophet. It is likely that since the more ecstatic endowment of the prophet would have seemed more exalted, the teacher who possessed it would usually have been called a prophet;[6] but even he would probably have found it impossible to distinguish between his "prophecy" and his "teaching." Both were inspired by the same Spirit and both were concerned only with the truth and relevance of the gospel.

This virtual identity—or at least extensive overlapping—of function is indicated in the way Paul actually describes prophecy and the prophet.

In I Cor. 14:1 ff. he is concerned to show the superiority of prophecy to tongues. The prophet, he says, "speaks to men for their upbuilding and encouragement and consolation." But would he have described the work of the teacher in different terms? It is true that a "teaching" seems to be distinguished from a "revelation" in 14:26: "When you come together, each one has a hymn, a teaching, a revelation, a tongue, or an interpretation." And in 14:6 Paul implies the same differentiation when he asks: "How shall I benefit you unless I bring you some revelation or knowledge or prophecy or teaching?" But in I Cor. 13, the gift of "teaching" is not mentioned, and "prophecy" seems to cover the entire field of revealed truth. We note also that if prophecy has first place in I Cor. 12:28, teaching is at least *mentioned* first earlier in the same chapter: "To one is given through the Spirit the utterance of wisdom, and to another the utterance of knowledge [are two kinds of teachers being designated?] according to the same Spirit, to another faith, . . . to another gifts of healing, . . . to another the working of miracles, to another prophecy, to another the ability to distinguish between spirits, to another various kinds of tongues [note the variety of functions even among the extreme ecstatics], to another the interpretation of tongues."

A comparison of this list of items with that in I Cor. 12:28 will confirm many other indications not only of the manifoldness and rich variety of the forms the ministry took, at least in the Pauline churches, but also of the way functions were sometimes exercised by different persons and sometimes combined in one person. When in Gal. 6:6 Paul reminds his readers that he "who is taught the word" should accept some responsibility for the financial support of "him who teaches," we may suppose that "prophets" as well as "teachers" are included in the provision. We do not need to decide whether Paul is supposed to be a "prophet" or a "teacher" at Antioch (in Acts 13:1-3). As a matter of fact, he was both; perhaps each of the prophets and teachers at Antioch was both. And the *Didache*, although it seems to know (in 11:1-2 and 13:2) a special class of teachers, can still say of the prophet: "If he does not do what he teaches, [he] is a false prophet" (11:10).

C. H. Dodd makes a careful distinction between preaching (*kerugma*) and teaching (*didache*)[7] in the early church. Such a distinction has merit in helping to bring out the full content of the message of the primitive prophets and teachers; but it would not do to identify the "preaching" with the prophets and the "teaching" with the teachers. Both the preaching and the teaching, as Dodd describes them, belonged to the function of each group. The preaching—in the sense of the proclamation of the good news of God's saving action in the life, death, and resurrection of Christ—was perhaps in a peculiar sense the work of the apostle and those associated with him, for they were the great missionaries of the early church and were principally responsible for proclaiming the gospel where Christ's name was not known. But the prophets and teachers in local churches, although responsible for the spiritual edification of the congregation itself, were also expected to do the work of evangelists as they had opportunity. Services of the church aimed in large part at the persuading and winning of unbelievers were certainly held. It is clear that the Christian movement spread chiefly through a constantly widening extension of the influence of the churches which had been established in metropolitan centers. The leaders in this extension must have been the prophets and teachers. The work of evangelism and the work of edification was then, as it is still, in considerable part one work.

It must not be assumed that all the "ministers" of the primitive church were men; women undoubtedly shared in both the gifts and the labors of the ministry. Paul, to be sure, says rather flatly (in I Cor. 14:34) that "women should keep silence in the churches," intimating that this was the rule in the churches generally; but earlier in the same letter (11:5 f.) he seems concerned only that a "woman who prays or prophesies" shall be veiled. This apparent discrepancy is difficult to understand and has never been really satisfactorily explained. Antecedently, however, it is unlikely that women should not have functioned as teachers and prophets. Would not the gifts of prophecy and teaching have been sometimes, and quite unmistakably, bestowed on women? And if so, could they have refrained from prophesying, or would the churches have dared require that they should? It is likely that Prisca was such a prophet or teacher; she is presented in some such role in Acts 18:26. And the same book tells of prophetesses at Caesarea (21:9).

As to the prominence of women in the administrative and pastoral work of the churches, there can be no question whatever. Phoebe in Rom. 16:1 is called a *diakonos* of the church at Cenchreae. If this final chapter of Romans is pseudonymous and late (as I think it is), Phoebe is being called a "deaconess," for we know that there were deaconesses in some at least of the second century churches; but even if the chapter is from Paul's own hand (as is generally supposed), Phoebe is being identified as an active servant of the church. In the same chapter "Mary" is described as having "worked hard among you," and "Tryphaena and Tryphosa," are called "those workers in the Lord." These are in effect deaconesses. Similarly, the "widows," about whom we hear in the Pastoral Epistles (I Tim. 5:3 ff.), as well as in Polycarp (4:3) and elsewhere, were deaconesses in fact. At first, the widow was probably merely the beneficiary of the church, one of the needy whom it supported from its common fund; but she soon became, where her strength and health permitted, one of its regular ministers. As such she visited the sick, comforted the bereaved, dispensed the charity of the church, and in other ways helped those in special need. Although her services were not confined to women, it is obvious that she could often be especially helpful to them and especially useful to the administrators of the church in dealing with them.

A distinction is often proposed between the "general" and the "local" ministry in the early church. There can be no question about the propriety of the distinction, but where exactly the line should be drawn is not so clear. Taking Paul's list in I Cor. 12:28, some students have regarded the apostles, prophets, and teachers as belonging to the "general" ministry, and the rest, including the bishops and deacons (that is, the "administrators" and "helpers") as local. Others have drawn the line of distinction between the prophets and the teachers, only the apostles and prophets belonging to the general ministry. What we have just been noting about the interrelatedness of the prophetic and teaching functions will suggest the difficulty of separating the teacher and the prophet from each other; and, if they belong together, it seems on the whole more plausible to regard them as belonging to the local ministry. Certainly they must in the beginning have had their primary locus in some congregation although there would have been nothing to prevent, and much to encourage, visits by a person with distinguished gifts as a preacher (such, I think, we would call either "prophet" or "teacher") to other churches. Often he would have been invited to make such a visit. It should also be recognized that some of Paul's associates in apostolic work —as, for example, Apollos and Timothy—would have been prophetic persons. It is to be assumed that such persons were associated with other apostles. And it probably goes without saying that the apostles themselves were almost certainly also prophets and teachers.

Later it is clear that there was a great number, a distinct class, of wandering prophets, depending for their support upon the churches they visited, many of them imposing on the early Christians' reverence for the Spirit and for Spirit-filled persons, some of them actual charlatans. Lucian, a pagan writer of the second century, writes satirically about such a rascally prophet and the gullibility of the Christians whom he exploited. The *Didache* lays down some rather shrewd rules for distinguishing the true prophet from the sham: "No prophet who orders a meal in the Spirit shall eat of it: if he does he is a false prophet. . . . whoever shall say in the Spirit 'Give me money [or something else],' you shall not listen to him." And if a visiting prophet (called in the *Didache* an "apostle") stays as long as three days, he is a false prophet (chap. 11).

It would seem, too, that the writer to the Ephesians, not so late as the *Didache,* but a generation after Paul's time, thinks of the prophet as belonging to what we are calling the general ministry. At any rate, he thinks of him as being very close to the apostle. It is interesting to compare with I Cor. 12:28 f. the statement in Eph. 4:11. "Some should be apostles, some prophets, some evangelists, some pastors and teachers." We note at once the absence of any reference to the healers, the wonder-workers, the speakers in tongues, and those gifted in interpreting these outpourings. Although the epistle is filled with allusions to the Spirit, the writer does not know, or at any rate does not highly esteem, the more ecstatic gifts by which Paul set great store. It is true that he still speaks of the "prophets," but he seems to place them in the same bracket with the apostles, thus relegating them to the early period of the church's beginnings. Just as there are no longer "apostles" in the same sense as in the days of Peter and Paul, so there are no longer "prophets" in the original high meaning of that term. The church, he tells us, is "built upon the foundation of the apostles and prophets"—prophecy has passed away along with tongues and miracles (although, I repeat, the Spirit is very fully present and active). "Evangelists" take the place of both. "Pastors and teachers" are grouped together. Do they represent the "local ministry"? Are the "pastors" the "administrators" and "helpers" of an earlier time (the "bishops" and "deacons" of the same and a later time,) and have these taken on the functions and responsibilities of the teacher as well?[8] Ephesians was probably written at Ephesus in the last decade of the first century and whatever the answers to our questions, that document may be thought of as representing the situation of the churches at the very center of Paul's "diocese" a generation after his death.

Let it be noted that in all of this discussion so far we have been dealing with functions or with vocations, but not with offices. For Paul there were teachers and prophets, but hardly the *offices* of teacher and prophet. More obviously the healers, speakers in tongues, miracle workers, were not "officials" of the church. Even the "bishops" and "deacons" of Phil.

1:1 are not to be thought of as officials. There is more basis for regarding the apostle as filling an office because it was not his personal spiritual endowment which primarily qualified him as an apostle, but his ability to meet certain specifications of a more objective kind—namely, he must have "seen the Lord" and been commissioned by him. His authority, therefore, was not merely the self-authenticating authority of the Spirit which possessed him, but inhered also in the relationship he sustained with the historical event in which the church began.

Of the several ministries of the local church, it is natural that those of the "administrators" and "helpers" should have been the first to receive official status. These are the least obviously spiritistic of them all, the most clearly susceptible of being filled by human election or appointment. Thus the "bishops" and "deacons" can be thought of as being, at least in the area of the church which Paul's letters had earlier represented, the first official ministers. These ministers, where prophets and teachers in the more traditional sense were not to be found or were found untrustworthy, would tend to take over the more spiritual functions of preaching and of presiding at the Eucharist and other services of worship. The *Didache* says much, as we have seen, about the prophets and can call them "your high priests"; but it recognizes the possibility that a church at a given time may not have a prophet (13:4). It is such a situation the author has in mind when (in 15:1) he writes: "Appoint . . . for yourselves bishops and deacons worthy of the Lord, meek men, and not lovers of money, and truthful and approved for they also minister to you the ministry of the prophets and teachers."

With this development of definitely official bishops and deacons, possessing priestly and teaching as well as administrative responsibilities and prerogatives, the strictly primitive phase of the history of the church's ministry comes to an end.

V

We have proceeded thus far without mentioning at all a term of great importance in this study or, for that matter, in the study of the ministry in any period—namely, the elder or the presbyter (*presbyteros*). This omission has been possible because elders are not referred to in any of Paul's letters, nor are they mentioned in Ephesians and the *Didache*, the other sources upon which we have thus far been principally relying. On the other hand, "elders" are mentioned in I Peter as the "shepherds" of the flock of God (5:1-3). According to James, "the elders of the church," who will pray and anoint with oil in the name of the Lord, are to be called on in cases of illness. The author of Revelation may be supposed to reflect a familiar order in the church when he speaks of the "twenty-four elders" around the heavenly throne (4:4). The Pastoral Epistles, although they speak also of "bishops," have much to say about the elders of the church, and the same thing is true of I Clement. And, most important of all, the book of Acts seems to represent government by "elders" as characteristic, not only of the Jerusalem church, but also of the churches generally in the primitive period.

It happens that all of these documents are relatively late—that is, considerably later than Paul—and might be supposed to reflect a post-Pauline development in the church's polity. Since many of these later references to elders apply to churches within the area of Paul's earlier work and even, especially in the case of I Clement, to a church actually founded by Paul, one must acknowledge a measure of truth in this supposition. I Clement is, of course, a letter addressed by the church at Rome to the church at Corinth about A.D. 95, and one might argue that it is the polity of the Roman, rather than of the Corinthian, church that is reflected there. This is undoubtedly true to some extent; but one can hardly suppose that the picture of church order at Corinth which the letter presents is substantially mistaken. There were, then, "elders" at Corinth at the end of the first century. The same thing can be said of Philippi, another of Paul's churches, at the beginning of the second, if we can trust Polycarp's reference to the "elders and deacons" there in his letter to that church (5:3). The book of Revelation may most naturally be taken as representing the Christianity of Asia (the very center of Paul's field of work) in the same general period; and the Pastoral Epistles, wherever they originated, are certainly thought of by their author as standing in the Pauline tradition. We may suppose, then, that a system of government in local churches by councils of elders had established itself very generally by the end of the first century, even in the Pauline churches, whose usages in an earlier period we have been studying thus far.

It is impossible, however, to regard this system as having its origin so late as this. Whatever our view of the date of Acts and of the purposes and methods of its author, it is all but impossible to suppose that he is not following early and authentic sources in his account of the life of the primitive community in Jerusalem; and the allusions to "James and the elders" or "the apostles and elders" are too frequent and integral to be seriously doubted. Nor can we regard the "elders" as simply the "older men"—although it cannot be denied that the term is sometimes used in the New Testament in that quite nonofficial sense. In Acts, as well as in I Clement and the Pastorals, they are the principal ministers of the church; and the probability is that the term was in use in that sense in the Judean church long before it had spread into the territory of Paul's mission.

This probability is confirmed by a very important *a priori* consideration. Jewish communities, large and small, were governed by councils of elders, the so-called sanhedrins. These "elders" were the only "ordained" officials of Judaism in the New Testament period—the priests and Levites being such by birth and the scribes not having yet attained full recognition as official representatives of the cultus.[9] Moreover, the elders were by all means the most important Jewish officials both in Palestine and in the diaspora, the oversight of all the interests of the communities being entrusted to them. Not only is it impossible to suppose that the term "elder" as used in the early church is not related to this Jewish usage, but it is almost equally difficult to doubt that the most primitive Jewish Christian communities followed this familiar and universal Jewish pattern in their organization. The pattern moved presumably in a westward direction till in the time when Acts, I Clement, and the Pastorals were written it had become very generally established.

How are we to think of the "elders" as related to the several functions and functionaries we have noted in the Pauline churches? Sometimes in the literature of the period (as, for example, Acts 20:28; Titus 1:5-7; I Clem. 44:4-6) the term "elder" seems equivalent to "bishop"; and it is not unlikely that the word *episkopos* ("bishop") was sometimes used to make intelligible to Gentiles the meaning of *presbyteros* ("elder"), which would have sounded strange to them as a title of office. But we must assume that, generally speaking, the word "elder" was a more inclusive term than any we have so far considered.[10] "The apostles and elders" of Acts—like the Jewish "chief priests and elders" referred to in the same work—are all "elders," and they constitute the essential governing body of the Jerusalem church. It is not unlikely that Luke thinks of the Jerusalem elders as exercising a kind of supervision over all the churches just as the Great Sanhedrin in Jerusalem held primacy over all the Jewish sanhedrins. The appointment of the Seven in Acts 6:1-6 is probably to be understood as the enlarging of the council of elders to represent the Jews of Hellenistic origin who had become members of the Jerusalem church. There were undoubtedly at Jerusalem prophets and teachers, as well as administrators and helpers (we can be less sure of the various kinds of ecstatics); but in all probability all of them belonged among the "elders" of the church. Was there a definite number of these? The Jewish sanhedrins varied to some extent in size, and there is no reason to suppose that the number of Christian elders was fixed. The more important the gifts of the Spirit were in determining function and role, the more fluid the number of elders would need to be. But as the primitive enthusiasm waned, or became corrupted, and the Spirit was thought of as conferred through ordination (rather than as being a prior condition of it), a body of fixed size, at any rate in a particular congregation, would become established as the norm.

We may suppose that as this pattern of a council of governing elders moved westward in the closing decades of the first century (it may have reached Rome in the far West earlier and more directly), it absorbed the more primitive ministries—and this meant particularly the "bishops" and "deacons," since, as we have seen, the bishops and deacons were already taking over the teaching and liturgical functions of the prophets and teachers. Sometimes, as we have seen, the term "elder" seems to be used interchangeably with "bishop;" sometimes it would appear that the "presbytery" included both elders who supervised and elders who served, that is, both "bishops" and "deacons." No doubt both polity and nomenclature varied from time to time and from place to place.

These boards of elders, like the Jewish sanhedrins, had general oversight of the affairs of the congregation and were responsible for guiding and ruling it. All of the many functions we have mentioned as belonging to the administration of a primitive congregation—and we remember that these were becoming constantly more numerous and complex—are now the responsibility of the elders in their corporate capacity. And as the Pastorals and I Clement make abundantly clear, the elders—at any rate those "elders" who are also "bishops"—are fully responsible for teaching and for the conduct of worship and the Eucharist. I Clement represents them as successors of the apostles (42:3-4, 44:1-3), and the same status is implied in the Pastoral Epistles. Both writers, as well as I Peter, Polycarp, and the *Didache,* are concerned that these rulers shall be worthy of the reverence to which the office entitles them—that they shall be men of good character and reputation, devoted to Christ, sober, not married a second time (or does this mean "undivorced"? [11]), free from pride and covetousness, discreet, responsible, trained in and loyal to the apostolic tradition, competent to teach, true officiants of the church's worship. (See, e.g., I Clem. 44:3; I Tim. 3:2 ff; II Tim. 3:10-4:5; Titus 1:5 ff.; I Pet. 5:1 ff.; Poly. *ad Phil.* 6:1; *Didache* 15:1-2.)

And the deacons, who assisted in both the administrative and liturgical tasks of the elder-bishops, were to be persons of similar kind (I Tim. 3:8 ff.; Poly. *ad Phil.* 5:2).

VI

One further stage in the development of the early ministry needs to be traced. This is the rise of monepiscopacy—that is, the pattern of a single bishop, or pastor, at the head of each church. We are so accustomed to this pattern—despite our controversies about episcopacy—that we may not realize that it does not clearly emerge till the opening years of the second century. The first witness to it is Ignatius, a prophet of the church of Antioch in Syria, who has become the bishop in the sense of the single head, of the church in that city. During his passage across the provinces of Asia and Macedonia on his way, under guard, to Rome, and presumably martyrdom, he had occasion to write a number of brief letters, especially to the churches of Asia which had sent deputations to visit and befriend him; and these letters are among the very few sources we have for the history of the church in the early decades of the second century. They reveal, not only that Ignatius was the single bishop of Antioch, but also that the several churches of Asia—at Ephesus, Philadelphia, Magnesia, Smyrna, and elsewhere—had likewise single rulers: Onesimus, for example, is "bishop" in Ephesus, and Polycarp in Smyrna. It is clear that each of these churches had a body of elders and a corps of deacons; but presiding over both and over the congregation as a whole is the bishop.

It appears even in Ignatius' letters that this system of a threefold ministry was not universal, for in his letter to the Roman church he says nothing about its bishop. Similarly, his colleague and friend, Polycarp, in writing to the church at Philippi speaks of their "elders and deacons" but does not mention their "bishop," thus strongly suggesting that monepiscopacy was not established in Macedonia at that time. Moreover, it can be argued that the vigor Ignatius shows in defending the significance and prerogatives of the bishop indicates that, even in Asia, the system was of recent origin. Indeed, if III John is to be understood as a protest again the new system, as many interpreters hold, it shows us this development in the very midst of its occurrence, probably in some Asian church. If we may assume that monepiscopacy was of longer standing and was more firmly established in Ignatius' own church, the indications would be that the single bishop pattern, like the elder pattern, moved in a westward direction from Palestine or Syria across the church.

Again as in the case of the elders, this direction is antecedently likely because of what we gather from our most primitive sources about the organization of the Jerusalem church. Acts, as we have seen, tells us of the "apostles and elders" there; Paul, who describes a visit of his own to Jerusalem, speaks of the "pillars." But both let us know that among the heads of the Jerusalem church (whoever they were and by whatever name they were called), there was one supreme head, namely James the Lord's brother.[12] He was apparently more influential even than Peter. Hegesippus is the source of the tradition, preserved for us by Eusebius, that James was succeeded by another relative of Jesus and that indeed a kind of dynastic line was established in the Palestinian church. Although this dynastic feature is unique, the office and role of James and his successors may well be the prototype of the later monarchical episcopacy. If so, it is not strange that the pattern should have early established itself at Antioch (although apparently not in Syria as a whole: witness the *Didache*) and that Asia should have adopted it before Macedonia or Italy. But its progress was steady and fairly rapid. By the end of the second century it was established virtually everywhere.

The rise and rapid spread of monepiscopacy cannot be explained, however, simply by the example of Jerusalem. We must recognize that the form served certain practical needs of the churches. A system of government through a council of elders could be cumbersome; and with the increasing complexity of the congregations' operations and the growing need for both unity and efficiency in the face of increasing persecution by the state and the more vigorous activities of the gnostic teachers —in such a situation the conception of a single head of the church, the guardian of its unity and the responsible agent of its decisions, would have appealed to many congregations. There would also have been felt a need for guardians of the tradition, persons authorized to speak for the apostles, to fill the place of highest authority they had left vacant. We have seen that I Clement regards the elders as the authorized successors of the apostles; how much simpler and how much more appropriate if the authority of this succession could be located in single individuals! And supporting such claims would be the fact that in some cases actual lines of connection between particular apostles and particular bishops could be traced. Many find the origin of the office of monepiscopacy in the function of presiding at the Eucharist which, it is argued, some one person must have performed from the beginning. This president gradually took on other functions, pastoral, administrative, and teaching, until the monepiscopal pattern had fully emerged. But whatever the causes of it or the process by which it came about, or however different these may have been in different parts of the church, monepiscopacy was firmly established in most churches before the end of the second century and by the end of the third century prevailed everywhere. With the establishment of monepiscopacy went the doctrine that a certain priestly power inhered in the office of the bishops, who were the successors not only of the apostles but also of the Old Testament high priests.[13] But the development of such doctrines falls largely in the second and later centuries. Even Ignatius says nothing about the apostolic succession of the bishops, although we cannot argue too surely from his silence that he does not accept it.

The first "bishops" in the monarchical sense were bishops of local churches; they were not diocesan superintendents in the later sense. But the roots of the later development must have been present wherever the church was situated in what was, actually or potentially, a center of expansion; and this would have been true of any large city. There would have been many congregations—at any rate, house congregations—in such a city as Ephesus or Antioch in the early second century; and therefore the bishop of Ephesus or the bishop of Antioch would have been more than the head of a single congregation. Although Harnack[14] is no doubt right in denying that there were in the beginning provincial organizations of churches presided over by single bishops and in insisting that the tendency in the second and third centuries was for every church to have its own bishop, nevertheless one must recognize some similarity, and perhaps some connection, between the apostolic oversight of many churches at the middle of the first century and the early second century episcopal oversight of the several congregations in a given city—and between both and the later diocesan episcopacy. In a significant article M. H. Shepherd, Jr.,[15] argues that Ignatius in urging monepiscopacy was motivated largely by hostility to the gnostic teachers operating among the house churches in various cities. His purpose was to bring all of these house churches in a single city area under a single leader, "who would have complete control and jurisdiction over all liturgical assemblies where baptism and the Eucharist were administered, discipline meted out, and instruction given." But a discussion of such matters falls more appropriately within the following chapter of this book.

FOR FURTHER READING

(In addition to titles mentioned in the notes for this chapter)

Dobschutz, E. von, *Christian Life in the Primitive Church*, New York and London, 1904.

Dunkerley, R., ed., *The Ministry and the Sacraments*, London, 1937.

Easton, B. S., *The Pastoral Epistles*, New York, 1947.

Harnack, A. von, *The Constitution and Law of the Church in the First Two Centuries*, New York and London, 1910.

Hatch, E., *The Organization of the Early Christian Churches*, London and New York, 1892 (4th ed.).

Hort, F. J. A., *The Christian Ecclesia*, London, 1897.

Kirk, K. E., ed., *The Apostolic Ministry*, New York, 1946; London, 1947.

Leitzmann, H., "Zur Altchristlichen Verfassungsgeschichte," *Zeitschrift für wissenschaftliche Theologie*, LV. Frankfurt, 1914.

Lightfoot, J. B., "The Christian Ministry" in *St. Paul's Epistle to the Philippians*, London and New York, 1894.

Lindsay, T. M., *The Church and the Ministry in the Early Centuries*, London, 1907 (3rd ed.).

Linton, O., *Das Problem der Urkirche in der neueren Forschung*, Uppsala, 1932.

Lowrie, W., *The Church and Its Organization in Primitive Times; An Interpretation of Rudolph Sohm's Kirchenrecht*, New York and London, 1904.

Manson, T. W., *The Church's Ministry*, Philadelphia, 1948; London, 1948.

Rawlinson, A. E. J., "The Historical Origins of the Christian Ministry" in *Foundations*, London, 1914.

Streeter, B. H., *The Primitive Church, studied with special reference to the origins of the Christian Ministry*, New York, 1929.

II

The Ministry of the Ante-Nicene Church (c. 125-325)

GEORGE H. WILLIAMS

In the New Testament epoch we saw three types of ministry unfolding within the Christian churches: (1) the inspired or vocational role of the apostle (and evangelist), prophet, and teacher;[1] (2) the cultual and eleemosynary service of the presbyteral "presidents" (protobishops), deacons, and widows, and (3) the originally perhaps honorific,[2] then disciplinary and administrative office of the presbyters from whose ranks the bishops were drawn. We know that these three kinds of ministry of the New Testament epoch were modeled in part on Jewish and pagan precedents and we shall take note of the extent to which they were elaborated in self-conscious polemical parallelism alongside these rival institutions on the assumption that Christians were the militia of Christ under the heavenly Emperor and the true or new and ongoing Israel of God.

Of these three ministries, that of the presbyterate had been so taken for granted that, as we have seen, presbyters were never directly mentioned by Paul or even, much later, by the *Didache*. Yet the early organization of Christian assemblies on the synagogal pattern can be readily inferred, if not so amply documented.[3] Not until the presbyters, from being the venerable rank of the first or most revered converts, became functionaries did they invite comment in our earliest documents. In the meantime, the other two ministries seemed more distinctively Christian and are therefore more amply attested in the earliest period; for the outburst of prophecy and the proclamation of the gospel were felt to be the distinctive signs of the new age that had opened, while the liturgical life of the community centered in the re-enactment of the Supper with its host or president and servers.

Amid the diversity of ministries in the New Testament epoch there was yet no true priesthood, for Christ was the only high priest and his the consummatory and definitive sacrifice ending all sacrifices. Moreover, priesthood, as defined by both Jewish and pagan usage, was hereditary or civilly bestowed; and to such a status the earliest Christian ministrants did not or could not aspire. But gradually the principal officiant at the cultual re-enactment of the Supper came to be so closely associated with Christ (Ignatius of Antioch) in the sacrifice of Calvary and its liturgical commemoration, the Eucharist, that by contagion and imputation the eucharistic president himself became looked upon as at least analogous to the high priest of the Old Covenant and the spokesman of the entire royal priesthood which is the Church. Though he was normally one of the presbyters, the cultual president acquired, through his supervision of the deacons, a pre-eminence over the other presbyters in their corporate capacity as the "municipal" council of Christians whose ultimate citizenship was in heaven. In the meantime, conflicting and sometimes irresponsible claims and vagaries put forward by certain prophets and teachers conspired to bring also the surviving "charismatic" ministries under the oversight of the bishop in order to assure the theological solidarity of the Christian community ever in peril of its life from a hostile populace and an intermittently persecuting magistracy.

Thus it was the bishop, as chief pastor of the local church, who came to represent the fullness of the ministry. He was prophet, teacher, chief celebrant at the liturgical assembly, and chairman of the board of overseers of the Christian "synagogue." But he could never perform his functions unaided. It was still the entire church, acting in him as the head and with the deacons and presbyters as the more important organs, that embodied the full ministry of Christ in the world. Thus by the end of the New Testament epoch the original three ministries, "charismatic," cultual, and disciplinary, had been so reassessed, redefined, and re-integrated that we begin to discern the emerging outlines in each community of a threefold, corporate ministry made up of a sacerdotal (i.e., "sacrificing") bishop, ruling presbyters, and liturgical-eleemosynary deacons. During the period of somewhat less than a hundred years recounted in Chapter I these three functionaries, and particularly the bishop, had begun to absorb several of the diverse ministrations alluded to by Paul. At this stage the bishops and presbyters together constituted the "clergy" (klēros). The ministry of the church was a more inclusive term than "clergy;" but only remnants of the charismatic ministry survived in certain free teachers and the exorcists.

With the completion of this consolidation of a threefold ministry the next development was the delegation of the sacerdotal ("sacrificatory") powers of the bishops to the presbyters. By the time of the Council of

Nicaea (325), the bishop, though remaining pastor in his own church, had turned over some of his functions to the several presbyters in the surrounding parishes not under continuous episcopal care, with the consequence that the presbyter himself became a priest. That is, on becoming chief pastor in his own local church, the presbyter became, like the bishop, a *sacerdos* or *hiereus*. Significantly, the bishop retained his unique baptismal role in the regenerative act of baptism somewhat longer than his eucharistic pre-eminence; and even after finally giving up the baptizing of all catechumens outside his own parish, he preserved, at least in the West, the confirmation thereof as a distinct and essential ceremony, while in the East it was he alone who could bless the oils used by priests in baptism and confirmation. In the originally perhaps undifferentiated act of the imposition of hands he also retained in most centers the exclusive right to the laying on of hands *in ordination*. At this stage the bishops and presbyter-priests together constituted the priesthood (*sacerdotium*), while the older term "clergy" had become enlarged to embrace most of the ministries of the church, including most of the so-called "lower orders." Only a few "lay" ministries had failed to be clericalized.

The process of breaking down the primitive cultual monopoly of the bishop with the consequent approximation of parity of bishop and priest in respect to their *ministry,* as distinguished from their *jurisdiction,* proceeded unevenly, more rapidly in the big cities than in the small towns, more readily in the West than in the East. It was accompanied by a variety of adjustments and accommodations among the older ministries and by the elaboration of new ones within the local churches and the growth of metropolitical, eventually also patriarchal, conciliar, and imperial control of the local bishop in the measure that the Church aspired to organize its forces in accordance with the new Empire-wide assignments and responsibilities. The proliferation of lower orders below the rank of deacon and the erection of a hierarchy above the level of the bishop, accompanying the establishment of Christianity as the moral cement of the Empire in the reign of Constantine, brought about the gradual disaggregation of the corporate ministry in a face-to-face fellowship. Thereupon the various orders of the clergy came to be thought of as the ecclesiastical counterpart of the succession of officers or the *cursus honorum* through which a magistrate normally advanced in the service of the State. Thus the ministry became more of a career than a calling. The ministrant became much less an organ of the local church and spokesman of the community before God and much more of a professional cleric, appropriately trained and promoted, even from one parish to another.

In the meantime, as bishop and metropolitan became involved in their new imperial assignments, many of the faithful felt estranged by clerical accommodation to the world; and monasticism developed with its own special ministry to the saints within and the seekers without. Thus by the end of the Patristic period the saintly or charismatic anchorite emerges as an alternative curer of souls; the abbot takes his place alongside the bishop and the parish priest as a third kind of chief pastor.

With this generalization for the Patristic period as a whole, we turn in this chapter to the evolution of the clergy in the ante-Nicene period (c. 125-325).

Without going back over the ground covered in Chapter I, it will be useful to pick out several passages which mirror the image of the proto-bishop and his subordinate colleagues about a hundred years after Jesus' death.

Ignatius of Antioch (d. before 117), who was the earliest exponent of monepiscopacy and the threefold ministry (*Trallians* 3:1), considered himself alternatively as the representative of God and the image of Christ for his people.[4] In his role of chief pastor of the flock, the bishop is the type of God (*Magnesians* 6:1; *Smyrneans* 9:1) and specifically of God the Father (*Trallians* 3:1). Ignatius enjoins the faithful to be "obedient to the bishop, as Jesus Christ was to the Father . . . for where the bishop is, there is the Catholic Church" (*Smyrneans* 8: 1 f). Indeed, God Himself is the *episkopos* of all and especially the bishop himself (*Polycarp*, 1), and whoever lies to the bishop does not just deceive the human visible bishop but he despises the invisible one (*Magnesians* 3: 1 f). In this frame of reference Ignatius thinks of himself as instituted by the Spirit of God. There is no thought of his being a successor of an apostle. He is a prophet. And it is the presbyters, ranged about him in council, who are the type of the apostles, while the humble servers, the deacons, are the type of the Suffering Servant, Jesus, and the widows (forerunners of the deaconesses) are the type of the Spirit (*Magnesians* 6:1).

In his personal conduct, however, the bishop is also, according to Ignatius, the image of Christ. Ignatius expects, for example, the faithful to be "subject to the bishop, as to Jesus Christ" (*Trallians* 2:1). Being the vicar of Christ, by whose presence the Church Catholic is made complete and without whose presence or authorization the Eucharist, instruction, and even marriage are invalid, the bishop is expected to live out in his life the fullness of Christ. That is why Ignatius yearns for a Christlike martyrdom in Rome, while dissuading lay Christians from putting their lives unnecessarily in jeopardy. Because this imitation of Christ is peculiarly an episcopal duty, he pleads with the Roman Christians not to interfere in his behalf lest, instead of becoming one with the Word of God, he once more be only the echo (Rom. 2:1).

In a contemporary, Polycarp of Smyrna (d. 156),[5] the self-image of the chief pastor was not quite so vividly perceived as in Ignatius. At his martyrdom Polycarp was content to style himself a loyal lieutenant of the heavenly Emperor Christ with whom he will presently co-rule at the last judgment (Phil. 5:2).[6] Although in his *Letter to the Philippians* (c. 135) Polycarp does not mention bishops but only deacons and presbyters, nevertheless his own effectual position must have been very much like that of Ignatius. Surely, in describing the ideal presbyter, Polycarp is picturing someone like himself (6:1):

The presbyters must be tenderhearted, merciful toward all, turning back [the sheep] who have gone astray, visiting the sick, not neglecting widow or orphan or poor man, abstaining from all anger, respect of persons, unrighteous judgment, being far from all love of money, not hastily believing [anything] against any one, not stern in judgment, knowing that we are all debtors because of sin.[7]

From a self-portrait, let us turn to a precious reminiscence of "the blessed and apostolic presbyter" Polycarp from the pen of Irenaeus, who vividly conjures up for posterity his boyhood memory of the "presbyter" who was a disciple of the apostles:

. . . I can tell the very place where the blessed Polycarp used to sit [note the posture of the bishop as teacher or preacher upon his *cathedra*] as he discoursed, his goings out and his comings in, the character of his life, . . . the discourses he would address to the multitude, how we would tell of his conversations with John and with the others who had seen the Lord, how he would relate their words from memory . . . and I can testify before God that if that blessed and apostolic presbyter had heard the like [the Gnostic vagaries], he would have cried aloud and stopped his ears and said, as was his custom: "O good God, for what sort of times hast thou kept me, that I should endure these things?", and he would have fled the very place. . . .[8]

Besides this glimpse of presbyter-bishop Polycarp as teacher, the same source preserves for us a picture of Polycarp as liturgical "president" or eucharistic host. Only one presbyter could preside at the Eucharist. When Polycarp was in Rome to discuss with Bishop Anicetus the vexing question of the conflicting dates for the celebration in Rome of Easter in the diverse ethnic house "parishes" (the immigrants from Asia observing the Johannine usage), the two bishops ended their deliberations amicably, each holding to his own usage. In parting they held communion with each other, and in the church "Anicetus yielded the celebration [of the Eucharist] to Polycarp obviously out of respect." [9] Although Irenaeus did not call Polycarp bishop, but rather presbyter, his contemporary Ignatius did,[10] as did also his own immediate followers, though perhaps more characteristically they wrote of Polycarp as an "apostolic and prophetic teacher." [11]

It is interesting that Polycarp's own description of the deacon was very similar to that of his ideal presbyter-bishop. He likened deacons in relationship to their "presbyter" (bishop) as Christ to God (Phil. 5:3); and described them further as "blameless before His righteousness, as the servants of God and Christ and not of men, not slanderers, not double-tongued, not lovers of money, temperate in all things, compassionate, careful, walking according to the truth of the Lord, who was 'the servant of all'" (5:2).

Whether the *Didache* is itself primitive or in its present form the composition of a "mild Montanist" of the late second century,[12] it no doubt authentically preserves the memory of the high esteem in which the charismatic ministry and notably that of the prophet was once held, when it speaks of the prophet as the "high priest" (13:3), to whom, as in the Old Testament, every first fruit of the wine vat, the threshing floor, or the pastures is due. It was indeed acknowledged that in the absence of a high priestly prophet the congregations should elect bishops and deacons; and the delineation of the ideal bishop (15: 1 f.), which picks up phrases from I Tim. 3 and Titus 1, is repeated by many of the later church orders and mirrors of bishops.

The search for an Old Testament source and sanction for the Christian ministry is found also in Clement of Rome, where the emergence of monepiscopacy was longer delayed than at Antioch, but where the authority of the chief presbyter was comparable to that of Polycarp in Smyrna. Though, in his *Epistle to the Corinthians,* Clement speaks of Christ as the effectual High Priest (36:1; 61:3), he regards the chief celebrant (protobishop) at the Supper as also the type of the Old

Testament Aaronic high priest and at the same time the embodied image of Christ the celestial High Priest after the order of Melchizedek; the deacons discharge in the New Dispensation the role of the Levites (40:5):

For the high priest has been given his own proper services, and the priests been assigned their own place [of dignity, seated on either side of the chief celebrant], while to the Levites their ministrations are given.

In making this identification with the Old Testament high priesthood and the Levitical order, Clement was prompted (42:5)[13] by his confidence that the appointment of *episkopoi* and deacons had been prophesied in his Septuagintal Isaiah 60:17.

For the great church of Alexandria in the time of Clement and Polycarp we have no comparable record, but we may infer that on the model of Jesus and the Twelve and following the example at once of James and the elders of Jerusalem, of the Sanhedrin of Jerusalem,[14] and perhaps of the organization of the neighboring huge Jewish community of Alexandria itself, the twelve presbyters of the Alexandrian church thought of themselves as both a sanhedrin and a college of Twelve. Very late accounts[15] of the "peculiarities" of Alexandria make plausible this description of a presbyteral constitution with the twelve choosing from their midst one to be bishop and consecrating him.

Thus, to sum up the meager evidence for the end of the New Testament epoch and the beginning of the Patristic period, there were at least five competing images in which a chief pastor of a Christian church might see himself mirrored *c.* 125: as an elder of a Christian sanhedrin, as an apostle, as a prophet, as a high priest, or as an epiphany of God or Christ to the Christian people.

Passing from these writings, which in part chronologically overlap the documentation provided by the New Testament, we turn to the Apologist Justin Martyr, whose incidental references give us the first firm evidence after the Apostolic Fathers as to the nature and function of the ministries of the Church. In his works we glimpse the teacher, the lector, the protobishop, and the deacon at work in Rome around 150.

The bishop is regularly called by Justin the "president," though this usage may have been dictated by a concern to avoid specifically ecclesiastical language in addressing the pagan world. In arguing with the Jews, it is evident that Justin regards the whole Christian community as "a high-priestly race of God," who collectively take the place both of the Aaronic priesthood and that of the eternal Melchizedek, through their eucharistic offerings in the name of Christ. The fact that Melchizedek,[16] the priest-king of Jerusalem (already identified with Christ in Hebrews), offered bread and wine (Gen. 14:18) made it natural for the royal priestly people to think of their cultual celebrant and spokesman, by assimilation, as their high priest. Justin lifts the curtain upon the action of such a high priest, though he calls him quite neutrally a "president," in a Roman Christian assembly at worship early on Sunday morning, presumably in the house of one of the more prosperous members.[17]

> . . . the memoirs of the apostles or the writing of the prophets are read as long as time permits. When the *lector* has finished, the *president* in a discourse invites [us] to the imitation of these noble things. Then we all stand up together and offer prayers. And . . . bread is brought, and wine and water, and the president similarly sends up prayers and thanksgiving to the best of his ability, and the congregation assents, saying the Amen; the distribution and reception of the consecrated [elements] by each one takes place and they are sent to the absent by the *deacons*. . . . This food we call Eucharist. . . . For we do not receive these things as common bread or common drink, but as . . . flesh and blood of that incarnate Jesus. . . . Those who prosper, and who so wish, contribute, each one as much as he chooses to. What is collected is deposited with the president, and he takes care of orphans and widows, and those who are in bonds, and the strangers who are sojourners among [us], and, briefly, he is the protector of all those in need.

The concern of the bishop for the impoverished and the imprisoned is likewise attested by Bishop Dionysius of Corinth with special reference to Soter, who became bishop in Rome (166-74) not long after the time of Justin's foregoing delineation:

> For this has been your custom from the beginning [he writes to the Roman community]: to do good in divers ways to all the brethren, and to send supplies to many churches in every city, now relieving the poverty of the needy, now making provision, by the supplies which you have been in the habit of sending from the beginning to the mines.[18]

Incidentally, Dionysius, like Justin, calls the bishop a "president." Dionysius goes on to characterize him as a loving father exhorting all the brethren who come to Rome as his children. Dionysius also mentions the activity of bishops as correspondents and apologists, whose writings were frequently and thoughtfully read and preserved in the assemblies to which they were sent.[19]

In Justin Martyr's description of the president, deacon, and lector at worship there is no mention of presbyters; this may be accounted for by his concentration on the cultual rather than disciplinary and administrative aspects of the Christian community. In addition to his sketch of the cultual ministry, however, we have from Justin some glimpse into the charismatic ministry of the lector and the teacher.

In the foregoing depiction of the service of worship at Rome c. 150, besides the bishops and deacons, only the lector is mentioned. He is seen reading from the Scriptures as long as time permits. In later church orders he is often ranked with the prophets:

> And if there is a lector, let him too receive [an allowance] like the presbyters, as ranking with the prophets.[20]

On the basis of this and similar statements some scholars have held that the readership was originally one of the inspired orders, gradually depressed as the church became more literate.[21]

Of the teacher, Justin has more to say. Himself a teacher, wearing the philosopher's mantle in succession to several teachers under whom he had studied,[22] Justin thought of himself also as the heir of the prophets of Israel and the superior of the contemporaneous teachers of the Jewish line, the rabbis. He held that the prophetic gifts had been "transferred" to Christian teachers,[23] although he acknowledged that there could be false teachers, as there had once been false prophets. Like his more speculative contemporary Ptolemy, a moderate Gnostic teacher, he undoubtedly thought of himself as standing in "the apostolic tradition" in a "succession" of teachers.[24] Like pagan teachers and rabbis, Justin laid hands upon the head of each disciple on the completion of the course.[25] At his trial, Justin, philosopher-prophet-teacher, describes the "school" where he has been teaching for the examining prefect, who will presently put him and several of his students to death. It is apparently his home, his local "parish house" in Rome:

> I live above the bath of a certain Martin, the son of Timothinus, and during all this time (this is my second stay in the city of Rome) I have not known any other assembly but the one there.[26] And whoever wanted to come to me, to him I communicated the words of truth.[27]

One of the students apprehended with Justin declared that he had received his elementary "training" in the "good confession" from his parents but that he "gladly" heard Justin's "discourses."

Winsome and heroic exponents of the church doctrine though Justin and others were, bishops could not long safeguard the orthodoxy of the faith with free-lance teachers; and to cope with the Gnosticism of some of them, the claim was put forward that the bishop himself was pre-eminently the teacher of the Church in succession to the apostles. Thus it was in his magisterial rather than his cultual role that the bishop took his place upon the apostolic *cathedra*. Or rather, the bishop's seat came in the course of time to be at once a doctoral (magisterial) chair, a liturgical bench, and a judicial throne. It was two outside churchmen who made the apostolic claim for the teaching authority of the see in Rome, namely: the Syrian Hegesippus, who was concerned to ascertain the true apostolic doctrine as it was preserved in the episcopal succession, notably in Rome up to Eleutherus (174-89); and especially the presbyter and later bishop of Lyons, Irenaeus (d. 177 or 8). Irenaeus attached importance to his demonstration of a continuous succession in apostolic instruction because of the pre-eminence of the Roman church, but he was convinced that a similar succession could be ascertained for the other great Christian centers. As it happens, Irenaeus used the designations "bishop" and "presbyter" interchangeably, because the corporate presbyterate was for him the ultimate guarantee against vagaries in doctrine, but in any given church like his own or that of Rome he surely had in mind the chief pastor or president of the presbytery when he spoke alternatively of bishops and presbyters as the bearers of the "certain gift of faith." [28]

So deeply implicated had Irenaeus become in the doctrinal or magisterial aspect of the episcopate that the cultual and disciplinary functions of the ministry remain obscure in his surviving works. Only once does he say that the apostles "instituted bishops" in their place of government,[29] to whom, accordingly, obedience is due.[30] Like Justin, he seems to regard the whole church as priestly: "I have shown that all the disciples of the Lord are Levites and priests." [31] But since also like Justin he holds that the Eucharist consists of "two realities, earthly and heavenly," the manufactured bread receiving the Word of God,[32] it was natural for Irenaeus to think of the bishop or president of the presbytery as a priest in this representative capacity; but the word is not used by him. He does speak of the chalice as the *compendii poculum*,[33] which may allude to the recapitulatory character of the Eucharist as a sacrifice. For just as Justin construes the Eucharistic prayer as the Christian apologetical counterpart of the pagan *sacrifice*,[34] so Irenaeus speaks of the Eucharistic gift as offered at an *altar*. But the primary altar is still thought of as in heaven.[35]

It is not until the communion table has become explicitly an altar that the Eucharistic president becomes explicitly a priest (*sacerdos, hiereus*). The first to mention the table as an altar seems to be the apocryphal Acts of John. The first to call a Christian cleric a priest [36] was Polycrates of Ephesus; and he does it, strangely, in calling (*c.* 190) St. John, the beloved of the Lord, not only a teacher but also a priest (*hiereus*) "who wore the sacerdotal tiara." [37]

In the *Apostolic Tradition* of Hippolytus (d. 235 or 6),[38] which presumably transcribes Roman usage about 200, Justin's "president" and Irenaeus' presbyter-bishop is now clearly a high *priest*, teacher, and judge. But his solidarity with his people is no less pronounced. In this very early church order the bishop is chosen by the people and ordained by bishops invited from other communities. He is nominated or chosen by the laity,[39] perhaps out of their satisfaction with his earlier ministry as a deacon in the community (e.g., Eleutherus had been a deacon under his predecessor), perhaps because of his valor as confessor (Callistus),[40] less likely because of his learning (Hippolytus, as antibishop). Formal confirmation (consent)[41] took place on a Sunday, the people of God (*laos*) being assembled together with the presbytery and such neighboring bishops as might attend. The consecration (*cheirotonia*) was performed by the imposition of the hands of several bishops while the presbytery stood by in silence, praying for the descent of the Holy Spirit in the imposition of the hands. Whereupon one from among the assembled bishops (and presbyters [42]), at the request of all present, laid his hands upon the bishop-elect, offering the prayer. The two separated acts of laying on of hands at episcopal consecration (probably our earliest evidence of consecratory imposition) may betray a double origin of *cheirotonia*, namely, that derived from the Jewish presbyters and that of the apostles. In the group act of imposition of hands tactile succession in the presbyterate would be the motivation; in the imposition and prayer of a single bishop the intent would be the invocation of the Holy Spirit [43] in the spiritual restoration of the apostolate. For from the words of the ordaining prayer it is clear that the second act was thought of as comparable to the setting aside of Matthias as apostle, and that the new bishop was thought of as becoming a high priest and princely shepherd of his flock, authorized to bind and to loose like an apostle, that is, to forgive sins, and possibly to cure diseases.[44]

The ordination was completed with the kiss of peace all around and then the new bishop moved on to celebrate the Eucharist.

Whether the new bishop might forgive the gravest sins—apostasy, murder, and adultery—*once* after baptism was a major issue in the church of Rome and elsewhere. Bishop Callistus (217-22), of whom his rival Hippolytus paints a highly colored picture in his *Philosophoumena*, seems to have argued for the plentitude of episcopal (or was it papal?) power in this respect.[45] Perhaps because he had once been a slave he did not oppose the marriage of high-born Christian ladies to slaves and freedmen and gave episcopal countenance to what the state regarded as invalid marriages. Solely as a confessor, Callistus could claim the right to forgive the lapsed (those who had apostasized during persecution), but it is more likely that Callistus claimed the right of forgiveness as the successor of Peter, the incumbent of the see closest to the bones of the·prince of the apostles, to whom the power to bind and loose had first been given. In addition to assuming the full Petrine prerogative as bishop, Callistus also suggested that by a process of monopolization, the spiritual man of Paul (I Cor. 2:15) is pre-eminently the bishop, who judges all things and is judged by none.[46]

Leaving Callistus, let us return to Hippolytus' ideal bishop. In the *Tradition* Hippolytus does not stress episcopal apostolicity, except as it is alluded to in the ordination prayer. But in the *Philosophoumena* he sounds more like Irenaeus. Speaking about Gnostic errors, he writes:

These, however, will be refuted by none other than the Spirit conveyed in the church which the apostles were the first to receive. Subsequently they imparted it to those who accepted the faith aright; of these men we ourselves are the successors sharing the same spiritual endowment, the same high priesthood, the same teaching authority, being in fact accounted as guardians of the church.[47]

Besides the magisterial authority and the supervision of catechetical instruction, the bishop as chief pastor had at this time among his major duties the protracted ritual of baptism. Assembling on the Saturday of Holy Week the catechumens duly prepared by their teachers, the bishop exorcised the evil spirits and thereupon breathed upon the face of each neophyte, sealing him with oil on the forehead, ears, and nose. At the immersion, beginning at cockcrow, the bishop was assisted by presbyters and deacons, one of the latter going into the water naked with the neophytes. After the neophytes had dressed themselves and joined the larger company, the bishop confirmed them with the laying on of hands and anointment with consecrated oil. It was the bishop's unique role in the baptismal action of rebirth that made it natural for all the faithful to revere the bishop as a spiritual father. As early as the apocryphal *Epistle of the Apostles* (140-60) Jesus is represented as encouraging his disciples to assume the titles of father and master (despite their protestations in view of Matt. 23:9 f.) expressly because of the "episcopal" role in baptism.[48]

At the weekly Eucharist the bishop of the *Tradition* occasionally received oils, cheese, and olives over which he offered appropriate prayers, while first fruits and even flowers (only the rose and the lily)[49] were offered when they came in season. At the Paschal Eucharist the deacons brought up to the bishop in addition to bread and wine, also milk and honey. Besides the weekly Eucharist the bishop participated in private *agapes,* whenever someone wished to bring an offering. On such occasions the bishop broke the loaf, tasted, and handed pieces to each of the faithful present. The bishop met each morning with the deacons and presbyters, praying with and instructing the laity who happened by; and thereafter each one went about his own business. The bishop of the *Tradition* was still very much one of the clerical presbyterate (*klēros*). Up until the middle of the third century the inscriptions refer to the Roman bishops as presbyters. Nevertheless, the presbyters of the *Tradition* were inferior to the bishop presbyter.[50]

The presbyters proper of the Roman *Tradition* may have been elective as they were in North Africa. In their ordination the other presbyters imposed their hands along with the bishop, further indication that *cheirothesia* (the imposition of hands) may well have been presbyteral in origin. Hippolytus himself, however, interpreted this inherited custom differently, holding that the bishop alone ordains (*cheirotonia*), while the presbyters merely seal or bless. The ancient prerogative of collegiate rule is prominent in the formulary of presbyteral ordination with its petition for purity of heart to enable the presbyter to govern and give counsel, to be "filled with the Spirit" as "the presbyters of Moses" (Num. 11:16). They are first after the bishop to partake of the communion, seated in the place of honor, perhaps the only ones for whom there were seats.

The qualifications for entry into the presbyterate do not come out in the *Tradition,* except that a confessor [51] who physically suffered in his witness to the faith in persecution is ranked as a presbyter or deacon by a kind of ordination in blood and in the Spirit without the laying on of hands (*cheirotonia.*)[52]

In the *Tradition* the deacons were expressly not of the "clergy" (*klēros*).[53] Therefore in their installation (*katastasis*) only the bishop laid hands upon them. They did "not receive the Spirit which is common to all the presbyterate [bishop and presbyters] in which the presbyters share. . . ." Nevertheless, "the bishop and his deacons were of one mind, shepherding the people diligently with one accord." The deacon's functions were at once liturgical, administrative, and eleemosynary, that is, as broad as the bishop's but always in his service. In his installation prayer the deacon is likened to Christ. In still later formularies of this type the memory of martyr-deacon Stephen is evoked. To anticipate, further, the Syrian *Didascalia*, assembled perhaps fifty years after the *Tradition*, goes on:

. . . let the deacon make known all things to the bishop, even as Christ to His Father. But what things he can, let the deacon order, and all the rest let the bishop judge. Yet, let the deacon be the hearing of the bishop, and his mouth and his heart and his soul. . . .[54]

That the deacon is the type of Christ we have already met in Ignatius and Polycarp. In the *Didascalia* the mediatorship of the deacon between the bishop and the laymen is especially prominent:

. . . let them have very free access to the deacons, and let them not be troubling the head at all time, but making known what they require through the ministers, that is through the deacons. For neither can any man approach the Lord God Almighty except through Christ.[55]

Deacons also ministered to the sick and the dying, reporting to the bishop; "for the sick man is much comforted that the high priest has mentioned him [in the liturgical prayers]." In some cases the deacons took charge of the cemeteries and catacombs.[56]

Associated with the deacons but without their liturgical duties were the widows. The widow was, in the *Tradition*, set apart (*katastasis*) for prayer and for the ministry to women but expressly not ordained (*cheirotonia*) because she "does not offer the oblation nor has she a liturgical ministry." Hippolytus groups the following along with the widow in the same general class of nonliturgical ministrants who, not belonging to the clergy proper (*klēros*), were only instituted or recognized, not ordained: the lector, the virgin, the subdeacon, and the healer (exorcist).

In the *Tradition* Hippolytus does not mention the teacher except in connection with the catechumens, and here he distinguishes between "lay" and "ecclesiastical" teachers, though to both he concedes the rite of laying on hands, as a sign of the catechumen's having completed the course. In Hippolytus' *Commentary on Daniel* we find the teachers still serving in charismatic autonomy. The teachers here constitute a distinct estate or rank, mentioned before the clergy proper, and called collectively "the choir of teachers." [57] This phrase significantly preserves Hellenic usage according to which, in allusion to the inspiring Muses, teachers constitute a *choros*.[58]

For a still more advanced stage in the development of the ministries of the Church we turn from Rome to North Africa, where the former lawyer and impassioned presbyter [59] Tertullian (d. after 220) brought to theoretical completion the development we have been following when he called not only the bishop *high priest* but also the concelebrating presbyters *priests*. But the latter are *sacerdotes* only by delegation, when they or the deacons perform that which is peculiarly the rite of the high priest by his license.[60] Here, as in so much else, Tertullian coins the Latin words and formulates the concepts that will become general much later. It is before the feet of presbyters that the penitents bow in the elaborate and humiliating once-for-all "second baptism" of penance known as *exomologesis*.[61] Here we glimpse the traditional judicial function of the Jewish and early Christian presbyters developing into the penitential discipline of priests. Tertullian has a high view of the teachers of the Church, associating them with the virgins and the martyrs. This esteem for the charismatic ministries became especially prominent when Tertullian fell under the influence of Montanism, and contended that only the confessors, apostles, and prophets are spiritual men who may judge all, forgive all, and be judged by none. As a Catholic and a legalist he had once deplored the confusion of the heretical sects as to the relative positions of the laity and the priesthood —today one is a deacon who is tomorrow a lector; the presbyter of today the layman of tomorrow.[62] But as a converted Spiritualist he held that "where three are, a church is, albeit they be laics." [63] In exigencies, baptism and the offering of the Eucharist by a layman are valid. Tertullian gives us a vivid picture of a woman ecstatic who regularly prophesied in a certain Montanist assembly for worship at which Tertullian himself was the preacher:

> For, seeing that we acknowledge spiritual *charismata* or gifts, we too have merited the attainment of the prophetic gift. . . . We have now amongst us a sister whose lot it has been to be favored with sundry gifts of revelation, which she experiences in the Spirit by ecstatic vision amidst the sacred rites of the Lord's Day in the church; she converses with angels, and sometimes even with the Lord; she both sees and hears mysterious communications; some men's hearts she understands, and to them who are in need she distributes remedies.[64]

Tertullian, then, provides us successively with both an advanced catholic sacerdotal view of the office of the bishop and presbyter and a radical Spiritual doctrine of the priesthood of all believers.

Turning to the development of the ministry in Egypt in the period of Hippolytus and Tertullian, we find a markedly different conception and practice, insofar as Clement of Alexandria (d. before 215), our chief source, supplies evidence.[65]

We have already noted the peculiarity of the constitution of the Alexandrian Christian community with its sanhedrin of twelve presbyters who elected the bishop from among their own number. It is possible that this bishop came to be consecrated by the hand of his deceased predecessor who was suitably robed and propped in his episcopal throne for a final gesture of legitimation and benediction.[66] Up through most of the lifetime of Clement all Egypt had only one bishop.[67] The village communities were under presbyters. Only during the episcopate of Demetrius (189-232) did some of these centers acquire bishops, in part as a consequence of the introduction of the Roman municipal system, in part as a calculated counterweight to the powerful Alexandrian presbyterate. We may have in the *Sacramentary* of Bishop Serapion of Thmuis in the Delta (despite its late date)[68] some of the formularies and usages introduced in the period of Demetrius. Herein, in contrast to all other church orders, the deacon is mentioned first "as servant in the midst of the holy people," the presbyter upon whom "we [other presbyters or bishops or both] stretch forth the hand" that "he may be able to be steward of thy people and an ambassador of thy divine oracles and reconcile thy people to thee who didst give of the spirit of Moses upon the chosen ones [the elders];" and finally the bishop who is ordained as "shepherd" of the flock "in succession to the [Old Testament] prophets, patriarchs, and the New Testament apostles." No other ministries are mentioned in the *Sacramentary,* and the sacrificatory role of none of them is alluded to.

It is barely possible that Clement of Alexandria himself was such a presbyter as here described; he calls himself one, though this is hard to reconcile with what else we know of his work. His renown, of course, is that of an ecclesiastically independent charismatic teacher, head of a school of theology frequented by adults, many of them well trained in philosophy. What he says about the Christian teacher is therefore especially instructive. But we wish first to see the parochial clergy through his eyes.

He preserves for us what he calls an instructive tale about the apostle John, in whom we can see Clement's ideal of the forgiving pastor seeking the lost sheep. Having entrusted a comely child to be brought up by a certain presbyter, John returned after many years only to find that the boy had turned delinquent and, as the leader of bandits, was harassing the neighborhood. John at once set out to seek his charge in the mountain lair and was attacked by the very band itself. Whereupon he rejoiced in his plight, for in the mutual recognition of tears and remorse, John was able to restore the youth to the church.[69]

In this tale Clement uses bishop and presbyter interchangeably. And although he recognizes a threefold ministry (once, however, listing them: presbyters, bishops, and deacons), he seems mostly to have thought in terms of two orders only, the presbyterate with a presiding bishop and the diaconate. He was disposed to find within this primarily twofold ministry a counterpart to what he called the "meliorative" and the "ministrative" services in society at large. He likened the meliorative presbyters to physicians for the body and philosophers for the soul, while the ministrative deacons corresponded to children in their duties toward parents and to subjects toward rulers. This distinction and classification from which Clement seemed to derive some satisfaction does not in itself appear to us particularly enlightening, except for its being linked with Clement's view that behind the orders of the Church are the ministering angels:

. . . according to my opinion [he writes] the grades (*prokopoi*) here in the Church of bishops, presbyters, deacons are imitations of the angelic glory, and of that economy which the Scriptures say, awaits those who, following the footsteps of the apostles, have lived in perfection of righteousness according to the Gospel. For these taken up in the clouds, the Apostle writes (I Thessalonians 4:17), will first minister [as deacons], then be classed with the presbyters, by promotion in glory (for glory differs from glory [I Corinthians 15:41]) till they grow into a "perfect man" (Ephesians 4:3).[70]

This parallelism between the celestial and ecclesiastical hierarchy was later to be elaborated.

At the same time there was bound up with this a conception and practice as far from hierarchical clericalism as the spiritual autonomy of the monk is from the autocracy of the prelate. For in this very text and a related place [71] Clement goes on to say that though the Christian gnostic or seeker will conform to church life as it is ordered by the ordained clergy, spiritually, he is already on his way to becoming himself an angel, indeed, divine:

As both these services [meliorative and ministrative] are performed by the ministering angels for God in their administration of earthly things, so they are also performed by the gnostic himself.

In heeding the provisions of the clerical church, the (Christian) gnostic inwardly liberates himself at length to qualify by his spirit, very much like the confessors in the *Tradition* of Hippolytus, for the clerical honor, if not for all the clerical functions:

He, then, who has first moderated his passions and trained himself for impassibility, and developed to the beneficence of gnostic perfection, is here equal to the angels. . . . Those . . . who have exercised themselves in the Lord's commandments and lived perfectly and gnostically according to the Gospel may be enrolled in the chosen body of the apostles. Such a one is in reality a presbyter of the Church and a true deacon of the will of God, if he do and teach what is the Lord's not as being ordained, nor regarded as righteous because a presbyter, but enrolled in the presbyterate because righteous. And although here upon earth he be not honored with the chief seat, he will sit down on the four-and-twenty thrones, judging the people, as John says in the Apocalypse.[72]

Here we have in an ascetic-intellectual form the same ideas expressed by Callistus and Tertullian, namely, that the confessor as the truly spiritual is judge of all things and judged by none.

Clement's gnostics constitute a kind of spiritual Israel, twelve from the Jews, he goes on to say, and twelve from the Greeks. The heirs of this conception of a spiritual ministry were, of course, to be the monks even more than the teachers of the Church; teachers were to become more amenable to ecclesiastical supervision. And like their counterparts, the confessors, the monks will be presently considered able to forgive the sins and guide the consciences of those less accomplished than themselves. (In appealing to this angelic and gnostic tradition the monks will one day threaten the penitential functions of the ordained clergy.)[73]

It was Origen (d. 253) who carried on these ideas as successor of Clement and who integrated Clement's informal adult study group as the upper division or advanced theological school within an episcopally supervised catechetical school.[74] He readily called fellow presbyters *priests,* but in this he seems to have been motivated more by his typological interest as an exegete to make the institutions of the Old and the New Testament correspond than by a deep recognition of the sacrificatory role of the cleric at the altar. For, as in the case of Clement, he took the spiritually enlightened pneumatic or gnostic Christian as the true counterpart of the old Aaronic priest. Thus he readily called the apostles and the disciples of Jesus even in the lifetime of their teacher "true priests" because of their gnosis received directly from the master. In his spiritualization Origen saw the true Church founded on Peter (Matt. 16:18 f.) in the sense that every perfected Christian beholds Christ transfigured.[75]

Nevertheless, to reach the perfection of the apostolic pneumatic, Origen did not depreciate the external ministries of the Church. No doubt, like Clement, he sensed the angelic ranks shimmering behind the visible orders of the clergy. His devoted pupil, Bishop Firmilian of Caesarea, writes about the harmony of the angels "united to [us bishops], who rejoice at our unity."[76]

We have numerous glimpses of Origen as a closely attended preacher, fascinating his congregation with his exegetical skill. A stenographic transcript has recently come to light of his participation as a theological consultant and authoritative teacher in a discussion with a Bishop Heraclides in the presence of other clergy and the faithful.[77] Origen had, at the time of this discussion, already left Alexandria for Caesarea, where he was to perish a martyr as a result of torture in the Decian persecution. Bishop Demetrius had deposed him from the headship of the Alexandrian School and suspended him from the presbyterate in two synods (231, 232) over which he presided, determined as he was to bring catechetical instruction and advanced theological studies even more strictly under episcopal supervision. Origen was, in a sense, the last of the Christian charismatic and independent teachers.

The teacher and catechist by the mid-third century had everywhere lost much of his former independence. Therefore Origen of Alexandria and Caesarea should be described as teacher at this point.

Passing reference might also be made to Malchion, who was the principal opponent of the powerful heresiarch Bishop Paul of Samosata at the synodal deliberations over the heterodoxy of Queen Zenobia's prime minister. Though only a teacher of the Greek rhetorical school in Antioch, he was regarded as the peer or, better, as the instructor of bishops in the realm of doctrine.[78] Mention might also be made here of the high ideal of instruction of Pseudo-Clement:

Let the catechists instruct, being first instructed; for it is a work relating to the souls of men. For the teacher of the word must accommodate himself to the various judgments of the learners. The catechists must therefore be learned and unblamable, of much experience, and approved. . . .[79]

"Bishop" Clement is spoken of as discharging the doctoral role.

But it is Origen who best exemplifies the ideal of the *doctor ecclesiae*. He thought of the old order of teachers as each a "Peter" by gnostic faith and as compositely embodying the teaching authority of the Church. Collectively they were the magisterial Rock of the Church.[80] At Caesarea, whither he fled because Bishop Demetrius claimed to possess the plenitude of magisterial authority, Origen guided the same kind of school as that which he had worked out in Alexandria. While we have no detailed picture of instruction in Alexandria, we do have a rather vivid description of his courses in Caesarea, which we may take as representative of the two schools, and, in a measure, of the best catechetical instruction in general at the middle of the third century. This description is preserved in the laudatory letter written by Gregory the Wonderworker, who paid his respects to his great teacher in a document most important for the history of education in general.

In the beginning of his address [81] delivered before all of the pupils of the school and no doubt in the presence of the Bishop of Caesarea and other ecclesiastical dignitaries, Gregory lauds philosophy, and then moves on to describe the character of the teacher himself whom he so much admires. Gregory describes his own soul as being "knit to the soul of Origen," as the soul of Jonathan was to that of David. Origen guarded him like an angel and was able to hover over him and guide his every thought, rejecting this, encouraging that, and, by the Socratic method, to bring out the inadequacies of Gregory's first thoughts concerning any number of subjects. One marvels at the extent of the instruction.

Dialectic was the first course in this school, and it is described as the art of the husbandman who cultivates various kinds of fields. Origen took each mentality, each personality, seriously and cultivated it according to its special needs. After dialectic had been satisfactorily taken care of he passed on to the natural sciences, including also geometry and astronomy.

He explained each existence, both by resolving them very skillfully into their primary elements, then by reversing the process and detailing the constitution of the universe and of each part, and the manifold variation and change in every portion of it, until carrying us on with his wise teaching and arguments, both those which he had learned and those which he had discovered, concerning the sacred economy of the universe and its faultless constitution, he established a reasonable, in place of an unreasoning, wonder in our souls. This divine and lofty science is taught by the study of Nature most delectable to all.

This was followed, then, by philosophy. It was Origen's view that all philosophers should be read, except those who were manifestly atheists. The coverage of Greek philosophy was intended to be complete. With philosophy, of course, went ethics and the inculcation of the pagan virtues of temperance, justice, courage, and wisdom. Gregory compares his revered master with other teachers:

I have often marvelled at such while they demonstrated that the virtue of God and of men is identical, and that on earth the wise man is equal to the supreme God. These teachers are incapable of conveying wisdom so that one should do the works of wisdom, or temperance so that one should actually make choice of what he has learned; similarly with justice; and still more with courage. It was not in this fashion that our teacher discussed the theory of the virtues with us: rather he exhorted us to their practice, and that more by his example than by his precept.

Origen himself was quite explicit about another aspect of the teacher's task—freshness of interpretation. Commenting on the law which forbade the Israelites to eat yesterday's meal, he admonished the priests and teachers of the Church "not to set forth stale doctrines according to the letter, but by God's grace ever to bring forth new truth, ever to discover the spiritual lessons." [82]

Origen held that the Christian teacher should not take payment from students for what is revealed to him by grace, because this would be "selling doves in the temple, that is, the Holy Spirit." [83] Origen asks only for leisure in the temple. The life of the mind or the Spirit is a great construction requiring peace:

. . . such a structure of thought as may contain the principles of truth, a sermon for example or a book, is best built at a time when, God giving good aid in its construction to him who purposes so excellent a work, the soul rests calm in the enjoyment of the peace which passeth all understanding, free from all disturbance, like the sea without a wave.[84]

So much for the ideal Christian teacher.

Although the ideas of Clement and Origen about teachers, gnostics, and angels are important for the later theories both of prelacy and the pastoral function of the monks, we must return to Rome and Carthage for the more immediately significant developments in the history of the ancient ministries of the Church.

Cyprian, sometime lawyer, fiery martyr-bishop of Carthage (249-53), whose rich pastoral correspondence survives *in extenso,* is at once the picture for us of a third-century pastor of a flock scattered and bewildered by two violent and systematic persecutions (Decian and Valerianic) and at the same time a major theorist of the nature and function of the ministry. He did not call the bishop *high priest* as did Tertullian, reserving that dignity for Christ alone, as the eternal Melchizedek.[85] The sacrificatory office of the bishop is clearly stated, however, when he says: "The Lord's passion is the sacrifice which we offer." [86] Unlike his master, Cyprian was concerned as a bishop to check any presbyteral or other derogations from episcopal authority. He considered the presbyters sacerdotal only as they participated in the sacrificatory office of the bishop by delegation. Perhaps it was because he thought of the bishop primarily as administrator and judge rather than as teacher and liturgical celebrant that he was so intense in his treatment of martyrs and confessors. On the one hand he exalted martyrdom as meritorious and on the other hand he contested the claim of the confessors to forgive the lapsed independently of the bishops. Ignatius of Antioch, it will be recalled, had striven to witness to Christ by a martyr's death in Rome and thus to qualify to co-rule and judge with Christ in his kingdom. Cyprian's ideal is likewise a martyr bishop, but because he must counter the rival claims of the confessors to bind and to loose by virtue of their witnessing to Christ, Cyprian must, unlike Ignatius, reach back explicitly to the prerogatives of the apostles and notably Peter.[87] Cyprian called Peter a bishop [88] and regarded every bishop as filled with the Holy Spirit [89] and as the vicar of Christ, succeeding by vicarious ordination to the apostles.[90] Thus Cyprian found the essence and fulfillment of the Church in the bishop:

. . . they are the church who are a people united to the priest and the flock which adhere to its pastor. Hence you ought to know that the bishop is in the church and the church in the bishop.[91]

Finding the unity of the local church in the Bishop, he found the universality of the Church in the confraternity of bishops; themselves *one* in the episcopacy of Peter. For Christ founded the Church upon Peter before Calvary and then after the Resurrection (John 20:22 f.) extended the foundations to include all the apostles and the bishops after them, alike endowed with the power of binding and loosing. Cyprian was fully participant in the growing confraternity of bishops, his colleagues, as he called them; but, though he was strategically located in the first see of North Africa, he was foremost in insisting that each properly elected and ordained bishop was supreme in his own church,[92] unless morally derelict. For example, Cyprian urged that a certain lapsed bishop, still acknowledged by the repentant *lapsi* themselves as their rightful bishop, should no longer be admitted to his former rank either by the repentant faithful or the confraternity of bishops.[93]

A corollary of Cyprian's high view of the clergyman as the steward of God [94] was that the people of God had the power of choosing their bishops, presbyters, and deacons and rejecting the unworthy.[95] Moreover, even when the deacons came to monopolize all actions connected with Eucharistic offering, the Christian people of God, like eleven of the tribes of old Israel, still had the duty of tithing in support of the Levites. The clergy were to be entirely freed from secular cares and supported by the congregation. Thus even in the middle of the third century the laity preserved their "liturgy" of electing, of bringing the offerings or tithing, of identifying themselves with the prayers of their celebrants in antiphonal amens.[97] Moreover, their consent was sought in dogmatic and moral formulations.[98] Closely connected therewith was the people's prerogative in the recognition of martyrs which in the fourth century was to become the communal voice in the authoritative canonization of saints.[99]

Cyprian's scant decade of episcopacy opened as that of Bishop Fabian

(236-50) was being brought to a close in Rome. From Fabian's episcopate date several of the major constitutional changes in the Roman
community. It was he who assigned the now traditional seven deacons
to seven diaconal regions of the city to carry out, from recognized bases,
their diaconal ministry and administration.[100] We are fortunate in
having from the period just before and just after the pontificate of
Fabian in Rome and that of Cyprian in Carthage, three other important
descriptions of the corporate ministry of the churches around the middle
of the third century: a factual account, a legal codification (the Syrian
Didascalia), and a vivid metaphor.

The metaphor is supplied by a Christian novelist, Pseudo-Clement.
Writing *c.* 225 just about a hundred years beyond the development
reached in Chapter I, this Christian romancer likened the corporate
ministry to the officers and crew of a galley ship. Addressing the faithful,
he declared:

. . . if you be of one mind, you shall be able to reach the haven of rest, wherein
is the peaceful City of the Great King. For the whole business of the Church is
like unto a great galley, bearing through a violent storm men who are of many
places, and who desire to inhabit the one City of the good Kingdom. Let, therefore, God be your captain (*despotēs*); and let the pilot (*kybernētēs*) be
likened to Christ; the look-out man (*prōreus*) to the bishop; the sailors to the
presbyters; the overseers of the rowers (*toicharoi*) to the deacons; the stewards
(*naustologoi*) to the catechists; the multitude of the brethren to the passengers. . . .[101]

After vividly describing the hazards of the sea, Pseudo-Clement goes on:

In order, therefore, that sailing with a fair wind, you may safely reach the
haven of the hoped-for City pray so as to be heard. But prayers become audible
by good deeds. Let therefore the passengers remain quiet, sitting in their own
places, lest by disorder they occasion rolling or careening. Let the bishop, as the
look-out, wakefully ponder the words of the Pilot alone.[102]

The bishop of Pseudo-Clement's purple patch may have been content
to be lookout man under Christ the pilot, but in other writings from the
same period the bishop himself is already likened to a pilot.[103]

From the metaphor we pass to the factual account which is supplied
by Fabian's successor Cornelius. Besides the bishop himself, Cornelius

lists the exact number of the clergy in Rome at midcentury: forty-six presbyters, seven regional deacons, seven subdeacons, forty-two acolytes, fifty-two exorcists, lectors and doorkeepers, and some fifteen hundred widows.[104] A corresponding list at this time from the East, say Antioch, would not have mentioned exorcists as a separate group but in contrast would distinguish widows from virgins and deaconesses.

Deaconesses, subdeacons, acolytes, exorcists, and lectors were not in most places in the mid-third century considered truly clerical. Cyprian, for example, had spoken of lectors and exorcists, however honorable, as next the clergy (*clero proximi*). The clergy proper were elected and underwent ordination (*cheirotonia, cheirothesia, ordinatio*). The last term was first coined for ecclesiastical purposes by Tertullian. There seem to have been two distinct actions suggested by the Greek words which eventually became synonymous. Ministrants who were "next the clergy" (later to be construed as in the "minor orders") were in the ante-Nicene period for the most part only nominated or formally instituted or installed (*nominatio, katastasis*), undergoing no imposition of hands. They, with the teachers, widows, and virgins, constituted a kind of quasi-clerical class between the clergy proper and the remainder of the royal priesthood of God's elect.

Some of the lower orders mentioned here were survivals of the earlier and inchoate ministries of the primitive church; others resulted from the differentiation and depression within the established ministries. The subdeacon may have been from near the beginning distinct from the deacon.[105] Out of the diverse diaconal or subdiaconal functions developed the subdeacon, the doorkeeper, the gravedigger, and the acolyte. The acolytes may originally have borne the same relationship to presbyters as subdeacons to deacons. Among other things, they ran clerical errands.[106]

The exorcists were, in Cornelius' day, especially charged with the care of the mentally ill. The charismatic healers survive as a distinct order much longer in the West than in the East. In the *Apostolic Tradition*, as earlier, they were especially empowered by a revelation, as Hermas of Rome. Like confessors they were expressly not ordained,[107] but they themselves employed the imposition of hands with prayer as the principal action in their ministry of healing.[108]

In the East, at least, the widows preserved or acquired certain ministerial functions, like praying for their benefactors, visiting the sick, and laying hands upon them. In the somewhat later *Apostolic Church Order* Cephas purportedly gave the following instructions:

Let three widows be appointed; two to wait upon prayer, concerning all who are in temptation, and for revelations concerning anything that may be needed; but one to attend upon the women that are tempted in sickness; and let her be ready to minister, and watchful, announcing what may be needed to the presbyter, not a lover of filthy lucre, not given to much wine, that she may be able to be watchful for nightly services, and for whatever other good deeds she may wish to perform.[109]

The obtrusive reference to filthy lucre was apparently necessary, for the *Didascalia* makes it quite clear that the widows as a class were strenuously interested in their church doles, spitefully attentive to who got what—not widows but wallets, the Greek text puns.

The deaconesses of the Eastern churches were drawn from this not entirely promising class, but increasingly from the more affluent and well-born. The apocryphal *Acts and Martyrdom of Matthew* has the apostle conferring the dignity of *diakonissa* upon the seventeen-year-old princess of a royal household converted to the faith. The *Didascalia* recalls the ministering women about Jesus and finds a continuing place for them. Ignatius had likened deaconesses to the Holy Spirit and this feeling about them continued. They visited women isolated in pagan households and assisted in the ritual of baptism of women, especially in the prebaptismal anointment.

Turning to the clergy proper and returning specifically to Rome during the episcopate of Cornelius, we find the presbyters heading the local assemblies of the house churches, called today the titular churches (from the inscription of ownership or occupancy above the doorway, the *titulus*). As many as eighteen of these titular churches date from the mid-third century. In the larger of the titular churches more than one presbyter served, the chief pastor being the *presbyter prior* or *primerius*. Because of the far-flung constituency of the Roman Christian community, almost from the beginning, the Eucharistic assemblies were local. But the eucharized bread (*fermentum*) from the bishop's altar was carried by acolytes to the titular churches as a symbol of the unity of the Roman Church. It is not known when the Eucharist came to be celebrated in its entirety by the presbyters of the "parish" churches apart from the bishop. But the sacerdotal action apparently fell within the competence of the priest sooner than baptism, which was linked to the bishop more closely because of its more solemn and definite character as the initiatory rite and because it took place at a special season and in a special locale where water was available and relative security assured.[110]

In the Eastern churches the presbyters were more commonly nominated by the bishop [111] than elected by the people as in Cyprian's North Africa and in Rome. This seems to accord roughly with the Jewish practice of the sanhedrin which co-opted new members of the presbyteral council. One Eastern church order gives the number of the presbyteral college as twenty-four (cf. Rev. 4:4 and *passim*).[112] Another indicates the apostolic number twelve,[113] natural enough in view of the frequent comparison of presbyters with apostles from the time of Ignatius.

The age of thirty was eventually requisite for becoming a presbyter, and the Council of Neocaesarea (*c.* 315) adduced as the reason that "our Lord was baptized at the age of thirty and then began to preach." The functions of mid-third-century presbyters may be most vividly pictured in Pseudo-Clement's exhortation to what he calls "philanthropy:"

Love all your brethren with grave and compassionate eyes, performing to orphans the part of parents, to widows that of husbands, affording them sustenance with all kindliness, arranging marriages for those who are in their prime, and arranging for employment for the unemployed, and alms to the incapable. . . . Feed the hungry, clothe the naked, visit the sick and the prisoners—help them as you are able—and receive strangers into your homes with alacrity. . . . You will do all these things if you fix love into your minds; and for its entrance there is only one fit means, namely, the common partaking of food.[114]

The mid-third-century bishop, not only in Rome, but everywhere, was a majestic figure. In the generalized portraiture of Syrian canon law, the *Didascalia*, the bishop, is "head among the presbytery," "pastor," "the watchman" set over the church. In the almost contemporaneous Pseudo-Clement he is an "ambassador" of God, the "president of truth" who by the laying on of hands (*proem.*, ii) has been entrusted with "the chair of Moses," "the chair of Christ" (*proem.*, xvii) and "the chair of the apostle" (*proem.*, ii). According to the *Didascalia*, he should be at least fifty years of age at his election, not necessarily educated, married not more than once with children whose discipline should testify to his competence. He

is your chief and leader; he is your mighty king. He rules in the place of the
Almighty; but let him be honored by you as God, for the bishop sits for you in
the place of God Almighty.[115]

The *Didascalia* is still quite prepared, as was Ignatius, to liken the
presbyters to the apostles, because, in effect, the bishop sits among them
as Christ, God incarnate. Yet the apostolic authority of the bishop is
also very much present when the *Didascalia* declares elsewhere:

> For the king who wears the diadem reigns over the body alone, and binds and
> looses it but on earth; but the bishop reigns over soul and body, *to bind and loose*
> on earth with heavenly power. . . .
> Therefore, love the bishop as a father, and fear him as a king, and honor him
> as God.

As a father he begets children in the regeneration of baptism. In the
imposition of hands and the blessing with confirmatory chrism he is
the type of the heavenly Father above the Jordan, saying: "Thou art
my son, this day have I begotten thee."

Bishops in another aspect of their lives are to take Christ, specifically
Christ the suffering Servant, as their model and to become "imitators
of Christ." Turning from the people directly, the *Didascalia* urges the
bishops for their part to take thought that they "be quiet and meek,
and merciful and compassionate, and peacemakers, and without anger,
and teachers and correctors and receivers and exhorters; and that you
be not wrathful, nor tyrannical; and that you be not insolent, nor
haughty, nor boastful." The *Didascalia* further enjoins the bishop:

> And let him be scant and poor in his food and drink, that he may be able to
> be watchful in admonishing and correcting those who are undisciplined. And let
> him not be crafty and extravagant, nor luxurious, nor pleasure-loving, nor fond
> of dainty meats. And let him not be resentful, but let him be patient in his
> admonition; and let him be assiduous in his teaching, and constant in reading the
> divine Scriptures, that he may interpret, and expound the Scriptures fittingly.
> And let him compare the Law and the Prophets with the Gospel. . . . But before
> all let him be a good discriminator between the Law and the Second Legislation,
> that he may distinguish and show what is the Law of the faithful.

The bishop was also a preacher, seated upon the magisterial *cathedra*.
It should be said, however, that preaching in the ante-Nicene period
was a responsibility shared by several of the ministers, not the bishops

alone. It will be well at this point to say more about preaching in general in the ante-Nicene Church.

Revelatory preaching seems to have been limited to prophets, especially numerous in the New Testament epoch. *Missionary* preaching, with a view to conversion, was the responsibility of all the ministers of the Church in the measure that they had ability and opportunity. A third kind of preaching was the dying or *testamentary* speech of church leaders and martyrs, echoing the farewell addresses of the patriarchs and of Jesus himself at the Last Supper.

The fourth and most common kind of preaching was *cultual*. Such preaching was directed to catechumens, to neophytes after their baptism, and to the faithful during the liturgical assembly. It is the direct ancestor of the sermons we know today. The earliest example of a congregational sermon was that of an Egyptian lector preached at a group baptism, namely, *II Clement*. Three principal forms of cultual preaching have been recently distinguished.[116] The first is the encomium or eulogy, originally on Christ and subsequently on the martyrs and saints, delivered on a festal occasion, and modeled on Greek exemplars. Melito of Sardis' recently recovered *On the Passion* is an example of a paschal encomium. The second type of cultual sermon was the homily or expository discourse, brought to a fine art by Origen on the basis of Philonic precedent. The third form of the sermon was thematic based upon the Stoic and Cynic diatribe. It was destined to become the regnant type of liturgical sermon in the fourth century.

With this excursus on preaching we may return to another of the ante-Nicene bishop's functions. The bishop was a judge. His judicial function as vicegerent of God and interpreter of the Law along with the whole clergy is very well delineated in the *Didascalia*. All Christians are reminded that they must not take altercations among themselves before pagan tribunals, nor should the church "admit a testimony from the heathen against any of our own people." The bishop, with the presbyters and deacons continuously present, hears suits and gives judgment only on Mondays so that there may be a whole week for a Lord's Day reconciliation between the "parties," expressly not called "brethren" until they are reconciled. The bishop is reminded that he must not be a respecter of persons and he and his associates are enjoined to judge "as you also are surely to be judged, even as you have Christ for a partner and assessor and counsellor and spectator with you in the same cause." The clergy as judges are urged "diligently" to keep the parties in the mood of friendliness, to take heed of the spirit and past behavior of the contestants, but to bear in mind the possibility that the accused person may have "formerly committed some sin, but is innocent of this present charge." Remarking on the scrupulosity, the caution, and the willingness of the civil judges who deliberate long and arduously, who draw the curtain to take thought and counsel much together, and who fairly interrogate the accused even though a murderer, the *Didascalia* goes on to counsel the bishops not to be "in haste to sit in judgment forthwith, lest you be constrained to condemn a man."

With this delineation of the bishop as judge, preacher, and teacher we could complete our survey of the ministries of the ante-Nicene period, if we were content to remain in the cities where Christianity was most at home and where its characteristic institutions evolved to meet the needs of largely urban populations. But as Christianity penetrated the countryside, it was hampered because it was unable to manage the two principal sacraments, so closely linked with the bishop. There were at least three possible solutions: (1) to delegate the sacerdotal functions of the bishop to resident priests, as was being done in the large cities, (2) to develop rural diaconates, and (3) to encourage the rural bishops (*chorepiskopoi*).

The village bishop of limited powers was probably a relic from the days before the municipal bishops had assimilated all their prerogatives and powers and therewith set the episcopal pattern. Instead of encouraging, the new forces operative in the Church sought to limit the powers of the rural bishop and to demote him with a designation implying inferiority: *chorepiskopos*. This "revolution" or differentiation within the episcopal order was obscurely completed by the middle of the third century,[117] and therewith obliged the church to work out other means of bringing the gospel and the sacraments to the countryside. But the *chorepiskopos* is too interesting a relic to put to one side without further examination.

The *Apostolic Church Order*, c. 300, surely reflects earlier usage[118] when it has Peter provide for the election of a *chorepiskopos* thus:

If there should be a place having a few faithful men in it, before the multitude sufficiently increase to vote (psēphisasthai), who shall be able to make a dedication to pious uses for the bishop to the extent of twelve men, let them write to the churches round about them, informing them of the place in which the multitude of the faithful [assemble and] are established that their chosen men in that place may come, that they may examine with diligence him who is worthy of this grade.[119]

After describing the qualifications for the office very much as a bishop is described in other church orders, except that here the want of ability in letters is clearly stated to be no bar, the *Order* goes on in the same infelicity of style to give some obscure instructions about the ordination of presbyters by the *chorepiskopos*. Rural bishops had been accustomed to ordaining in emulation of the municipal bishops but by *c.* 314 at the Council of Ancyra in Galatia [120] (canons 13, 32, 42) they were firmly enjoined not to ordain presbyters and deacons outside their own "parishes" without written consent from a full bishop. Otherwise their sacramental powers remained complete. About 315 at the Council of Neocaesarea (canon 74) their relationship to the full bishops was declared to be that of the seventy (disciples)[121] to the Twelve. Their itinerancy may be suggested by the comparison with the disciples (later canons confirm this impression), and they are expressly noted for "their devotion to the poor." By 325 at the Council of Nicaea (canon 8) the process of demoting the *chorepiskopos* was furthered in admitting lapsed bishops to the Catholic chorepiscopate if the Catholic bishop of the local see deemed fit.

Nevertheless, though threatened by successive canonical legislation inspired by the city bishops, the *chorepiskopoi* in the East continued to serve a useful purpose in extending the ministry of baptism and the Eucharist into the countryside in the period before the delegation of full sacerdotal power to the presbyters could be effected.

Long before the process was completed there had been a class of rural presbyters whose sacerdotal powers were only *ad hoc* and who lost their status whenever the municipal bishop or the town presbyters happened to make a visitation (Neocaesarea, canon 12).[122] The earliest reference to rural presbyters (and also rural teachers) is in a letter of Bishop Dionysius of Alexandria (*c.* 247-64).[123] Whether these numerous Egyptian presbyters also had only delegated *ad hoc* sacerdotal powers (baptism and Eucharist) is not certain but probable.

The remaining ante-Nicene experiment in delegating episcopal functions to meet the needs of the rural constituencies was the enlargement of the scope of the diaconate, since the deacon from the beginning had been the attendant or the representative of the bishop. The evidence for this tendency is meager and largely inferential and Western. The Council of Elvira (306, canon 77) regulates deacons who are improperly governing the faithful in certain localities without direct episcopal supervision and without priests. Here the regulation concerns only baptism. The Council of Arles (314), however, knows of many places in which deacons offer the Eucharist and it seeks to abolish the practice (canon 13). Several of the church orders of the third century give additional evidence of trying to keep deacons in their zeal from exceeding their proper duties. Then at the Council of Nicaea in 325 (canon 18) it was decreed that deacons henceforth should not communicate the presbyters.

This canon did not, to be sure, touch upon the rural diaconate, and the Council as a whole was content to leave the chorepiscopate as it had been limited by Ancyra and Neocaesarea, but by implication it confirmed the emerging pattern of the sacerdotal, parochial presbyterate as the constitutional solution of the pastoral problem of both the big city and the countryside. Canon 18 should therefore be before us in full, as it marks an epoch; in a few lines it records what has happened:

It has become known to this holy and great council that in localities and cities the deacons distribute the Eucharist to the presbyters, though it is contrary to the canon and the tradition that they who may not themselves offer the sacrifice should distribute the body of Christ to those who do offer the sacrifice. It has also become known that some deacons receive the Eucharist before the bishops. All that shall be discontinued now and the deacons shall remain in their place, knowing that they are servants (*hyperetai*) of the bishop and in rank subordinate to the presbyters. They are to receive the Eucharist in accordance with their rank, after the presbyters, a bishop or presbyter administering it to them. The deacons also are not to sit in the midst of the presbyters; for what has happened is contrary to rule and order. If anyone, after these ordinances, still refuses to obey, let him cease from the diaconate.[124]

In abolishing the practice of deacons' communicating the presbyters, the Nicene Council characterized as against tradition what had, in fact, been primitively the natural function of the servants of the bishops, namely, to pass the bread and wine and first of all to the *liturgically nonparticipant* but revered and seated elders (presbyters) of the congregation.

This canon thus provides a point of easy reference for the summary of the evolution of the ministry in the two hundred years traced since the close of the New Testament epoch. The bishop and the presbyter are in this canon alike *sacerdotes* who offer the Eucharistic sacrifice. The deacon who at the primitive Eucharist served the presbyters as the venerable elders of the Christian fellowship is now a member of the third order down from the episcopate in a society of clearly demarcated clerical ranks. For while this process was going on and presbyters were becoming priests in their own right, the primitively cultual bishops assumed more and more of the disciplinary functions of the presbyters and the magisterial functions of the teachers. The city bishops have, moreover, dissociated themselves from the rural bishops who are being depressed as a kind of intermediate order between bishops and presbyters. The city episcopate is well on the way to monopolizing the rite of the imposition of hands in ordination, a practice once associated with both pagan teachers and Jewish elders and rabbis and by now projected into apostolic times as the unique function of the apostles *qua* bishops. At the Council of Arles the Western bishops had decreed that henceforth at least three consecrating bishops were necessary for the elevation of a cleric to their rank, and this is repeated at Nicaea, bringing, for example, the ancient presbyteral constitution of Alexandria to an end.

Metropolitans, the bishops of provincial capitals, are emerging as authoritative in their presidency of the provincial councils. In the measure that bishops have taken counsel with one another in correspondence and councils,[125] they have developed a sense of catholic confraternity and solidarity whereby they are beginning to feel somewhat apart from their local presbyteries. Collectively in their councils they are the organ of the Holy Spirit. It may be significant in this connection that the first councils were convened in Asia Minor to wrest control of the Church from the hands of the Montanist prophets who claimed to speak through the authority of the Spirit. Canon 5 of Nicaea requires two provincial synods a year made up exclusively of bishops. Spiritual men, exercising their divine, disciplinary, and doctrinal authority, they are collectively able to judge all things and be judged by none.

III

The Ministry in the Later Patristic Period (314-451)

GEORGE H. WILLIAMS

With the sudden cessation of imperial persecution the ministry was obliged to accommodate itself quickly to the demands and the expectations of a patronizing magistracy. With the establishment of the Church in the favor of one Emperor (by 314 in the West and 324 in the East), and the prospect of a rapid enlargement of the membership of the churches and the proliferation of new duties and opportunities and temptations, a new phase in the evolution of the ministry had dawned. In the complete change of religious climate most of the new patterns of priestly behavior and pastoral rule which were to prevail for a millennium in both Eastern and Western Catholicism until challenged by Protestantism were laid down in the period between the Council of Arles in 314 and the Council of Chalcedon in 451.

We began our survey in Chapter II of the two hundred years' development of the ministry after the close of the New Testament epoch by distinguishing three kinds of ministry: the charismatic, the cultual, and the disciplinary. We saw how the cultual ministry, which was originally twofold with protobishops (or presiding presbyters) and deacons, absorbed several of the functions of the other two, until at length only remnants of the first survived, while the presbyterate was in the process of even more radical metamorphosis. For by the Council of Nicaea the old collegiate, disciplinary presbytery in each city was well on its way toward disaggregation. The city "parish" (*paroikia*[1]) was becoming a diocese (though not yet in name) under its bishop while the presbyters were more or less permanently assigned to outlying communities or the regional churches in the case of the more populous cities. These segments of the episcopal "parish" were on their way to becoming parishes in our later sense. Thus presbyters were becoming priests at the very same time they were relinquishing their corporate judicial and disciplinary authority in the bishop's church, while the bishop had become the chief judge; and the law itself was being codified in canons at councils at which bishops alone decreed.

Thus in place of three basic, though overlapping ministries of the primitive church (sometimes concurrently discharged by the same person) we found at the end of the two centuries of evolution three main orders of the clergy: the episcopate, the priesthood, and the diaconate and an ever-growing series of lower orders. Bishops and presbyters together belonged to the priesthood (*sacerdotium*) in respect to their function at the altar; to the presbyterate, wherever it remained intact as a corporate entity, in respect to local discipline. All three, bishop, priest, and deacon, constituted the clergy, while others pressed for the same dignity, notably the subdeacon (soon to be classed with the major orders). In the meantime, ordination, which set the clergy apart from the laity, had acquired the significance of a kind of second baptism or a second penance in blotting out all but carnal sin (Neocaesarea, canon 9)[2], a step toward construing the clerical state as a superior stage of Christian achievement both morally and spiritually, and a step also toward the doctrine of the indelibility of ordination.

Celibacy was becoming more and more a mark of the clergy, though the process was not even, and there were many sections of the Church that limited their scruples to second marriage only. Celibacy had long been esteemed a laudable state for the clergy. It was not, however, until the Spanish provincial council of Elvira (306) that continence as distinguished from celibacy had been made obligatory. Yet in a corresponding Eastern council, that of Ancyra (314), the bishop and presbyter might enter marriage before ordination; only the deacon might do so afterward on condition that he have declared his intentions before ordination.

The evolution of the episcopate as a ministerial order distinct from the presbyterate, virtually completed by the time of the Council of Nicaea, was formalized in the conciliar canons between Nicaea and the Council of Chalcedon, though not without resistance.

It was at the Council of Antioch in Encaeniis (341)[3] that the character of the fourth-century episcopate was most clearly and significantly defined. Almost all its canons dealt with episcopacy and were authoritatively made a part of canon law by the Council of Chalcedon.[4] These canons made clear that the bishops of a province, meeting semiannually in synod under the presidency of their metropolitan, constituted a collegium with a relationship to the metropolitan much like that of the second-century collegiate presbytery in relation to the bishop of the local church. According to canons 4 and 18 to 23,[5] a new bishop is elected and ordained by the metropolitan and the provincial bishops in synod; and, when thus elevated, he enjoys the rank and ministry of bishop even if he is not accepted by the people of his see.[6] Yet he may be deposed by the same synod for other reasons. In these canons of an Arianizing council [7] the relation of the bishop to his people has been seriously attenuated. In 380 at the Council of Laodicea election by the people [8] was expressly forbidden (canon 13), though the rights of the laity in election survived in many places, especially in the West. In the Eastern *Apostolic Constitutions* the communal voice in the election of a bishop has been reduced to the thrice-iterated consent of the people and presbytery to receive a synodally chosen bishop as their ruler (archōn).[9] In the *Testament of Our Lord*,[10] the formality is reduced to the thrice-recited "He is worthy!" (*axios!*) which still resounds at the enthronization of a Greek bishop.

With the widening gulf between the bishop and his people went the elimination of the *chorepiskopoi* and therewith the pattern of greater fellowship and intimacy between bishop and people which had survived outside the great cities. The Council of Sardica (canon 6) decreed (343) that *chorepiskopoi* should no longer be appointed; and Laodicea (canon 54) sought to replace all rural bishops with visitors under the supervision of city bishops. It should be remarked that the repeated efforts to control and eventually to suppress the chorepiscopate were prompted in part by the recurrent involvement of the rural bishops, because of insufficient stipends, in part-time economic activities inconsonant with the episcopal dignity. Despite this consolidation the feeling that each (city) bishop stood in succession to the apostles was still largely confined to the apostolic sees. The Syrian Constitutor of the *Apostolic Constitutions* (c. 380) could, for example, still think even of the presbyters of Antioch (for this would have been his model see) as taking the place of the apostles rather than the bishop. He called the presbyters "the sanhedrin and senate of the church," [11] and he thought of Christ as the universal Bishop and High Priest.[12] To be sure, Chrysostom, Epiphanius, and Theodore of Mopsuestia among others contended that bishops were but presbyters with greater jurisdiction and the power of ordination.[13] Jerome and Ambrosiaster were particularly pleased to recall that even the ordaining power had once been exercised by presbyters in ante-Nicene Alexandria. But these were not representative contentions, for the provincially organized and ecumenically minded episcopate had bcome fully conscious of participating in a *ministry*, as well as a *jurisdiction,* different from that of their subordinate presbyter-priests.

As we have noted, as early as the Council of Nicaea bishops had taken upon themselves the full responsibility for the authoritative definition of dogma in their corporate capacity as the organ of the Holy Spirit. To this doctrinal function had been added the disciplinary and legislative powers to bind and loose by canons deemed superior in authority to locally received traditions and the consensus of local churches in which the laity and the presbyters had customarily voiced their assent in adjudications and in doctrinal formulations.

The bishops were also assigned local judicial duties by the new Christianized State. In the period of persecutions it had been natural that Paul's injunction not to seek adjudication outside the Christian community should be observed; and usages in this connection were codified in manuals of church discipline. Yet even in the period of imperial patronage, when the ordinary courts themselves came to reflect Christian principles, bishops continued to enlarge the judicial aspect of their office. All Christians, at the beginning of the Constantinian era, were directed (318, 333) to the courts spiritual presided over by bishops; and thus two codes of law and two separate though mutually influential "Christian" systems of adjudication were elaborated in the course of the fourth century. Only in 398 did Emperor Acadius for the East and in 408 Honorius for the West limit the scope of the episcopal court in respect to Christian laymen to those cases in which both parties sought it in preference to the regular tribunal. Canon 9 of Chalcedon was content to constrain clerics from carrying their grievances before secular tribunals (except as a final resort, the throne in Constantinople). In the meantime, bishops had come to be appointed occasionally, as it were *ex officio,* the emperor's "personal" *defensores* of the municipalities to protect the local populations, Christian and otherwise, from any unfair practices of the local or provincial officialdom of the Empire. At Chalcedon by canons 4 and 8 bishops also acquired the right of direct supervision and appointment in respect to all monasteries, the surviving chorepiscopacies, poorhouses, and hospitals in their "dioceses." [14]

The diaconate, in contrast, had by the end of the Patristic period been atrophied insofar as it could no longer be considered a terminal or life ministry. It was merely a rung in the clerical ladder; moreover, the deacon had become the assistant of the parish presbyter-priest [15] as well as of the bishop. For the most part the presbyter had become the principal beneficiary of the devolution of episcopal powers. Nevertheless, in Rome and perhaps in other very large sees, the deacons, who were held to the apostolic number of seven but with quite unapostolic prerequisites and powers, tried intermittently to take precedence over the more numerous and less highly remunerated presbyters. During the pontificate of former deacon Damasus, Ambrosiaster wrote a little tract *On the Arrogance of the Roman Deacons*.[16] Besides the propitious factor of the relatively small number of deacons, mention also should be made of their close association with people in their everyday necessities as a common consideration in their election to the episcopate. Hence some of the jealousy of the presbyters. As late as the *Testament of Our Lord* (variously dated from 350 to 450) the deacon is said to be "counsellor of the whole clergy" at the very point in the reworking of Hippolytean material where the deacon had been hitherto expressly stated *not* to be participant in the counsel of the clergy. In the fifth-century *Canons of Hippolytus* certain deacons are set aside as instructors of the catechumens and are called *doctores ecclesiae*. In this same milieu the deacons were also charged with preaching, like the Syriac Father Ephrem (d. 373), teacher in Nisibis and in the refugee "School of the Persians" in Edessa. In view of their close assocation with the neophytes, deacons frequently baptized in the absence of priest or bishop (though the practice was forbidden in the *Apostolic Constitutions*).[17] Deacons continued in most areas their eleemosynary functions but many of these had been taken over by the ever-growing number of minor or more specialized clerical functionaries.

In the meantime, the female diaconate was undergoing significant expansion, but exclusively in the East. Beginning with the obscure reference of canon 19 of Nicaea respecting Paulinian [18] deaconesses and ending with canon 15 of Chalcedon which prohibits the ordination (*cheirotonia*) of a deaconess *before* the age of forty we have the canonical framework of the most significant period in the expansion and elaboration of the ministry of women before modern times.

According to the *Apostolic Constitutions* she had to submit to a careful examination before proceeding to ordination. A representative prayer for the latter is preserved in the "Clementine" Liturgy embedded in the *Constitutions* and reflecting Antiochene usage *c.* 350 to 380. The "constitution" is ascribed to the apostle Bartholomew who instructs a bishop thus:

Thou shalt lay thy hands upon her in the presence of the presbytery and of the deacons and deaconesses, and shalt say:
O eternal God, the Father of our Lord Jesus Christ, the Creator of man and

of woman, who didst replenish with the Spirit Miriam, and Deborah, and Anna, and Huldah; who didst not disdain that thine only-begotten Son should be born of a woman; who also in the Tabernacle of the testimony and in the Temple, didst ordain women to be keepers of thy holy gates, do thou now also look down upon this thy servant, who is to be ordained to the office of a deaconess, and grant her thy Holy Spirit . . . that she may worthily discharge the work.[19]

At a somewhat later date we know from the Byzantine ritual for the ordination of the deaconess that the bishop invested her with a diaconal stole and that after communicating, she herself replaced the chalice on the altar. The mid-fourth-century Council of Laodicea speaks (canon 10) of female presidents (*presbytides*). These, however, are no longer to be appointed in the church. In view of the survival of Montanists in the region—and this Council deals with them—it is possible that these *presbytides* represent the Catholic counterpart of the Montanist prophetesses. The deaconesses from Nicaea to Chalcedon and thereafter seem to have been recruited almost exclusively from the upper classes; and, although in *The Testament of Our Lord* they are by way of exception regarded as markedly inferior to the widows (*presbytides*)[20] "who sit in front," the highborn deaconesses are almost everywhere else clearly distinguished from widows in being ministers rather than the recipients of church welfare.

Virgins did not become a clearly distinct order until the middle of the fourth century.[21]

Of the increasing number of clerics in minor orders and other special functionaries of the fourth- and fifth-century ecclesiastical bureaucracy, a partial list must suffice. Among these numerous ministries, several were commonly singled out as the *seven* degrees or orders ordained by Christ and sanctified by his having himself served variously in the grade of (1) gravedigger, (2) doorkeeper, (3) lector, (4) subdeacon, (5) deacon, (6) presbyter, and (7) bishop.[22] These seven ministerial degrees could also be made to correspond to the seven gifts of the Holy Spirit. There was also a tendency to assimilate these clerical degrees to the *cursus honorum* of the Roman civil servant. But, as in the imperial bureaucracy, so in the clerical career, it was not always necessary to start at the bottom of the ladder. Moreover, though the number seven recurs in the ancient lists, the lower degrees were not fixed. Exorcist and acolyte were possible alternatives. In the East, at least, the singers constituted a special order. Interpreters were assigned to preachers in rural areas where the languages of the Empire were not sufficiently well known for the missionary preacher to dispense with the local dialects. Visitors of the sick and custodians of the episcopal residences emerged as special classes of servants and ministrants of the church. In this period the archpriest emerged as the chief representative of the bishop in respect to priestly functions in the cathedral church, comparable to the archdeacon in administrative and eleemosynary affairs. The Council of Chalcedon (canon 26) advanced beyond the Council of Antioch (canon 24) in regularizing episcopal property and decreed that every episcopal establishment should have a steward (*oikonomos, vicedominus*) drawn from the cathedral clergy whose task it was to manage the estates and income of the basilica, to keep the bishop's personal property distinct from that of the see, and to safeguard the cathedral holdings during a vacancy of the see. Other functionaries of the large sees were the notaries, the archivists, and the emissaries (*apokrisiarioi, nuntii*), the latter representing the bishop at the residence of his superior (the metropolitan, exarch or patriarch).

The household of the bishop had become so large that new patterns were bound to emerge for the common life of cathedral clerics. Eusebius of Vercellae (d. 370) and Augustine (d. 430) were pioneers in the West in introducing the model of the monastery into the cathedral.

In the late fourth century short-cropped hair or the tonsure, borrowed from the Egyptian monks, began to be the outward sign of all clerics.[23] Already by the middle of the fourth century the clergy were wearing a distinctive garb.[24] Among the higher clergy the insignia and distinctive garments and accoutrements of dress were made to correspond to those of the secular ranks of society, the *clarissimi* (of the senatorial class), the *spectabiles,* and the *illustres.* Within the last rank there were the five grades of *illustrissimi, magnifici, excellentissimi, glorissimi,* and *nobilissimi* (of the blood royal). The Synod of Arles, for example, addressed the Pope as *glorissime.* The insignia and prerogatives of rank and precedence, such as the use of a certain kind of sandal, rings, pallium, and maniple, seem to have been in part appropriated by the clergy and in part formally bestowed by the emperor. With the enhancement of the dignity of the bishop and the extension of his judicial authority under the patronage of the Empire, the old *cathedra* upon which the ante-Nicene bishop had sat in his capacity as teacher, was gradually converted into a veritable throne, imitative of that of the emperor.[25] It is quite possible that the courtly protocol and the sartorial details of the so-called Donation of Constantine are a reasonably accurate description of the dress, insignia, and prerogatives of the chief bishop of the West in the late imperial period, that even the account of the bestowal of these privileges primarily errs in fictionally ascribing to one emperor what was probably done by several in the course of the fourth and fifth centuries, and that once the fictional monopolization of these prerogatives by one bishop is removed, the Donation is recognized as supplying us with a picture of a late imperial prelate.[26]

Let us turn from the prelates inextricably involved in the protocol of late imperial society and from the more specialized ministries of the various orders to the pastoral office as conceived by four great episcopal pastors of the fourth century: Chrysostom and Basil for the East; Ambrose and Augustine for the West. In one sense none of these was typical, for one was called from a high post in civil service; two were pre-eminently monks; all of them were prelates of important sees and knew the life of the capitals; and none of them had climbed the clerical ladder from the lowest rungs. But taken together they give us a fairly complete picture of the city pastor in the period of imperial patronage.

John Chrysostom (c. 345-407) vividly delineates his pastoral functions in his sermons and in his *Treatise on the Priesthood* (c. 386). Born of a family high in the imperial administration, Chrysostom enjoyed an extended liberal education in philosophy and rhetoric. He was able to extricate himself from being prematurely, as he thought, elevated to the episcopate. After becoming a monk instead, he became successively deacon and presbyter in Antioch, and then in 397 Bishop of Constantinople.

Despite his own monastic formation, this eloquent preacher to the turbulent, variegated "audiences" of the two Eastern capitals was certain that monks were not the best fitted for the role of priests, but rather those "who, though having their life and conversation among men, yet can preserve their purity, their calm, their piety, and patience, and soberness, and all other good qualities of monks more unbroken and steadfast than those hermits do themselves." [27] Chrysostom describes the ideal bishop:

He must be dignified yet modest, awe-inspiring yet kindly, masterful yet accessible, impartial yet courteous, humble yet not servile, vehement yet gentle, in order that he may be able easily to resist all these dangers[28] and to promote the suitable man with great firmness, even though all men gainsay him, and reject the unsuitable with the same firmness, even though all favor him; he must consider one end only, the edification of the Church.[29]

Chrysostom well understood the scope and exactions of the pastorate:

A priest must be sober and clear-sighted and possess a thousand eyes in every
direction.[30]

Since he must consort with men in all walks of life, he must himself be
"many-sided" yet guard against becoming a dissembler. To enter upon
the ministry the conscientious would-be cleric must pass the "test of
bravery of soul," which should be "robust and vigorous." [31] Chrysostom's
initial reluctance to accept the responsibilities of the episcopate, or
rather his recoiling from it as something dreaded and perilous, was an
attitude he shared with many of the other great episcopal pastors of the
fourth century. Some of their protestations of utter unworthiness strike
the modern reader as pathological; and some of the ruses whereby they
sought to escape being "captured," "snared," and "seized" for the
episcopate seem theatrical. Closer scrutiny of their behavior and arguments, however, gives us perhaps a clearer idea of the ministry in
Christian antiquity than any other approach. Reluctance rather than
readiness was taken as a sign of valid vocation.

Chrysostom, knew, for example, that the contest between Damasus
and Ursinus for the episcopacy of the Roman church in 367 had cost
the lives of 137 persons in Santa Maria Maggiore and that many other
unworthy men had sought or had been advanced to the episcopate. He
despairingly lists some of the improper or fatuous reasons sometimes
put forward in favor of such candidates, like their wealth, family connections, their being recently converted from the other side, their
fashionable large-mindedness, their ecclesiastical pull.[32] But basically,
the reluctance of the high-minded to be elected bishop was their own
extremely high view of the office and the spiritual dangers it involved.

There was first of all among just such men a great yearning to work
out their own salvation, often in devotion to "Christian philosophy," i.e.,
monasticism. Besides Chrysostom, one thinks of such reluctant bishops
as Ambrose, Martin of Tours, and Augustine. Involvement in pastoral
cares withdrew them from the contemplative life.

Secondly, there was deep feeling that the pre-eminent qualification of
the true pastor was his readiness to perish for his sheep. Chrysostom
regards Paul as the ideal pastor in this and other respects and cites
Paul's eagerness to incur eternal punishment that his kinsmen after the
flesh might be saved. Chrysostom could not be certain whether he had
this degree of love for the brethren.

Thirdly, there was a dread lest in assuming the responsibility for the eternal life of the brethren with the apostolic power of binding and loosing, the pastor himself might be adversely judged at the Great Assize.

And fourthly, there was the holy fear that bordered on awesome dread which surrounded the priestly act at the Eucharist. This was a feeling which seems to have been especially characteristic of Chrysostom and others in the Antiochene and related traditions,[33] and we shall do well to pause with Chrysostom before the fourth-century altar.

Chrysostom compares the chief celebrant at the altar with Elijah on Mount Carmel:

Picture . . . before your eyes Elijah and the vast crowd standing around him, and the sacrifice lying on the altar of stones. All the rest are still and hushed in deep silence; the prophet alone is praying. Then of a sudden the flame is flung down from heaven upon the offering. This is a wonderful and awful picture. Pass from that scene to what is now performed. You will see things not only wonderful to look upon, but transcending all in *terror*. The priest stands bringing down not fire, but the Holy Spirit; and he offers prayer for a long space, not that a fire may be kindled from above and destroy the offering, but that grace may fall on the sacrifice through that prayer and kindle the souls of all. . . . Can any one despise this awful rite? Do you not know that no human soul could ever have borne the fire of that sacrifice, but they could all have been brought utterly to nought, had not the help of the grace of God been lavishly bestowed?[34]

And the help that comes "when he invokes the Holy Spirit, and offers that awful Sacrifice," are the angels who "surround the priest and the whole sanctuary . . .; and the place around the altar is filled with heavenly powers in honor of Him who lies there." [35] Nay more. As in Clement of Alexandria, the ranks of the clergy are themselves the sacerdotal counterparts of the angels:

Although the priestly office is discharged upon the earth, it ranks among celestial ordinances. And this is natural; for no man, no angel, no archangel, no other created power, but the Comforter Himself appointed this order, and persuaded us while still in the flesh to represent the angelic ministry. Wherefore the priest must be as pure as if he were standing in heaven amid those powers.[36]

This identification with angelic action is made in connection with the Eucharist.

In connection with repentance priests are declared to be even superior to the angels, for priests "have been entrusted with the stewardship of things in heaven, and have received an authority which God had given neither to angels nor to archangels." Thus with their power to bind and loose (penance), to regenerate (baptism), and to distribute the Body of the King, which enables one "to escape the fire of hell" and "obtain the crowns" of heaven—in these actions every priest is raised above parents, kings, and even angels.[37]

This exaltation of the priest in his office of forgiveness may well be connected with the fact that Chrysostom occupies a nodal point in the evolution of the penitential discipline. As the spiritual counselor of the citizens of a sophisticated capital, Chrysostom sought an alternative for the humiliating public penance (*exomologesis*) with its several stages or stations of readmission to communion. Even this repentance for a major sin was permitted by the Church at large only *once* after the cleansing bath of baptism (the latter frequently postponed for this reason, as in the case of Chrysostom himself, until adulthood). His contemporaries such as Ambrose still held to one faith, one baptism, and one (public) penance. But Chrysostom, perhaps because of his monkish understanding of the range of inward sinfulness, came to believe in the iteration of penance and in a diversified therapy for sinners.[38] "It is not right," he said, "to take an absolute standard and fit the penalty to the exact measure of the offense, but it is right to aim at influencing the moral feelings of the offenders," for surely "no one can, by compulsion, cure an unwilling man." [39] As a curer of souls, Chrysostom thought of himself as a physician dispensing medicaments to those who voluntarily submitted to his art and of the church as a hospital whither the sinner might have to repair for more than one serious sin:

> Show thy charity [he urged a fellow priest] towards the sinner. Persuade him that it is from care and anxiety for his welfare and not from a wish to expose him, that thou puttest him in mind of his sin. . . . Urge him to show the wound to the priest; that is the part of one who cares for him, and provides for him, and is anxious on his behalf.[40]

Besides his penitential and liturgical functions the bishop was, for Chrysostom, pre-eminently a teacher and preacher. As teacher he wards off heresy. Chrysostom himself could preach effectively to a large and diversified congregation on the *homousios* or the impropriety of resorting to synagogues for special ritual services. The preacher must toil long on his sermons in order to gain the power of eloquence. Yet he must be indifferent to praise. And if the presbyter or deacon is better than his bishop in the homiletical art, the latter must, for the glory of the church, adjust himself to the disparity of gifts. The golden-tongued presbyter-preacher of Antioch and his aged bishop Flavian co-operated in an exemplary way in this respect and notably in the crisis of 387 when, after a tax riot and the breaking of the royal statues by the populace, the whole of Antioch huddled in terror of Emperor Theodosius' wrath. The bishop's intercessory journey to the Emper and Chrysostom's famous series of sermons on the statues stand out as an example of the priestly role in appeasing the anger of rulers. Chrysostom further exemplified the role of the priest as prophet when, as Bishop of Constantinople, he rebuked the Empress Eudoxia as Jezebel and again as Herodia, not, however, without incurring deposition and exile once and then a second time.

Besides the royal wrath, Chrysostom knew well the lesser hazards of the prophetic priesthood. The priest, he observed, is ever judged by his parish as though he were an angel and not of the same frail stuff as the rest of men. If there be the slightest bit of stubble in the building of his life, it will be licked up by the inflammatory envy of vexed parishioners or rival clerics and the whole edifice can be "scorched and utterly blackened by the smoke."

The Western counterpart of Chryostom was Ambrose (339-397), bishop of Milan. Like Chrysostom, Ambrose was born in the family of a high official but differed from the sometime monk of Antioch in having been recruited directly and spectacularly from the ranks of imperial administration. He too was self-deprecatory about his qualifications and after his elevation wrote *On the Duties of Ministers* in the same year (386) that Chrysostom wrote *On the Priesthood*. But despite the title, Ambrose, in adapting the Stoicism of the *De officiis* of Cicero, had more in mind a compendium of Christian ethics of which the clergy would be the most exemplary embodiment than a manual on the ministry. Thus after paying respects to his careful working through of the four pagan virtues, as they applied to Christians, and the three specifically Christian virtues, we must turn elsewhere for Ambrose's conception of the pastoral and priestly role.

Ambrose was a notably eloquent preacher, converting Augustine who had come to hear him simply as a master of the rhetorician's art. Like

Chrysostom, whose name is given to one of the liturgies of the Greek Church, Ambrose devoted himself to the liturgy in theory (*De mysteriis,* possibly [41] *De sacramentis*) and in practice (the liturgical *cantus Ambrosianus,* based upon the ancient Greek modes).

Ambrose had an exalted view of the episcopate. The bishop is both a *sacerdos* and a *propheta* in the *Old Testament* sense. In a letter to his sister, Ambrose sets forth his view that both the stern, prophetic rebuke and the healing, priestly ministry are combined in the episcopal office. Referring to the rod of the almond tree in Jeremiah 1:11, he observes that the priest and prophet must proclaim things bitter and hard like the almond husk but inside is sweetness. The authority of the *sacerdos* is derived by apostolic succession from the incarnate Christ; the authority of the espicopal *propheta* stems from the eternal Christ. In Elijah, who worsted the priests of Baal on Mount Carmel, Ambrose beholds the union of the two vocations.

In calling down the fire to consume the sacrifice, Ambrose sees the Old Covenant counterpart of his own act as priest in summoning the Holy Spirit to the Christian altar, and repeating the incarnate Christ's words of institution.[42] In the rebuke of Ahab and Jezebel he finds the parallel to, and sanction for, his denunciation of Valentinian II and his Arian mother. Or again, if he is rebuking an orthodox emperor, he may identify himself with Nathan pointing the finger at David. Ambrose states his conviction as to the prophetic function of the bishop very well in a letter to Theodosius: "There is nothing in a priest so full of peril as regards God, or so base in the opinion of men, as not freely to declare what he thinks."

The authority of the bishop, while greatly enhanced by personal rectitude, does not, according to Ambrose, depend upon his own merits but upon those of Elijah, and Peter, also of Paul, and ultimately of Christ. Ambrose emphatically asserted that Paul was not inferior to Peter in the apostolate, "second to none." And interpreting Matt. 16:18 f., Ambrose singled out Peter's *faith* rather than his being first as determinative in the founding of the Church upon him and says that it was *representatively* that Peter responded for all the apostles to Jesus' pre-transfiguration inquiry. Elsewhere [43] Ambrose argued that Peter accepted the sheep from Christ along with all subsequent bishops; indeed, in Peter the whole future episcopate was present, receiving proleptically what Peter at that time assumed personally. In the analogous Johannine commission of Peter (John 21:5 ff.) Ambrose laid stress upon the thrice-asseverated *love* of Peter for the resurrected Jesus as distinguished from the *faith* in the pre-resurrection Matthaean episode as the basis of Peter's pre-eminence among the apostles and of his authority to rule the flock of Christ and bind and loose on earth. Ambrose thereupon declares: "The care of these sheep, this flock, not only for that time did the blessed apostle Peter take upon himself but also along with us he received them, and all of us [bishops] with him received them." He goes on to explain to the clerical brethren listening that they should more fully realize that "there can be found nothing in this world more excellent than priests, nor more lofty than bishops," for they are as gold compared to princes, who are like lead.

Augustine, building in part on Ambrose who had converted him, was as Bishop of Hippo both an exemplary pastor and preacher and as a theologian a major theorist concerning the nature and function of the priesthood. Reluctantly, however, we pass over his own exemplification of the pastoral ideal so attractively delineated in the *Life* by Bishop Possidius of Calama.[44] We can only mention the fact that Possidius characteristically uses *ministri* alike for priests, bishops, and deacons. He shows how Augustine, like Ambrose, was raised to the episcopate by the spontaneous action of the *plebs* after the aging Greek-speaking bishop of Hippo had asked for a coadjutor. We see in the *Vita* how much of Augustine's time was spent as an arbiter of Christian cases (without, apparently, the presbyters counseling with him as in the roughly contemporary Eastern church manuals), how he often interceded for prisoners, how he preached and debated, how he occasionally healed by the imposition of hands, how he dined with his clerics at the episcopal table with moderation but never abstemiously, under a motto on the wall which enjoined all guests to refrain from gossip. But the most vivid aspect of the *Vita* is its preservation of Augustine's own words concerning the self-sacrifice of the pastor in times of persecution or invasion (the Vandals). Herein he gives voice to what we might call the professional ethic of the clergyman who, like the captain, must go down with his ship, or, like the shepherd, give his life for his flock; for ". . . the ties of our ministry, by which the love of Christ has bound us not to desert the churches . . . should not be broken."[45]

God forbid [he goes on] that this ship of ours should be prized so lightly that the sailors, and especially the pilot, ought to abandon it when it is in danger, even if they can escape by taking to a small boat or even by swimming.

He vividly describes the plight of the people and the duties of their ministers:

> . . . when these dangers have reached their height and there is no possibility of flight, do we not realize how great a gathering there usually is in the church of both sexes and of every age, some clamoring for baptism, others for reconciliation, still others for acts of penance: all of them seeking consolation and the administration and distribution of the sacraments? If, then, the ministers are not at hand, how terrible is the destruction which overtakes those who depart from this world unregenerated or bound by sin!

He stresses the solidarity of pastor and flock:

> . . . when the danger is common to all, that is, to bishops, clergy and laymen, let those who are in need of others not be abandoned by those of whom they are in need. Accordingly, either let them all withdraw to places of safety or else let not those who have a necessity for remaining be left by those through whom their ecclesiastical needs are supplied, so that they may either live together or suffer together whatever their Father wishes them to endure.

Apart from his own embodiment of the ministerial ideal, Augustine's contribution to the development of the priesthood was his sacramental concept of the ministry whereby the validity of a cleric's sacramental action was seen to be independent of his personal character.[46] For his theory of the validity of the sacrament *ex opere operato*, Augustine drew upon the thinking of the anti-Donatist Bishop Optatus of Mileve who had contended for the objective validity of baptism as long as the action and intention were formally correct. But Augustine also drew upon the thinking of a leading Donatist lay theologian Tichonius and also Donatist Bishop Parmenian who had been forced to "catholicize" in trying to make sense of the schisms within rigoristic Donatism! The moderate Donatists knew of an invisible universal Church of the pure and righteous and sought to demonstrate the validity of Donatist ordinations on either side of their schism. From all this, Augustine, in his effort to win back the Donatists for the Great Church, developed the theological basis for maintaining that an indelible *character dominicus*, comparable to the military brand (*character militiae*) or the regal imprint on a coin (*signum regale*) is imparted by any formally correct ordination.[47]

Hitherto there had been considerable ambiguity and difference of opinion about the ordinations of heretical and schismatic clerics prepared to reunite with the Church catholic. The Council of Nicaea (canons 8, 9, and 10, and the synodal letter), dealing variously with the Novatianist and the Meletian clergy and with *lapsi* who should never have been ordained on moral grounds, left open the question as to what constituted valid ordination and what constituted the difference between election (*eklogē*), recognition or installation (*katastasis*), imposition of hand (*cheirothesia*), and ordination proper (*cheirotonia*). Nor did Nicaea make a distinction between the deposition from clerical rank and the mere suspension from clerical acts of one who had been validly ordained.[48] Gregory of Nyssa, among others, gave expression to an Eastern view of the nature of ordination (*c.* 376) when he compared the change of a cleric at ordination to the sacramental action whereby bread becomes the Body of Christ:

> The same power of the word . . . makes the priest venerable and honorable, separated. . . . While but yesterday he was one of the mass, one of the people, he is suddenly rendered a guide, a president, a teacher of righteousness, an instructor in hidden mysteries, metamorphosed in respect of his unseen soul to the higher condition.[49]

But Gregory did not develop a doctrine of the indelibility of ordination, while the weighty contemporaneous *Apostolic Constitutions* supply an ordaining prayer beseeching God never to withdraw his Holy Spirit.[50] At the Council of Chalcedon (canon 29) the Eastern fathers will presently give evidence of continuing uncertainty as to whether, for example, a bishop for disciplinary reasons may be reduced to the rank of presbyter, or whether he should be eliminated from the clergy altogether and classed as a layman.

In the meantime Augustine, for the West, by separating the question of orders from the nature of the Church and schism (to the end that he might contribute to the healing of the North African schism), made ordination wholly a permanent possession of the individual apart from the community in which and through which it was conferred. In thus individualizing ordination Augustine witnesses indirectly to the extinction in the West *c.* 400 of the older catholic feeling for the corporate ministry of the local church.[51] Within four centuries the hereditary priesthood of Israel had been replaced by the indelible priesthood of Christendom, valid not by inheritance and birth but through a kind of rebirth in the solemn rededication of ordination in the descent of the

Holy Spirit, an action which also represented a tactile succession going back to the apostles.

With this conception of the role of the clergy articulated by Augustine, the ministry of the Church was prepared for a new phase in its evolution, destined to find fresh forms and functions as it faced the breakdown of Empire in the West and the incursions of the barbarians. Monks were to emerge as the principal missionaries, bishops to become administrators of vast dioceses, while within the cathedral and the parish new functions and functionaries were to develop in a society in which the city was not for a long time to come to be again the basic civil unit.

But in the East the ministry could still evolve within the familiar structure of a Christian Empire, truncated though Byzantium might be.

Before closing our survey of the ministries of the Patristic period in the East down to the Fourth Ecumenical Council (451), we must say a word about the ministry of the monastery in the post-Nicene period. The institutional church, in accommodating itself to imperial establishment and the arduous assignment of embracing the whole of the population of a given territory within its ministrations, left to the still pneumatic or the new charismatic ministry of the monks an important pastoral role. The monk was a successor of the ante-Nicene confessor with his power to forgive.[52] It is one of the anomalies of the evolution of the monastic ideal that they who withdrew to the wilderness, for the most part dispensing with the ministries of the organized parishes and thinking of themselves as "laymen," were presently to become the tutors and models of the "secular clergy." The monastic or "regular *clergy*," in their submission to a rule which was construed as a kind of higher ordination, were eventually to be esteemed by themselves and by the world as clergy *par excellence*.[53] But since this development belongs as much to the next chapter, a few words must here suffice concerning the pastoral function of monks to those outside the community of anchoritic or cenobitic discipline.

Evagrius Ponticus (d. 399), who systematized the thought of Clement of Alexandria, of Origen, and the Cappadocian Fathers, as it applied to the monastic life, distinguished between the "righteous" of the organized church and the "perfect," or "philosophers," i.e., the monks and hermits of the monastery and the cell. He taught it as a duty of the perfect to show a pastoral concern for the often shepherdless rigorist and heretical groups rejected or even persecuted by the Great Church. Frequently the most saintly seers among the monks and hermits were sought out by heretic and catholic alike because as holy men they were able to mediate the grace of healing, forgiveness, and spiritual counsel which the faithful sometimes found wanting in their institutionalized clergy. Occasionally these pneumatic curers of souls presumed to arrogate to themselves the administration of the sacrament of penance.[54] And the fierce abbot Shenoudi (d. 466) of the White Cloister of Atripe, ruling omnipotently over several thousands of monks, could think of himself in the language of Ignatius and the *Apostolic Constitutions* in the image of the Father who begets or regenerates his monks by the act of bringing them out of the world and admitting them to the monastery church. "Abbot" (Father) was originally a pneumatic designation indicative of charismatic achievement and authority.[55]

Shenoudi was unchallenged lord of his vast monastic church. But for the most part the Great Church and the monastic church worked out a *modus vivendi*. Indeed, most monasteries came to have priests appointed by neighboring bishops to communicate the monks; for, though the Eucharist had no place in the high monastic theory of self-discipline, it did have an adventitious place in the life of each monk. The Eastern churches, in part, solved the latent conflict between the clergy of the world and the monks by recruiting their higher clergy from the monasteries. Basil of Caesarea, who established the Basileiad, a veritable city of asylums for orphans, the sick, and the aged, and brought his own monks under a rule, is perhaps the best early representative of the "philosopher" bishop. He was a philosopher both in the sense of being a major philosophical theologian and more specifically of being a monk in the intellectual tradition of Clement and Origen. His *Addresses, Detailed Rules,* and *Short Rules* for monks, and his *Moralia* alike for monks and married Christians (for he made no basic distinction between the two in the achievement of perfection except continence) are admirable specimens of Basil's method as pastor and spiritual counselor.

It remains to point up a few emphases in the priesthood of the first half of the fifth century, exclusively in the East, within and without the Empire. We have already observed in Chrysostom the sense of majesty which the priest experienced in the discharge of his duties at the altar. This sense was intensified in his successors in the Antiochene and allied traditions. We can best understand the almost numinous character of the priesthood in the Greek Church today and in some of the extant

Oriental churches surviving from the fifth century by looking at this aspect of the ministry more closely. Theodore, Bishop of Mopsuestia (d. 428), a friend in his youth of Chrysostom, wrote of the central action in the ministry of every priest:

We are ordered to perform in this world the symbols and signs of the future things so that, through the service of the Sacrament, we may be like ones who enjoy symbolically the happiness of the heavenly benefits, and thus acquire a sense of possession and a strong hope of the things for which we look. . . . We must picture in our mind that we are dimly in heaven, and, through faith, draw in our imagination the image of heavenly things. . . . Because Christ our Lord offered Himself in sacrifice for us and thus became our high priest in reality, we must think that the priest who draws nigh unto the altar is representing His image. . . .[56]

Because of the august nature of his duty Theodore declared that the officiating priest has need of the prayers and the antiphonal amens of the faithful, for they are all one body together and he but their "eye" or "tongue," and when they respond "And with thy spirit," "the priest obtains more abundant peace from the overflow of the grace of the Holy Spirit" and from it receives help for his "awesome task." [57]

Narsai, Nestorian head of the Syrian school at Edessa (437-57) and refounder of the school in Nisibis, conveyed even more movingly the numinous sense of the office of the priest. Ambrose and Chrysostom, each in his own way, had likened the priest at the Eucharistic altar to Elijah on Mount Carmel. Narsai seized upon the image of Isaiah in the Temple with the burning coal to express the sacred terror experienced by the priest in the mediation of the divine, for Isaiah saw in the coal "the Mystery of the Body and Blood, which, like fire, consumes the iniquity of mortal man." He goes on:

The power of that mystery which the prophet saw the priest interprets; and as with a tongs he holds fire in his hand with the bread. . . .The power of the Spirit comes down unto a mortal man, and dwells in the bread and consecrates it. . . . His power strengthens the hand of the priest that it may take hold of His power; and feeble flesh is not burned up by His blaze.[58]

Narsai beheld in the altar at once a tomb and a throne; in the basilica, a sepulcher and a throneroom:

All the priests who are in the sanctuary bear the image of those apostles who met together at the sepulcher. The altar is the symbol of the Lord's tomb, without doubt, and the bread and wine are the body of our Lord which was embalmed and buried. . . . And the deacons standing this side and on that and brandishing [fans] are a symbol of the angels at the head and at the feet thereof.

In another order it is a type of that Kingdom which our Lord entered and into which He will bring with Him all His friends. The adorable altar thereof is a symbol of watchers and men in the clear day of His revelation [i.e. judgment].[59]

With "trembling and fear for himself and for his people" the priest is attorney and advocate, "an object of awe even to the seraphim," and standing before the "awful King, mystically slain and buried," he gives with his own hands the Body of the King to his fellow servants, and then inwardly exclaims:

O corporeal being, that carries fire and is not scorched! O mortal, who being mortal, dost distribute life! Who has permitted thee, miserable dust, to take hold of fire! And who has made thee to distribute life, thou son of paupers?[60]

Narsai saw the mediatorial role of the priest in communicating the divine forgiveness in succession to that of the first "twelve priests" of the New Dispensation, the Twelve Apostles. Christ was concerned to enlarge God's ongoing Israel as the community of judgment and forgiveness. The priesthood of *all* believers is suggested in a moving passage:

. . . and instead of the People He called all people to be His. . . . To this end He gave the priesthood to the new priests, that men might be made priests to forgive iniquity on earth.[61]

Divinely charged with the forgiveness of sins, the priest is likened to a physician whose art it is to heal both hidden and open diseases, to give health to both body and soul. Nor may he limit himself to the altar. By his preaching "he sails continually in the sea of mankind; and much he warns every man to guard the riches of his soul."[62] He must move among his people and preside at all the great moments of human life for "without a priest a woman is not betrothed to a man; and without him their marriage festival is not accomplished; without a priest the defunct also is not interred." [63]

Writing within the fifth century but after the Council of Chalcedon was the anonymous Syrian Monophysite of strong Neoplatonist convictions who propagated his theory of the priesthood among other things, by writing under the name of Dionysius, Paul's convert of the Areopagus. Pseudo-Dionysius' interpretation of the ministry was not immediately accepted in the East, but it should be mentioned here since it is comparable in significance to, though quite different from, Augustine's conception of the indelibility of ordination and the *ex opere* validity of the sacraments administered by the priest. In brief, Pseudo-Dionysius in his *On the Ecclesiastical Hierarchy* systematized the speculation about the angelic host which we have several times adverted to and he found in the threefold ministry of bishop, priest, and deacon the earthly counterpart and, as it were epiphany, of the three angelic grades, worked out in his book *On the Celestial Hierarchy*. It was the invisible angelic action that gave efficacy to the action of all priests. Dionysius' theory was not alone influential in the East, but by way of translations, also in the medieval West.

From the beginning of this survey we have had occasion to call attention to the differences between the Western and the Eastern ministries. Among other things, the Latin West seems to have been the first to begin the delegation of the sacerdotal powers of the bishop to the presbyter and to have conserved longer the role of the exorcist. The East developed the chorepiscopate and the female diaconate and revered longer the independent teacher and lector.[64] But there are even more important differentiations between the Eastern and the Latin (and increasingly Germanic) West which we may appropriately characterize as this survey of the ministry in the Patristic period is brought to a close. Both traditions claimed alike apostolic and angelic sanction.

The Eastern clergy, however, were particularly conscious of being the associates or imitators of the angels (in the tradition of Ignatius, Clement of Alexandria, Chrysostom, and Pseudo-Dionysius). Theodore of Mopsuestia's characterization of the ministry will serve as a generalization for the East:

Because the priest performs things found in heaven through the symbols and signs, it is necessary that his sacrifice also should be as their image and that he should represent a likeness of the service in heaven.

In the West, whose apostolic see could claim the sanction of both the prince and the prophet among the apostles, the tendency was rather to stress (in the tradition of Clement of Rome, of Callistus, of Tertullian, of Cyprian, of Ambrose, and of Augustine) the Covenantal sanctions of the ministry in succession both to the apostles and to the Old Testament prophets and priests.

Perhaps the best exemplification of this conception of the ministry was Leo the Great, Bishop of Rome from 440 to 461, the formulator of the christological dogma of Chalcedon. In a sense somewhat different from the Christ whom he defined, the true priest is himself, according to Leo, fully human and fully divine.[65] Leo held that the ministries of all bishops and their subordinate priests have validity in the measure that they participate in the communion of the universal bishop (the Pope), for they are called "to share a part of the pastoral care of the Bishop of Rome but not in the plenitude of his power."[66]

Through the holy prince of the apostles Peter the Roman Church possesses the sovereignty (*principatus*) over all churches in the whole world.[67]

As vicar of Peter and *consul Dei*, Leo was the Covenantal heir of the authority of the Jewish high priest and the prince of the apostles and the residuary legatee of the power of the *populus Romanus*.

In his sermon (lxxxii) on the Feast of SS. Peter and Paul, Pope Leo movingly declared that the *pax christiana*, built upon the Word, and which is manifest in harmony with the see of Peter, is the Christian counterpart of the older *pax Romana*, which was first built upon the weapons of Romulus and Remus. And it was the leading motif of his pontificate, amid the debris of Empire and the gathering shades of civilization, that he and all clergy in communion with him had it as their dual task to civilize the nations and to sanctify the hearts of men.

IV

The Ministry in the Middle Ages

ROLAND H. BAINTON

No more compact summary of the results of the previous chapter is to be found in the contemporary literature than Chrysostom's tract *On the Priesthood*[1] from which some quotations already have been given. It was written to justify the decision to remain a monk rather than to undertake the more onerous tasks of a parish minister. What a reversal of values comes here to light! At first monasticism was deemed the most rugged form of the Christian life, the very successor to martyrdom. Now the priesthood had come to be regarded as more arduous and monasticism was defended as the safest way to heaven, for though here one might not rise so high, neither could one fall so low. Chrysostom proceeds in his tract to enumerate the many features of the stupendous office.

The priest first of all, said he, has sacramental functions. He stands before the altar bringing down not fire from heaven but the Holy Spirit. At his hands the Lord is again sacrificed upon the altar and the people empurpled with that precious blood. Only by eating of the flesh of the Lord and drinking of his blood can man escape the fires of hell. How tremendous then is the office of the priest through whose hands alone this saving rite can be administered! Vastly greater is he than an earthly parent who generates only unto earthly life, whereas the priest regenerates unto life eternal. To him has been given an authority exceeding that of angels and archangels.

He has likewise a disciplinary function, for he must excommunicate the unworthy, and whatsoever he shall bind on earth shall be bound in heaven. He is to serve likewise as a judge, and much of his time will be consumed in adjudicating the disputes of his flock. He is also an administrator of the property of the Church which is to be used for the entertainment of strangers and the care of the sick.

He is the instructor of his people through the pulpit; a skilled theologian, he must be able to refute the heretics and the pagans. As a preacher he will have to compete with tragedies and musical entertainments. He has a pastoral function and must be able to mingle with men in all walks of life. If he does not make a round of visits every day, unspeakable offense will ensue. He must distribute his smiles with utter impartiality and not beam inordinately upon anyone in particular. The virgins are under his care, and he must endeavor to confine them to their homes, save for inexorable necessity. The widows will try his patience, since they are garrulous and querulous. The married women he must visit when sick, comfort when sorrowful and reprove when idle, and in all of this scrupulously guard himself, recognizing that chaste women may be even more upsetting than the wanton.

Thus far Chrysostom. His picture is comprehensive and illuminating. It leaves out much which was to accrue to the priesthood in a later time. The distinction between the clergy and the laity is implied but is not spelled out. Already it had been made clear. Although Constantine as a layman was accorded a large share in the calling and direction of councils, yet when his son Constantius undertook to enforce decisions contrary to Nicene orthodoxy, he was roundly reproved by Bishop Hosius on the ground that emperors may not burn incense.[2] And the Emperor Theodosius was twice reproved by Ambrose, once when after the massacre of Thessalonica he approached the church; secondly when, already absolved for the bloodshed, he ventured to go beyond the chancel and take his place among the priests.[3] Constantine had conferred special immunities upon the clergy, subsequently curtailed when they precipitated too great a rush for holy orders.[4] Still the clergy remained a caste.

Their functions and deportment differed from those of the laity. Not only the monk but also the minister had a code. Priests should not meddle in business and if they did, were to be shunned as the plague.[5] The bishop of course was responsible as an agent for the goods of the Church and the Church, even before Constantine, held property as a corporation. The goods were not vested in the bishop personally and for himself he must abstain from all private commercial transactions. Again he must not be a magistrate, and when Paul of Samosata, in the late third century, became a Ducenarius of Zenobia of Palmyra the very pronunciation of his title evoked a shiver of disapprobation.[6] The objection arose largely from the fear that the magistrate might have to pass sentence of death or torture. Consequently, to deter the mob from making him a bishop, Ambrose, at that time a Pretorian prefect, held

an impromptu court and passed a severe sentence to show that one who
so acted according to the law was disqualified for the service of the
gospel.[7] The throng as a matter of fact was not deterred, and that in
itself was a step toward the Middle Ages. Above all, the minister should
never be a soldier. Ambrose was quite clear on that score, although he
did not condemn soldiers and even exhorted the emperor to a campaign
and almost a crusade against the Arian barbarians.[8] The minister then
should not be a merchant, a magistrate, or a militiaman.

The monk, whose role appeared to Chrysostom relatively easier, was,
however, acquiring enlarged functions which blurred the differentiation.
By St. Jerome scholarship and monasticism were combined and the role
of the Benedictines was thus foreshadowed. Likewise after the sack of
Rome, when refugees streamed into the East, Jerome's monastery
became a hostel. He tells us also of high-born Roman matrons, who
having embraced the religious life, dedicated themselves to ministering
in hospitals to sufferers from the most loathsome diseases.[9] The cell had
thus become expanded to encompass the study, the hostel, and the
hospital.

The Church throughout the Empire had acquired a high degree of
universality and centralization which served as a model to be surpassed
in the high Middle Ages, but only after a long period of obscuration.
The bishop of Rome enjoyed a certain presidency of love. His church
was regarded as the purest custodian of the primitive tradition because
founded by the two pillar apostles, Peter and Paul. The bishop of Rome
by the middle of the fourth century was deemed to have been the
successor of Peter, not simply as the founder but as himself the first
bishop of Rome. His successor in the see wielded the power of the keys
to him committed. Actually the early ecumenical councils were not
summoned by the bishops of Rome nor did they attend. At the same
time Rome exerted a preponderant influence upon their decisions and
when the orthodox were intimidated or persecuted they looked to Rome
as their protector and asylum.

After the barbarian invasions in the West great changes ensued. The
traditional functions of the priest described by Chrysostom all continued
but the once forbidden tasks also were added to his portfolio. In consequence, although in a formal way the line between the laity and the
clergy was accentuated, in function the two more nearly approximated
each other, doubly so because the laity assumed a larger role in the
founding, supplying, and reforming of churches. The monks likewise
extended their functions when many became priests. In the meantime,

priests became celibate and thus the regular and secular clergy were less to be distinguished. The term "regular" was applied to the monastics because they followed the *regula* or rule, the term "secular" to the parish clergy because they served *in saeculo,* in the world. The word had not yet acquired the connotation of secular in the sense of worldly.

These great changes were occasioned by a vast alteration in the social structure as a result of the barbarian inroads.[10] Centralization and public order broke down. The invasions menaced goods and life. After the main incursions subsided sporadic raids of pillaging Norsemen continued and even major thrusts from the Danes in the West and the Magyars in the East. When the barbarian kingdoms became established they warred upon one another and within them barons preyed upon barons. Security had to be sought on some walled promontory in the company of bellowing and offensive herds. The disorders interfered with commerce. A further and even more serious setback was occasioned by the Mohammedan invasion commencing in the sixth century which made of the Mediterranean an Islamic sea.[11] The decline of commerce meant also that there was a decline of cities and a reversion to an agricultural economy with exchange in kind rather than in coin.

The invaders were either Arian Christians or pagans, in neither case orthodox subscribers to the Nicene creed. This meant that they did not accept the leadership of Peter's successors. The Arians had no centralizing focus comparable to Rome and their missionaries had attached themselves in the north to the tribes. When these were converted to the Nicene faith they still retained or tended to retain the decentralized organization. An assertion of authority on the part of the Roman church was all the more difficult because the city of Rome geographically was no longer at the center of the Christian world, as in the days when the extremities were Spain and Syria. After the Mediterranean was lost to Islam, Rome came to be on the periphery of the new world of the West. The center was at Metz in Germany and the other extremity at Hadrian's wall in Scotland.

The task of converting and Christianizing the northern peoples was stupendous in view of the disorder, hampered communication, and nonviable currency. New methods were imperative, and new functions, imperceptibly at first but inevitably, accrued to the Church and to the clergy. Rome could commission missionaries to the North but thereafter they were on their own. No missionary boards could finance them with bank drafts or postal money orders. They would have to be self-sustain-

ing and there was only one way by which they could support themselves
in a rural society and that was on the land. They acquired ground
already domesticated or themselves undertook to fell the forests or drain
the swamps. No agency of the Church was so well adapted to this task
as the monastery and it can be no accident that whereas Christianity
went into Ireland under episcopal auspices, when the curtain rises for
the second scene, the form disclosed is monastic. Groups of monks
could form a community and establish a self-sufficient life with their
own fields, vineyards, graineries, fish ponds, rabbitries, and orchards. As
late as the high Middle Ages the Cistercians profoundly affected the
economic life of Europe by their projects of reclamation. Waters were
gathered behind dikes into ponds stocked with fish, bogs were transformed into "golden meadows," greenhouses introduced new plantings,
and forests were discriminately cut with an eye to conservation.[12]

In all of this one sees much that was new in the functions of the
clergy. Chrysostom had not enumerated among the ministerial cares the
maintenance of a suitable temperature in a greenhouse. The three
activities which the Early Church had forbidden to the clergy came to
be appropriated. The first was business. To be sure, in the first centuries
the bishop was the administrator of the Church's goods but in the Middle
Ages he was more, and the Church's business was so enlarged, so
intricate, and so geared into all of the property and commercial activities
that the difference at this point between the cleric and the lay was no
more than that the former was more successful.

The bishop of Rome became a great business administrator. In the
days of Gregory I (590-604) vast possessions not overrun by the Lom-
bards were still in the hands of the Church, timber and grain lands in
Sardinia, Sicily, Calabria, and northern Italy. We find the bishop of
Rome sending the churches lumber and lead, supplying the populace
of Rome with grain, *panem* if not *circensem,* and supporting a great
concourse of nuns presumably refugees in the city. In order to manage
these huge estates an imposing bureaucracy had been developed with
a whole hierarchy of managers, *rectores patrimonii.*[13] The letters of
Gregory afford a striking contrast to those of Augustine who was concerned with the cure of souls rather than with the care of estates. The
epistles of Gregory read like the correspondence of a dean. Every letter
renders a decision.

To the north in Gaul and later in Germany the secular clergy came
in suprisingly short order to be endowed with fantastic estates, as much
as one-third or one-half of the land in the kingdom. Frequent expropri-

ations by rulers like Charles Martel were speedily recouped by fresh donations. These gifts were now vested not in the Church as a corporation but personally in the bishop or the abbot.[14] Of course, he still thought of himself as acting for the Church. In any case, immense amounts of his time would have to be devoted to oversight and collection.

The fate of the monasteries was not different. The Benedictines began with a regime of manual labor for each of the brothers, but when lands were given with the laborers thrown in the monks did not drive them off in order to do the work themselves but accepted the serfs with the soil. The monk then became a squire or, if his tastes so dictated, perchance a scholar with a lily hand. In the high Middle Ages, when the new monastic orders produced wine, wool, and grain beyond their needs, they began to dispose of the surplus in the channels of trade, outfitted convoys on the roads, and flotillas on the rivers. Altogether they were the most enterprising businessmen of their day.[15]

Functions of government devolved upon churchmen. There was no conspiracy for power, simply the discharge of a job to be done. In Italy the popes reluctantly took over the role of the Caesars. By reason of the invasions any control in Italy, even in the areas still free of the invaders, was but tenuous when exercised from Constantinople or even Ravenna. Gregory I, precisely because of his immense resources, found himself doing what formerly government had undertaken. The debilitating practice of feeding the Roman populace went back to the days when rival contestants for office distributed largesses of food to the public. In the end the Empire was feeding the citizens. When then the sovereign at Constantinople could no longer function in this way, the Church of Rome wafted the wheat from the plains of Africa. If Roman citizens were captured by the barbarians who had the gold for their ransom if not the bishop of Rome? And if he thus dealt with the barbarians, how inevitable that he should make agreements and even treaties with their rulers? Little wonder that Pippin, the king of the Franks in 754, recognized the actual conditions when he conferred upon the pope the keys of ten cities that over them he might exercise civil rule. This date is commonly taken to mark the beginning of the estates of the Church over which the pope was temporal lord until 1870. His authority was restored in 1929 over the diminished area of Vatican City.

In the north churchmen likewise assumed functions of government. Since the clergy were the only literate class the kings of the Franks drafted them as civil servants. The precedent was thereby laid for many a subsequent figure who combined the role of a high ecclesiastic and a prime minister or chancellor of the realm, men like Sully, Ximenes, Woolsey, and Richelieu. The amazement of Henry II can well be divined when his favorite Thomas à Becket refused to conform. Bishops and abbots became rulers in their own domains when the feudal system became established and taxes, military levies, and the administration of justice devolved upon the holders of land. So long as churchmen held vast estates they could not escape obedience and service to their overlords nor responsibilities and protection for the underlings. They had become prince-bishops and prince-abbots.

Under such circumstances they could scarcely obviate involvement in war. In the days of the invasions even abbots as well as bishops donned armor over their cassocks to repel raiders. Monasteries were begirt with walls. Sometimes even nuns entered the fray and in the conflict of baron with baron the churchman behaved like his neighbor. In the days of Henry II in Germany, for example, a robber baron so devastated the archdiocese of Treves that the archbishop fled. The Emperor thereupon selected a hardfisted young noble, raced him through the grades of the hierarchy until he was made the archbishop of Treves. He promptly distributed the goods of the Church to knights who formed a small standing army and repulsed the marauder.[16]

Such behavior at least prior to the year 1000 was looked upon as a defection from the Christian ideal. The view that the soldier could himself be esteemed as a servant of the Church, that the knight should be inducted with a religious ceremony and that churchmen might even participate in conflict with the sword as well as with the cross, was the outcome of a great peace crusade. In the first half of the eleventh century churchmen sponsored the Truce of God and the Peace of God whereby the time for active hostilities was so restricted that warfare became a summer sport and the number of combatants so reduced as to make of it an aristocratic pastime. This was the intent, but many barons took the oath and did not keep it. Then churchmen raised a disciplinary army of enforcement, a peace militia. Here was the notion of the holy war, under the auspices of the Church in order to suppress war. This concept was basic for the Crusades. Urban II began his famous exordium with a plea for peace. "Let Christians," he urged, "stop shearing each other and go against the common enemy of the faith!" And all the assembly shouted, *"Dieu le veult!"* [17]

The prohibition of clerical participation broke down. An example is given in the case of a priest in the Frankish army on the first crusade.

At Constantinople quarrels with the Greeks led to a skirmish between vessels in the Bosphorus. Anna, the daughter of the Greek emperor, relates with horror that a priest from the bow of his ship hurled missiles against her father's admiral till even stones were exhausted. When the Frankish vessel was captured this priest, severely wounded, embraced the opposing commander saying that with better weapons he would have won, then expired and went to hell, according to Anna, because as a priest he had taken weapons.[18] The West, however, did not condemn him. Even before the crusade Leo X led his forces against the Normans. The aversion even of monasticism to war collapsed with the founding of the Hospitalers, Knights of St. John, and the Templars with the enthusiastic blessing of that great monk St. Bernard.

This change in clerical functions excites wonder but even more remarkable was the success of the papacy in uniting the diverse and warring factions of France in the first crusade: the knights of Langue d'Oui and Languedoc, the Normans of Normandy, and the Normans of Sicily and southern Italy, Godfrey and Baldwin, the Roberts and Tancred, Raymond of Toulouse, and Adhemar of Puy. What united them was the conviction that *God* willed it.

How did the Church ever come to persuade them of this? The attempt would hardly have succeeded had not the Church been fired with a flaming zeal to Christianize the very fabric of society and to accomplish this end first of all by emancipating and purifying herself. The Gregorian reformers were deeply aware of all the corruptions inherent in the very processes of Christianization. The Church had to be of the people in order to win the people and in so doing all too readily became like the people. The warring of bishops and abbots was understandable enough in a disorderly society and might be condoned as self-defense. Yet all too often it became predatory. The immense episcopal baronies had originated innocently out of the very necessities of the situation. Then they had become so lucrative as to tempt the avaricious and the ambitious. The manning of churches by lay patrons, at first a boon, had become a bane, when through their power of lay investiture they consecrated superfluous sons in order to enlarge their domains. The centralizing of political authority in the hands of the emperor was stabilizing but if to this end he determined episcopal appointments his eye might be less directed to saintliness than to amenability. The marriage of the clergy was supported by the sanction of eminent churchmen such as St. Ambrose but introduced the possibility of a hereditary episcopacy.

To cure all of these ills two drastic reforms were launched. The one aimed at the independence, the other at the purity of the Church. The clergy were to be emancipated from lay control. They were not to be subject to the civil courts. Justice for churchmen should be administered by the Church. The tonsured were to be exempt from lay authority, and even though guilty of theft, rape, and murder should enjoy benefit of clergy. The practice of assigning all ecclesiastics to the bishop's court is discernible in England only after the conquest and was a result of the Gregorian reform. Popular sentiment supported this exemption because the secular courts were so severe. On a single gallows one might see twenty men hanging for trivial offenses. The bishop could not impose the death penalty. He might adjudge the accused guilty and turn him over for punishment to the civil power. Commonly, however, he exacted only purgation. He might condemn the culprit to an ecclesiastical prison, but still, there would be no taking of life.[19]

Again the clergy should be free from all lay interference both in the inception and conduct of their office. The Church should determine appointments and the new incumbents should swear fealty only to the pope. Such demands might have been readily conceded if the Church had not owned one-half of the land on which all political institutions were based. Church lands, moreover, were not consolidated but dispersed in strips and patches which if withdrawn from the emperor's control would leave him with an inchoate and unmanageable domain. The Church might easily have been accorded independence had she been willing to renounce her endowments but she argued that so many donations had been given in trust and were not to be alienated to the sons of perdition.

But if the bishops were not to be appointed by lay patrons nor to swear allegiance to lay rulers, by whom then were they to be inducted and invested? A special machinery was developed by the Church to meet this need, namely, the College of the Cardinals. The suggestion had been made long since in the spurious Decretals of the ninth century which significantly emanated from the lower church clergy of France who desired the centralization of Church government and the enhancement of the papacy as a defense against the highhandedness of overlords, alike lay and clerical. The proposal was made that the pope be fortified by a college of assistants; thereby the central administration would be strengthened and the local metropolitans set down a notch in the hierarchy.[20] Not until the eleventh century was the idea implemented and the Cardinals established with the function of choosing popes quite independently of any lay directives.

By this move the hierarchy was further elaborated and the gradations within the clergy still more accentuated. In one respect, however, the cleavage within the ranks was diminished. When the altar was moved to the rear of the apse the bishop no longer stood behind the communion table but took his place with the other clergy in the choir stall. Though he had there a throne, he was still but one in a row.[21]

While the clerical body was being welded, the line between the clergy and the laity was heightened. There were two postures at communion. The priest stood; the people kneeled. And there came to be two positions. The priest at the altar; the people before the altar rail. Only the priest partook of both elements. From the laity the wine came to be withheld.

But nothing did so much to set the clergy apart from the body of the faithful as did the imposition of celibacy. In the earlier period it had not been demanded. The Bishop of Mans, for example, had been openly married and called his wife *Episcopissa*. In 966 Rutherius declared that all of the clergy in his area were married and some of them more than once. If the decree prohibiting repeated marriages were enforced only boys would be left in the Church. He endeavored to institute a reform but was driven to seek the sanctuary of an abbey. At the same time, for centuries an incompatibility had been sensed between sexual relations and ministry at the altar and the married priest was enjoined to abstain during the period of his ministration.[22] The Gregorian reform, partly for practical reasons to break up the system of hereditary bishoprics and partly for ascetic reasons because virginity was rated higher than marriage, undertook to make the reform universal. Opposition was intense but the rule became canon law.

Coincidently a device was introduced to demark the clergy as a special class by imposing upon them a distinctive dress which would serve both to enhance their prestige and to guard their morals by setting them apart. Complaint was made of those clad in scarlet, wearing rings, "with short tunics, ornamentally trimmed, with knives and basilards hanging at their girdles." The rules prescribed that the head must be tonsured, the beard closely trimmed, sleeves must be short, coats long, and colors somber. There was as yet no specific uniform for the clergy as to street attire save for the distinguishing mark of the tonsure.[23]

These reforms occasioned much stout resistance particularly from the civil government. There was no serious objection to having the clergy dress differently nor did civil rulers too much care if the priests were unmarried, save that celibacy terminated a system by which the noble and royal houses had profited. Vastly more serious from the point of view of the state was the abolition of lay investiture. For how could a king be sovereign in his own domain if he could not count on unqualified obedience from subordinates who controlled one-half of the land? Plainly France, Germany, England, and Spain would be ruled from Rome. Again, exemption from the civil courts constituted a serious threat to the administration of even-handed justice throughout the realm, particularly in a society where the ratio of the clergy to the laity was estimated as somewhere between 1 to 50 and 1 to 25.[24]

This opposition, though serious, was cowed. Henry II of England, who in resisting clerical immunities occasioned the murder of an arch-bishop, had to do penance at his tomb. Henry IV in Germany hurled defiance at Gregory VII when the pope categorically insisted on the imposition of clerical celibacy and the abolition of lay investiture. The emperor for his truculence was placed under excommunication and his subjects released from their oaths of obedience. The emperor thereupon found himself devoid of subjects; in order to recover his scepter he must stand a suppliant in the snow at Canossa.

The line though tortuous, runs from this dramatic papal triumph to the dazzling pontificate of Innocent III in the thirteenth century when the objectives of the Gregorian reform were accomplished to an astounding degree.

A culture had emerged properly designated as Christendom. The Christian faith, save for a remnant of the Jews and occasional heretics, was dominant from Caledonia to Calabria. And the lord pope was more effectively the head of the society than was any civil ruler. St. Peter's vicar exalted the lowly and abased the proud. Never did he claim to rule as a temporal sovereign, save of course in the papal states and in those areas which became fiefs of the papacy, namely Sicily, Portugal, and England. Elsewhere he claimed jurisdiction only over sin, but inasmuch as most human endeavor is tainted with sin, the pope's area of possible jurisdiction was large.

This authority was exercised without direct force of arms. The pope might indeed call upon one prince to discipline another. The popes had not been above leading armies to repel the Normans. But Innocent III did not undertake to police the world. He ruled by admonition and the spiritual weapon of excommunication carrying with it the exclusion from blessedness in the life eternal.

When this point in a church history course is reached, the class gasps and inquires how the pope ever came to exercise such authority that at his word an emperor excluded from the altar should be deemed by his subjects unfit to govern Christian folk. Truly one cannot but be amazed that excommunication should have been so seriously regarded as to have become a political weapon. This never could have taken place if the Church for centuries had not been training the populace on remote farms and in distant hamlets. A host of unrecorded emissaries must have instilled this faith.

The first stage in the fashioning of Christendom was the conversion of the northern peoples. Seculars and regulars alike contributed. The task of these missionaries differed little from that of the first Apostles, save that the audience was different. The gospel now was addressed not to the cultivated philosopher or the ecstatic initiate of the mystery cults but to cruder folk: Druids scarcely beyond human sacrifice, Teutons worshiping Thor within the sacred Oak. From fragmentary remains of that time one would judge that Christ was presented as the Redeemer on the rood, by death conquering death and insuring for man blessedness in the world to come. One recalls the sermon of Paulinus when he pointed to the swallow flitting through the Saxon banqueting hall from darkness to darkness as a parable of the life of man, were it not that Christ has shed light and hope on the darkness beyond.[25] Again King Oswy at Whitby is claimed to have decided for the Roman representative because he was the agent of St. Peter, holder of the keys to the gates of heaven.[26] At the other extremity of the empire Cyril and Methodius impressed the Bulgar king by a picture of the judgment to come. The power of the death-conquering Christ was reinforced by the intercession of the saints whose relics were a part of the missionary's equipment. Among polytheistic peoples the saints readily became the successors of the gods. The pacific aspects of Christianity proved no deterrent to a warlike folk who saw in Peter the doughty knight with his broad sword cleaving clean the ear of the high priest's servant.[27] The ethical demands of the gospel were laid with emphasis upon unbridled peoples, witness the early development of the penitentials. Not only were penalties imposed on earth but punishments and rewards offered in the life to come. The Pauline doctrine of justification by faith apart from works was too precarious a word to commit to these undisciplined hordes.

Conversion was by peoples rather than by individuals. The desirability of this method is much debated in our own day. Frequently

the churches have demanded a personal commitment and an understanding of the faith as a prerequisite for baptism. The result has been
that converts have suffered a complete social dislocation and, disowned
by their own people, have had to find a home within a European or
Europeanized community. This was not the course adopted in the
winning of the West. Commonly kings and queens were converted and
at their behest whole peoples received the waters of baptism. Such conversion was of necessity highly superficial and genuine Christianization
had to come afterward.

Only then did the real work begin. Once more the regulars and the
seculars shared. We have already noted how readily monasticism
adapted itself to the rural economy and how the monks altered the
contours of the land. They ministered likewise to the folk round about
by draining their swamps and by training their children; in some cases
also by serving their churches. The monk, however much he might
cherish seclusion and prize contemplation, was never actually withdrawn from the social fabric. No pope of the twelfth century, for
example, was so influential as the monk St. Bernard. So frequently was
he called upon to leave the cloister that he referred to himself as a bird
out of his nest. His critics called him a frog out of his pond. Whether
he was rebuking the Count of Champagne or the King of France,
settling the papal schism or fomenting the Second Crusade, this inde-
fatigable, inexorable, and irresistible abbot so swayed his fellows that
mothers are said to have hidden their sons at his approach.

But the monks were not dedicated primarily to the service of the
community and the ministry of the abbot was first of all to his own sons
in the cloister. The letters and the sermons of St. Bernard rebuke the
foibles of monks with an itch for singularity, who enjoy better the singing of one psalm alone in the choir when the brothers are asleep than
an entire psalter in the company of the brethren. Again the monk is
rebuked who seeks to distinguish himself by spectacular austerity, and
lacking a mirror, is continually scrutinizing the visibility of his ribs.[28]
Bernard is again the lyrical preacher as he discourses on Christ the
bridegroom in the Canticles or as he dwells with rapture on the vision
of the ineffable.

When society became more stabilized, increasingly the needs of the
people were met by churches whether in cities, towns, or hamlets. In
the urban centers there were cathedral churches staffed by a considerable
corps of the clergy responsible for the cure of souls in the area and
sometimes, as in the case of Chantry priests, committed to saying masses

for designated persons living or dead. The cathedral churches were manned sometimes by seculars, sometimes by regulars. In England the great secular cathedrals were St. Paul's, York, Lincoln, Salisbury, Exeter, Hereford, and Lichfield. These were governed by a dean and a chapter. The regular cathedrals were at the same time Benedictine abbeys, namely, Canterbury, Durham, Winchester, Norwich, Ely, and Worcester. The monks in theory elected the abbot, and he was also the bishop.[29]

The bulk of the population lived in the villages, and in ecclesiastical parlance belonged to vicarages. The term arose because the incumbent was commonly a substitute. Many changes brought the system to pass. In the early Middle Ages a landlord frequently built a chapel and appointed to it a rector, assigning certain lands for his support. Out of this arrangement grew the tithe system, but inasmuch as the private chaplain to the landlord was frequently expected to be his boon companion in hunting and hawking and sometimes did not reside at all but delegated his functions to a vicar, the bishops struggled to emancipate the rural churches from lay control. One expedient was to assign them to monasteries, which became themselves the rectors and the recipients of the revenues.[30] Sometimes they undertook to provide for the cure of souls from their own ranks, but of this arrangement there was grievous complaint inasmuch as the only baptismal font was located at the monastery, and the villages might be a dozen miles away. In case of extremity an infant might die on the road. Therefore a substitute for the rector, a vicar, was assigned to the parish.[31] His living was precarious since the monastery continued to appropriate approximately two-thirds of the income.[32] Such exactions were not wholly without warrant, at any rate in medieval eyes, because the monasteries were engaged in prayers for the living and the dead and also in extensive hospitality. Yet the bishops generally fought the monasteries on behalf of the vicars and themselves, and if there were no monastery in the picture, the bishop made his own levy. On the Continent the bishop often took one-fourth or one-third of the income, and when such imposts were replaced by free gifts these in turn became involuntary. An effort was made on one occasion to restrict a bishop to not more than a bushel of barley, a keg of wine, and a pig worth sixpence.[33] The bishop also could plead necessity, for his obligations, too, were heavy. One bishop reported that he had to entertain three hundred guests on a single day, not to mention sixty or eighty beggars.[34] Then, too, there were scholars whose educational expenses could be defrayed only through a church living, and when the average vicarage comprised, as in England, four thousand acres,[35] why should it not support more than the vicar? All of this was plausible enough, yet the net result was that the vicar had in part at least to support himself by the cultivation of his own glebe, which was expected to yield one-half of his income.[56] There are references to vicars so poor as to be driven to steal. One need not greatly marvel that they were on the lookout for more lucrative benefices and did not too long remain in a particular cure.[37]

Neither should one be altogether amazed if vicars who lived so precariously were not distinguished for erudition. The story is told of a dean who conducted an examination of his subordinates. He called on one to parse the opening sentence of the canon of the Mass, *Te igitur clementissime Pater*. *"What governs Te?"* he was asked. *"Pater,"* was his reply, *"because the Father governs everything."* The dean marked him down as *sufficienter illiteratus*. Yet when the laity were interrogated as to the sufficiency of their parson in the role of preacher and teacher, they gave him a favorable report, and one may well conceive that he who could not parse the Latin Mass might be able to instruct his flock in the rudiments of faith and conduct.[38]

The parish priest at any rate was the most instructed person in the community. To him men turned as counselor, teacher, lawyer, doctor, and friend. His foremost function was the performance of the Sacraments. Baptism was deemed essential for salvation. If a priest were not present, a midwife might administer the rite using Latin, good or bad, or even English provided there were the intent to baptize.

For adults the great sacrament was the Mass. It was conducted in Latin, and the people did not understand the lines. In any case much of the liturgy was inaudible. The congregation was encouraged to occupy itself with private devotions so that two parallel services were taking place coincidently. At the same time the dramatic acts of the liturgy, such as the elevation of the host, were readily intelligible and besides the Church was richly endowed with symbolism that it might be "a book to the lewd [ignorant] people that they may read in the imagery and painture that clerks read in the book."[39]

The ignorance of the people is not, however, to be exaggerated. They understood much. They knew that the Mass arose from the Supper which the Lord shared with his disciples before he suffered. They knew that it re-enacted the suffering of the Lord. On the altar the cross of Calvary was again set up. If he who there suffered was God then the incarnation also had to be repeated. The very bread and wine were changed not to the sight of the eye, the touch of the hand, or the taste of the mouth but in substance into the very flesh and blood of God. The faithful in eating partook of His very life. The gospel was reduced to one central event—the Passion. And the Passion meant the forgiveness of sins, communion with the ever-dying and ever-risen Lord. The Mass was celebrated not simply on behalf of those attending but also for the souls departed whose bodies lay beneath the stones in the cathedral floor. Here the Church Militant met with the Church Triumphant and earthly pilgrims were rapt into the company of the saints in heaven.

Quite as influential as the Mass in the Middle Ages was the sacrament of penance involving contrition, confession, and satisfaction. In the confessional the priest came into direct contact with the parishioner and subjected him to a thoroughgoing spiritual examination in faith and in morals:

The clergy were taught to probe into the most secret places of a man's life so that his confession might be full and nothing kept back from God. Some of the questions which he was told to put to the penitent were very searching. "Have you ever borrowed things and not returned them?" "Have you taught your children the Creed and the Lord's Prayer?" "Have you without devotion heard any predicacion?" "If your children are 'shrewes' have you tried to teach them good manners?" "Have you ever ridden over growing corn?" "Have you left the churchyard open so that beasts got in?" "Have you eaten with such main that you have cast it up again?" This was indeed a searching cross-examination, from which no one could hope to emerge faultless.[40]

Yet the outcome was not despair. Confession expunged sins so that the devil was compelled to erase them from his record.[41] Alongside of the sacraments were the sacred ceremonies, often immemorial usages reaching back into a remote pagan antiquity, invested now with Christian symbolism, teaching men the sacred meaning of the seasonal round. At Christmas

children stole into church to see the crib. . . . At Candlemas the congregation marched around the church with their lighted candles. All received ashes on Ash Wednesday that they might understand the defilement of sin. On Maunday Thursday, great men washed the feet of the poor. On Good Friday men crept to the Cross in humble adoration of Him who had died for them. On Easter Eve the new fire was hallowed from which the Paschal candle was lighted. At Rogationtide the fields were blessed and religion consecrated the daily toil. At Whitsuntide the dove descended from the roof of the church, while clouds of incense perfumed the air. At Corpus Christi time were the glad processions of those rejoicing in Emmanuel, God with us. At Lammas the loaf . . . was presented as an act of thanksgiving. On All Hallows five boys in surplices chanted *"Venite omnes virgines sapientissimae"* in honour of those who had gone in to the marriage supper of the Lamb. On St. Nicholas Day or Holy Innocents a boy pontificated, reminding all of the command to turn and become as little children![42]

Such customs at their best served to hallow the terrestrial pilgrimage.

Of all the means at the disposal of the Church for the instruction and edification of the flock none was more efficacious at its best than preaching. The Church expected it of the parish priest and strove to give him aid and counsel in the task. One of the great manuals of the art of preaching was *The Pastoral Rule* of Gregory the Great. The pope there instructs the pastor first as to how he shall demean himself:

He is to be discreet in keeping silence, profitable in speech, a near neighbor to everyone in sympathy, exalted above all in contemplation; a familiar friend of good livers through humility, unbending against vice of evil doers through zeal for righteousness; not relaxing in his care for what is inward from being occupied in outward things, not neglecting to provide for outward things in his solicitude for what is inward.

The pastor is then counseled to adapt the Word to the hearer, and the manual proceeds by setting up series of contrasting pairs. Those who are well should be enjoined to employ the health of the body to the health of the soul. The sick are to be admonished to consider themselves the sons of God subject to the scourge of discipline. The meek must not be suffered to grow torpid in laziness nor the passionate to be deceived by zeal for uprightness. Let the humble hear how eternal are the things they long for, how transitory the things they despise; let the haughty hear how transitory are the things they court, how eternal the things they lose. These and many other injunctions deal with eternal types and *The Pastoral Rule* was therefore of use in any culture, but it certainly was not addressed specifically to the condition of the parson in the Middle Ages.[43]

Jacob of Voragine, who flourished in thirteenth-century Italy, pointed out that times had changed, and whereas preachers in the early days of the Church were like fishermen, who in one cast of the net drew in a multitude, today the preacher is more like a hunter, who with great labor and outcry catches but a single animal. If in fishing the catch is not large, the reason may lie with the fish. There are those who adroitly avoid the net of preaching. In other words, the problem is how to get at them at all. The fault may lie also with the fisherman:

They fish at the wrong time, they fish too deep, they fish with poor tackle or broken nets, or they fish in the wrong place. Those who fish among riches, pleasures, and honor, are fishing in the wrong place. Those who look for death-bed repentances, or try to instruct others when they themselves are ignorant are fishing at the wrong time. Those who look for money or honor throw their hooks too low, and those who preach in word while their lives do not correspond, fish with broken nets.[44]

A booklet entitled *Instructions for Parish Priests* by John Myrc (Mirk), written in English somewhat earlier than 1450, is rather remarkable for enjoining preaching and then saying so little about it. The opening section is a reminder to the priest that his preaching will be in vain if his life is evil.

> For little of worth is the preaching
> If thou be of evil living.

He must be chaste, eschew oaths and drunkenness.

> Taverns also thou must forsake
> And merchandise thou shalt not make.
> Wrestling and shooting and such manner game
> Thou must not use without blame.
> Hawking, hunting and dancing
> Thou must forgo for anything
> Cutted clothes and peaked schoon[shoes]
> Thy good fame they will for-done.
> Markets and fairs I thee forbid
> But it be for the more need.
> In honest clothes thou must gone [go]
> Basilard and baudrick wear thou none.
> Beard and crown thou must be shave
> If thou would thy order save.
> Of meat and drink thou must be free

> To poor and rich by thy degree.
> Gladly thou must thy psalter read
>   And of the day of doom have dread.
> And ever do good against evil
>   Or else thou might not live well.
>
> Women's service thou must forsake
>   Of evil fame lest they thee make.
> . . . Thus this world thou must despise
>   And holy virtues have in vise [view]
> If thou do thus, thou shallt be dear
>   To all men that seen and hear.
> Thus thou must also preach
>   And thy parish gladly teach
> When one hath done a sin
>   Look he lie not long therein
> But anone that he him shrive
>   Be it husband, be it wife
> Lest he forget by Lenten's day
>   And out of mind it go away.[45]

The poem then goes on to discuss excommunication, baptism, the Mass, behavior in church, payment of tithes, articles of belief, and above all how to conduct confession. One might indeed infer from these instructions that although preaching was enjoined, it was either not too highly regarded or else considered too simple to require elaboration. All of which raises the question how much preaching there was in the Middle Ages. Owst, who has written two superb volumes on the subject as it bears on England, points out that Gasquet considered the office of preaching to have been adequately fulfilled, whereas Coulton held that it was shamefully neglected. Owst concludes that there could scarcely have been so much contemporary complaint of neglect if Coulton were not more nearly right. But then again H. Maynard Smith warns that we are in danger today of passing from a sentimental view of the Middle Ages seen from a sanctuary where the sun irradiates the stained-glass windows, to a realistic view of the Middle Ages as seen from a gutter on a gloomy day. At any rate the literature of complaint and denunciation demonstrates that some people were fully alive to the need of preaching in the parishes and did their best to remedy the deficiencies. On the other hand, the activity of the friars in invading the parishes in order to supplement the work of the priests, particularly at the point of preaching, is itself the proof that they were indeed remiss.

Or if not remiss, they were incompetent or impeded. Opportunities for anything beyond a grammar-school education were scant. The printing press was not available to supply cheap and plentiful tools, and congregations were inattentive and disorderly. Inasmuch as the church was the only large covered building in the community, it was used for buying and selling. Even during the services gallants ogled the ladies, women gossiped, pickpockets stole and prostitutes solicited.[46] The preacher was driven to meretricious devices for attracting attention such as suspending the eggs of ostriches in the churches.[47] When the congregation dozed, a preacher cried, "There was a king named Arthur," and as ears pricked up, he castigated the hearers for listening only when titillated by tales.[48]

A favorite device was that of playing one portion of the audience against another, all the more readily because men and women were seated separately, and the various professions were distinguishable by their costumes. Gibes at the women were especially relished. In the sermon manuals one finds several examples. For instance, there is the tale of a man who, desiring to be relieved of his wife without culpability, departed on a journey leaving with her two boxes of candy, one poisoned, the other harmless. He instructed her under no circumstances to touch the box which he and not she knew to be fatal. On his return, as he expected, she was dead. But this sort of raillery could not be overdone because the women predominated in the audience, and if the laugh were on them, their feelings must then be relievd by castigation of the men for gluttony, drunkenness, swearing, and the like.[49]

Most of the illustrations in the extant handbooks are fantastic allegorizations of the characteristics of animals applied to humankind or stories of preposterous miracles by the saints or the Virgin Mary. The moral pointed by the tales was, however, perfectly sound, and sometimes the examples were taken from real life as in the case of a judge who received from one of two litigants an ox while his wife received from the other a cow. The verdict was in favor of the latter, and when the former complained, he was told that the cow would not suffer the ox to speak.[50] Just what this illustrates is another matter. A further example is devoid of ambiguity. In this instance a homily tells of a lady that had two "little doggis," loved them so that she took great pleasaunce in the sight and feeding of them: and she made every day dress and made for them dishes with sops of milk, and often gave them flesh. But there was once a friar that said to her, that it was not well done that the dogs were fed and made so fat, and the poor people so lean and famished for hunger. And so the lady for his saying was wroth with him, but she would not amend it. So the lady came to a bad end, as she deserved.[51]

Preaching at its worst must have been banal, at its best superb. The note of prophetic denunciation against extortion is not lacking in the sermons of those who stood face to face with the extortioners. Take this excerpt from a sermon in *The Handbook of Bromyard*. The despoiled, he says,

With boldness at the last judgment will they be able to put their plaint before God and seek justice, speaking with Christ the judge, and reciting each in turn the injury from which they specially suffered. Some of them were able to say, as the subjects of evil lords—"We have hungered. But those our lords standing over there were the cause of this, because they took us from our labours and our goods." Others—"We have hungered and died of famine, and those yonder did detain our goods that were owing to us." Others—"We have thirsted and been naked, because those standing opposite, each in his own way, so impoverished us that we were unable to buy drink and clothing." Others—"We were made infirm. Those yonder did it, who beat us and afflicted us with blows." Others—"We were without shelter. But those men were the cause of it, by driving us from our home and from our land; . . . or because they did not receive us into their own guest-houses." Others—"We were in prison. But those yonder were the cause, indicting us on false charges, and setting us in the stocks." Others—"Our bodies have not been buried in consecrated ground. Those yonder are responsible for this, by slaying us in numerous and in various places. Avenge, O Lord, our blood that has been shed."

Bromyard adds:

Without a doubt the just Judge will do justice to those clamouring thus. Terrible as is the indictment of the wronged, terrible likewise will be the fate of the oppressors. Many who were here on earth are called nobles shall blush in deepest shame at that Judgment-seat, when around their necks they shall carry, before all the world, all the sheep and oxen and the beasts of the field that they confiscated or seized and did not pay for.[52]

Raoul Ardent celebrates in his sermon the foolishness of the Cross. God, he says,

hid His divine power in human weakness, and His wisdom in foolishness. For to men it has seemed foolishness that God became man, that the Impassible suffered, that the Immortal died. Therefore, the wisdom of God, by foolishness, conquered the craft of the Devil. . . . Let us, therefore, brethren, learn from the example of our Redeemer to conquer the evil of this world, not by pride, but by humility, by patience, and gentleness. Let us learn to conquer the wisdom of this age, not by craftiness, but by the foolishness of God. For indeed, to this age it seems foolish and futile to despise the world, to reject the age, to forsake all things, to love poverty and inferior station, to desire things invisible. And yet, this foolishness conquers the wisdom of both the devil and man.

Bernard of Clairvaux declares contemplation to be vain if it produces not the fruits of holiness. He inquires:

Does it appear to you that two persons have equal and similar love towards Christ of whom the one sympathizes indeed piously with His sufferings, is moved to a lively sorrow by them, and easily softened by the memory of all that He endured; who feeds upon the sweetness of that devotion, and is strengthened thereby to all salutary, honourable, and pious actions; while the other, being always fired by a zeal for righteousness, having everywhere an ardent passion for truth, and earnestly desiring wisdom prefers above all things sanctity of life, and a perfectly disciplined character; who is ashamed of ostentation, abhors detraction, knows not what it is to be envious, detests pride, and not only avoids, but dislikes and despises every kind of worldly glory; who vehemently hates and perseveres in destroying in himself every impurity of the heart and of the flesh; and lastly, who rejects, as if it were naturally, all that is evil, and embraces all that is good? If you compare these two types of affection, does it not appear to you that the second is plainly the superior?

Bede the Venerable chanted the ineffable joys of the celestial city:

O truly blessed Mother Church! So illuminated by the honour of Divine condescension, so adorned by the glorious blood of triumphant martyrs, so decked with the inviolate confession of snow-white virginity! Among its flowers, neither roses nor lilies are wanting. Endeavor now, beloved, each for yourselves, in each kind of honour, to obtain your own dignity—crowns, snow-white for chastity, or purple for passion.

With how joyous a breast the heavenly city receives those that return from fight! How happily she meets them that bear the trophies of the conquered enemy! With triumphant men, women also come, who rose superior both to this world and to their sex, doubling the glory of their warfare; virgins with youths, who surpassed their tender years by their virtues. Yet not they alone, but the rest of the multitude of the faithful shall also enter the palace of that eternal court, who in peaceful union have observed the heavenly commandments, and have maintained the purity of the faith.[53]

Whether the preaching of the friars was basically different from that of the parish priest is not easy to determine. Perhaps because the former were itinerants, they could be freer in denunciation, since on the morrow they would be up and off. Because they had been impelled to come in the first place to the parishes out of missionary zeal, their sermons were more fervent. They were renowned for their ability to allay feuds at home and to promote crusades abroad. The Franciscan Salimbene gives a vivid account of the revival called the Great Alleluia in northern Italy in the early thirteenth century.

Brother Benedict of Parma . . . called the Brother of the Horn . . .was like another John the Baptist to behold. . . . His beard was long and black and he had a little horn of brass, wherewith he trumpeted; terribly did his horn bray at times, and at other times it would make dulcet melody. He was girt with a girdle of skin, his robe was black as sack-cloth of hair, and falling even to his feet. His rough mantle was made like a soldier's cloak, adorned both before and behind with a red cross, broad and long, from the collar to the foot, even as the cross of a priest's chasuble. Thus clad he went about with his horn, preaching and praising God in the churches and open places; and a great multitude of children followed him, oft-times with branches of trees and lighted tapers. . . . [He would cry] "Alleluia, alleluia, alleluia!" Then he would sound his trumpet; and afterwards he preached, adding a few good words in praise of God.

Brother John of Vicenza, another of the preachers in the revival, had the reputation of being able to raise the dead. When then the Florentines heard he was coming to their city, they exclaimed, "For God's sake let him not come hither for we have heard how he raiseth the dead, and we are already so many that there is no room for us in the city."[54]

How much such preaching accomplished is difficult to assess. A modern author, writing about Franciscan preaching in Italy, describes the popularity of the evangelists whose engagements had to be regulated by the popes. He tells of the great audiences of eighty thousand assembled at one time, of the feuds reconciled and crusades launched.[55] All of this failed to inaugurate the millennium but one may surmise from the very survival of the Church that preaching did much to sting the callous, hearten the discouraged, fortify the faint, and enrapture the questing. Witness Chaucer's gentle picture of the faithful parish priest and the testimony of an anonymous English poet who to his bishop rendered this testimony:

> He preached on so fair manner
> That it was joy for to hear
> And when his sermon ended was
> The folk with mikel joy up rose
> And thanked Jesus in that place
> That gave their bishop so much grace.[56]

In a remarkable way the Church succeeded also in enlisting the laity in her service. One recalls the dramatic account of how the nobles assisted in the building of the cathedral at Chartres by harnessing themselves to carts that like beasts they might pull loads of wine, oil, grain, stone, and timber, both for the building and the builders. One reads how they pulled in silence save for the confession of sins and suppliant prayer.[57] Another chronicle relates how the villagers constructed their own parish church:

Inasmuch as the Castle Church of Clitheroe, being their parish church, was distant twelve miles, and the ways very foul, painful, and perilous, and the country in the winter season so extremely and vehemently cold, that infants borne to the church are in great peril of their lives, and the aged and impotent people and women great with child not able to travel so far to hear the Word of God, and the dead corpses like to remain unburied till such time as great annoyance to grow thereby, the inhabitants about 1512, at their proper costs, made a chapel-of-ease in the said forest.[58]

Nor should one forget the guilds which contributed this stained-glass window or that. Nor the architects of the cathedrals, laymen largely, who dreamed in stone and compelled the medium both to conform to its nature in carrying weight and to defy its nature by seeming to soar after the illimitable. The strolling players, the jongleurs, even the troubadours sang not only of amours but related the legends of the saints. By a tale thus told, Peter Waldo was converted.

Nor are the rulers, who so often quarreled with churchmen to be regarded as the sons of Belial. They represented themselves as reformers, often genuinely. At any rate, they functioned as equal partners in a Christian society endowed with the two swords, temporal and spiritual, each responsible to and for the other. Henry IV in the investiture controversy complained of Gregory VII as one who had stepped out of his proper role by fomenting war. This emperor was a traditional, early medieval Christian who objected to the new trend whereby the clergy were embracing weapons or stirring up warriors to battle under the banners of the Church. Moreover, Henry's father had displaced and replaced bishops, not primarily in order to advance political interests but because the unworthy were desecrating the see of St. Peter. Lay princes and town governments felt a very real responsibility for the morals of the churchmen in the areas under their jurisdiction. The great conflict of the Middle Ages was not between Christ and Lucifer but between St. Peter and Caesar, a Christian Caesar like Constantine and Theodosius with a genuine concern for the Church. In fact one can talk about a priesthood of all believers even in the Middle Ages, in this sense that each according to his station had a share in, and a responsibility for, a Christian world order.

At the same time there was much to disappoint in so magnificent an achievement; success itself bred corruption. The very process of Christianizing Europe entailed the paganizing of the Church. Legend has it that the missionary Boniface was about to strike with his ax the sacred Oak of Thor as the pagans stood by expecting the god of thunder to smite the blasphemer with his bolt. Instead lightning struck the tree splitting it into four equal parts whereby it was the more readily cut up into planks for the construction of a church.[59] Here is a symbol of the way in which paganism was incorporated into Christianity. Sacred oaks became churches, and the gods, if they did not survive as fairies, were transmuted into saints. In the field of morals bellicosity was not subdued but only enlisted for crusades.

Even reforms recoiled. The whole history of monasticism is the story of trying to keep poor. The Benedictines at first lived by their labor but when serfs came with the soil the monks became, as we noted, administrators or scholars or contemplatives, and perchance even simply drones. The Cistercians tried to revive the original pattern insisting on manual labor and undertaking to break in wastelands. They were so successful that their produce exceeded their needs and they entered into commerce and waxed fat. Francis and Dominic tried a new way. They would labor; they would beg, but the wages and the alms should not exceed the daily needs. The orders grew. Supplying five hundred brethren by daily begging proved to be a very precarious assignment. Begging therefore was allocated to experts. And then the Church offered to take the onus of owning property and of allowing the Franciscans to enjoy the use. The Conventual Franciscans accepted this subterfuge. The Spirituals refused and the order was rent. In the end and almost of necessity the moderates came to predominate.[60]

The great Gregorian reforms achieved an astounding success and yet only at the price of dilution. The peace campaign ended in crusades and crusades fell into disrepute when the very dregs of Europe were enlisted for the Holy Land, when Christian princes were willing to sell Christian slaves to the Turks, when the financing of crusades became a racket, and when disasters made men doubt whether after all *Dieu le Veult*.[61]

The imposition of clerical celibacy in the Middle Ages met with only restricted success. Many of the clergy refused to abandon their wives but this gallant gesture degenerated into a system of clerical concubinage condoned and even taxed by the Church. A medieval prince-bishop frivolously remarked that as a bishop he was celibate but as a prince he was the father of a large family.[62] The very papacy was invaded by laxity, witness the license of Renaissance popes. The prevalence of irregularities is revealed in the story that word reached a concubinous vicar of an impending visit from the bishop to terminate the relationship. The vicar's lady, carrying a basket, intercepted the bishop on the way, who inquired where she was going. She replied that she was taking a present to the bishop's lady at her lying in.[63] The bishop paid his call without raising the question. On another occasion when after a revival in Wales the clergy resolved to put away their concubines, the bishop actually forbade them because he would lose the revenue derived from the tax on such infractions of the canon law.[64] The abolition of clerical concubinage was a major item on the docket alike of the Protestant and the Catholic reformers of the sixteenth century.

When so many reforms proved abortive, the very zeal by which they had been engendered kindled a new effort for the correction of abuses. Curiously the thirteenth century is not only the high period of the papal theocracy but also of sectarian movements. There were other factors to be sure than Christian reformatory zeal. The heresy which most disturbed Innocent III was a revival of ancient Gnosticism with its sharp disparagement of life in the flesh. The Cathari owed their origin to contacts with another Gnostic group the Bogomili of Bulgaria with whom the Crusades had brought them in contact. These folk, however, thought of themselves as Christian, employed the Gospels, and outdid the most monkish of monks in their austerities.

The critique of the Cathari cannot be brushed off by branding them as heretics, when there were other sectaries who made the same complaints and who very definitely were not heretics but only schismatics, and schismatics only because cast out against their will. Such was the case of Peter Waldo, a product of the rising mercantile class in southern France in the twelfth century. He sold his goods, gave to the poor, and dedicated himself to a life of poverty. All this was perfectly regular and would have received the approbation of the Church without the least cavil, but he felt an urge to acquaint himself with the Scriptures and then to inform others. He began to preach. Since he was an unauthorized layman, he was subjected to a theological examination. A contemporary records that he was asked, "Do you believe in God the Father Almighty?" "Yes," he replied. "Do you believe in Jesus Christ, His only Son, our Lord?" "Yes," was the answer. "Do you believe in the Virgin Mary, the Mother of Christ?" "Yes," he responded. There was a roar of consternation, for he should have called Mary the Mother of God. The expression "Mother of Christ" indicated that he was a Nestorian heretic. He was refused permission to preach but he defied the order and thus became the originator of a schismatic group.[65]

A generation later St. Francis was in a similar position, but this time Pope Innocent III, perhaps mindful of the blunder of his predecessor, granted a quasi permission, and the saint became the father of a great preaching order. The line between the sectaries and the new monastic preaching orders was always tenuous. St. Francis believed his Rule to have been given by the Holy Spirit and many of his followers preferred on that account the Rule to the Church. The Fratichelli became schismatics. Among the Dominicans Savonarola was a prophetic proclaimer of diluvial doom on a generation scornful of the way of salvation. In general the sermons of the sectaries were marked by a strong ethical emphasis and a recurrent note of denunciation of those churchmen whose lives identified them as anti-Christs and limbs of Lucifer—so Wycliff, so Hus and their respective followers .   .

Against the heretics and the schismatics the Church invoked the Inquisition. Churchmen should inquire and pass sentence. Civil rulers should implement their decisions at the stake. The Inquisition was deemed a department of the cure of souls. Its object was not to burn heretics in the body but to save them by the fear of a brief temporal fire from the unquenchable flames. The whole technique of the Inquisition was designed to break down the suspect that he might confess, adjure, be reconciled, and saved. Of course, it was also important that he should supply the names of others that they too might be subject to the pressures needful for the saving of their souls.

Such methods intimidated some but served only to stimulate in others a more passionate rebellion. We are frequently disposed to accept unqualified their strictures on that Church which occasioned their criticism and which sought by such means to stifle their complaints. We must remember, however, that the Church cannot have been devoid of vitality when she was able to bear such sons. They might be her undoing. They were at the same time the witness to her residual integrity.

A veritable symbol of the late Middle Ages is Dante Alighieri who even better than the great Aquinas conveyed the mood of a life lived *sub specie aeternitatis*. Dante was a layman. Likewise he was an imperialist and not a papalist, exiled from Florence because he favored the emperor rather than the pope. In his political theory he desired to restrict the Church severely to the spiritual sphere. Highly versed in the universal language of the Church, the Latin tongue, nevertheless, he composed the great poem of medieval faith in the language of the common folk. The *Divina Commedia* is written in the Italian vernacular. He desired the continuance of the great Christian society under the two luminaries, the Church and State, yet he was as critical of particular popes as were the prophetic reformers. In the tradition of the Spiritual Franciscans he portrayed Christ upon the cross, deserted by all save *La Donna Poverta*.

V

The Ministry in the Time of the Continental Reformation

WILHELM PAUCK

The Nature of the Ministry

Nothing is more characteristic of Protestantism than the importance it attaches to preaching. To be sure, also before the Reformation, the sermon played a great role in Christian life. As Jesus himself had done, the apostles and the earliest Christian missionaries spread the gospel by preaching. The greatest Christian leaders of the ancient church, John Chrysostom and Basil of Caesarea, Ambrose and Augustine, were not only ecclesiastical rulers and theologians but masters of the pulpit. In the Middle Ages, preaching did again and again have a great influence, though it was not as general as it had been earlier. Just prior to the Reformation, it came once more into general vogue. But preaching had never been in the very center of Christian life.

Only the new understanding of the gospel achieved by Luther and his fellow Reformers led to such an emphasis upon the proclamation of the Word that henceforth the very reality of the church was grounded in preaching. The seventh article of the Augsburg Confession, in which Melanchthon summarized the faith of the Lutherans for presentation at the diet of Augsburg in 1530, defined the church as "the congregation of the saints in which the gospel is rightly preached and the sacraments are rightly administered." Somewhat later, Calvin wrote: "Where the Word is heard with reverence and the sacraments are not neglected there we discover . . . an appearance of the Church." [1] Formulations of this kind are to be found in the creeds of most Protestant communions. Indeed, we do not go wrong when we define the Protestant conception of the church thus: Where the Word of God is rightly preached and heard and the sacraments are rightly administered and received, there is the church. Protestants attribute priority to the Word of God (i.e., the Christ of the Bible) and they assert that the Word is communicated by preaching and by the administration of Baptism and the Lord's Supper. They assume, furthermore, since faith comes by hearing which is not merely a listening to speech but also an understanding of it followed by decision and action, that when people hear and accept the gospel preached to them, they recognize themselves and each other as members of the church, i.e., the people of God.

The basic criticism which the Reformers directed against Roman Catholicism was that, instead of permitting the Word of God to run a free course among men, the Papists confined it to a historical man-made institution, the Church of Rome. Luther especially was persuaded that the Pope was the very Anti-Christ, because he claimed to be the only authoritative interpreter of the Bible and thus bound it to his office. Calvin regarded the Roman Church as a victim of superstition and idolatry because, in his judgment, it relied for the ordering of its practices on human inventions and not on the Bible. In his eyes, the ceremonialism of Roman Catholicism was an evil because it was the practice of an irreligious religion and not that of obedience to the will of God revealed in Christ.

The Reformers went on to object that, because the Papal Church did not give the Bible its due, it did not properly understand the gospel as the good news of the forgiveness of sins and, therefore, it educated its people to seek salvation not by faith but by good works, not by a trusting reliance on the divine promise of forgiveness as proclaimed by the Bible, but by the performance of all sorts of religious acts as prescribed by the priesthood.

"Three great abuses," wrote Luther,[2] "have befallen the service of God. First, God's Word is not proclaimed; there is only reading and singing in the Churches. Second, because God's Word has been suppressed, many unchristian inventions and lies have sneaked into the service of reading, singing and preaching, and they are horrible to see. Third, such service of God is being undertaken as a good work by which one hopes to obtain God's grace and salvation. Thus faith has perished and [instead of believing the gospel] everyone wishes to endow churches or to become a priest, monk or nun."

Luther's conception implied a tremendous simplification of Christianity. In the last resort, only two things mattered: The Word of God and faith. Or, as he put it: "The sum of the gospel is this: who believes in Christ, has the forgiveness of sins." Faith in Christ can be real only if it depends on the Bible. Nothing, therefore, is as important for religion as to make the Bible accessible and to proclaim its message. The

Reformers staked everything on this understanding of the nature of Christianity.

Against this background, we must see the new conception of the ministry. The very term "minister," i.e., *minister verbi divini* (servant of the Word of God) makes sense only in connection with the ideas we have been discussing. Strictly speaking, every Christian is or should be a minister of the Word of God by virtue of his faith. It is therefore not surprising that, at the very beginning, Luther was led to propose the doctrine of the universal priesthood of all believers, thus doing away with the distinction between clergymen and laymen.

This teaching is an eminently social one: every believer in the gospel is a priest, i.e., a mediator and intercessor between God and men. He must transmit to others the power of the gospel that has laid hold of him. He must express his faith in loving social action and thereby communicate it to others. All Christians are such ministers; they cannot but bring about a new kind of society—the fellowship of believers.

"God has placed his Church in the midst of the world among countless undertakings and callings in order that Christians should not be monks but live with one another in social fellowship and manifest among men the works and practices of faith." [3] This was the conclusion Luther drew from the idea of the universal fellowship of believers.

All Christian believers, therefore, are ministers, servants, priests, by virtue of their faith in the Word of God, but not every one of them can or should assume the function of preaching, teaching, and counseling. For the sake of order, certain ones must be set apart from the group of believers to undertake the office of the preacher.

This was the new conception of the ministry that was to determine the whole history of Protestant Christianity. "We are all priests," wrote Luther, "insofar as we are Christians, but those whom we call priests are ministers [*Diener*] selected from our midst to act in our name, and their priesthood is our ministry." [4]

The institution of a separate hierarchical priesthood was thereby overcome in principle and together with it the distinction between the clergy and the laity, between *rectores* and *subditi* (rectors and subjects). How many difficulties the Reformers encountered when they tried to translate this idea into fact, we shall see in what follows. The point to be kept clearly in mind when one deals with the Reformers' conception of the ministry is that they regarded the function of the leader of the congregation, whose task was to be primarily preaching, as an assignment or office [*Amt*] which, to be sure, set him apart from his fellow Christians but only by their appointment, in order that he might perform a duty that each one of them was entitled to fulfil. Moreover, they regarded this office as a service to be rendered in the name of God and not in the name of men. Once appointed to the office, a minister could not be removed from it by the congregation that had called him, except if he disregarded or defied the Word of God.

This was a high conception both of the ministry and of the power of the congregation over the ministry. We must admit that it has only rarely been fully realized by Protestant churches in the course of their history. At the time of the Reformation, the condition of the congregations was such that they could not in fact exercise this power. As we shall see, they had a part in calling their ministers, but it never happened that they deposed them and judged them in the light of the Word of God. The declaration of the principle was the result of Luther's belief at the beginning of his career as a Reformer that any true Christian and particularly a congregation of Christian believers would be able to see that the institutions and practices of the Roman Church were irreconcilable with the gospel. He wrote in his tract *On the power of a Christian congregation over its preachers:* [5] "We conclude then, that a Christian congregation that has the gospel, possesses not only the right and power but also owes it to the salvation of souls according to the baptismal bond it has entered into, to shun, avoid, depose, and withdraw from the authority which the present bishops . . . exercise; for it is publicly manifest that they live and govern in opposition to God and his Word."

In this connection, we should also mention that Luther asserted that every Christian has the power of the keys, i.e., to forgive sins, but that no one should exercise this power unless publicly authorized to do so. This notion became the common property of the Reformation. These key sentences from Luther's early writings are representative of many others: "Where the Word of God is preached and believed, there is true faith, that (certain) immovable rock; and where faith is, there is the Church; where the Church is, there is the bride of Christ; and where the bride of Christ is, there is also everything that belongs to the Bridegroom. Thus faith has everything in its train that is implied in it, keys, sacraments, power, and everything else." [6] In other words, a man of faith has all the spiritual powers which in Roman Catholicism belonged to the clergy alone. "All of us who are Christians have this office of the keys in common." [7] "Every Christian has the power the pope, bishops, priests and monks have, namely, to forgive or not to forgive sins. . . . We all have this power, to be sure, but no one shall dare exercise it publicly except he be elected to do so by the congregation. In private, however, he may use it." [8]

Such a view of the rights of the individual Christian and of the congregation implied the rejection of clericalism, which therefore never appeared in the course of the Reformation. Indeed, it has not held sway in Protestantism at any time, although it has often happened that the ministers dominated and determined the life of the churches.

Whenever and wherever, in the course of the Reformation and later, such domination became a fact, it was caused chiefly (apart from many other factors which we do not need to explore here) by the prominence attributed by Protestants to the preaching office. In Protestantism, the preachers tend to be the spokesmen and representatives of the church and the church is often a preachers' church. This is a great danger and threat to the Christian religion, not unrelated to clericalism, but nevertheless not as deadly. For clericalism tends to identify the church with the priestly-sacramental clergy to such an extent that it is no longer, in fact or conception, the people of God. Modern Roman Catholicism, for example, finds it most difficult to interpret the church as the people of God when, by defining it as the *corpus Christi mysticum,* it bases its reality on the sacraments and the priests. But when, as in the case of Protestantism, the church is dominated by the preachers, the people must nevertheless be reckoned with in a very real sense, for even a preachers' church is nothing without people to preach to. Preaching cannot be and is not undertaken unless there is a congregation to address, while, in Roman Catholicism, the sacraments can be and are celebrated even if there is no congregation present. In any case, the possibility that the church will become a preachers' church inheres in the Reformers' insistence that preaching the gospel is the source and fountain of all Christian life. It was most characteristic of them that they thought of God as a speaking God (*Deus loquens*), of the gospel as a tale or spoken message, of the Bible not as a book but as preaching, and of the church as a gathering of people who listen to the Word of God being spoken to them. Luther once called the church building a *Mundhaus* (mouth or speech-house). [9]

The significance the Reformers attached to the preaching office is reflected in all their writings. Here are characteristic statements of Luther: "Next to the preaching office, prayer is the greatest office in Christianity. In the preaching office God speaks with us. In prayer I speak with God." [10] "God speaks through the preacher. When we preach [*lehren*] we are passive rather than active. God is speaking through us and it is a divine working [that is happening]." [11] "The preaching office is the office of the Holy Spirit. Even though men do the preaching, baptizing, forgiving of sins, it is the Holy Spirit who preaches and teaches. It is his work and office." [12] "A Christian preacher is a minister of God who is set apart, yea, he is an angel of God, a very bishop sent by God, a savior of many people, a king and prince in the Kingdom of Christ and among the people of God, a teacher, a light of the world. There is nothing more precious or nobler on earth and in this life than a true, faithful parson or preacher." [13]

Calvin expressed the same judgment and in equally superlative terms: "Neither the light and heat of the sun, nor any meat or drink, are so necessary to the nourishment and sustenance of the present life, as the apostolical and pastoral office is to the preservation of the Church in the world." [14] God "chooses from among men those who are his ambassadors to the world, to be the interpreters of his secret will, and even to act as his personal representatives. . . . When [therefore] a contemptible mortal, who had just emerged from the dust, addresses us in the name of God, we give the best evidence of our piety and reverence toward God himself, if we readily submit to be instructed by his minister who possesses no personal superiority to ourselves." [15] "On the one hand, it is a good proof of our obedience when we listen to his ministers, just as if he were addressing us himself; and on the other hand, he has provided for our infirmity, by choosing to address us through the medium of human interpreters, that he may sweetly allure us to him, rather than to drive us away from him by his thunders." [16]

Similar judgments can be found in the writings of the other Reformers. In view of the fact that they were all preoccupied with the preaching office and its importance for the church, it is surprising that they did not produce more books and tracts dealing specifically with the ministry. The most outstanding book of this kind was a work of Martin Bucer, entitled *Pastorale, i.e., On the true Care of Souls and the right Pastoral Ministry and how the same is to be established and performed in the Church of Christ.* [17] It is an exposition of the various functions of the ministerial office in the form of a plea addressed to the magistrate of the city of Strassburg for the establishment of a truly reformed church under adequate ecclesiastical leadership. Earlier, Zwingli had published a tract on the ministry under the title *Der Hirt (The Shepherd,* or *Pastor).* It is mainly an argument against the Roman Catholic priesthood, its vices and its inadequacies in the administration of pastoral care. The norm of his exposition is to be found in the following characteristic sentence:

"The Christian people never lived more piously and purely than at a time when no human addition or authority [*Zwang*] was added to the Word of God." [18]

In this connection, we must mention that the Reformers customarily spoke of the minister as pastor (shepherd, in relation to certain New Testament passages, e.g., John 10:2 and 10:16; Hebrews 13:20; I Peter 2:25), but they called him most frequently "preacher" (*Prediger* or *Praedikant*). The term "pastor" came into general use only during the eighteenth century under the influence of Pietism, especially in Lutheranism. The German Reformers also adhered to the medieval usage and called the preacher *Pfarrer,* i.e., parson (derived from *parochia*—parish, and *parochus*—parson). The common people most generally called the ministers "preachers," but they also continued to use the terms to which they had been accustomed under Roman Catholicism, i.e., "priests," et cetera. This was natural in view of the gradual transition from the old order to the new. In certain regions, basic structures relating to the organization of the parishes and to the polity of the church developed by Roman Catholicism were preserved in the changeover to the Reformation, not only in certain parts of Germany, but chiefly in the Scandinavian countries, especially Sweden, not to speak of England. Here, the old names and titles of the ministerial office were naturally retained. The term "minister" was gradually introduced into English-speaking countries by the Nonconformists and Dissenters. Dependent upon Calvinism, they distinguished the Protestant "ministry" from the Anglican "clergy."

The Ministry in the Context of Evangelical Church Orders

The actual formation of the early Protestant ministry was determined by the course the Reformation took in the various regions first of Germany and then of other European countries. The general ideas and principles which we have been decribing were at work everywhere, but the forms they assumed depended on many different circumstances. When Luther's views of the gospel and of Christian faith and life as well as his criticisms of the Roman Church took hold of others, the discussion of the issues of the struggle in books, tracts, and pamphlets led to concrete action aimed at the abolition of Roman Catholic orders and practices. Priests and monks who had become evangelical preachers generally took the initiative. But even when the spokesmen of the Reformation had won a following among the common people and when they had gained the open or concealed support of princes and magistrates, they could not readily proceed to institute a new order. They were face to face with many difficulties. The Roman Church was firmly established in the common life. Innumerable ties linked it to the political and social order, to economics and law, to mores and customs. New church orders could not come into being except by a transition in the course of which much that was old and traditional had to be preserved. Moreover, Luther was outlawed by Papacy and Empire and everything he represented was officially condemned together with his person. Only in 1526, did the evangelical minority among the princes and estates of the German Empire risk the cautious introduction of the Reformation in their territories. Indeed, the acts of the Reformers were without legal sanction until the Peace of Augsburg in 1555. Until then, the expansion of the Reformation and the formation of evangelical churches were possible only because the Pope and the Emperor were unable to execute the ban they had pronounced upon Luther and his cause. Both were entangled in the conflicts of European politics. In fact, they were politically at odds with each other so frequently that they both became the involuntary allies of the Reformation. They could not stop its progress so long as they schemed against each other. Under these circumstances, it required skillful engineering on the part of the friends of the Reformers among the princes and political leaders to make way for a new order in the church.

Moreover, there was no preconceived and overall plan for the building of evangelical churches. Luther had no program when the role of reformer was forced upon him. No one among his followers had a strategic plan of action. At first, Luther himself thought that, if the worst abuses of the Roman Church could be undone and room given in the world to the preaching of the Word of God, true Christians would arise who would gradually form new congregations and proceed to build a new church order. Throughout his life, he never entirely abandoned the notion that "the Word must do it." But he saw very soon that an actual reformation could not be carried out except with the help and authority of the princes and political magistrates. In 1520, he appealed to the Christian nobility to act as "emergency-bishops" because the regular bishops had failed to care properly for the church. As time went on, he reluctantly acknowledged and agreed that the public authorities had to assume the responsibility for all ecclesiastical change. The territorial princes and the magistrates of the towns took the necessary steps to introduce the Reformation.

The first of such steps were taken early in the twenties of the sixteenth century, but new forms of the church were produced only gradually and were of considerable variety. In the towns, changes could be effected comparatively quickly, because they were close-knit autonomous administrative units. But even there, workable patterns of an evangelical church order emerged only in the course of several decades. In the territories of the princes, the situation was much more complex, even though here the decision lay in the hands of the monarch alone. Scores of communities and localities were involved and many different ancient feudal rights and customs had to be respected.

Here one proceeded on the basis of visitations. They were first instituted in 1526 in the electorates of Saxony and Hesse. Under the authority of the princes, commissions of theologians and of public officials trained in law inspected the conditions of the churches in the various parts of the territories in order to lay the ground for their reorganization. They found widespread confusion. The old order had collapsed. The barons had appropriated much of the ecclesiastical property. They and the common people showed little interest in the church and had ceased to support it. They no longer paid tithes and fees and made no gifts of goods or money. After the tragic suppression of the Peasants' Revolt in 1525, the peasants were largely alienated from the Reformation and they resented or passively resisted the actions of the Reformers and of the lords as well. The worst feature of the situation was that there was little adequate local leadership. Monasteries had been forsaken, and whole parishes were without ecclesiastical leadership. Many priests who had turned to the Reformation and had become evangelical preachers were incapable either of preaching or of rebuilding the congregations. There was no common understanding about the ways by which the Reformation was to be realized. Confusion prevailed in the celebration of worship services and sacraments. The changes made were often arbitrary and inspired by the whims of individuals. Ecclesiastical discipline-and Christian morality were no longer maintained. The jurisdictional and administrative power which the Roman Catholic bishops had exercised, either directly or through episcopal officials, had disappeared—with dire effects, particularly upon the institution and the practices of marriage.

But, in many places, ardent adherents of the Reformation were at work, preachers who had studied in Wittenberg and in other evangelical centers or who had come under the influence of the Reformers through their writings. Since 1522, Luther's German translation of the New

Testament was in circulation. He had also published his *Church Postil Sermons* as examples of evangelical preaching. Numerous tracts written by the Reformers continually came from the printing presses. Thus the new understanding of the gospel was kept alive.

Soon a diversity of Christian doctrines and practices arose which embroiled the Reformers themselves in controversy with one another. We need to concern ourselves here only with the so-called sectarians, because it was in opposition to them that the new church orders assumed a special uniformitarian character. Luther found it necessary to oppose the spiritualism and mysticism of his colleague, Karlstadt, the "heavenly prophet" who was the first in Wittenberg to attempt the introduction of a Biblical order of service in place of the Roman Mass. He also had to defend himself against Thomas Müntzer, the "Schwärmer," who felt that Luther lacked the radicalism and the resolute will to carry the Reformation through to a complete abolition of the Papist priesthood and to the establishment not only of new churches but also of a new social order, if necessary by revolution.

A similar opposition arose against Zwingli, who, since 1519, had prepared the way for the Reformation in Zürich by Biblical preaching. In 1523, he began to introduce a new order with the sanction of the public authorities and he completed it in its first form two years later. Under the leadership of Conrad Grebel, some of his most ardently evangelical adherents objected to his program (which in fact was the only feasible one) to effect the Reformation by the co-ordination of Church and State and the building of an evangelical people's church to which every citizen and subject of Zürich had to belong and to whose order all were expected to conform. They advocated instead the idea that a church truly reformed according to the Bible could not be anything else but a community of believers who, having been awakened and reborn by the Holy Spirit, were resolved to follow Christ and to practice a life of uncompromising discipleship, declining to rely on political power for the maintenance of religion and refusing to bear arms, to use physical coercion of any sort, to appeal to the courts, to swear oaths, et cetera. The issue between them and Zwingli became joined, when they neglected to present their children for baptism, convinced that only believers' baptism was the true sign of entrance into membership of the church. When they were ordered to abide by the common custom of infant baptism, they chose to set themselves apart in a community of the reborn, using a very simple form of baptism as the seal of faith. Because they thus appeared to "rebaptize" one another, though they themselves regarded infant baptism as no baptism at all, they were dubbed Anabaptists. They were vigorously and cruelly suppressed in Zürich, but what they had begun spread rapidly. From 1525 on, Anabaptists were active wherever the Reformation took hold. They founded communities of regenerate disciples who were resolved as simple Bible Christians to dedicate themselves to a life of faith and love. Their missionary zeal made them agents of Christian awakenings. Their gatherings in private houses, in barns, in forests and open fields were often revivals.

Their presence where the churches were in process of being reformed, added to the general confusion. As believers wholly committed to the Christian way, they refused to identify themselves with the publicly instituted churches, whether they were Roman Catholic or Evangelical. They disobeyed the commands of the political authorities that they attend the officially sanctioned church services. At the same time, they vigorously criticized the Reformers for their alleged failure to produce fruits from their preaching of the gospel.

The Reformers opposed them with fervor and even with violence. They now found themselves compelled to interpret the gospel not only in contrast to Roman Catholicism but also in opposition to these sectarians. Indeed, the greatest expositions of the faith of the Reformers (for example, Calvin's Institutes) were conceived in opposition to Roman Catholicism on the right and to the Anabaptists on the left.

On can understand this rejection of the Anabaptists only if one is mindful of the fact that, when the Reformers were confronted with the task of building church orders of their own, they found it inevitable to adhere to the principles and practices of religious and creedal uniformity. They maintained the tradition that had prevailed throughout the Middle Ages and had shaped all institutions, namely, that peace, concord, and unity could not prevail in a sociopolitical community unless all its members were bound together by the same religious confession. Though they knew from personal experience and continually professed that faith cannot be coerced, and though they were themselves in dissent from Roman Catholicism, which heretofore had furnished the religious bond of unity, they demanded conformity from all who lived in the confines of the territories and communities where they were developing new church orders. Dissenters were ordered to emigrate. The Protestant estates did not protest when first at Speyer, in 1529, and then at Augsburg, in 1530, the Diet of the Empire invoked the old heresy laws against the Anabaptists. The Protestants themselves did not prosecute the sectarians on the charge of heresy but rather put them on trial for sedition and disturbance of peace. Their crime was that they dared set themselves apart from the "people's churches" and that they formed conventicles and met in secret. The evangelical churches were thus formed as territorial or state churches. Each of them became a closed unit, subject to the political authority of its own government, the prince, or the city council. All subjects or citizens were expected under penalties of law to conform to the established order.

In the course of time, it was generally agreed everywhere in these churches that the ultimate source and norm of the church and of the Christian life was the Bible; that nothing, therefore, was as important as the preaching and teaching of the Bible and that, because there was no authority higher than the Bible, Biblical preaching was not subject to regulation by political authority (except if it led to secession from the common order!). Everything else, however, particularly matters relating to the external organization of the church, was to be under governmental regulation. This arrangement gave the preachers as the spokesmen and interpreters of the Bible considerable freedom to preach but it confined them at the same time to the established church order and made their actions subject to political administration.

The orders which thus came into being were a far cry from what Luther had envisaged at the beginning of the Reformation but they were also the result of the conviction of Luther and the other Reformers that there were not yet enough Christians in the world. In 1526, Luther had written in the preface to his *German Mass:*

Those who earnestly desire to be Christians and confess the gospel by word and deed, should register their names and gather in a house by themselves in order to pray, read, baptize, receive the sacrament [of the Lord's Supper] and to practice other Christian work. In such an order, those who could not behave in a Christian way, could be recognized and one could punish, reprimand, expel or banish them according to the rule of Christ, Mt. 18. Here one could also levy upon the Christians a common contribution of alms, which readily given could then be distributed among the poor according to the example of Paul, Cor. 9. . . . But I cannot and do not yet dare organize or establish such a congregation or gathering. For I have not yet available a sufficient number of Christian people [for such an undertaking] and, as a matter of fact, I do not know and see many who insist that it be done.

As they actually developed, the evangelical church orders were of several types. We must distinguish between the territorial churches (A), and those of the towns (B).

A. The church orders of the princely territories of Germany were of three types:

1. In Saxony, and in dependence upon it in most principalities of northern Germany, the ministers were held solely responsible for preaching, catechetical teaching, and the administration of the sacraments. They were relieved of all responsibility for the external organization and administration of the Church. They were supervised by Superintendents who, generally speaking, were the successors of the archdeacons and deans of the Roman Catholic order. These Superintendents were appointed by the ruler and were commonly ministers of a parish in a district town. It was their task to examine the ministers before they were called to serve a church, to ordain them and to supervise and advise them in their work. They convened the ministers of their districts in synods, which were permitted to concern themselves solely with problems and issues relating to the ministry. Everything else lay in the hands of Consistories (there were three in Saxony, established after 1555). Each of these consisted of two theologically trained and two juristically trained councilors as well as other minor officials, among whom there had to be some who were skilled in financial administration. Responsible to the prince, they regulated all affairs of the church, external and internal, except that they lacked the power of ordination and had to respect the preaching office insofar as it was bound to the Word of God. But they controlled the training for the ministry, the observance of the creeds and of the orders of divine services. They administered the finances and properties of the churches and exercised all jurisdictional authority, especially with respect to marriage laws and customs.

In this system, the congregations had no status providing for active responsibility. They were entirely at the receiving end. Some church orders of this type provided for the exercise of a veto on the part of the congregation (or at least its representatives), especially in connection with the appointment of ministers, but these provisions were in fact ignored. The congregations were the objects of ministerial and pastoral labors and consistorial administration. The ministers, themselves hemmed in by regulations issued by higher authorities, were the sole voices of the church.

2. Similarly in the church order of Hesse (first introduced in 1531 and revised in 1537, 1539, and 1566), the highest ecclesiastical authority

lay in the hands of the prince, but it was less bureaucratic and more representative in character. In the local congregations, the people were given a voice through the office of elders who were selected from their midst. Actually this office rapidly declined after it had first been instituted in 1539. The church was governed by Superintendents (at first six, later four) who exercised full episcopal authority in their districts, supervising ministers and congregations, administering church properties and dispensing discipline and jurisdiction. The first Superintendents were appointed by the Landgrave, and their successors were named in the following manner: the ministers of a district proposed three of their number as candidates for the office to the Superintendents who then elected one of them, proposing his name to the prince who had the right either to confirm or to veto the election. The ministers of each district were convened annually by their Superintendent; every second year there was held a General Synod attended by the Superintendents, one minister from each district elected by his synod, and the official representatives of the prince.

3. The church order of Württemberg (completed in 1533) was bureaucratic in character. The church was governed by a commission of councilors acting on ducal authority. They engaged a number of Visitators (theologians and lawyers) under a director, the church councilor. It was his duty to inspect the churches regularly with regard to all external affairs. In their purely spiritual work the ministers were led by Superintendents who resided in the district towns. The highest spiritual officials were four General Superintendents who were set over the Superintendents and were appointed by the prince.

The object of all these orders was to establish churches according to the standards of the Reformers! The prince as the *praecipuum membrum ecclesiae* (chief member of the church) assumed the authority which formerly had belonged to the bishops. Only preaching and the administration of the sacraments were exempt from his power, and he himself was subject to the Word of God, the highest authority. The bureaucratic officials through whom he exercised the *landesherrliche Kirchenregiment* (the church government of the ruler) were the instruments of what turned out to be a patriarchal government. The prince generally took a very personal interest in the affairs of the church. When one reads the records and documents of sixteenth-century church administration, one cannot but be surprised at the innumerable details which were submitted by the church officials to the prince for his personal decision. He was ultimately responsible for the punishment of wayward ministers, the settlement of quarrels in synods, the disciplining of church members who objected to their ministers or refused to observe the church rules, et cetera. He was in fact the patriarch of his people who through his personal government led them in Christian ways. For the success of his rule, he had to rely not only upon the administrative officials but chiefly upon the local ministers and the heads of families. In their own spheres, these were as patriarchal as he was in his. The most important parts of this scheme were the local parish ministers, for they occupied a position in between the ruler and the families.

Strenuous efforts were made to produce well-trained, effective parish ministers. Secondary schools and universities were maintained in order to train them. In 1525, Philip of Hesse founded the University of Marburg in order to raise an educated ministry. The University of Wittenberg, the school of Luther and Melanchthon, fulfilled a similar purpose for Saxony. When Württemberg became Protestant, its university at Tübingen was given the same role, and the same pattern was followed elsewhere. It was believed that a humanistically and theologically trained minister who had been taught how to interpret the Bible would effectively lead the common people in Christian faith and life, chiefly through his preaching and teaching.

B. The church orders of the free towns were different, primarily because these communities had a social character of their own. They were ruled by oligarchical-republican governments and were engaged in commercial pursuits. Here too public affairs were managed and administered through person-to-person relationships, even more so than in the territories of the princes, but the structure of governing authority was not patriarchal. When, therefore, the city councils and their executive officers assumed control of the evangelical churches, and it was generally through their decision and sanction that the Roman Catholic order was abolished and the Reformation introduced, the church government took on a less bureaucratic character. The political magistrates jealously guarded their prerogatives: they were intent on not having their control of the common life restricted and curtailed. They insisted, therefore, that the preachers as the leaders of the churches should be subject to their guidance. But the preachers, nevertheless, had much more leeway of action than their colleagues in the monarchical lands enjoyed. They were able to assert their own iniative. The goal of the towns that had introduced the Reformation was to establish a Christian commonwealth (*respublica Christiana* or *civitas Christiana*). In the pursuit of this aim, the preachers were able to display a much greater independence from the governments than the church leaders of the princely territories found possible. As advisers to the princes, certain ministers could exercise great power; particularly the Reformers themselves had a deep influence upon the rulers: Luther and Melanchthon in Saxony; Bugenhagen in Pomerania and Denmark; Krafft in Hesse; Brenz in Württemberg; et cetera; but the preachers of the towns were able to press their demands for the regulation of the Christian life much more forcefully upon their magistrates as in the cases of Bucer and his colleagues Hedio, Zell, and Capito in Strassburg; Rhegius in Augsburg; the brothers Blaurer in Konstanz; Zwingli in Zürich; Oecolampadius in Basel; and of course Calvin in Geneva.

We must not imagine that they dominated the towns. There the great issue was the institution of Christian discipline; i.e., the subjection of all phases of life, personal and social, private and public, to the moral-religious demands of the gospel. In the territorial churches, this concern was not so acute. One relied on the prince and trusted that he would exercise a Christian responsibility in his rule. In this connection, we should note that Luther was doubtful whether public life and particularly government could be Christianized. It was also hoped that the local ministers would control and shape the behavior of people, especially in family relations, by preaching and a conscientious administration of the sacraments. But in the towns, the introduction of Christian discipline, at least as it was understood by the preachers, amounted to the regulation of the whole common life by laws designed to render the church omnipresent. In order to comprehend this undertaking, one must be mindful of the fact that the citizens of medieval towns were accustomed to live under strict and amazingly detailed regulations issued and executed by their governments.

Nevertheless, the people of the towns were not exactly friendly toward the plans of the preachers. To be sure, the city councils were prepared to assume many of the functions which, under Roman Catholicism, had been fulfilled by the bishops in the administration of marriage laws, poor relief, education, et cetera. They were also ready to introduce and to supervise evangelical church orders. But they shied away from the demand for Christian discipline, particularly if the preachers insisted that its administration was their prerogative and that it should be as unencumbered by governmental interference as preaching the Word of God was recognized to be. Though the magistrates of the evangelical towns were wont to emphasize, sometimes from a high sense of mission, that the town governments were Christian, they hesitated to institute church discipline, because they feared that the preachers might constitute themselves as a second legislative and governmental body. Indeed, they suspected that a new "Papism" might arise. They were widely supported by the people themselves who, though by no means hostile toward religion, were unwilling to submit to a Puritan regime of the preachers. It is reported that, in Strassburg, they said: "One must let the world be the world, at least a little!" (*Man muss dennoch die Welt ein wenig die Welt sin lassen*).[19]

It is most instructive to consider what took place in Strassburg. The Reformation was introduced there in the early twenties of the sixteenth century. Its agents were a group of distinguished preachers who had all been converted from Roman Catholicism to the gospel. Each of them was a highly educated and competent person. They all, Caspar Hedio, Matthias Zell, Wolfgang Capito and others, wielded great influence, but their leader was Martin Bucer. In the course of time, he became the spokesman of the Strassburg church, and related it to the Reformation movement everywhere. He adopted practices that had been established elsewhere (particularly in Zürich and Basel) and introduced them in Strassburg, but he also transmitted the new patterns developed there to other places, like Konstanz, Ulm, even Hesse, and particularly Geneva.

After the city government, yielding to evangelical preaching, had permitted the people of the several parishes in the city to elect their own preachers and then had encouraged them to establish an evangelical order of worship, it proceeded to reorganize the property of the church, assigning its income to the maintenance of church buildings, the payment of ministers' salaries, education, and poor relief. In 1529, the Council issued a detailed mandate of morals (*Sittenmandat*), and then established a marriage court. In contrast to Zürich, the preachers were given no responsibility as "judges." Two years later, after the preachers had demanded that the magistrate further the health of the church by legislation (their most important suggestion was that, in each parish, elders should be appointed to supervise the people of their own congregation but particularly the ministers), the city council ordered the appointment of three church wardens (*Kirchenpfleger*) in each of the seven parishes in the city, two to be chosen from the city government and one from the citizens. These wardens were to be elected by the city council and were to be responsible to it. They were charged to supervise the ministers "in their life, teaching and preaching" and to attend the synods, which, it was hoped, would meet henceforth twice a year, "in order that they might further the gradual upbuilding of a real Christian congregation." After the first synod had met in 1533 and promulgated a confession of faith, the city council proclaimed a definite church order (1534), incorporating in it most of the earlier regulations. The office of the church wardens was strengthened. They were now made responsible for the preservation of true doctrine, given a more important part in the nomination of ministers, and empowered to admonish people who disregarded the church laws. Neither they nor the ministers nor the congregations were given power of excommunication. Moreover, they continued to be functionaries of the city council.

This office of the church wardens proved to be ineffective, in part because it was both ecclesiastical and political, in part because those appointed to it fulfilled their duties only formally, but chiefly because the magistrate was really not interested in seeing it succeed. The preachers, therefore, pressed for greater independence of the church from the government in order to make Christianity more effective in the common life. Particularly Bucer, who had a high sense of the church as a moral community, fired one memorandum after another at the city council, demanding for the church the full institution of church discipline. In 1539, he argued that the church should be constituted according to the law of the New Testament and that therefore four offices should be established: preachers, elders (responsible for the administration of discipline and for the religious and moral supervision of church members), teachers and deacons (responsible for poor-relief). The council did not choose to adopt his proposal. In 1546 and 1547, he went so far as to propose the formation of fellowships (*Gemeinschaften*) of earnest Christians in each parish. Such fellowships were to be voluntarily formed by church members who had responded to an appeal from the ministers, but no one was to be permitted to join without making a clear confession of his faith. Young people were to become members only after a period of thorough instruction in the Christian religion and on the basis of a solemn confession of faith before the whole fellowship. (Here is the first pattern of the Protestant practice of Confirmation, later introduced into Lutheranism under the influence of the Pietist, Spener). The fellowship was to elect elders who together with the ministers were to administer discipline according to Matt. 18:16 ff. The minister and the elders should have the right to supervise the life of the members of the fellowship, to admonish, and, if necessary, to excommunicate them by excluding them from prayer and the Lord's Supper and, in certain cases, from the preaching service. The fellowship

was to manifest itself chiefly in the common celebration of the Lord's
Supper, for which all members would be expected to make themselves
ready by attending a special preparatory service of penance, confession,
and absolution.

Bucer had the support of a minority of his fellow ministers. The
others feared that the building of an *ecclesiola in ecclesia* might disrupt
the officially established church and disturb the unity of the commonwealth. It did not take the magistrate long to reject these proposals.
Bucer thus lost his long battle for the establishment of an effective
church discipline. His proposal of an inner church fellowship, which
reminds one of the plan that Luther had entertained and quickly
rejected at the beginning of the Reformation, represented a final, even
desperate, effort to obtain for a minority in the church what he had
hoped to realize on behalf of the whole community.

The church order as he saw it was to be based on the following
principles: The government is responsible for the temporal and eternal
welfare of its subjects, because it is endowed with the sword, and has
power over life and death. It therefore must regulate also the affairs of
religion. Indeed, it is charged with the *custodia utriusque tabulae* (the
custody of the two tables of the law), i.e., it has power to order and
supervise men's duties toward God as well as toward one another, but
only insofar as external order is concerned. It must institute true
religion and abolish all religious abuses, idolatry, and superstition. At
the same time, it must maintain a just and moral public order con-
comitant with religion. But its power of coercion does not extend to the
affairs of eternal life and it therefore must maintain and respect the
right of the church, under the Word of God, to regulate preaching, the
administration of the sacraments, absolution, excommunication, and the
ordering of divine services. In his tract *On the True Care of Souls,* Bucer
put the matter in this way: "The secular sword and power must be under
the spiritual sword and power. And this spiritual sword is the Word of
God. . . . When the pastors rightly handle this spiritual sword, namely
the Word of God, . . . all men must with complete obedience be
subject to them, i.e. to the Word of God and of Christ which they teach
and according to which they pass judgments. They must now let themselves be judged and governed not by men who happen to be ministers,
but by Christ, the heavenly King, who by 'his Word [rules] in and
through his ministers.'"

In these sentences, Bucer formulated succinctly the conception of a
Christian commonwealth which guided him throughout his career and

which inspired the leaders in other Reformed city-states: Christ is the governor of the city and he governs through his Word. His vicars are the preachers who administer the Word. To them, the teachers and interpreters of the Word of Christ, the sociopolitical order must be subject. Under the Word of God, the civil government must maintain order by means of the sword, i.e., by means of the power of public law and coercion. Under the Word of God, the church must also constitute itself as a fellowship of faith through preaching, teaching, celebration of the sacraments, spiritual disicipline, and benevolence. Both must be free in their own sphere but not separated from each other, for their ultimate source, authority, and norm is the same: the Word of God.

This ideal hovered over the church orders of all towns in which the Reformation was introduced. It was nowhere completely realized, chiefly because the civil governments refused to yield an independent control of public life to the preachers. In Geneva Calvin succeeded in making it real. He had to make concessions to the political government, to be sure, but the compromise to which he gave his assent, did not invalidate the ideal. He too was compelled to enter into long conflicts with those who wanted to prevent the church from administering discipline, but he won—and was thus enabled to accomplish what in Zürich, Basel, Strassburg, and other places remained either a plan or a fragment or an inffective compromise.

Calvin submitted the *Ordonnances Ecclesiastiques* (Ecclesiastical Ordinances) to the Genevan government, when, in September, 1541, he returned to the city, at its invitation, for his second pastorate there. After detailed negotiations, which produced changes, the Ordinances were adopted in November of the same year and henceforth had the force of law.

The outstanding feature of this church order was the provision of four church offices, namely, of preachers, teachers, elders, and deacons, according to the institution of Christ, i.e., by divine law. Calvin here proceeded on the principle, which he had most probably adopted from Bucer, that the New Testament (in Rom. 12; I Cor. 12; and Eph. 4) prescribed a definite form of the church. Exegetically, he argued that the New Testament passages provided for some church offices that were valid only for the beginnings of the church, e.g., apostles, prophets, et cetera, and others that were at all times, i.e., preachers, elders, et cetera.

The preachers as a body were constituted as the *Compagnie Vénérable* (Venerable Company). New ministers were examined by them and recommended by them to the congregation to be called and elected. The city council had the right to approve the election. Until he died (in 1564) Calvin was the president of this body of ministers. The function of the pastors was to preach, teach, administer the sacraments, and enforce church discipline. In the latter task, they were joined by the elders, all twelve of whom were also members of the city government, two of the Small Council, four of the Council of Sixty, and six of the Large Council. Though named to the eldership by the magistrate, they were officers of the church and as such not responsible to the city government. Together with the ministers, they constituted the *Consistoire* (Consistory) which administered church discipline. Pastors and elders were charged to supervise the religious and moral life of the people of their districts (the city was divided into twelve districts) and to bring all irregularities to the attention of the Consistory for action (hearings, admonitions, reprimands, exclusion from the Lord's Supper, and excommunication). If criminals were discovered in connection with the administration of church discipline, the persons involved were handed over to the secular government for trial and punishment. The Consistory was entitled to hear all marriage cases but it could not make legal decisions concerning them. This was the duty of a civil marriage court to which one of the ministers was attached as a consultant. Despite the fact that the Consistory was a partnership between the church and the secular government, Calvin saw to it that it operated as the disciplinary body of the church. In the course of time, its right to pronounce excommunication from the church (this did not also entail the civil ban) without the sanction and approval of the civil government was challenged, but Calvin succeeded in maintaining the freedom of the ecclesiastical function of the Consistory. Gradually, it imposed, under his guidance, a strict and very minute discipline upon the people of Geneva.

The teachers also were officers of the church. Their chief responsibility was the Academy, a humanistic and theological institution for the training of young men for the ministry. It began to flourish, when in 1559 Theodore Beza, who was to become Calvin's successor as the leader of the church of Geneva, assumed its rectorship. Finally, the church also administered poor-relief and benevolences of all kinds through the deacons.

It is no wonder that this church order became the most influential of all that were produced by the Reformation. Its most remarkable administration under Calvin made Geneva, according to the words of John Knox, "the greatest school of Christ on earth." The fact that the four ministerial offices on which the structure was based were regarded as divinely prescribed, made it possible to transplant this polity, basically unchanged, to other countries and places, where Calvinism became established. Thus the Genevan church order served as the pattern for the Protestant churches of France, Holland, Hungary, Scotland. Furthermore, the ideal of the Christian commonwealth which it embodied became that of the English Puritans and their descendants, particularly among those denominations which later shaped American Protestantism.

The Functions and Standards of the Early Evangelical Ministry

At the beginning of the fourth book of the *Institutes*, in which he deals with the church, Calvin likens the church to a mother and he suggests that no one can be a Christian unless he gives himself continuously into her care. "Our infirmity," he writes, "will not admit of our dismission from her school; we must continue under her instruction and discipline to the end of our lives." And, he continues, "though God could easily make his people perfect in a single moment, yet it was not his will that they should grow to mature age, but under the education of the church." [20]

In writing this, Calvin was thinking of the church as it comes into being through the Word of God as it is preached, taught, and applied to private and public, individual and social life. Under the Word of God, therefore, the church is the educator—not by itself, but "by the instrumentality of men," the ministers, to whom is assigned "the preaching of the heavenly doctrine" and the administration of the whole divine order prescribed by it.

Calvin's doctrine of the church implied a high conception of the ministry. He was unique among the Reformers because he regarded the polity of the church as divinely instituted. However, they all held a high doctrine of the ministry, and they all agreed with Calvin that the church as the school of Christ becomes real through the ministry of the Word.

The primary ministerial function was *preaching*. And what a load of it the ministers of the era of the Reformation had to carry! In his *German Mass* Luther described the practice prevailing at Wittenberg as follows: On Sunday, there were three services. At the early morning service, at five or six o'clock, there was a sermon on the Epistle of the day. At the main service, at eight or nine o'clock, the minister preached on the Gospel of the day. The sermon at the Vesper service in the afternoon was based on the Old Testament. It was the practice to expound the whole book consecutively, Sunday after Sunday. Monday and Tuesday were the days of the Catechism, and on each of these days, the sermon was devoted to an exposition of parts of the Catechism, the Decalogue, the Creed, the Lord's Prayer, or the sacraments. The early morning service on Wednesday was centered on the Gospel of Matthew. On Thursday and Friday, the Epistles were expounded. On Saturday, a late afternoon Vesper service was held, and the Gospel of John traditionally furnished the text of the sermon. In other places the practice was similar. In the evangelical churches of the cities and towns, at least one service with sermon was held every day. In the villages, particularly those that were incorporated in a township, there were, naturally, fewer services. For example, the parish of Wittenberg comprised thirteen villages besides the town. The preaching services there were held by an assistant preacher, called deacon (generally a theological student) who visited each place at regular intervals. Let us mention, by the way, that the parish minister of Wittenberg had three (and, since 1533, four) assistants. He could, of course, count on being helped in his preaching chores by the members of the Theological Faculty.

Luther preached regularly in the town church. Many of the sermons that were later published and included in his *Collected Works* are transcripts of stenographs taken at these occasions. They are representative of the type of preaching generally practiced among the early Protestants. They are all expository homilies and, in large part, paraphrases of the Biblical text, interlaced with interpretations of key doctrines and with moral admonitions that were designed to make the Bible live as the mirror of God's self-disclosure.

In other respects, Luther's style of preaching was not typical. As he did in all his works, he communicated his own person in his sermons, yet without superimposing himself on the message he wanted to convey. The vivid imagination and the sharp observation of men and nature that marked his mind; his acquaintance with common speech and his joy in the use of proverbs; indeed, his capacity to express in creative speaking with a skill that only a poet and genius possesses the whole range of human emotions from awe in the presence of the numinous to the feelings of the body—all are reflected in his sermons (as also in the commentaries, his work of the lecture room), not consistently, of course, and not every time, yet most impressively in the *Church Postil Sermons*, one of the products of his exile on Wartburg Castle, written in order to furnish to the preachers of the Reformation examples of Biblical preaching. There is nothing parallel in the work of another preacher of the Reformation. Zwingli spoke directly and naturally, yet too intellectually; Calvin preached with remarkable consistency, always concerned to bring to the fore all that was contained in the passage he was expounding, but he was always impersonal; Bucer was rambling and long-winded and because, as he spoke, all kinds of ideas were awakened in his well-stored mind, he could never be a popular preacher. We know the sermons of scores of other men of the Reformation. Most of them do not reflect anything extraordinary. And we do not know anything about the work of hundreds of other preachers, but we may be sure that only comparatively few had mastered the art of preaching.

It is understandable that ministers were permitted and specifically encouraged to use sermons published by others, even if they could not memorize them and had to read them aloud from the pulpit. Luther's *Postils* and other sermon collections "useful and of advantage to unskilled pastors and preachers" could be bought at the book markets. A volume of sermons for all occasions, written by the Reformer of Augsburg, Urbanus Rhegius, was most popular.

At the beginning of the Reformation, there were many pastors, converts to the gospel from Roman Catholicism, who had no experience in preaching and could not learn how to do it because they were too old or because they lacked training and education. The Visitators and Superintendents who shaped and directed the new evangelical church orders were instructed to help them with advice and counsel, to provide them with books and to assign readings, in many cases of the Bible itself. Melanchthon, who from 1526 on was a leading member of the Visitation Commission of electoral Saxony, once told one of his classes that, at a Visitation examination, he had asked a minister who earlier had been a monk, whether he taught his people the Decalogue and that he had received the answer: "That book I have not yet been able to get." Melanchthon did not say what he did to help the man. As the Reformation progressed, provisions were made for the training of ministers at schools and universities. This ministerial education did not provide specifically for training in the art and skill of preaching. The assumption was that if one had learned to read and interpret the Bible and could defend and expound a Biblical theology, he would also be able to preach. Perhaps it was this sort of training which made for the length of some of the sermons in early Protestantism. During the latter part of the sixteenth century, it was not unusual for a sermon to last two or three hours. Of Bugenhagen, the first evangelical minister of the parish church of Wittenberg and the first Superintendent of the church of electoral Saxony, it is reported that, during a visit to Denmark where he helped to introduce the Reformation, he once preached for seven hours! [21] This was certainly not the common custom at this or any other period, but Bugenhagen had a reputation as a preacher who took a very long time in the pulpit.

Luther certainly was not in favor of overlong sermons. He was too mindful of the capacities of his congregation! He often said, in his *Table Talk,* that when he was in the pulpit, he thought of "little Jack and little Betty" (*Hänslein und Elslein*) and of the maids and menservants in the pews.[22] He knew that "to preach simply is a great art." [23] His rule for good preaching was as follows: "First of all, a good preacher must be able to teach correctly and in an orderly manner. Second, he must have a good head. Third, he must be able to speak well. Fourth, he should have a good voice, and, fifth, a good memory. Sixth, he must know when to stop. Seventh, he must know his stuff and keep at it. Eighth, he must be willing to risk body and soul, property and honor. Ninth, he must let everyone vex and ridicule him [*sich von jedermann lassen vexieren und geheuen*]." [24]

These rules show that he was well acquainted with preaching and preachers. But how many ministers could observe them? It is probable that a great number among them resembled the parson Dionysius Brunn of Moisall in Mecklenburg about whom a Visitation Commission of 1544 made the following report: "There is not much knowledge or intellect in the little man. He preaches from memory, it is true, but he has a strange way and is very faulty in his pronunciation and, besides, he shouts. He swallows the last words and syllables, and he has an odd way to over-use certain words; he repeats them again and again in his sermon. Consequently, he is unpleasant to listen to; indeed, he hurts one's ears. The poor congregation cannot possibly comprehend what he is saying." [25]

Another minister who had no trouble in making himself understood had difficulties of another sort. In a sermon, he once advised his congregation that they should whistle when they heard someone tell a lie. "A little later, he preached on the creation of man and, desiring to be as graphic and plain as possible, he said: 'When God Almighty had made heaven and earth, he rolled in one a lump of clay and fashioned it into the likeness of a man and then leaned it on a fence to harden.' When an insolent peasant heard this, he whistled very loudly right in the church. The parson noticed it and said: 'What! Do you think, peasant, that I am lying?' 'No,' replied the peasant, 'but who had made the fence when there was not yet any man on earth?' " [26]

When the Visitations disclosed that the chief trouble of the evangelical churches was the ignorance of the common people, steps were taken to use the public services also for purposes of instruction. Catechisms, which were produced everywhere, served as the basis of *teaching*. It was customary in many churches, when the sermon was ended, for the minister to lead the congregation in a recital of the Catechism or parts of it. Luther had written his *Smaller Catechism* to be memorized by young and old alike and the larger one to be read aloud at home or in church. Shortly after they were published in 1529, they were put into general use. In Wittenberg, it became the practice (which was instituted elsewhere) to hold, four times a year, preaching services on the Catechism. For two weeks, the Catechism was explained seriatim in daily sermons. Practices of this sort made it inevitable for preaching generally to assume a catechetical character. The ministers directed their sermons to the end of stimulating a right faith on the basis of a correct knowledge of evangelical doctrines. They did not try to arouse conversion experiences in their listeners nor did they cultivate religious emotions or sentiments. Early Protestant preaching was doctrinal and became more and more so. Only among the Anabaptists did Christian awakenings and revivals occur under the influence of Biblical preaching, Bible readings, and hymn singing. The movement of the Reformation at large was not a "great awakening." It was the goal of the Reformers and of the early Protestant ministry to inculcate right Christian teaching and "pure doctrine" in the minds of men. This is why as preachers they were primarily teachers.

The predominance of teaching became apparent also in the general work of the ministry. The administration of the sacraments was always accompanied by some kind of instruction. In Lutheran churches, young people were not admitted to the first communion service without having been examined by the minister on their faith. In St. Gallen, Switzerland, children between the ages of seven and fourteen had to attend lessons every Sunday afternoon in order to be instructed by the minister in the Catechism, in preparation for their first communion. In the services of confession and penitence which practically everywhere preceded the celebration of the Lord's Supper the people were examined on their faith. Practically all Lutheran church orders prescribed such a *Glaubensexamen*. To be sure, this "examination" was but part of the confession without which no one could take the sacrament. In Lutheran churches, where the sacrament was celebrated in connection with every main Sunday service and where only those who chose to do so communed, the confessional had a private character. People who intended to take the sacrament had to inform the minister beforehand, and he was not allowed to admit them without having held with them a service of confession. They were not expected to confess their sins in detail, but those who were in need of counsel were encouraged to make complete confession of all that burdened them.

In Geneva, the Lord's Supper was regarded as a service of the whole congregation that everyone had to attend. Calvin had originally proposed that it should be held once every month in the city, each parish observing it once every quarter of the year but on different Sundays, and that, in addition, it should be observed in every parish at Christmas, Easter, and Pentecost. But the Ecclesiastical Ordinances as they were actually adopted prescribed the celebration of the Supper only on the three great feast days and the first Sunday in September. Here, too, a confessional service was held preceding the celebration of the sacrament. Meeting as the congregation of God, all were individually confronted with their responsibility worthily to approach the Lord's table. The ministers did not admit anyone who was not in good standing in the church. The communion service was thus placed in the context of church discipline. To be excluded from it was the chief consequence a person had to bear on whom the Consistory had pronounced the sentence of excommunication. Moreover, none of those who had been cited to appear before the Consistory because of irregularities in faith or morals was permitted to take communion, unless evidence was given of his having corrected the faults.

In this connection, there developed, in Geneva, a regular practice of the *care of souls*. The Ordinances prescribed that each minister accompanied by an elder should regularly call in the homes of his parish. In 1550, an order was issued that the ministers should visit each home at least once a year. Beza commented on the effect of the order by saying: "It is hard to believe how fruitful it proved to be." [27]

In other towns attempts to introduce a similar practice were made, but apparently the plan was generally not carried out. According to the regulations of most church orders, the care of souls for which the ministers were responsible by virtue of their office was limited to regular visits in the hospitals and prisons. The ministers visited the sick in their homes only if they were asked to come. People were encouraged to inform the ministers when members of their families were ill, and especially when they were near death, and then to invite them to call. It seems that the ministers made no uninvited sick calls in order to avoid the impression that people required the services of a priest when they were about to die. Where church discipline was instituted, the regular visits of ministers and elders produced a sense of Christian mutuality and a spirit of churchmanship not matched elsewhere.

Among all the Reformers, it was Bucer who saw this most clearly. Throughout his career, he aimed to actualize the church as a real community of love. To what an extent he characteristically interpreted this concern in terms of instruction, he reveals in this passage of his book on *The Care of Souls:* "One must not confine Christian teaching and exhortation to the church service and the pulpit, for there are many who let remain general what is there offered as a general teaching and admonition and who interpret and understand it with respect to others rather than with respect to themselves. Hence it is necessary to instruct the people at home and to give them individual Christian guidance. Those churches therefore have acted wisely who pursue an individual approach in teaching everyone penitence and faith in Christ the Lord." [28] In the church of Geneva, Calvin turned the same concern in the direction of *discipline:* "As the saving doctrine of Christ is the soul of the Church, so discipline forms the ligaments which connect the members together and keep each in its proper place. . . . [For there would occur] a dissolution of the Church . . . unless the preaching of the doctrine were accompanied with private admonitions, reproofs and other means to enforce the doctrine and prevent it from being altogether ineffectual." [29] "For the doctrine then obtains its full authority, and produces its due effect, when the minister not only declares to all the people together what is their duty to Christ, but has the right and means of enforcing it upon them whom he observes to be inattentive, or not obedient to the doctrine." [30]

These sentences, which accurately reflect the practices of the Genevan church, imply that the minister occupied an office of great authority. And this was the case not only in Geneva but also elsewhere. He had the power to preach, to bind and to loose, and to administer the sacraments. In these three respects, the Augsburg Confession (Art. 28, 5) defined the *power of the keys (potestas clavii)*. Its definition applied generally to Reformation Protestantism. By virtue of it, the minister had the right to proclaim the ban. But one was careful to distinguish this power of excommunication from that used in Roman Catholicism.

Luther wrote in the Smalcald Articles (Art. 3, 9): "The great ban [maior excommunicatio] as the Pope calls it, we regard entirely as a secular punishment, and it does not concern us. But the small, i.e., the true Christian ban is this that one must not permit apparent, obstinate sinners to partake of the sacrament and other common acts of the Church, unless they mend their ways and avoid sin." In Lutheranism, this power was used by the minister on behalf of the church, in private rather than in public, but, in Calvinism, it was employed publicly by the minister and the elders in the church. Yet also here, excommunication was understood as a measure of discipline rather than as a punishment. "For," Calvin wrote, "excommunication differs from anathema; the latter, which ought to be very rarely or never resorted to, precluding all pardon, execrates a person and devotes him to eternal perdition; whereas excommunication rather censures and punishes his conduct." [31]

The power and authority of the minister was regarded as divine. It was believed that he did not speak and act in his own name but in the name of God. Calvin went so far as to treat acts of contempt or ridicule of the ministry as serious public offenses. He saw in them an expression of disregard of the divine order, and he was sure that such contempt threatened all order.

But though divine in nature, ministerial authority was bestowed by the congregation. This was the principle that was enacted when persons were inducted into the ministerial office. The methods of calling and ordaining a minister differed greatly from place to place and only gradually assumed a definite form.

The Confessio Helvetica Posterior of 1566 (written in 1562 by Henry Bullinger, the successor of Zwingli), summarizes the prevailing conception of the ministry in a representative way though it speaks only for the Swiss Reformed Church (Art. 18): At all times, God has used ministers for the gathering and establishment of the Church and for its government and maintenance. The origin, institution, and function of the ministry is therefore very old and willed by God himself. It is not a new order nor is it man-made. While God leads the hearts of his elect to faith inwardly by the Holy Spirit, he teaches them outwardly by the Word through his ministers. Christ called the apostles to preach the gospel and, by his command, they ordained pastors and teachers throughout the churches of the world and, by their successors, he has been teaching and governing the Church until now. Only such persons are qualified to become ministers who possess adequate and holy learning, pious eloquence (pia eloquentia) and simple prudence and are persons of moderation and honesty. They must be called and chosen by a legitimate ecclesiastical election (*electione ecclesiastica et legitima*), i.e., they must be carefully chosen by the church or by persons delegated by the church for this purpose, in an orderly proceeding without disturbance, sedition, or contention.[32]

The basis of this conception was the rejection of the *ordinatio absoluta* of the Roman Church, i.e., ordination to the priesthood without reference to a call to a specific office. At the very beginning of the Reformation, Luther had argued that the ministry made sense only in relation to a local congregation. Rejecting, therefore, the Roman Catholic sacrament of ordination as an induction into the status and order of the priesthood, he insisted that no one should be ordained to the ministry unless he had a call from a congregation. This view became the common property of the Reformers. It was not always observed in practice, and it often was lost sight of in the complex and confused efforts to raise and train a Protestant ministry. However, in principle, the congregational call of the minister was henceforth more important than his ordination. Indeed, in early Protestantism, ordination was nothing else than the confirmation of the calling and election of the minister. The importance which was attached to the choosing of the minister is impressively reflected in a passage of Calvin's *Institutes* where he writes: "Whenever a controversy arises respecting religion, which requires to be decided by a council or ecclesiastical judgment; *whenever a minister is to be chosen,* in short, whenever anything of difficulty or great importance is transacting; . . . it is a pious custom and beneficial in all ages, for the pastors to exhort the people to public fasts and extraordinary prayers." [33]

When one considers the actual conditions that prevailed in the local congregations at the time of the Reformation and is mindful of the fact that the people themselves for many reasons lacked initiative so that, as objects rather than as subjects of action, they were dependent upon the leadership of the princes, magistrates, and church governments, one can understand why the actual calling of the ministers was in fact rarely the result of their decision. According to the regulations of the various church orders, the patrons, Superintendents, ministers' convents, or officials of the church governments actually chose, examined, and elected the ministers, and the secular governments often appointed them. However, care was taken to have the candidate at least presented to the congregation (or its deputies) he was to serve.

In Wittenberg and the electorate of Saxony, the method of calling and ordaining a minister remained fluid until about 1535. Until then the early teaching of Luther was followed according to which ordination was nothing else than the confirmation of the call to the ministry in a particular congregation. When a minister had received a call, he was examined on his fitness for the office. Competent persons administered this examination: neighboring ministers; Visitation commissions; Superintendents; et cetera. If he was found to be qualified, he was elected and then, with prayer and the laying on of hands, commended to the congregation in its presence. The laying on of hands was understood as a gesture of intercession on behalf of the minister. After 1535, ordination, still interpreted as *confirmatio vocationis,* became a separate ritual. As such it was now an act of the church government, performed generally by the Superintendent, with prayer and the laying on of hands, in the presence of the congregation. No candidate for the ministry could be thus ordained, unless he had been called and elected and until he had passed an examination, the examiner being the Superintendent, later the Theological Faculty of the university.

Soon after ordination became a separate rite (it was, by the way, not repeated, when the minister accepted a call to another parish), the requirement of an ordination vow was introduced. In Wittenberg, the ordinand vowed (since 1533) that he would keep himself to the Apostolic, Nicene, and Athanasian Creeds and to the Augsburg Confession, but there was not yet a fixed formula. Regulations of other early Lutheran church orders prescribed that the candidate for ordination should vow that he would preach the pure gospel of Jesus Christ without any additions (*ohn allen zusatz*) and that he would obey the Superintendent.

In Zürich, the early practice of calling and ordaining a minister, according to an *Order for Preachers* written by Leo Jud and Henry Bullinger, was as follows: A commission of examiners consisting of two ministers, two members of the City Council, and two laymen experienced in the reading of the Bible, examined the candidates who either had been proposed or had applied to be called to a vacant ministerial office. They inquired into their way of life and doctrine. On recommendation of this commission, the City Council elected the minister. The Dean (or senior minister) of Zürich then ordained him by the laying on of hands in the presence of the congregation, and a magistrate commended him to the people. At the next Synod meeting, the ordained minister had to vow that he would faithfully preach and teach the gospel and Word of God according to the Old and New Testaments, that he would be obedient to the government, and that he would keep the secrets of his ministerial office.

In Calvin's Geneva, the *Compagnie Vénérable* examined the candidates for the preaching office. In order to qualify, they had to be "men of sound doctrine and holy life." The ministers then nominated the candidate of their choice to the congregation who called and elected him. When the City Council had confirmed the election, the candidate was ordained, the pastors laying their hands on him. Calvin explains in the *Institutes* that the significance of the imposition of hands is "to admonish the person ordained that he is no longer his own master but devoted to the service of God and the Church." [34]

What Calvin has to say about the call to the ministry in the *Institutes* reflects not only his own high sense of the dignity of this office, but also the practices that prevailed in Geneva. He writes: "In order, therefore, that any one may be accounted a true minister of the Church, it is necessary, in the first place, that he be regularly called to it, and, in the second place, that he answer his call, that is, by undertaking and executing the office assigned to him." [35] "I speak of the external and solemn call, which belongs to the public order of the Church; passing over that secret call, of which every minister is conscious to himself before God, but which is not known to the Church. This secret call, however, is the honest testimony of our heart that we accept the office offered to us, not from ambition or avarice, or any other unlawful motive, but from a sincere fear of God and an ardent zeal for the edification of the Church. . . . In the view of the Church, . . . he who enters on his office with an evil conscience, is nevertheless duly called, provided his iniquity is not discovered." [36] "We find, therefore, that it is a legitimate ministry according to the Word of God, when those who appear suitable persons are appointed with the consent and approbation of the people; but that other pastors ought to preside over the election, to guard the multitude from falling into any improprieties, through inconstancy, intrigue, or confusion." [37] "Whoever, therefore, has undertaken the government and charge of one Church, let him know that he is bound to this law of the Divine call; not that he is fixed to his station so as never to be permitted to leave it in a regular and orderly manner, if the public benefit should require it; but he who has been called to one place, ought never to think either of departing from his situation, or relinquishing the office altogether, from any motive of personal convenience or advantage. But if it be expedient that he should remove to another station, he ought not to attempt this on his own private opinion, but to be guided by public authority." [38]

The *supervision* of the ministers, to which we have repeatedly referred, was a constant problem. It was particularly acute so long as the evangelical churches had not yet recruited and trained their own ministers. During the period of transition from Roman Catholicism, especially during the third decade of the sixteenth century, the method of visitation proved to be the only feasible one. The theological members especially of the Visitation Commissions concerned themselves with the standards of the ministry. They advised the congregations on proper proceedings, counseled the ministers, and enforced discipline among them. If necessary, they could invoke the assistance of secular authorities, and these generally responded by applying coercion. Many unfit ministers, e.g., former priests or monks who had forsaken the old order not for spiritual reasons but for material ones of all kinds, and also spiritual adventurers of all sorts who lacked adequate preparation; were dismissed from their "posts." When conditions were stabilized, Superintendents were installed. They assumed the spiritual functions which formerly the bishops had exercised, their chief duty being the supervision of the ministers of their districts. They supplemented the training of the ministers by assigning readings to them and by subjecting them to regular examinations. By the middle of the century, most ministers were university-trained in some fashion, and the theological faculties began to wield considerable influence on the standards of the ministry—but they also created a climate of theological controversy with dire consequences for edifying preaching!

In Zürich, since 1528, a synod was held twice a year. All preachers from town and country were expected to attend it. It met in the presence of several members of the City Council. Its sole agenda was the *censura mutua,* i.e., the ministers subjected one another to criticism and mutual counsel on their life and work. The congregations had the right to send one or two delegates to the synod, but only if they had complaints of their minister's teaching or behavior. It seems that the congregations made little use of this privilege, and the synods became ministers' conferences.

In Strassburg, the church wardens were at first responsible for the supervision of ministers. When, in 1533, synods were introduced, they were ordered to attend them in order to assist in the building of a common church order. In 1543, a Church Convent was established, of which Bucer was the permanent superintendent and Hedio his permanent deputy. Its other members were two ministers, one deacon and one teacher. All these were elected annually. The Convent met once a month. It surveyed the life of the church and particularly the work of the ministers. How effective it was, we do not know.

In Geneva, Calvin had provided in the Ecclesiastical Ordinances for a weekly *Conférence des Ecritures* (Bible Conference) of the ministers. Its chief purpose was *censura mutua*. One of the ministers had to preach a sermon which was then discussed and criticized by the others. But all aspects of the ministry were subject to being reviewed. The members of the "Venerable Company" were charged to maintain certain standards for themselves and for one another. Heresy; deviation from the established ecclesiastical order (*rébellion contre l'ordre ecclésiastique*); blasphemy; drunkenness; playing prohibited games; and dancing were regarded as irreconcilable with the ministry. Moreover, the ministers had to avoid arbitrary exegesis of Scripture; presumptuousness; preoccupation with speculative problems (*curiosités à chercher questions vaines*); indolence in the study of Scripture; tardiness in the denunciation of vice; avarice; irascibility; cantankerousness; unseemly dress. Also in this case, regrettably, we do not know what the actual proceedings and their results were.

The Social and Economic Status of the Early Protestant Ministers

All the ideals and doctrines, developments and practices we have been describing produced a new social and vocational class: that of the Protestant minister. He did not belong to the caste of the clergy, set apart as a special group in the social order. He became identified with the middle class, the burghers. No members of the nobility became Protestant preachers—in contrast to the medieval tradition. The Roman Church recruited its higher clergy chiefly from the ranks of the feudal lords and barons. When the Reformation deprived the evangelical churches of political and economic power, the ecclesiastical career ceased to be attractive to the sons of the upper classes, because in it they could no longer hope to satisfy either political ambition or the desire for riches and an opulent way of life. As soon as the evangelical churches were in some way established, the preachers were recruited from the ranks of the small burghers. A comparatively large number of them came from families of teachers and sextons, others from the ranks of clerks, printers, typesetters, and weavers. Significantly enough, the peasants were hardly represented among them, partly because, after the Peasants' Revolt, most of them had become estranged from the Reformation, and partly because it was difficult for them to come up even to the lowest standards of education the Protestant church governments required.

The great differences in social rank and position which characterized the Roman Catholic clergy had no chance to develop among the evangelical ministers. Yet they too were not all of the same social or professional status. It took a long time to establish educational standards for the ministers and to enforce them. For many years, the new churches lacked adequately trained preachers. Until 1544, even the Theological Faculty at Wittenberg admitted poorly educated men, even mere artisans, to ordination. Many theological students did not finish the full course of study but were nevertheless assigned to parishes. At the middle of the sixteenth century, most churches of the Reformation had, in fact, a ministry of two ranks, one of trained and one of untrained men. The former, many of whom held the theological doctor's degree or a lower academic title, became parish ministers in the towns or court preachers. They wielded considerable influence. Indeed, they were the "conscience" of the new profession.[39]

Many of the country preachers were poorly trained. For a long time, it was customary to examine those who wanted to qualify for service in rural parishes much less strictly than those who aspired toward ministerial positions in the towns. When a country parson wanted to be transferred to a town parish, he had to submit to a new examination.

The Visitations showed that many preachers were rough and uncouth fellows, careless and sloppy in their way of life and manner of dress and inattentive to their duties. The most common complaint about them was that they drank too much. It was frequently reported that preachers spent their time sitting around in taverns and that many of them had the habit of staying at wedding parties until the last keg of beer was consumed. Mathesius, famous for his sermons on Luther's life, tells of a preacher who took a jug of beer with him into the pulpit! In 1541, the Hessian Superintendents sent the following petition to the Landgrave Philip: "In view of the fact that there are current many complaints about parsons who scandalize people by their excessive drinking and other disgraceful vices and yet remain unpunished as well as unreformed, we suggest that the jail at the cloister of Spisskoppel be restored and that the parsons who persist in their vices be given the choice either to leave their parishes or to be confined in this jail for a period of time the length of which shall depend on the nature of their offence, in order that on water and bread they may undergo corrective punishment." [40] Unfortunately, we are not told whether the Landgrave acted on this petition or, if he caused this jail for parsons to be built, whether any elected to be confined there.

Many of the troubles and vices to which ministers became subject were undoubtedly caused by the poor economic conditions under which they had to live. It took a long time to reorganize church property and income. During the confusion that accompanied the initial introduction of the Reformation, the princes, nobles, town magistrates and even the peasants had appropriated much of the landed endowments and properties of the churches. Later, the barons and the peasants did not continue to pay the customary dues and excises, and people generally, who, in former times, had supported the church by paying fees for private masses, prayers, indulgences and other religious goods and services, now ceased to make contributions—in part, because they rightly thought that the teachings of the Reformers prohibited them, and, in part, because they simply took advantage of the new order. What income remained for the parish ministers was in most cases insufficient to support them. As late as in 1531, Luther said of the parsons: "They are now poorer than before [i.e., in Roman Catholicism], and if they have wife and children they are beggars indeed." It is no wonder, then, that the preachers turned to all sorts of devices in order to eke out a living. They practiced handicrafts or turned to farming, keeping gardens and cattle, sheep and pigs. Many availed themselves of feudal privileges with which their parishes were endowed, for example, by taking over from monasteries and other Roman Catholic establishments brewing rights, et cetera.

In the course of time, the income of the preachers was, of course, regulated. In Hesse, Landgrave Philip ordered that rural ministers should be paid 50 to 60 gulden and the preachers in the towns 70 to 80 gulden. In addition, they were to receive certain amounts of meat, corn and grain, wood, et cetera. Duke Maurice of Saxony set the salaries of town and country ministers at the amount of 200 and 90 gulden respectively, later reducing them to 150 and 70 gulden. The parish minister at Wittenberg (Bugenhagen) received (since 1529) annually 200 gulden and later 300 gulden, plus 75 bushels of corn. In addition, he had an income of 40, later 50 gulden as a professor in the university. The first (i.e., highest ranking) minister of Augsburg was paid (since 1544) 250 gulden; the other ministers received 200 gulden and the deacons 100 to 150 gulden.

Nothing shaped the social status of the Protestant ministry as decisively as the fact that they were permitted and indeed encouraged to marry. The evangelical parsonage assumed a character by which the Protestant ministry was radically distinguished—in social terms—from the Roman Catholic clergy. The family life of the ministers became the symbolical expression of the communal character of the evangelical faith. Ministerial households often exemplified the practical application of the Reformers' new understanding of the Christian religion, namely, that the faith in Christ must be practiced in mutual love and service in the natural, social setting of human life and in ordinary, secular pursuits. Thus the married ministry came to demonstrate that family life together with the manifold social activities it engenders can be a more effective vehicle of religion and the service of God than asceticism, celibacy, and otherworldliness.

There was not one of the Reformers who did not get married. And every one of them was an advocate of the institution of marriage, insisting particularly that ministers of the Word of God should be married men, who would preside over their parishes as fathers of families. The most noted marriage was, of course, that of Martin Luther with Katharine von Bora (on June 13, 1525). It was a particularly happy union, though Katharine was almost sixteen years younger than her husband. In his ebullient, unreserved, communicative way, Luther let the world share in his happiness as well as his sorrows (three of his six children died in infancy or in childhood), and all Protestants, but especially the Lutherans, have thought and still think of him, the Reformer and enemy of the Pope, as *the* Protestant parson in the midst of his family circle in the Black Cloister of Wittenberg! The families of some of the other Reformers were no less notable. The homes of the Strassburg Reformers were famous all over Europe for the generous hospitality that was there extended to Protestant refugees and travelers from many lands.

Nor should the women who presided over these households be forgotten. Katharine von Bora assumed responsibility for the economic security of Luther and his children and she took efficient care of him in the many sicknesses of his later life. Katharine Zell, the wife of the popular senior among the preachers of Strassburg, was a fearless and temperamental defender of tolerance. She did not hesitate to speak up when the ministers or the City Council saw fit to exile a man because of his religious views without taking into account his personal character. She readily entertained religious nonconformists in her home and let it be known that in her Christian judgment, character and honorableness mattered more than orthodox doctrine. Anna Weisbrücker, the wife of the Augsburg Reformer Urbanus Rhegius, mother of thirteen children, was a woman of learning. She knew Latin, Greek, and Hebrew, and used and cultivated her knowledge throughout her married life. Wilbrandis Rosenblatt, the second wife of Martin Bucer (his first wife died during the great epidemic of the plague in 1541) had been married three times before, and two of her husbands had been ministers and Reformers closely related to Bucer. As a young widow, she had married John Oecolampadius of Basel and, after his death, she became the wife of Bucer's colleague and friend Wolfgang Capito (he too perished in the plague of 1541). One can readily imagine that women like these contributed their share to the life and work of the ministry, helping to integrate it in the common social life!

A telling symbol of the new religious and social status of the Christian minister of the Age of the Reformation was his manner of dress. The gown of the secular scholar, commonly worn by the men of learning among the burghers and called *Schaube,* became the outward sign of ministerial vocation and social status. Zwingli was the first to introduce it in Zürich, during the autumn of 1523. In the afternoon of October 9, 1524, Luther too began to wear it. Clothed in the *Schaube,* he then preached from the pulpit which he had ocupied in the morning for the last time wearing the monk's cowl.

Henceforth, the scholar's gown was *the* garment of the Protestant minister. It symbolizes all the changes that were wrought by the Reformation in the nature and the work of the ministry.

FOR FURTHER READING

The best sources for the development of the Protestant ministry at the time of the Reformation are the works of the Reformers, especially their letters. The early church orders together with the documents and letters dealing with the history of their formation and first application are also mines of information.

There are studies on several aspects of the early evangelical ministry, but no monograph on the subject as a whole is available.

Two highly illuminating studies on the history of the Protestant ministers of Germany have been mentioned. They contain brief chapters on the Reformation.

Paul Drews, *Der evangelische Geistliche in der deutschen Vergangenheit,* 2nd ed. (Jena, 1924).

Hermann Werdermann, *Der evangelische Pfarrer in Geschichte und Gegenwart,* (Leipzig, 1925).

VI

Priestly Ministries in the Modern Church

EDWARD ROCHIE HARDY JR.

I

Robed in the vestments of his office, the Bishop has taken his seat near the Holy Table. Before him stand the young men "whom we purpose, God willing, to receive this day unto the holy Office of Priesthood." In the final exhortation he warns them, in the impressive phrases of Tudor rhetoric, "of what dignity, and of how great importance this Office is, whereunto ye are called." They are

to be Messengers, Watchmen, and Stewards of the Lord; to teach, and to premonish, to feed and provide for the Lord's family; to seek for Christ's sheep that are dispersed abroad, and for his children who are in the midst of this naughty world, that they may be saved through Christ forever.

A great treasure is to be committed to their charge—

For they are the sheep of Christ which he bought with his death, and for whom he shed his blood. The Church and Congregation whom you must serve is his Spouse, and his Body. And if it shall happen that the same Church, or any Member thereof, do take any hurt or hindrance by reason of your negligence, ye know the greatness of the fault, and also the horrible punishment that will ensue. Wherefore . . . see that ye never cease your labour, your care and diligence, until ye have done all that lieth in you, according to your bounden duty, to bring all such as are or shall be committed to your charge, unto that agreement in the faith and knowledge of God, and to that ripeness and perfectness of age in Christ, that there be no place left among you, either for error in religion, or for viciousness in life.

Earnest prayer and daily meditation on the Holy Scriptures is necessary for those who hope to rise to such an ideal, and so the candidates are reminded

> how ye ought to forsake and set aside, as much as ye may, all worldly cares and studies . . . to give yourselves wholly to this Office, whereunto it hath pleased God to call you . . . and draw all your cares and studies this way that so, by prayer for the assistance of the Holy Ghost, and by daily reading and weighing the Scriptures, ye may wax riper and stronger in your Ministry; and that ye may so endeavour yourselves . . . to sanctify the lives of you and yours, and to fashion them after the Rule and Doctrine of Christ, that ye may be wholesome and godly examples and patterns for the people to follow.[1]

Then after solemn prayer, introduced by the Carolingian hymn *Veni Creator Spiritus,* the bishop and assisting priests lay hands on the ordinands, with words based on the commission given to the apostles in John 20:22-23:

> Receive the Holy Ghost (for the Office and Work of a Priest in the Church of God, now committed unto thee by the Imposition of our hands). Whose sins thou dost forgive, they are forgiven; and whose sins thou dost retain, they are retained. And be thou a faithful Dispenser of the Word of God, and of his holy Sacraments; In the name of the Father, and of the Son, and of the Holy Ghost. Amen.[2]

Such for four centuries have been the solemnities with which the Church of England and others of the Anglican Communion have continued the Order of Priests as, according to the Preface to the Ordinal, it has existed "from the Apostles' time." I do not intend to discuss here the theological question whether there is indeed such an Order in the Church of Christ, or the more technical problem whether the Anglican rites have adequately provided for its continuance. I shall assume, moreover, that in formal usage as in common speech the English word "priest" is, like the French *prêtre,* the equivalent of *sacerdos* or *hiereus,* in spite of its etymological derivation from *presbyteros.* Nor, except incidentally, do I intend to discuss the question of the proper relation of presbyters to the higher Order of Bishops, or to deacons and other Major or Minor Orders below them. In the Catholic tradition the fullness of the Christian priesthood properly belongs to the episcopate, presbyters possessing a share in it by delegation. However, in practice most priestly functions are commonly exercised by the presbyter, only certain special rights, including the crucial privilege of ordination, being reserved to the bishop. Such an order of priests is for the larger part of Christendom, today as in the past, central in the liturgical life and pastoral work of the Church. A full treatment of the subject would probably center around the priestly ideal as preserved in the Roman Communion and the Eastern Orthodox Churches. Within the limits of this volume, however, I must confine myself to the tradition which I know from within, with some reference to the Roman and Eastern traditions as they have been influences upon it.

The Christian priest, like the Jewish, stands for men in things pertaining to God (Heb. 5:1); with the same inheritance intensified by the apostolic mission, he also speaks for God to man. So as George Herbert wrote in that classic of Anglican pastoralia, *A Priest to the Temple: or the Country Parson,* in the 1630's—

A Pastor is the Deputy of Christ for the reducing of Man to the Obedience of God. This definition is evident, and contains the direct steps of Pastorall Duty and Auctority. For first, Man fell from God by disobedience. Secondly, Christ is the glorious instrument of God for the revoking of Man. Thirdly, Christ being not to continue on earth, but after he had fulfilled the work of Reconciliation to be received up into heaven, he constituted Deputies in his place, and these are Priests. And therefore *St. Paul* in the beginning of his Epistles professeth this, and in the first to the Colossians plainly avoucheth that he *fils up that which is behinde of the afflictions of Christ in his flesh for his Bodie's sake, which is the Church.* Wherein is contained the complete definition of a Minister. Out of this Chartre of the Priesthood may be gathered both the Dignity thereof and the Duty: The Dignity, in that a Priest may do that which Christ did, and by his auctority and as his Vicegerent. The Duty, in that a Priest is to do that which Christ did and after his manner, both for Doctrine and Life. [Chapter I]

The dignity of the priest comes from his union with the priestly work of his crucified Master, and is therefore only truly realized when the priestly life is in a real sense a life of sacrifice. It is this which the contented churchmanship of the eighteenth century seemed to fail to realize —one thinks of such amusing illustrations as Adam Smith's discussion of the ministry in England and Scotland on the basis of its economic status [3] or the even more startling defense of diversity of orders in the Church by Archdeacon Paley on the ground that it "may be considered as the stationing of ministers of religion in the various ranks of civil life." [4] When the Catholic tendencies in Anglicanism were reinvigorated by the Oxford Movement in the nineteenth century it seemed in retrospect that "quiet worldliness" was the particular blot of the English Church.[5] Famous examples are the blameless but barely ecclesiastical parsons who figure in the novels of Jane Austen. Yet even in 1827 it was natural for a Christian poet to pray

> Oh! by Thine own said burthen, borne
> So meekly up the hill of scorn,
> Teach Thou Thy Priests their daily cross
> To bear as Thine, nor count it loss![6]

More formally, it is recorded of George Horne, who became Bishop of Norwich in 1790, that he was accustomed to read over the solemn words of the service for the Ordering of Priests on the first Sunday of every month, on which practice his biographer observes that "the imitation of this example may be practiced with ease, and will be attended with advantage."[7] The Oxford Movement reinvigorated but did not invent the tradition of the priestly ministry in Anglicanism.

II

By definition of the term, a priest is a minister of divine worship, a servant of the altar; it was primarily the development of Christian worship into an ordered liturgical action which naturalized the term *sacerdos* for the presiding Bishop or the presbyter who takes his place. Cautious though George Herbert's post-Reformation Catholicism sometimes is, he does not hesitate to emphasize the reverent care to be given to the church building—

that all things be in good repair: as walls plastered, windows glazed, floors paved, seats whole, firm, and uniform; especially that the Pulpit and Desk, and Communion Table and Font, be as they ought for those great duties that are performed in them. Secondly, that the Church be swept and kept cleane, without dust or Cobwebs, and at great festivalls strawed, and stuck with boughs, and perfumed with incense. [Chapter XIII]

Aftr the storms of the sixteenth century, the Anglican revival of the seventeenth brought with it a renewal of love for the glory of the House of God. The solemnity of Bishop Andrewes' chapel became the model for cathedrals, and as far as possible for parish churches, under the guidance of Archbishop Laud. The harshness of Laud's methods has been exaggerated. Still they were not such as to win popularity for a movement he represented. But with the Restoration his liturgical arrangements became the standard of dignified Anglicanism, as illustrated by the London churches rebuilt after the Great Fire of 1666. The pulpit is indeed prepared to be the parson's throne as Herbert calls it, but the church's center of dignity is the railed-in Holy Table at the east end, backed where resources allowed it by a carved and perhaps painted reredos.

In connection with the care of churches, as with the pastoral labors of the clergy, the eighteenth century has sometimes been unduly denigrated. Nevertheless, there was certainly much carelessness and neglect, and Newman's rhetorical picture of the situation confronted by the leaders of the Catholic Revival is not wholly unjustified:

The author of the *Christian Year* found the Anglican system all but destitute of this divine element, which is an essential property of Catholicism—a ritual dashed upon the ground, trodden on, and broken piecemeal;—prayers clipped, pieced, torn, shuffled about at pleasure, until the meaning of the composition perished, and offices which had been poetry were no longer even good prose;—antiphons, hymns, benedictions, invocations, shovelled away;—Scripture lessons turned into chapters;—heaviness, feebleness, unwieldiness, where the Catholic rites had had the lightness and airiness of a spirit;—vestments chucked off, lights quenched, jewels stolen, the pomp and circumstance of worship annihilated; a dreariness which could be felt, and which seemed the token of an incipient Socinianism, forcing itself upon the eye, the ear, the nostrils of the worshipper; a smell of dust and damp, not of incense, a sound of ministers preaching Catholic prayers, and parish clerks droning out Catholic canticles; the royal arms for the crucifix; huge ugly boxes of wood, sacred to preachers, frowning on the congregation in place of the mysterious altar; and long cathedral aisles unused, railed off, like the tombs (as they were) of what had been and was not; and for orthodoxy, a frigid, unelastic, inconsistent, dull, helpless dogmatic which could give no just account of itself, yet was intolerant of all teaching which contained a doctrine more or a doctrine less, and resented every attempt to give it a meaning—such was the religion of which this gifted author was—not the judge and denouncer (a deep spirit of reverence hindered it)—but the renovator, as far as it has been renovated.[8]

It is often observed that the Oxford Movement strictly so called, from 1833-45, was concerned with the theological bases of the Catholic

Revival rather than with its liturgical and missionary expression. Like most generalizations, this is only very partially true. The Tractarians were certainly interested in preaching the Gospel of new life in the mystical Body of Christ to the poor as well as to the academic and clerical world—as shown by the title of the series of *Plain and Parochial Sermons by the Authors of Tracts for the Times*. Newman introduced the weekly celebration of the Holy Communion at St. Mary the Virgin's, Oxford, for the first time in an Anglican parish church since the early eighteenth century. The mission chapel at Littlemore, usually remembered in connection with Newman's dramatic farewell sermon in 1843, was for some years before that a conspicuous illustration of Tractarian ideals of ministry to the underprivileged and simple parochial worship. Under the guidance of Newman's first curate at Littlemore, J. R. Bloxam, Littlemore exemplified the arrangement, partly based on the Laudian traditions preserved in some college chapels, which has become standard in modern Anglicanism—the altar with cross and candles in the center and the pulpit and lectern on either side.[9]

The Gothic Revival in architecture was promoted as much by religious as by aesthetic considerations. It aimed to recover the sense of the church as primarily a place of worship rather than a preaching hall; its influence on the scene of priestly ministry is confluent with the Oxford Movement's revival of the sense of the authority and responsibility of the apostolic commission. The Cambridge ecclesiologists who founded the Camden Society in the 1830's are parallel to the Oxford Tractarians rather than dependent on them. As with the Oxford leaders, their influence spread rapidly. As early as 1839, the Bishop of New York praised the return in several new churches to the older style of the central altar, in contrast to the common arrangement of American colonial church buildings in which the pulpit either blocked the Holy Table from the front or dominated it from behind.[10] The interests of the Cambridge group were continued in the many-sided ministry of John Mason Neale (1817-66)—the scholar who was content to take up his lifework as pastor to a few old people at Sackville College, from which his influence became world-wide through his literary work in a number of fields, and his foundation of an Order devoted alike to the ideals of monastic piety and to missionary, charitable, and educational service, the Sisters of the Society of St. Margaret. Neale's career is an outstanding modern example of a life of joyful sacrifice and service inspired by the specifically priestly ideal of the Christian ministry. He was also one of the first Anglicans to revive the traditional eucharistic vestments.

Though they originated from the daily Roman costume of the early Christian centuries, since the Middle Ages the alb and chasuble (and their Eastern equivalents) have symbolized the objectivity of the worship which the priest offers at the altar, as well as the unity of this particular priest here this morning with his colleagues of every age and every land. Indeed the same principle is true of the less solemn vesture which seventeenth-century Anglicans defended against Puritan attacks. Any priest may say, in the words of a young cleric of a century ago who was criticized by a lady in his parish for the tone of authority he assumed with his surplice, "Madam, when I have this on I am nineteen hundred years old." [11] Ritualism, as it is somewhat improperly called (since the area involved is that of ceremonies rather than of the spoken ritual itself) has never been defended on merely aesthetic grounds— though these are not to be despised, since God is not glorified by ugliness, and beauty is one aspect of the truth in which he is to be worshipped. Ancient ceremonies display the ancient faith, as later developments of ceremonial exhibit its progress; in stately cathedral or in mission to the poorest, the offering of all that man has to offer in worship is part of man's response to the fullness of the Gospel of God. Detailed manuals like Dearmer's *Parson's Handbook* or Fortescue's *Ceremonies of the Roman Rite* are guides to one essential part of the priestly work of leading men in their response to the glory of God, and of bringing mankind within the sphere of divine grace.

III

No sharp distinction can be drawn between the work of the priest as leader of worship and his pastoral task of guiding men along their way to God. A connecting link is the administration of the sacraments. Sacraments are administered in an atmosphere of worship, while the proper preparation of candidates for the Sacraments is an important part of pastoral care. Herbert balances "The Parson in Preaching" with "The Parson in Sacraments," speaking of the central Sacrament of the Eucharist in surprisingly concrete terms:

Especially at Communion times he is in a great confusion, as being not only to receive God, but to break and administer him. [Chap. XXII]

Both adults and children are to be prepared by proper exhortations for their Communions; for the time of "first receiving" Herbert repeats and enforces the medieval rule of a minimum age of discretion:

When any one can distinguish the Sacramentall from common bread, knowing the Institution and the difference, he ought to receive, of what age soever. Children and youths are usually deferred too long, under pretence of devotion to the Sacrament, but it is for want of Instruction; their understandings being ripe enough for ill things, and why not then for better?

Herbert's pastoral directions make no mention of Confirmation, which in Stuart as in medieval England had to be secured whenever one was fortunate enough to find a bishop in the neighborhood. The association of this rite with fully responsible profession of faith led gradually to a postponement of the age of First Communion, from which modern practice has again turned toward an earlier stage of life, before rather than during the excitements of adolescence.

The priest's library is an important help in his homiletic and pastoral activities. So Herbert's parson is devoted above all to study and meditation on the Bible, with the help of "Commenters and fathers," and has at least one "Comment" (Commentary) on each book. His own will reveals the presence on his shelves of "the Comment of Lucas Brugensis upon the Scripture" and the Works of St. Augustine.[12] In his preparation the parson will have read the Fathers, Schoolmen, and later Writers, "or a good proportion of all," to compile his personal "book and body of Divinity," which is "the storehouse of his Sermons." He will be versed in cases of conscience, as a matter of practical importance, and so presumably acquainted with the literature of the subject (Chapter V). Much of the literary production of Anglican divines during their enforced retirement under the Commonwealth reads like an attempt to fill up the country parson's shelves. Pearson's Lectures on the Creed (delivered in London in 1659) are an example of the "body of divinity," largely based on patristic sources, while many of Jeremy Taylor's works deal with matters of practical concern to the parish clergy. His treatises include works on Marriage, on Confirmation, and on the Holy Communion, and his ethical and devotional writings take up the principles of spiritual guidance as a pastor might want to know them in dealing with others, as well as assisting priest or people in their own inner life. In fact the whole series of English devotional manuals from Cosin's in 1627, which picks up the tradition of the medieval and Elizabethan Primers, down to Thomas Nelson's Companions (to the Altar and to the Festivals and Fasts), the work of a nonjuring layman under Queen Anne, may be considered as the provision of tools for the clergy in their pastoral work.

After the classic period of the seventeenth century the eighteenth was less productive in works of practical divinity, as distinct from the speculative and apologetic, and in books of devotion. A more prosaic age in English piety follows the epoch of Andrewes, Cosin, and Taylor, just as Roman Catholic writers in the eighteenth century do not reach the heights of St. Francis de Sales, Bossuet, or Fénelon. There are, however, splendid exceptions, such as the saintly Richard Challoner, Vicar-Apostolic of the London District, whose *Meditations for Every Day in the Year* were long standard among English Roman Catholics and also used by Anglicans, and among Anglicans Thomas Wilson, the self-denying Bishop of Sodor and Man, and William Law, nonjuring theologian and mystic. During some of his important Oxford years John Wesley was under Law's spiritual guidance. The Wesleys' interest in providing practical devotional material, especially in preparation for the Holy Communion, belongs to their Anglican inheritance. With the nineteenth century a revival of devotional as of theological traditions began. Early in the 1800's John Henry Hobart, later Bishop of New York, issued American editions of Nelson's *Companions*—Cosin's *Devotions* were reprinted in 1838 (the first edition since 1721), and Bishop Andrewes' *Preces Privatae* translated by Newman in 1840 (*Tracts for the Times,* No. 88). Beginning in the later years of the Oxford Movement Pusey embarked on the enterprise of enriching the Anglican tradition by adapting Continental manuals, French or Italian, for English use. In the last century the production of devotional literature on various levels has been continuous.

Some of this literature seems to envisage learned clergy dealing with a sophisticated public. But Herbert's parson is also equipped with "a slighter form of Catechizing, fitter for country people" (Chapter V); the straightforward tradition of religious instruction which the modern parish priest inherits from his medieval predecessor has never been forgotten. The eighteenth century thought of religious teaching largely in terms of moral advice given in sermons—the main duty of the clergy, says Paley, is "to inform the consciences and improve the morals of the people committed to their charge" until the Lord returns in judgment.[13] Nothing, writes Addison at the beginning of the century, is more pleasant than a country Sunday on which the rustic population assembles "to converse on indifferent subjects, hear their duties explained to them, and join together in adoration of the Supreme Being," [14] a typically Augustan description of the essence of religion. At the end of the century the High Churchman Bishop Seabury of Connecticut has a more definite idea of the content of religious instruction, though he is still a man of his age. The duties of the clergy as stewards of the mysteries of God, "that is, preachers of the 'great mystery of godliness, God manifest in the flesh' (I Tim. 3:16), which virtually contains in it all the mysteries or sublime truths of Christianity" are extensive.

> Their office, in short, as preachers or dispensers of the word, takes in all the revelations and dispensations of God to man, all the articles of christian faith, and all the particulars of christian practice.

Stewardship of the mysteries equally includes the right to admit men to the Church by baptism and "the power of administering the other sacrament, the sacrifice of the eucharist." [15]

Since 1800 the responsibilities assumed by the Anglican priest have increased rather than diminished. One can only refer to the Sunday School and more modern forms of religious education in America, in which the clerical share is important in spite of the considerable lay leadership. In England there are also numerous church schools, which in the first half of the nineteenth century almost became a national parochial school system, and which still give many of the clergy a definite place in the general educational system of the country. Moreover, there are now more sacred rites to be administered and prepared for than the eighteenth or even the seventeenth century realized. After as well as before the Reformation, Confirmation was administered in England with remarkable casualness and sometimes even disorder. Since the 1840's clergy have assumed responsibility for the preparing of candidates, and bishops for providing at least annual opportunities for the administration of the rite. This along with many other modern ecclesiastical procedures owes much to the example of Samuel Wilberforce, Bishop of Oxford 1844-69, of Winchester 1869-73, and founder of the modern Anglican episcopate both as a pastoral institution and an administrative enterprise. The Ministry of Absolution has always been provided for in the English Prayer Book, but though not infrequently practiced in the seventeenth century it became almost obsolete in the eighteenth, as shown by the disappearance of definite references to it in the American Prayer Book of 1789. (A partial recovery was effected in

1928.) None of the subjects treated in the *Tracts for the Times* was more definitely a return to lost traditions than this, which was boldly taken up fairly early in the series. Keble's Tract 17, for instance, "The Ministerial Commission a Trust from Christ for the Benefit of His People," lays special emphasis on the priest's right to declare pardon to the penitent in God's name to those who humbly desire it:

How then ought we to look upon the power which has been given us by Christ, but as a sacred treasure, of which we are Ministers and Stewards; and which it is our duty to guard for the sake of those little ones, for whose edification (2 Cor. xiii 10) it was that our Lord left power with his Church. And if we suffer it to be lost to our Christian brethren, how shall we answer it, not only to those that might now rejoice in its holy comfort, but to those also who are to come after us?

One of the episodes which brought on the crisis of the Oxford Movement was Pusey's suspension from preaching before the University after his sermon of January, 1843, on "The Eucharist a Comfort to the Penitent." Two years later when his suspension expired his turn came around again, and he continued his intended series with "Absolution a Comfort to the Penitent" and no man said him nay. Since then the hearing of confessions has found a regular if not universally accepted place in Anglican pastoral practice. Pusey himself exercised a widespread ministry as confessor, of which he ventured to write some years later:

If there is one part of our Ministry which God has blessed; if there be one part of our office, as to the fruits of which we look with hopefulness and joy to the day of our judgment, it is to the visible cleansing of souls, the deepened penitence, "the repentance unto salvation not to be repented of," the hope in Christ, the freshness of grace, the joy of forgiven souls, the evident growth in holiness, the Angel-joy "over each sinner that repenteth" which this ministry has disclosed to us. We have often in the subsequent growth in grace and "transformation" of the soul, by the "renewing of the mind," not been able to recall to ourselves the former self which we knew of, when first a person sought to hear, through our ministry, his Saviour's voice, "Thy sins be forgiven thee: go in peace."

> In these, a Pastor dare delight
> A lamb-like, Christ-like throng;

for his likeness has anew by Himself been traced upon them.[16]

The priest is celebrant of the holy mysteries, spiritual guide, teacher of the faith, hearer of confessions—and, as we shall see, the pastoral interests of the modern priest are even more extensive than his strictly ecclesiastical activities. Who indeed is sufficient for these things unless he maintains the closest union with his Lord and Master? Herbert's quiet pages are crossed here and there by surprisingly ecstatic expressions of union with the sufferings of Christ. The parson

is generally sad, because hee knows nothing but the Crosse of Christ, his mind being defixed on and with those nailes wherewith his Master was—

This sentence opens the chapter on "The Parson in Mirth" which admits that reasonable relaxation has its place, and may indeed be useful (Chapter XXVII). When despised, as he may expect to be, the parson reflects that

this hath been the portion of God his Master and of God's Saints his Brethren, and this is foretold that it shall be still until things be no more. [Chapter XXVIII].

Nor is the priest's way of life maintained only by occasional reflections. Prayer and fasting, holy study and meditation on Scripture, as well as sharing in public worship and Sacraments are its essential pattern and framework. So the English Prayer Book retains from its medieval sources the requirement that the daily Offices be recited privately, if not said publicly, by every priest and deacon. The traditional days of fasting were retained (Herbert comments in some detail on their proper observance, Chapter X), and since 1662 have been listed in the Prayer Book for reference. And as we saw at the beginning, the priest is reminded at his ordination of the importance of meditating deeply on the Scriptures as well as studying them formally.

Before noting more recent developments of the priestly rule, we may glance at some more general aspects of the cleric's life. The Reformation brought with it an acceptance of the propriety of the marriage of the clergy, but did not entirely abolish the principle that some are called to the celibate state. As Herbert observes, blending the medieval and the reformed traditions:

The Country Parson considering that virginity is a higher state than Matrimony, and that the Ministry requires the best and highest things, is rather unmarried than married. But yet as the temper of his body may be, or as the temper of his Parish may be, where he may have occasion to converse with women and that among suspicious men, and other like circumstances considered, he is rather married than unmarried. Let him communicate the thing often by prayer unto God, and as his grace shall direct him so let him proceed. [Chapter IX]

Indeed until the middle of the nineteenth century fellowships in the English universities were vacated by marriage (as, for instance, in the case of John Wesley, who remained Fellow of Lincoln until his marriage), a relic of medieval days when college fellows were necessarily celibate as either priests or possible candidates for the priesthood. Some English clerics accepted permanently the state of life then prescribed for a time. For much of the seventeenth century, as during part of the Anglo-Saxon period, the discipline of the English Church in effect resembled that of the Greek, with a married parish clergy presided over by a celibate episcopate. Some even spoke as strongly in favor of celibacy as Bishop Ken:

> A virgin priest the altar best attends,
> Our Lord this state commands not, but commends.[17]

Herbert himself was married during his brief parochial ministry, though his observations on the special problems of the celibate and how to meet them seem rather more sensible than his brief notes on marriage (Chapter IX). As is well known, the Eastern Church requires the clergy to assume either monastic or marital vows before ordination, and does not allow the remarriage of a clerical widower unless he abandons the exercise of his priesthood. The Latin Church requires the celibacy of the clergy, although this is now understood to be by acceptance of the obligation at ordination to the subdiaconate and not (as was widely held in the later Middle Ages) a matter of divine law.[18]

An interesting by-road of this subject is the call to celibacy felt by some of the eighteenth-century Anglican Evangelicals. At a time when the High Church clergy were as a rule contentedly married, some of the English Evangelicals revived the spirit of the preaching friar wholly devoted to the work of the gospel. Berridge of Everton spoke sharply on this matter—"No trap so michievous for the field-preacher as wedlock"—

and John Wesley's unhappy marital adventures were a warning to others as well as, occasionally, to himself.[19] Of the Oxford Movement leaders, the hereditary High Churchmen Pusey and Keble were married (though Pusey lived an almost monastic life after the death of his wife in 1839), while Newman's sense of a call to the celibate life came to him during his Evangelical days. A similar case is that of William Augustus Muhlenberg (1796-1877), an Evangelical Catholic as he called himself, who had a large share in bringing the influence of the Oxford Movement to the American Episcopal Church, but was as much influenced by his German Evangelical connections. As his biographer tells us, some years after his ordination he was contemplating the possibility of an "alliance with a lady of very suitable connection" when on his way to take the lady to morning service he chanced to stop for a moment in a Roman Catholic church, and

these words of the preacher fell upon his ear: "We have but one heart; if we had two hearts, we might give one to God and the other to this world; having but one, God must have it all." "Amen!" said William Augustus Muhlenberg's inmost soul; "Farewell, ———," and he neither took the lady to church nor sent her the book she had asked to borrow of him.[20]

Since the days of the Oxford Movement a certain number of the Anglican clergy have, whether or not under formal vows, considered themselves dedicated to the celibate life. My own impression is that outside of the actual Religious Orders the number has not increased during the present century. However, several societies of clergy bound by rules which include vows of celibacy (usually not formally lifelong, but taken for a period with the expectation of renewal), have been founded, such as the Oblates of Mount Calvary in America, associated with the Order of the Holy Cross, and the recently organized Company of Mission Priests in England.[21]

The social and economic status of the clergy has varied from time to time. In England down to the rearrangement of endowments which followed the Reforms of the 1830's (as in France down to the Revolution) much survived of the medieval situation; there was a clerical proletariat, whose standard of life approximated that of the skilled laborer, and a clerical aristocracy, who, whatever their origin, expected to live on a scale comparable to that of the nobility. A late example of this is afforded in the career of Henry Phillpotts, 1778-1869, one of the last of the pre-Reform bishops, appointed to Exeter in 1830. Since its endowed income of £2700 would not allow him to maintain the dignity expected, he secured permission to hold a canonry of Durham along with his bishopric, one of the last cases of the benefice *in commendam* by which medieval and later Bishops had often profited.[22] Phillpotts was an earnest administrator, and fought hard to raise the minimum salary for curates in his Diocese to £50.[23] Such a range of 100 to 1 within honorable incomes in the clerical profession would scarcely be found in our times.

In the eighteenth century £40 was considered a reasonable minimum for beneficed clergy. The Society for the Propagation of the Gospel paid its American missionaries £50, expecting their congregations to provide as much, with a house and perhaps a glebe. If regularly paid, which was not always the case, such an income would have ranked respectably among professional incomes in the colonies. Money has gradually declined in value since then; the Domestic and Foreign Missionary Society of the Protestant Episcopal Church, founded in 1820, in its early days thought of $500 as a generous salary for a domestic missionary, and the first American bishop to be supported wholly by his diocese (the Bishop of New York in the 1830's) received $2500. In recent years the clergy have found their place in the greater security of a welfare society, as shown by the provision of Pension Funds for the clergy (such as the efficient Church Pension Fund in America, organized in 1917) in lieu of earlier efforts to relieve their distressed widows and orphans. English bishops are now generally freed from the responsibility of maintaining the medieval mansions in which some of them still reside; their salaries are now with a few exceptions equalized at £2000-£2500, while most English dioceses achieve a minimum stipend for incumbents of £500 or better.[24] In available goods and comparable status this is probably somewhat but not much better than the "passing rich on forty pounds a year"[25] of two centuries ago. Herbert's Parson has servants and his wife maids, but this doubtless reflects his personal circumstances.

In modern times, even more than in the Middle Ages, it is possible to recognize the English clergy when you see them in the street. Canon 74 of the Canons of 1603 required the traditional clerical dress—cap, gown, and tippet—the "priest's gown" and square cap which the early Puritans had raged against in the 1560's. This was already worn mainly on formal occasions and in church; at home the clergy might wear any "scholar-like apparel," though expected to abstain from such indulgences as embroidered nightcaps, and in public they were at least not to appear without coats or cassocks. With a mixture of correctness and informality sometimes found in England today, a cleric-scientist of the period is recorded to have met his guests in "an old russet cloath-cassock that had been black in dayes of yore, girt with an old leather girdle, an old fashion russett hat that had been a bever *tempore Reginae Elizabethae*." [26] The cassock remained common clerical dress into the eighteenth century, but then except on formal occasions came to be replaced by black clothes of the ordinary cut. With a plain white stock or neckcloth this remained the distinctive costume of the Anglican cleric until the middle of the nineteenth century; Newman marked the definite renunciation of his Anglican Orders by coming to dinner at Littlemore one day in gray trousers. [27] The more serious clerics of the post-Oxford Movement period revived the cassock, though it has not come to be commonly worn except in church and on ecclesiastical premises. The modern clerical collar dates from about 1865, and in spite of its common description as "Roman collar" is apparently a convenient Anglican invention.

V

The otherworldly aspect of Christian life and discipline in general, and therefore of clerical life and discipline in particular, was an important concern of the authors of the *Tracts for the Times*. Tracts in the series were devoted to such topics as the value of fasting on the days appointed (18 and 66) and the importance of the recitation of the Daily Offices (84). An elaborate tract by Newman presented the beauty of the complete system of the Latin Offices—No. 75, "On the Roman Breviary as Embodying the Substance of the Devotional Services of the Church Catholic." The attractiveness of those Hours of Prayer, which the ordinary priest of the Latin rite has sometimes felt to be a burden rather than a joy, was one of the factors which led many of the Tractarian group to an increasing appreciation of the devotional treasures preserved in the Roman Communion. With some, including Newman himself, this was an important step toward final submission to the Roman obedience. Others who remained in the Anglican Communion prepared English adaptations of the medieval Sarum or modern Roman Breviaries, which became part of the daily prayer of the Religious Communities organized after 1845, and have been used by many of the clergy as supplements to the austere Anglican Offices. In recommending this practice H. P. Liddon writes of Psalm 119, which in the Sarum rite and until the reform of 1910 in the Roman was recited daily in the Little Hours of Prime, Terce, Sext and None:

The 119th psalm is at once infinitely varied in its expressions, yet incessantly one in its direction; its variations are so delicate as to be almost imperceptible, its unity so emphatic as to be inexorably stamped upon its every line. . . .

Nothing, we believe, so expresses the true spirit of ecclesiastics as the 119th psalm—the pure intention to live for God, the zeal for His glory, the charity for sinners, the enthusiastic love of the Divine law and the Divine perfections, the cheerfulness without levity, the gentleness without softness, the collectedness and gravity which is never stern or repulsive: in short,—the inward and outward bearing of the Priest of Jesus Christ.[28]

Usually the secular clergy say the Lesser Hours privately, but sometimes even a busy clergy house has lived on a semimonastic schedule, as for instance in Wellclose Square, in the 1860's:

The first bell for rising was rung at 6:30; we said Prime in the Oratory at 7; Matins was said at 7:30, followed by the celebration of the Holy Eucharist. After breakfast, followed by Terce, the clergy and teachers went to their respective work—some in school, some in the study or district. Sext was said at 12:45, immediately before dinner, when the household were again assembled. . . . After dinner, rest, letters, visiting or school work, as the case might be, and then tea at 5:30. After tea, choir practice, classes, reading or visiting again until Evensong at 8 P.M. After service the clergy were often engaged in classes, hearing confessions, or attending to special cases. Supper at 9:15, followed by Compline, when those who had finished their work retired to their rooms.[29]

W. G. Ward's book, *The Ideal of a Christian Church,* which brought on the formal crisis of the Oxford Movement in 1844-45, was largely a plea for the introduction to England of the devotional discipline and efficient pastoral methods so well exemplified, as he saw it, in the contemporary priesthood of France and Belgium. As has been shown, the English tradition had its own inheritance along these lines. No nobler statement of the ascetic priestly standards could be found, for instance, than in the private devotions of an Anglican Father whom the Tractarians greatly admired—Thomas Wilson, Bishop of the island Diocese of Sodor and Man from 1699-1755. A typical passage is this statement of ideals:

Fervency in devotion; frequency in prayer; aspiring after the love of God continually, striving to get above the world and the body; loving silence and solitude, as far as one's condition will permit; humble and affable to all; patient in suffering affronts and contradictions; glad of occasions of doing good even to enemies; doing the will of God and promoting His honour to the utmost of one's power; resolving never to offend him willingly, for any temporal pleasure, profit, or loss.[30]

But there was in early nineteenth-century Anglicanism an excessive degree of informality, a tendency to accept the cultured gentleman as an adequate substitute for the trained and devoted ecclesiastic. The example of the contemporary Catholic revival, and the documents of the classic period of seventeenth-century French Catholicism (an age when the Gallican and Anglican Churches had much in common) were a challenging contrast. How different, for instance, from systematic meditation according to the methods of Ignatius Loyola or Francis de Sales was the picture of

a worthy clergyman in his study,—he is resting his elbow on the table and reflecting on some portions of his Bible—making remarks at intervals to his wife.[31]

This comes from an essay, first published in 1856-57, which then offers detailed instruction in the art of meditation or mental prayer, and as a whole is the first clear and practical description of the ideal of priestly piety for the modern Anglican cleric. This classical pattern of Eucharist, Office, Meditation, and more informal prayers scattered through the systematic day's work has been commended to generations of budding clerics ever since. In Anglicanism discipline is accepted rather than imposed; and many priests have found value in membership in devotional societies bound together by a common rule of life, some independent and some associated with religious orders.[32]

As the meditation is within the day, so is the Retreat (as it is rather unhappily called) within the year, a special period of attention to eternal things. It was not unknown to seventeenth-century Anglicanism— though the examples recorded seem to be largely lay: Izaak Walton, Nicholas Ferrar, at the time a layman, and the great Christian gentleman, John Evelyn, who gave a week to devotion in London churches on entering his sixtieth year.[33] The clergy who visited the Ferrar household at Little Gidding to share in its round of devotion were retreatants of sorts. However, in the eighteenth century Bishop Wilson seems to regret the absence of any such opportunity when he observes that ancient bishops had places of retirement near their cities for Lent.[34] Informal retreats were known, as for instance the days spent in quiet by Samuel Wilberforce before his consecration to the episcopate in 1845. But organized facilities for retreats, such as Vincent de Paul had provided for the French clergy in the seventeenth century, were one of the desiderata of Ward's *Ideal*. They began, rather hesitantly, with a retreat-conference (in which there was discussion as well as prayer and meditation) arranged by Pusey at Christ Church, Oxford, in 1855. Soon thereafter they became in a more strict form a common feature of clerical life, for which a large country parsonage, a seminary like Wilberforce's Cuddesdon College, or a monastic house provided the setting.

One of the most significant achievements of the Council of Trent was the establishment of special institutions for the education of the clergy. The term "seminary" in itself comes from its canon directing the bishops of major sees to establish colleges for the training of youths destined for the service of the Church; as some proceeded to their work their places were to be filled so that the college might be a "perpetual seed-plot of ministers of God," *Dei ministrorum perpetuum seminarium*.[35] With a variety of local adaptations, the theological seminary has been a central institution in the preparation of the Roman Catholic clergy ever since—replacing the medieval system (not unlike that which still survives in Greece) of learned theologians trained in the universities and local clergy whose main preparation was an informal apprenticeship in the conduct of services. The Tridentine seminary did not aim at advanced theological studies, for which there were (and in some parts of Europe still are) Catholic university faculties; it was to concentrate on the practical side of ecclesiastical knowledge and on training in piety. Trent suggested taking boys at the age of twelve. The modern American custom is for boys to go from high school to a junior seminary, which is not necessarily residential. After a pretheological course of three or four years come four years in residence at the major seminary.[36] In American Protestantism the theological seminary originated in the early nineteenth century. Standards of theological education were rising and college courses became less adequate for the future minister. The seminaries of the Episcopal Church (starting with General in 1819 and Virginia in 1823) began under these circumstances, and gradually replaced (never quite completely) an older system of "reading for orders" under a learned clergyman. They have gradually added more of the Tridentine seminary's emphasis on spiritual discipline. As might be expected in the Anglican tradition, seminary piety usually centers in the regular use of the liturgical services of the Church.

In England the theological college originated in a spiritual rather than an academic interest. Some were established to prepare non-graduates for Orders, like the Missionary College of the Church Missionary Society, founded at Islington in 1815. But the theological colleges for graduates aimed mainly to give a year or so of disciplined study and prayer to men who had already laid the foundation of general theological knowledge in school and university. Chichester was founded in 1839; Wells in 1840. But its founder, its position, and the definite Tractarian influence of its early leaders gave major prominence to Cuddesdon, established by Bishop Wilberforce in 1854 across the road from his episcopal palace, six miles from Oxford. H. P. Liddon was its first Vice-Principal, 1854-59, and developed and enforced at Cuddesdon his austere standards of clerical life. A minor involvement of Cuddesdon in the ritualistic disputes led to his retirement in 1859, but the basic tradition continued—definitely settled in the days of Edward King, Chaplain, 1858-63, Principal 1863-73, who added to the spirit of discipline the radiant joy of holiness.[37] Later Professor of Moral and Pastoral Theology at Oxford, then Bishop of Lincoln from 1885-1910, King is one of the great priests and pastors of nineteenth-century Anglicanism. In recent years the English theological college has become a more formal academic institution, but still thinks of itself largely as a place of spiritual preparation. Two modern Religious Orders have introduced variants of the Tridentine system, begun originally about 1900 to provide for vocations to the ministry among those financially or perhaps socially unable to attend the universities. The Community of the Resurrection sends its students through a university course at Leeds before bringing them for theology to the College attached to the mother house at Mirfield; while the Society of the Sacred Mission at Kelham, which in fact developed out of the educational work of its founder, Fr. H. H. Kelly, provides preparatory as well as theological training in its own monastic establishment.

As already illustrated several times, clerical ideals overlap with those of the monastic life. The ascetic ideal has never been entirely extinct in Anglicanism, nor the forms of personal ministry which the monk can provide. Modern active Orders may of course engage in work which in itself does not differ from that of others—a Jesuit college for instance; but the Dominican motto *contemplata aliis tradere*, "to share with others the fruits of prayer," expresses the specific type of spiritual ministry appropriate to those whose main activity is the life of prayer. Nicholas Ferrar's community at Little Gidding was, in spite of its enemies' nickname "The Arminian Nunnery," rather a large and very pious household than a monastic establishment. However, it exemplified in its way the monastic ideal of a life devoted to prayer, work, and study. In the late seventeenth and eighteenth century similar aspirations were felt from time to time, but the only conspicuous Anglican ascetic is the controversial theologian, spiritual guide, and mystical writer William Law, who would certainly have found his place as a monk, or perhaps a hermit, in other ages of the Church. He did not actively exercise the priesthood which he received late in life from a Nonjuring Bishop,[38] but his career certainly belongs to the story of priestly lives and ministries. As chaplain and tutor in the Gibbon family he was an urgent director of souls in the worldly London of the 1720's. His summons to serious devotion and prayer is enshrined in his great work, the *Serious Call to a Devout and Holy Life*. This activity continued in his later years of retirement in the household of two good old ladies at King's Cliffe, when he also became the chief representative in England of his time of the mystical tradition, not very much appreciated in the eighteenth century even by the godly.

This crosscurrent of ascetic mysticism in the Age of Reason has its counterparts in other countries. French Jesuits were almost as formal and rational as their opponents, but produced the two great apostles of simplicity in prayer in that rationalistic age, de Caussade and Grou. A similar movement, even more extensive, arose in Russia, the revival of primitive monastic ideals in the spirit of the early Fathers of the Desert begun by Paissi Velichkovski (1722-94), a monk on Mount Athos and later Abbot of a Moldavian monastery. Paissi and his followers engaged in a great work of translation of ancient ascetic and mystical literature, and renewal of the spirit of ancient Orthodox piety. The monastic "elder" (*starets,* plural *startsi*) to whom people of all kinds come for advice became an important figure. Seraphim of Sarov, the last Russian saint to be canonized, is a conspicuous example of the type. The most famous series is that of the *startsi* of Optino, a monastery in Central Russia, which lasted from 1829 until the eve of the Revolution. A remarkable feature of the typical *starets* is the simple, down-to-earth character of his counsel—it is mysticism without fireworks, and often just simple common sense. The tradition is best known to the world at large through Dostoevski's Father Zossima in *The Brothers Karamazov,* although it is said that the monks of Optino when presented with the book did not recognize the portrait.[39]

In the Church of England the first revivers of the monastic life thought in terms of "Sisters of Charity." Orders of women practicing the mixed life of prayer and service were the earliest and are still perhaps the most typical Anglican foundations. Many of them were formed under the guidance of a priest as founder and chaplain, as Pusey was for the Sisterhood which survives as the Society of the Holy Trinity at Ascot, Canon Carter of Clewer for the Sisters of John the Baptist, Butler of Wantage for the Wantage Sisterhood, and John Mason Neale for St. Margaret's. W. A. Muhlenberg's Sisterhood of the Holy Communion in New York was more like the German communities of deaconesses, but out of it grew the more definitely monastic Community of St. Mary, inaugurated by Bishop Horatio Potter in 1865. Some Americans dreamed of missionary communities on the model of early medieval or Celtic missionary monasteries, but none of these survived as such—Bishop Ives' Order of the Holy Cross at Valle Crucis, North Carolina, broke up, and the mission begun at Nashotah, Wisconsin, in 1842 continued only as a seminary.

In 1865 the first monastic community of men in the modern Anglican communion came into being—the Society of Mission Priests of St. John the Evangelist, established by R. M. Benson at Oxford. Its main activity is the life of prayer under vows of poverty, chastity, and obedience, with such formal and personal ministries as are compatible with it. One of the leading members of the Society in the past generation was an outstanding expert in the study of the *Spiritual Exercises* of St. Ignatius, as well as in their adaptation for modern use. Other priestly Orders have followed—in America Holy Cross in 1844, in England the Community of the Resurrection, which reflects the intellectual, missionary, and devotional interests of its founder Bishop Gore, and Fr. Kelly's Society of the Sacred Mission. In the present century Anglican Communities following the rules of St. Benedict and St. Francis have been established both in England and in America. Some twenty years ago a writer on Anglican monasticism noted the absence of one classical form from Anglican piety, the strictly contemplative male Community (there are several such for women in England)—

in which, to men who have already received the grace of priestly consecration there is added a further vocation to a life of intensive devotion and of contemplation, in whom there would be united the right to sacrifice, the will to suffer, and the power to pray.[40]

Carthusian or Trappist Communities have not yet been raised up in *ecclesia anglicana,* but a beginning has been made in Sussex where the Bishop of Chichester has recognized and enclosed a small Community of the Servants of the Will of God.[41]

VI

From the most intensive aspects of the priestly life one may turn to its most extensive, to the priest as a minister of God not only in the sanctuary but in the world. Throughout its history the Christian ministry has been concerned for the temporal as well as the spiritual welfare of mankind; the definition of pastoral care which a church historian produced for sixth-century Gaul would apply to many other epochs as well:

Pastoral care of souls is that form of Christian charity exercised from day to day by a corps of consecrated men in a) maintaining Divine Worship for, b) communicating Sacramental Life to, c) providing inspirational guidance for, and d) procuring material benefits for that portion of mankind officially assigned to its charge.[42]

This would easily describe the program of Herbert's Country Parson, whose interests extend to the relief of the poor and the general well-ordering of the lives of his parishioners of every station—he is "a father to his flock" (Chapter XVI), a title which I believe Herbert is one of the first to apply to the parochial clergy.[43] The civic functions of Caroline prelates are not without significance in this connection. Part of Laud's policy was an effort to actualize the medieval ideal of regulation of economic life for the common good. The wide sweep of Bishop Andrewes' *Preces Privatae* shows a mind to which nothing in nature, society, or the world of grace is alien. Under the Restoration Thomas Ken both as priest and bishop ministered equally to the underprivileged and to those in high places—and his morning and evening hymns aimed to make the spirit of the priest's daily devotions available for the boys of Winchester School. The Seven Bishops who faced trial for their protest against James II's unconstitutional Declaration of Indulgence in 1688 became for a moment the voice of the nation. That they were guided by conscience and not mere politics was shown a year later when five of the seven, along with one other bishop, surrendered place and power rather than take the oath to William and Mary. The noble but tragic

nonjuring schism lost the Church of England some of her best leaders
—though even nonjurors could lead the nation through the pen, as
shown in Jeremy Collier's bold attack on the immorality of the stage,
and in the next century in the career of William Law.

After 1689 the Anglican cleric was more inclined to defend the order
of Church and State than to attempt to improve or guide it. Still, the
work of missionary and charitable societies is an important feature of
church life. The leading figure in this movement is Thomas Bray, who
after his brief experience as Commissary in Maryland organized the
Society for the Promoting of Christian Knowledge, the Society for the
Propagation of the Gospel, and a series of less conspicuous charitable
enterprises. The typical Hanoverian prelate may have basked on the
summit, except when he descended for an occasional charity sermon,
but many quiet pastors like Bishop Wilson were well aware of the
practical needs of their people. Bishop Seabury had recent as well as
ancient tradition behind him when he reminded the clergy of Connecticut and Rhode Island that they owed special attention to the sick
and afflicted, the poor and oppressed, though he seemed a little vague
as to what they could do for the latter class—

Though he [the faithful clergyman] may want power to rescue the oppressed
from the hand of violence, his mediation may be of real service.[44]

Like many others of the colonial clergy, Seabury himself had acquired
some medical skill as well as theological training. Also like many of his
brethren, he had taken a considerable part in politics, in his case as a
loyalist pamphleteer, though this belongs to his personal more than his
official career. The Anglican clergy were presented by the Revolutionary
movement with a special case of conscience revolving around the
prayers for the King in the Prayer Book—some continued with the full
service unless or until forcibly restrained, others felt they could only
perform occasional offices, and others with varying degrees of enthusiasm
or regret accepted the transfer of allegiance and modified the services
accordingly.

In the early nineteenth century the broader interests of the clergy
revolve around the various church societies, especially those for education and missions. In the last years of the Oxford Movement there is an
outburst of expansive activity, partly derived from the influence of the
Oxford leaders, partly led by others with some contacts with them.
G. A. Selwyn, Bishop of New Zealand from 1843-70, revived the ideal

of a truly Missionary Bishop (slightly earlier was the first American Missionary Bishop under that name, Jackson Kemper in the Northwest, 1835-70). Samuel Wilberforce was an energetically pastoral diocesan. Self-sacrificing priests faced the pastoral and social problems of England's teeming cities. Hook at Leeds is one of the earliest—soon comes Pusey's foundation of St. Saviour's in the same city, and the great London slum parishes such as St. Barnabas, Pimlico, St. Peter's, London Docks; and St. Alban's, Holborn. Butler from his parish at Wantage, Neale from his almshouse at East Grinstead, confronted the equally urgent problems of neglected country towns. As in the last two cases, the founding of Sisterhoods was often connected with this mission to the poorest. Two heroic figures of the end of the century are A. H. Stanton, pastor and preacher to London for fifty years, who spent his whole ministry as Assistant Curate at St. Alban's, 1862-1914, and the unconventional Father Dolling, whose ten great years were spent redeeming the almost barbarized area that surrounded St. Agatha's, Landport, in Portsmouth.[45]

Father Dolling is credited with the phrase that the Incarnation has something to do with the drains. In America Father Huntington laid the foundations of the Order of the Holy Cross while working in an East Side Mission in New York. Though later based in rural monasteries his Order has never lost its interest in human problems. Its foundations include a school in the mountains of Tennessee and a many-sided mission in the hinterland of Liberia. Members of the Order represent the Church at the great prison at Sing Sing and were instrumental in founding the Church Mission of Help, now a casework service usually known as the Episcopal Service for Youth. These activities are mentioned mainly as samples of priestly work. If the modern cleric often moves contentedly toward the vine-clad rectory in the fashionable suburb, or its equivalent, he at least must answer the question why he does not go and do likewise. Even broader than the vocation of the priests who serve the underprivileged is that of those who have been led to share in movements for social reform, F. D. Maurice's Christian Socialism grew directly out of his theology and his view of the Church as the Kingdom of Christ and the priest as its servant. The priest as reformer is represented by such great figures as Gore and Temple. Some lesser lights may illustrate concrete applications even better—Father Huntington who at some moments seemed almost to make the Single Tax an article of the Creed, Father William, friar of the Society of the Divine Compassion, leading a demonstration of the unemployed of

Plaistow in 1900, Basil Jellicoe describing his housing projects and recreational activities in Somers Town as an extension of his priestly work of consecrating bread and wine. The welfare state and the New Deal have reduced the call for some of the more conspicuous acts of priestly service among the poor. But modern urban and rural missioners still find enough concrete human needs as well as spiritual and ecclesiastical problems to meet.

VII

Some of the greatest examples of the glory of the Christian priesthood since the days of Ambrose and Chrysostom have been the leaders of the generation now just passed. One thinks of Charles Gore, scholar and theologian, monastic founder, pastor of three great dioceses—and always a missionary at heart, who hastened his death by a mission of service to divided Christians in India. One thinks of William Temple, who in more ways than one deserved the phrase humorously applied to him in early days, "not one, but all mankind in effigy," [46] Those who think of him first of all as philosopher, Christian socialist, ecumenical statesman, or evangelist should remember that it was the priesthood of the Church of England to which his life was primarily devoted, and by its traditions that he was inspired. Another many-sided figure is Frank Weston, Bishop of Zanzibar, lover of Africa and defender of Africans, theologian and monastic founder too, author of an appeal which the modern Catholic does not dare to forget:

You cannot claim to worship Jesus in the tabernacle if you do not pity Jesus in the slum. Now go out into the highways and hedges, and look for Jesus in the ragged and the naked, in the oppressed and the sweated, in those who have lost hope, and in those who are struggling to make good. Look for Jesus in them; and when you have found him, gird yourself with his towel of fellowship and wash His feet in the person of his brethren.[47]

Another such figure is that of Cardinal Mercier, professor and philospher, pastoral prelate of the metropolitan diocese of Belgium, voice of his country during the enemy occupation of World War I, who in his last years embarked on the bold experiment, destined perhaps to greater fruition in the future, of the Malines Conversations between Roman and Anglican divines. The principle of his life is expressed in the striking phrase with which he justified the holding of the Conversations—

si la verité a ses droits, la charité a ses devoirs; its center was the simple chapel in which he began each day with an hour's meditation.[48]

The modern priesthood, as this essay has sketched its ideal and to some extent its practice, is of course continuous with that of the ancient and medieval Church. However, as in many other areas of Christian life and thought, modern forms have been largely determined by the developments of the sixteenth and seventeenth centuries, the age of Reform and Counter-Reform. As in other cases, one naturally inquires whether some new word is not to be spoken today. I think there is, and that it is being found in the return to a more corporate understanding of the place of the Christian priesthood in the Church, in which we will both go back of the Middle Ages to the days of the early Christian community and forward into the future with new expressions of ancient life, bringing out of God's treasure things new and old. The individualism for which we commonly blame the Renaissance or Reformation is deeply ingrained in the thought and practice of the Middle Ages. It produces the tendency to think of the Christian minister as an individual practitioner who brings the grace of God to bear by preaching and sacrament and other ministries on a number of other individuals. The Liturgical Movement which has become so important in the Roman and Anglican Communions in the last fifty years reminds us that priest and people are brought by one Spirit into one Body. A document of at least semiofficial status, the reply of the English Archbishops to Leo XIII, describes the Prayer Book service in terms which suggest the point of departure of modern liturgical piety:

. . . we think it sufficient in the Liturgy which we use in celebrating the Holy Eucharist—while lifting up our hearts to the Lord, and when now consecrating the gifts already offered that they may become to us the Body and Blood of our Lord Jesus Christ—to signify the sacrifice which is offered at that point of the service in such terms as these. We continue a perpetual memory of the precious death of Christ, who is our Advocate with the Father and the propitiation for our sins, according to His precept, until His coming again. For first we offer the sacrifice of praise and thanksgiving; then next we plead and represent before the Father the sacrifice of the cross, and by it we confidently entreat remission of sins and all other benefits of the Lord's Passion for the whole Church; and lastly we offer the sacrifice of ourselves to the Creator of all things which we have already signified by the oblations of his creatures. This whole action, in which the people has necessarily to take its part with the Priest, we are accustomed to call the Eucharistic sacrifice.[49]

This is a step further toward emphasis on corporate action than we find, for instance, in F. D. Maurice's comparison of the Jewish and Christian priesthood written some fifty years before:

I do think a Melchisedec priesthood has succeeded to an Aaronical priesthood, even as the power of an endless life has succeeded to the law of a carnal commandment. I do think that he who represents the perfect sacrifice before God, and himself and his people as redeemed by that sacrifice, has a higher function than he had who presented the daily offerings, or made the yearly atonement before God. I do think he who is permitted to feed the people with this bread and wine has a higher work to do than he who came out of the temple to bless the people in God's name.[50]

Indeed, as the Archbishops observe, the pastoral function is in some sense more strictly peculiar to presbyters than the liturgical

seeing that it represents the attitude of God towards men (Psalm xxii, Isaiah xl. 10, 11, Jerem. xxiii 1-4, Ezek. xxxiv 11-31), while the latter is shared in some measure with the people. For the Priest, to whom the dispensing of the Sacraments and especially the consecration of the Eucharist is entrusted, must always do the service of the altar with the people standing by and sharing it with him. Thus the prophecy of Malachi (i.11) is fulfilled and the name of God is great among the gentiles through the pure offering of the Church—

as St. Peter Damian has pointed out that

this sacrifice of praise, although it seems to be specially offered by a single Priest, is really offered by all the faithful, women as well as men; for those things which he touches with his hands in offering them to God are committed to God by the deep inward devotion of the whole multitude.

So in similar terms Pius X exhorted the faithful not only to pray at Mass, but to "pray the Mass with the priest," whatever precisely that might mean.[51]

This emphasis on the common action of the Body of Christ, in the Liturgy and in common life, is the spiritual message of the modern liturgical movement. The priest is still essential in the priestly community, the *totus Christus* of St. Augustine; but rather as standing in the midst of the community as its leader than as confronting, dominating, or even serving the congregation (I Pet. 2:5, 5:3; I Cor. 1:24). So in modern churches the altar is often brought out from the east wall to which Laud had carried it back. Some have adopted the custom, preserved from ancient times in Solemn Papal Masses, of the celebrant's facing the people across the Holy Table. This is open to some objection, however, as stressing in a new way the distinction between priest and people. There is much to be said for the principle set forth by the English bishops at the Savoy Conference of 1661, that when the priest proclaims God's Word to the people he should face them, and when he leads them in prayer all should face the same way.

The liturgical movement will presumably call for a new kind of literature on the priesthood and its vocation, differing in emphasis from the pastoral guides of the last three centuries. An interpretation of the historic and biblical faith as bringing all human life to the altar of God, and of devotion, theology, art, and social reform as radiating from it, such as F. D. Maurice laid the foundations for a century ago and as A. G. Hebert sketched it in *Liturgy and Society* in 1935, calls for a new approach to the ideal of the priest. This has I think begun, and its beginnings can be traced in current literature. Efforts toward a new understanding of the life of the parish have significance for the priest as well.[52] Some individualistic forms of traditional priestly piety such as the private Mass are being questioned, and simpler yet more demanding forms of prayer than the formal meditation are being urged. The faith is ever old yet ever new, unchanged yet ever changing, and the Christian priesthood shares this combination of qualities.[53]

The breadth and depth of interests, the exacting and exciting character of the priesthood in the modern world, should appear even in this brief discussion. It is one particular form of the vocation which comes to all Christians to press on to the measure of the stature of the fullness of Christ. If one thinks largely of responsibility and labor, there are boundless joys too—perhaps the priest may take to himself the remark of a modern Chinese Christian about the mystic way, that "the sorrows are the sorrows of the ages; but the joy is the joy of eternity." [54] Moreover, within the priesthood there are numerous possibilities of specialization or expansion of interests. We have thought mainly of the pastor, but there is also room for the scholar, the teacher, the chaplain, or the social worker. Some have proposed experiments under modern conditions in ordaining men whose daily work would be "in the world" rather than "in the Church." More may yet come of the French experiment of worker-priests, at present suspended if not abandoned, or of the proposal for "voluntary priests" which has been put forward in England. But perhaps it is better to leave priest and layman to fulfill their vocations without mixing them; meanwhile, the Trappist monk going from the altar to milk the cows may serve to represent the principle that no honorable labor is unbefitting the priesthood as such.

To priests, as to all men, the hour of death finally comes, and what does life look like then? This subject, solemn but not necessarily depressing, is often propounded for meditation in retreats for priests. Legend has it that the worldly Patriarch Theophilus of Alexandria thought, as he came to his end, of a noble scholar who had left the palace classroom for a desert hermitage, and murmured, "How I envy you, Arsenius, you were always mindful of this hour." [55] Sometimes at least the end fittingly crowns the work. It is told of Newman's Roman Catholic diocesan, the straightforward English monk Bishop Ulla-thorne of Birmingham, that he said something on his deathbed about St. Benedict and the angels, and when asked if he saw them answered, yes he did.[56] Frank Weston returned from the plaudits of London crowds to die, as he would have wished to, in his mud and straw "palace" at Hegongo. Almost alone in his last agony, he was buried with a funeral that proud prelates might have envied:

. . . when we went out to take the body to the grave, Padre Canon Samwil Sehoza finished the prayers. Everyone you looked at, he was crying.

At the end of the prayers the body was covered up. Ah! alas! the lamentation which arose was very great. People cried very much. Then we returned to the house at a quarter-past six to thank the God Who had given us a good father, and now had carried him to a place of greater peace that he might rest from the troubles of the world. God grant him eternal rest and let light perpetual shine upon him.[57]

Of Charles Gore it is recorded that almost the last words heard from his lips were "transcendent glory:" [58] perhaps the theologian's unconscious mind turned to familiar topics, or perhaps the lover of God looked at last upon the face of Him in whom he had so long hoped and believed.

FOR FURTHER READING

A. CLASSICS

J. P. Camus, *L'Esprit du Bienheureux François de Sales,* 6 vols., published 1639-41—the best English selected versions of *The Spirit of St. Francis de Sales* are by H. L. S. Lear (London, 1872), and by C. F. Kelley (New York, 1952).

George Herbert, *The Priest to the Temple, or The Country Parson,* published 1652, J. B. Cheshire, ed. (New York, 1908); and in editions of Herbert's *Works.*

Thomas Wilson, *Sacra Privata,* published 1781; and vol. V of Wilson's *Works* in *Library of Anglo-Catholic Theology* (London, 1860).

B. MODERN

J. G. Barry and S. P. Delany, *The Parish Priest* (New York, 1926).

H. S. Box, ed., *Priesthood, by Various Writers* (London, 1937); historical and practical.

H. P. Liddon, *Clerical Life and Work,* (London, 1894).

Leo J. Trese, *Vessel of Clay* (New York. 1950).

Francis Underhill, ed., *Feed My Sheep, Essays in Pastoral Theology* (London, 1927).

C. BIOGRAPHICAL—a few suggestions among many

Vida D. Scudder, *Father Huntington, Founder of the Order of the Holy Cross* (New York, 1940).

John Ilyich Sergieff, *My Life in Christ* ("Father John of Cronstadt"), tr. (London, 1897).

H. Maynard Smith, *Frank, Bishop of Zanzibar 1871-1924* (London, 1926).

VII

The Ministry in the Puritan Age

The Puritan Age in England may roughly be defined as the century following the Reformation. It extended from the first years of Elizabeth's reign to 1660 when the restoration of the Stuarts brought to an end the attempt to fashion a Puritan state.

The Reformation in England had been much less drastic and far less systematic than the reforms introduced on the Continent. Worship was simplified, elements of "superstition" were removed, English replaced Latin, but much that was familiar was retained. The Articles of Religion were brief and, in the interest of comprehension, avoided precise definition. The structure of the church—with its dioceses and parishes, bishops and parish clergy—was left largely untouched. But this absence of drastic reform was deceptive. It served to cloak the far-reaching changes in thinking that had been introduced. Nowhere can this be seen more clearly than in the altered view of the clergy.

The sacerdotal aspect of the ministry was not in express words disallowed, but it was so effectually obscured as to fall out of general acceptance. The word "priest" remained, but it was carefully explained by Archbishop Whitgift to mean no more than presbyter, and it was carefully avoided in official documents. Except when referring to the Ordinal, the Canons of 1604 invariably employ the word "minister" instead of "priest." The suggestion of the official usage was emphasized by the destruction of the altars in the parish churches, . . . and the abandonment of the Eucharistic vestments.[1]

Formerly the clergy had been "priests," finding their primary responsibility at the altar; now they were "ministers," with preaching and pastoral care as their pre-eminent duties.

It is because there was this essential agreement as to the role of the clergy that it is possible to discuss the ministry in the Puritan Age without resorting to party distinctions. The English church, to be sure, did become divided into the two rival camps of Puritan and Anglican, but until the last years of our period the difference between them was not great. Henry Scougal, the Scottish Episcopalian, once observed that animosities frequently are greatest where differences are least, and this was true of the increasingly acute religious controversy which was to plague the life of England during the century following the Reformation.

Puritanism, which had its origin early in the reign of Elizabeth in an effort to push through a more thoroughgoing reform of the worship of the English church, was merely the most dynamic form of English Protestantism.[2] The points at issue were peripheral rather than central, and the Puritan and Anglican were more to be distinguished by a difference of mood and emphasis than by any fundamental theological disagreement. It is true that the Puritan made his primary appeal to the authority of Scripture and that the Anglican gave greater heed to the authority of tradition, yet even this distinction was a distinction in emphasis. Chillingworth could insist that the Bible was the religion of the Anglican, and no Puritan was ever indifferent to tradition as represented by "the best reformed churches abroad" and by John Foxe's accounts of the English martyrs. Moreover, the reason for the varying emphasis upon Scripture and tradition was not so much theological as psychological. It was rooted in a difference in temperament. The Puritan was zealous for reform; eager, impatient, and intense; insistent that all of life must quickly be reduced to conformity with God's will. The Anglican was more cautious and moderate; more aware of the power of habit and custom; fearful of precipitate action and desirous of making haste slowly. The Puritan never forgot Peter's word that one must obey God rather than men, while the Anglican remembered Paul's counsel that due regard must be given constituted authority. Thus some things which were intolerable for the Puritan were tolerable for the Anglican.

No one better represents the Anglican mood of caution and moderation and the stress upon the necessity for obedience to constituted authority than George Herbert. His "country parson" used and preferred "the ordinary church catechism, partly for obedience to authority, partly for uniformity sake that the same common truths may be everywhere professed." The mood of caution and moderation was also apparent in the hesitancy of the "country parson" to reject familiar usages. He was a lover of old customs and thought it foolish to reject practices, harmless in themselves, if the "people are much addicted to them." It was his policy, "if there be any evil in the custom that may be severed from the good," to pare the apple and give them "the clean to feed on."³

While this difference in mood between the Puritan and the Anglican did spell out some differences in ministerial practice, the differences were of a minor nature. They were mostly in matters of detail, in tempo of activity, and in the relative emphasis to be given specific tasks. But in terms of the definition of the ministerial function itself there was virtual unanimity.

A distinction of greater consequence was in process of development during these years, but its full impact upon the work of the minister was not to be felt until a later period. This was the emergence in incipient form of the evangelical pietism which was destined to become so influential a feature of religious life in the English-speaking world. The Puritan had found his major support through the emotional response awakened by his preaching, and he came to stress more and more the paramount importance of an awakened conscience and the work of grace in the heart of the believer. Thus it became his overriding concern that the Word be preached with power and effectiveness. The Anglican, on the other hand, was driven to defend his position by emphasizing the sacramental efficacy in the life of the community of the prayers and worship of the church.

I

When George Herbert set himself to the task of writing *The Country Parson,* his intention was not to describe a typical parson of the time but rather "to set down the form and character of a true pastor." His purpose was to give himself "a mark to aim at," a mark which he set as high as he could, "since he shoots higher that threatens the moon than he that aims at a tree."⁴ The surprising fact, however, is that there were so many pastors of the time, including Herbert himself, who closely approximated the ideal which he delineated so charmingly. In all ages, there have been the indifferent, indolent, unworthy, and scandalous among the clergy; and the age in which Herbert lived was no exception. But no one who has browsed through the biographical accounts of the ministers whose lives fell within the period from the death of Mary through the tumultuous years of the Civil Wars and Commonwealth to the deceptive calm of the Restoration can fail to be impressed with the deep devotion, earnest labors, and high conception of their task which characterized so many of the clergy. This is the more remarkable because the clergy were so very largely on their own, and the practice of their calling was left to their own voluntary efforts. Even had the disciplinary powers of the bishops remained unimpaired, it would have been difficult to legislate good preaching and conscientious pastoral care.

It was a busy life these parsons led. The pattern varied from parish to parish, but the weekly schedule of Herbert's "country parson" suggests the general scope of their activities. On Sundays, there were two services with preaching in the morning and catechizing in the afternoon.

> The rest of the day he spends in reconciling neighbors that are at variance, or in visiting the sick, or in exhortations to some of his flock by themselves whom his sermons cannot or do not reach. And everyone is more awakened when we come and say, "Thou art the man." This way he finds exceeding useful and winning. At night, he thinks it a fit time, both suitable to the joy of the day and without hindrance to public duties, either to entertain some of his neighbors or to be entertained of them; where he takes occasion to discourse of such things as are both profitable and pleasant, and to raise up their minds to apprehend God's good blessing.[5]

On weekdays, the afternoons were utilized "to visit in person, now one quarter of the parish, now another," to counsel, admonish, and exhort.

> There he shall find his flock most naturally as they are . . . whereas on Sundays it is easy for them to compose themselves to order, which they put on as their holiday clothes and come to church in same, but commonly the next day put off both.[6]

The mornings were for reading and study and the numerous other activities which were the pastor's lot. Mealtimes were the occasion for extending the hospitality of the table to his parishioners, taking them in turn "so that in the compass of the year he hath them all with him," but inviting those most often "whom he sees take best courses that so both they may be encouraged to persevere and others spurred to do well."[7]

This ideal which Herbert sketched was not easily attained, for the minister was caught up in many other activities of parish life. Not infrequently he was called upon to serve as schoolmaster to the parish children, and occasionally he might be prevailed upon to utilize his spare time for the instruction of adults as well. One minister is reported to have taught forty persons to read who were over forty years of age.[8] Nor was it unusual for a clergyman to be licensed to practice medicine, and whether licensed or not he was expected to keep a book of "physic" at hand and his wife a garden of medicinal herbs so that help could be given in emergencies. In similar fashion, he needed at least an elementary knowledge of law, for as the educated person of the community he was called upon to give legal advice, draft legal documents, and frequently adjudicate legal disputes. In the midst of all this, if his income was to be at all adequate, he needed a moderate knowledge of farming and, in some cases, had to be able to handle a plow and a spade with reasonable skill.

Given these circumstances, it was to be expected that many—quite apart from those who frequented the tavern, the gaming table, and the hunt—did not measure up to the specifications of Herbert's ideal parson. What is astonishing is that there were many who exceeded the rigorous routine he prescribed, who added a weekday lecture to the Sunday schedule of sermon and catechizing, or who, like Richard Greenham, "rose each morning at four, and spoke to his people at dawn every week-day morning." [9]

What was the aim of this busy activity? "The first and great work of the ministers of Christ," Richard Baxter declared, is "to acquaint men with that God that made them and is their happiness," [10] and there were few ministers who would have dissented. Henry Scougal, who was deeply indebted to Herbert in many ways, was to state it with greater force and beauty.

The great business of our calling is to advance the divine life in the world; to make religion sway and prevail, frame and mould the souls of men into a conformity to God and superinduce the beautiful lineaments of his blessed image upon them; to enlighten their understandings and inform their judgments, rectify their wills and order their passions and sanctify all their affections. The world lieth in sin, and it is our work to awaken men out of their deadly sleep—to rescue them out of that dismal condition. We are the instruments of God for effecting these great designs; and though we be not accountable for the success when we have done what lieth within our power, yet nothing below this should be our aim; and we should never cease our endeavors until that gracious change be wrought in every person committed to our charge.[11]

To understand in detail how these "ministers of Christ" went about the "great business" of their calling is the major concern of the following pages.

II

Thomas Fuller, whose comments on the events of his time are as discerning as they are vivid, noted that the secret of the growing influence of Puritanism in English life was to be found in the marked ability displayed by the Puritan preachers in the pulpit.

What won them most repute was their ministers' painful preaching in populous places; it being observed in England that those who hold the helm of the pulpit always steer people's hearts as they please.[12]

"Painful" preaching, of course, was good preaching—painstaking preaching, carefully prepared preaching—and all parties within the English Church were agreed as to its importance.

The century following Elizabeth's accession was one of the great ages of the pulpit. At a time when there were few, if any, organized social activities and when newspapers had yet to make their appearance as a source of information and diversion, a sermon could be a major event. Nor, in a leisurely age when time was of little consequence, did people object to sermons that on occasion extended well beyond the turning of the hour glass. George Herbert, however, suggested that the wise parson would not exceed "an hour in preaching," since "all ages have thought that a competency, and he that profits not in that time, will less afterwards; the same affection which made him not profit before, making him then weary; and so he grows from not relishing to loathing."[13] While the ordinary preacher had a captive audience—a shilling fine being levied upon absentees—and consequently could not take it for granted that he would have the attention of his auditors, a talented preacher could win unusually large congregations that came from far beyond the parish boundaries. One of the most noted of the preachers was Henry Smith—"commonly called 'the silver-tongued Smith,' being but one metal, in price and purity, beneath St. Chrysostom himself."[14] When Smith preached, reports Fuller, "his church was so crowded with auditors that persons of good quality brought their own pews with them, I mean their legs, to stand upon in the aisles." And "their ears did so attend to his lips, their hearts to their ears, that he held the rudder of their affections in his hands, so that he could steer them whither he pleased."[15]

The unanimity of emphasis upon the importance of preaching was striking. Herbert was insistent that his "country parson" should preach constantly—"the pulpit is his joy and throne." [16] It is true that at the Hampton Court Conference, when Dr. Rainolds urged that every parish should be furnished with a preaching minister, Archbishop Bancroft in a moment of petulance replied that the real need was for a praying ministry, since "preaching had grown to such a fashion that the services of the church were neglected." [17] The ensuing discussion, however, made it clear that neither Bancroft nor the King had any thought of disparaging the importance of the sermon. Indeed, the whole thrust of Whitgift's policy, with the active assistance of Bancroft, had been to raise up a preaching ministry in the church, and this endeavor had met with marked success.

The Elizabethan church had inherited the problem of widespread ignorance among the clergy. "Many knew little or no Latin and less Scripture—indeed, some could barely read the English services of the new Prayer Book." [18] The reason that not many of the clergy were preachers was the simple fact that not too many of them were able to preach. When Whitgift emerged into a position of influence, he immediately took steps to remedy this situation. More precise requirements for ordination were established, and appointments to parishes providing the most adequate incomes were restricted to licensed preachers or men holding advanced degrees. All nonpreachers were ordered to secure a Bible and a copy of Bullinger's *Decades,* and each day one chapter of the Bible was to be read and each week one of Bullinger's sermons; periodically they were to be examined by the archdeacons as to the progress they had made. In the interim between examinations by the archdeacons, the licensed preachers were to supervise the studies of the nonpreachers in their vicinity, making quarterly reports concerning their charges to the diocesan authorities.[19] In addition to these general measures, some of the bishops experimented with other means of developing a preaching ministry, most notably with "prophesyings"—patterned after the procedure adopted by Bullinger at Zurich—as a method of perfecting homiletical skill, but this expedient was ultimately frowned upon by the government and suppressed.

Several factors contributed to the furtherance of Whitgift's efforts to increase the number of preachers, and he achieved considerable success. When he became archbishop, fully two-thirds of the clergy were not university graduates, and the majority of these men had no university training at all. Not one-sixth of the clergy had sufficient training to be licensed as preachers. Fifteen years later, about half the clergy were licensed to preach, and a large number of those who were not had had some university training. "Only a small minority could compare in ignorance with the unlearned clergy of two decades earlier." [20] If the ignorant parson at the end of Elizabeth's reign was the subject of more unfavorable comment than he had been at an earlier time, it was partly due to the fact that he had become a less typical figure in the life of the church. Increasingly the normal expectation was that the parson both could and would preach, and if he were not qualified to do so, he was under obligation to see that preaching was provided in his parish at regular intervals.

If there was general agreement as to the importance of preaching, there was an equally strong conviction that it was an art which demanded careful preparation and great skill. "Preaching," Henry Scougal was to declare, "is an exercise that many are ambitious of, and none more than those that are least qualified for it."

It is not so easy a matter to perform this task aright; to stand in the presence of God and to speak in his name, with that plainness and simplicity, that seriousness and gravity, that zeal and concern, which the business requires; to accommodate ourselves to the capacity of the common people without disgusting our more knowing hearers by the insipid flatness of our discourse; to excite and awaken drowsy souls, without terrifying and disturbing more tender consciences; to bear home the convictions of sin, without the appearance of some personal reflection; in a word, to approve ourselves unto God as workmen that need not be ashamed, rightly dividing the word of truth.[21]

Richard Baxter had used strikingly similar words in affirming that "it is no small matter to stand up in the face of a congregation and deliver a message from the living God."

What skill is necessary to make plain the truth, to convince the hearers; to let in the irresistible light into their consciences, and to keep it there and drive all home; to screw the truth into their minds and work Christ into their affections . . . ; and to do all this so for language and manner as beseems our work, and yet as is most suitable to the capacities of our hearers. . . . So great a God, whose message we deliver, should be honored by our delivery of it.[22]

Scougal and Baxter were pleading for what, in the parlance of the time, was known as the "plain" style of preaching—a type of sermonic construction that was designed to reach both the minds and hearts of the people. This was in distinction to the so-called "witty" preaching which sought to impress the congregation by a display of erudition, making extensive use of classical allusions and delighting in literary flourishes. While there were practitioners of "witty" preaching in university circles and while it enjoyed a measure of popularity at court and other centers of fashion, the use of exotic words, obscure phrases, and complex rhetoric in the pulpit had few, if any, defenders. The objection to such preaching was that it served to confuse rather than to enlighten the hearers. They were apt to miss the point. "Painted obscure sermons, like the painted glass in the windows that keeps out light, are too often the marks of painted hypocrites," Baxter observed. "The paint upon the glass may feed the fancy, but the room is not well lighted by it." And when he remarked that for a person to "purposely cloud the matter in strange words . . . is the way to make fools admire his profound wisdom and wise men his folly," he was stating the common sense of the matter which was obvious to everyone.[23]

The first requirement of the "plain" style of preaching was that it should be intelligible. "If you would not teach men, what do you in the pulpit?" asked Baxter. "If you would, why do you not speak so as to be understood?" And "he that would be understood must speak to the capacity of his hearers and make it his business to be understood." [24] To make "a hard point easy and familiar," to make difficult doctrines as plain as one can, it is necessary to speak the natural and unaffected language of ordinary people and it is necessary to utilize imagery drawn from their own experience. Thus George Herbert notes that his "country parson" condescends even to the knowledge of tillage and pasturage, and makes great use of them in teaching, because people by what they understand are best led to what they understand not." [25] It was in the interest of intelligibility also that the use of anecdotes to illustrate doctrine was widely recommended and practiced.

The second requirement of the "plain" style of preaching was that it should touch the heart, awaken the conscience, and win assent. The aim of the preacher was not to shoot "his arrows over the people's heads but into their hearts and consciences." The goal was to persuade each of his hearers to ask the question which the Philippian jailer asked of Paul and Silas: "Sirs, what must I do to be saved?" But this was no easy task. Scougal was to observe that "the vulgar that commonly sit under the pulpit are commonly as hard and dead as the seats they sit on," and

Herbert had noted that they frequently "need a mountain of fire to kindle them." [26] Thus the words of the preacher—to use Roger Williams' felicitous expression—had to be "working words"—words that were convincing, forceful, and direct. They should strike "to the quick" and elicit an emotional response. "Lively and effectual words," they were sometimes called, words that would command attention, dig through to the very heart of man, awaken the deadest conscience, and bring conviction.

If the language was to be simple and direct and the words "lively and effectual," the method must be "plain and clear." The sermons must be carefully prepared, but even if written out in advance, the popular preacher seldom took more than "the heads of the discourse" into the pulpit with him. The sermon had three major divisions. First, the text was explained or "opened" in its context. Then, the text was "divided"; that is, "profitable points of doctrine" were drawn from it. Lastly, the doctrines were "applied" to the lives of the people. This was called the "uses." It was frequently remarked that those who wished to display their learning or who were fearful lest the gospel give offense spent the major portion of their time dividing the text and multiplying doctrines to the neglect of the "uses" wherein "a sermon's excellency doth consist." Those who wished to reach the heart emphasized the applications, and George Herbert was even to suggest that his "country parson"—in order to avoid the former temptation—found it both possible and profitable to proceed directly from the "opening" of the text to its application.[27]

It is obvious that the "plain" style of preaching, which was so widely commended, did not mean a colorless or prosaic style. It was plain because it was designed to be intelligible and moving and pointed. But it was a studied simplicity which was far from dull; and, in addition to its Biblical imagery, it reflected the life of the countryside, the household, the marketplace, and—especially among the preachers of East Anglia—the sea.

III

The Elizabethan legislation which provided for uniformity of ecclesiastical practice by prescribing the use of the Prayer Book gives no hint of the extraordinary confusion which was to continue to prevail in the actual services of the church. The variety of practice is described in a manuscript dated February 14, 1564:

Some say the service and prayers in the chancel; others in the body of the church. Some say the same in a seat made in the church; some in the pulpit with their faces to the people. Some keep precisely the order of the book; others intermeddle Psalms in metre. Some say with a surplice; others without a surplice.

The table standeth in the body of the church in some places; in others it standeth in the chancel. . . .

Some receive kneeling, others·standing, others sitting.

Some with a square cap; some with a round cap; some with a button cap; some in scholar's clothes; some in others.[28]

Nor was variation in practice by minister and people the only source of confusion. Peddlers still sold their wares in churchyards and even at the church door during the time of service. Inside, there was much walking and talking even when prayers were being said. Actual misbehavior, Usher reports, was not uncommon, "especially pushing people off the other end of the bench or knocking their stools out from under them." Moreover, the church buildings were not always properly equipped. Among other deficiencies in the parish church at Elme in 1605, it was noted that "the minister's seat in the church is not a comely and convenient seat, for it is open on both sides or ends so that the dogs run through it and trouble and disturb him in time of prayers and service." Nor was there "a ready or fit passage up into the pulpit there, but one must climb over men's backs when he goes up to preach." [29] This may have been unusual, but the church buildings on the whole were dirty and damp and unwholesome, some lacking adequate roofing and some with no flooring other than straw and rushes.

The disorder of the churches ought not to be unduly magnified, and the fact is that many of these conditions were being remedied. Extensive reconstruction of church buildings, including the laying of floors and the introduction of pews and other more suitable furnishings, was taking place, and a generous use of whitewash obscured the dirt if it did not prevent the seepage of water through the walls and into the foundation. The behavior of the people was not susceptible to prompt reform, but here also there were indications of improvement, most notably where able preaching was beginning to have effect.

The major problem was the necessity for an ordered worship. The authorization of the Prayer Book, the issuance of various sets of Injunctions, and the adoption of the Canons of 1604, all had been aimed at securing uniformity of practice, but progress in this direction was slow. Much of the noncomformity was due to carelessness, to the weakness of ecclesiastical administration, and to a lack of precise knowledge of what was required, but a portion of it reflected a concern on the part of some for an ordered worship of greater theological integrity than the prescribed worship seemed to them to possess. The tension here was not between order and disorder, but between differing conceptions of what the structure of ordered worship ought to be. Richard Baxter was as emphatic as Archbishop Laud in declaring that an essential part of pastoral work was "to guide our people and be as their mouth in the public prayers of the church and the public praises of God," and that this must be done with dignity and in due order.[30]

The communion service also suffered from the general laxness of practice. "A general fault it is among ourselves," complained Baxter, "that some are so careless in the manner" of their administration of "the holy mysteries or seals of God's covenant," and that "others do reform that with a total neglect."[31] For the most part, communion was celebrated only infrequently and attendance appears to have been disappointingly small. Conditions varied, of course, from parish to parish, but even George Herbert's model parson was not expected to summon his people to the table more than five or six times a year—at Easter, Christmas, Whitsuntide, before and after harvest, and at the beginning of Lent. The early Puritans did better, some of them achieving the goal of a weekly communion, although in time a monthly celebration became the rule.[32]

IV

Preaching, conducting public worship, and administering the sacraments constituted only a part of the pastoral office as it was defined in the post-Reformation years. Of equal importance, was the minister's responsibility for pastoral care and oversight.

Catechizing the people—instructing them in the essentials of the faith—was a statutory obligation which often became a tiresome task. It "is no small toil," said Scougal, "to tell the same things a thousand times to some dull and ignorant people, who, perhaps, shall know but little when we have done. It is this laborious exercise that does sometimes tempt a minister to envy the condition of those who gain their living by the sweat of their brows, without the toil and distraction of their spirits."[33] But, whether tiresome or not, Scougal was not disposed to suggest that catechizing was a task which could safely be neglected, and Baxter had expressed the hope that the time was at hand "when

it shall be as great a shame to a minister to neglect the private instructing and oversight of the flock as it hath been to be a seldom preacher." [34]

A striking feature of the age was the frank experimentation that was
being carried on in an effort to make sure that the ignorant were
instructed adequately and effectively. George Herbert reports that his
"country parson," who "values catechizing highly," followed the conventional procedure of dealing with the heads of the families privately,
while utilizing the time before or after the second Sunday service for
the public instruction of children, apprentices, and servants.

He exacts of all the doctrine of the catechism; of the younger sort, the very
words; of the elder, the substance. Those he catechizeth publicly; these privately,
giving age honor, according to the apostle's rule.

His one innovation was to insist that even the heads of the families be
present for the public catechizing:

First, for the authority of the work; secondly, that parents and masters . . .
may when they come home either commend or reprove, either reward or punish;
thirdly, that those of the elder sort who are not well grounded may then by an
honorable way take occasion to be better instructed. [35]

A more frequent innovation was to supplement the catechizing in the
church with more informal procedures in the homes. There are numerous instances of the minister's extending the hospitality of his table for
this purpose. There are also reports of more formal catechetical exercises
held by turns in "the richer men's houses" in the various parts of the
parish. Samuel Clarke reports the procedure followed in one parish:

In the morning when they first met, the master of the family began with
prayer, then was the question to be conferred of read, and the younger Christians
first gave their answers, together with their proofs of Scripture for them; and
then the more experienced Christians gathered up the other answers which were
omitted by the former; and thus they continued until dinner time, when having
good provision made for them by the master of the family, they dined together
with much cheerfulness. After dinner, having sung a Psalm, they returned to their
conference upon the other questions (which were three in all) till towards
evening; at which time, as the master of the family began, so he concluded with
prayer, and I gave them three new questions against their next meeting, which
being appointed for time and place, everyone repaired to his own home. [36]

Richard Baxter adopted an even more systematic procedure, and *The Reformed Pastor* was written primarily to urge his method upon his fellow ministers. Baxter was convinced that "we must use all the means we can to instruct the ignorant in the matters of their salvation," and it was evident to him that personal conferences and examinations were indispensable.

I am daily forced to admire how lamentably ignorant many of our people are that have seemed diligent hearers of me these ten or twelve years, while I spoke as plainly as I was able to speak. . . . Some that come constantly to private meetings are found grossly ignorant; whereas, in one hour's familiar instruction of them in private, they seem to understand more and better entertain it than they did in all their lives before.

His method was to have each family come to the manse at an appointed time when he could spend an hour questioning and instructing them. Copies of the catechism had been delivered to each home at the begining of the year and a week in advance the clerk notified the individual family of the questions to be discussed and of the hour at which they were scheduled to appear.

We spend Monday and Tuesday from morning to almost night in the work . . . , taking about fifteen or sixteen families in a week, that we may go through the parish, which hath above eight hundred families, in a year; and I cannot say yet that one family hath refused to come to me, nor but few persons excused themselves and shifted off. And I find more outward signs of success with most that come than of all my public preaching to them.

"I earnestly beseech you . . .," Baxter urged his fellow ministers, "for the sake of your people's souls, that you will not slightly slubber over this work . . ., but make it your great and serious business." It is a task that demands careful preparation, and you must "study how to do it beforehand as you study for your sermons." Nor was it a task that could properly be delegated to an assistant. Baxter confessed that he had been among those who had sought to have parliament "settle catechists in our assemblies," but he was not sorry that the project had not been adopted.

For I perceive that all the life of the work, under God, doth lie in the prudent effectual management of searching men's hearts and setting home the saving truths; and the ablest minister is weak enough for this, and few of inferior place or parts would be found competent.[37]

Pastoral visitation was a second aspect of the exercise of due pastoral care. This included visiting the sick, "helping them prepare either for a fruitful life or a happy death," but it also had as its objective becoming "acquainted with the state of all our people as fully as we can . . ., for if we know not the temperament or disease, we are likely to prove but unsuccessful physicians." [38] Herbert was convinced, as has been noted, that only by a systematic program of visitation could the pastor come to know his people as they "most naturally . . . are, wallowing in the midst of their affairs," and it was only by such intimate knowledge of their lives as could be gained in this fashion that he would be equipped to reprove and admonish them, and thereby lead them to mend their ways. [39]

Thus pastoral visitation was regarded in large part as but an adjunct of the exercise of pastoral discipline, and it was regarded as a doubly important adjunct because the proper ordering of family life was a major disciplinary concern. "We must have a special eye upon families," said Baxter, "to see that they be well ordered and the duties of each relation performed," for "if we suffer the neglect of this, we undo all. . . . You are likely to see no general reformation till you procure family reformation." [40] The problem, declared Scougal, is that "we, perhaps, see them once a week, and bring them to some degree of sobriety and a sound mind; but then their wicked neighbors and the companions of their sin do meet them every day and, by their counsel and example, obliterate any good impression that has been made upon them." Consequently, in the absence of being sustained by a well-ordered family life, we are apt to "lose more in a week than we are able to recover in a whole year." [41]

There were frequent complaints concerning laxity in the administration of discipline. Baxter's lament is not untypical.

In all my life, I never lived in the parish where one person was publicly admonished or brought to public penitence or excommunicated, though there were never so many obstinate drunkards, whore-mongers, or vilest offenders. Only I have known now and then one for getting a bastard that went to the bishop's court and paid their fees; and I heard of two or three in all the country in all my life that stood in a white sheet an hour in the church. [42]

It may be supposed that the occasion for these laments was not so much a question of discipline having decayed as it was a heightened sense of the importance of discipline. One of the problems, to be sure, was that the disciplinary procedures of the church were badly confused, but, as Baxter pointed out, there was sufficient opportunity for the pastor to discharge this responsibility if he so desired. "The great objection that seemeth to hinder some from this work is, because we are not agreed yet who it is that must do it: whether only a prelate, or whether a presbytery or a single pastor or the people." Yet, it is granted by everyone that "a single pastor may expound and apply the word of God," and so it is also evident that "he may rebuke a notorious sinner." This much was acknowledged by all parties. Baxter's urgent plea, therefore, was that the ministers should, "without further delay, unanimously set themselves to the practice of those parts of Christian discipline which are unquestionably necessary and part of their work." [43]

Actually, there was much more of this private or pastoral type of discipline than Baxter's words might lead us to believe. There were both the private endeavors of the minister to bring the sinner to repentance, requiring "a great deal of skill," [44] and the last resort to public reproof and admonition. Within the particular changing ecclesiastical structures, of course, there was always the possibility of a formal excommunication.

Discipline, as even Baxter agreed, was a pastoral responsibility which must be handled with great caution. Scougal called it "an edged tool," and suggested that "they had need be no fools that meddle with it." It is hard so to manage the business with such "care and prudence" that it "may neither encourage flagitious persons by our remissness nor tempt to irritate others by needless severity." [45] This, however, should not be used by a minister as an excuse for avoiding his duty.

When we have done all that we can by public and general exhortation, we shall effectuate very little without a more particular application to the persons under our charge. Interest and self-love will blind the eyes and stop the ears of men, and make them shift off from themselves those admonitions from the pulpit that are displeasing; and therefore we are commanded not only to teach and exhort, but also to rebuke with all authority.[46]

Nevertheless, the erring and the wayward should be dealt with patiently. "It is not to be expected that an hasty conference or an abrupt disputation should prevail with those who have been long habituated to false persuasions." The task of the minister, in dealing with disciplinary problems, is "first to study to combat the perverseness of the will, the prejudices of the world, the desire of victory and applause, their . . . unwillingness to yield," and then to "strive to render them meek and pliable and sincerely desirous to knew the truth." [47] Fortunately, much could be done by indirection, by "the due encouragement of those that are humble, upright, obedient Christians." Echoing the counsel of George Herbert, Baxter suggested that, if ministers would, "in the eyes of all the flock, put some difference between them and the rest by our praises and more special familiarity and other testimonies of our approbation and rejoicing over them," they would do much "both to encourage them and incite others to imitate them." [48]

When Thomas Fuller described William Perkins as "an excellent surgeon . . . at the jointing of a broken soul and at stating of a doubtful conscience," [49] he was voicing no small tribute, for pastoral counseling was everywhere regarded as one of the most important as well as the most difficult of all pastoral duties. The age, of course, was one which had intensified personal problems and the changing pattern of society created many new situations in which people felt the need of guidance in making moral decisions. The ministers, in turn, were acutely aware of their responsibility to help those who were beset by perplexity, anxiety, and indecision. "As the lawyer is (a counselor) for their estates and the physician for their bodies," so the minister is the "counselor for their souls," who "must be ready to give advice to those that come to him with cases of conscience." [50] "Of all divinity," Joseph Hall, Bishop of Norwich, declared, "that part is most useful which determines cases of conscience." [51]

Since it was recognized that "unskillful" counselors were apt to aggravate "griefs and perplexities," the clergy were constantly exhorted "to have a care to qualify themselves" for the task and to keep "some good sound body of casuistical divinity" always at hand. [52] Even though many of the more prominent divines—most notably William Perkins, William Ames, Joseph Hall, Jeremy Taylor, Robert Sanderson, and Richard Baxter—had busied themselves with the preparation of this type of literature, there was a continual demand for additional manuals or directories which would provide the clergy with guidance in dealing with the "cases of conscience" which they encountered in the course of their ministry.

These manuals follow a common pattern, taking up individual cases and indicating how they are to be resolved, and the directions they offer are remarkably similar in character. [53] The greater number of cases discussed deal with moral perplexities—questions involving family life, economic activity, military service, political issues, the relationship of master and servant, the right use of recreation—but spiritual perplexities—involving "the great case which the Jews put to Peter and the jailor to Paul and Silas" [54]—undoubtedly received equal attention in actual pastoral work. The greater amount of space devoted to the moral perplexities in the manuals is to be explained by the fact that the spiritual perplexities were not susceptible to being divided into as many distinct cases. Of this we may be sure: the moral perplexities were frequently as acute as the spiritual. "For," as George Herbert insisted, "everyone hath not digested when it is a sin to take something for money lent, or when not; when the affections of the soul in desiring and procuring increase of means or honor be a sin of covetousness and ambition, and when not; when the appetites of the body in eating, drinking, sleep, and the pleasure that comes with sleep be sins of gluttony, drunkenness, sloth, lust, and when not; and so in many circumstances of actions." [55] To resolve these questions and many more to the ease of one's conscience, a skillful guide was needed.

It was still a third type of "case" which provided the greatest challenge to the pastor. These were those instances of acute anxiety and despair, subsumed under the general category of "melancholy," which were characterized by gloomy brooding, undue desire for solitude, and even the suicidal impulse. Cases of melancholy appear to have been not uncommon, stemming in part, perhaps, from that general sense of the decay of the world which was a familiar feature of the Elizabethan climate of opinion, in part from the sense of rootlessness and estrangement which is characteristic of a transitional society, and aggravated no doubt by the searching, pointed preaching of the time. It was recognized that there were various types of melancholy, produced by diverse causes, and not susceptible to the same treatment. While successful treatment involved the adaptation of remedies to fit the specific malady, certain general directions for dealing with such cases were provided.

It was suggested that the person ought first to be directed to see a physician, because the cause might be a physical indisposition, perhaps nothing more than indigestion. "I have seen abundance cured by physic," said Baxter, "and till the body be cured the mind will hardly ever be cured." [56] If the melancholy persists, such persons are to be directed to consult "a skillful prudent minister of Christ . . . that is skillled in such cases," to whom they can confidently reveal their secrets and pour out without reserve the story of their distress.[59] They are neither to exaggerate nor to minimize their affliction, but to tell all that help may be given. The minister, in addition to resolving their doubts and praying with them, will choose for them some comforting gospel promises, most suitable to their condition. "A sick man is not usually fit to think

of very many things, and therefore two or three comfortable promises"
to "roll over and over" in his mind "may be the most profitable matter
of his thoughts." [58] The melancholy person is also to be urged to avoid
both solitude and inactivity. He is to surround himself with friends and
to busy himself in his calling, seeking out opportunities to engage in
physical labor and also to help others who are in an even more unfortunate condition. "It is a useful way, if you can, to engage them in comforting others that are deeper in distresses than they, for this will tell them
that their case is not singular, and they will speak to themselves when
comforting others." [59] Finally, "changing air and company and riding
abroad" may help, and securing a friend to read aloud "Dr. Sibbes'
books, and some useful pleasing history or chronicles or news of great
matters abroad in the world, may do somewhat to divert them." [60]

What of the role of the counselor in these various situations? Perkins
tells us that he must be patient and bear with the "peevishness" and
"distempered and disordered affections and actions" of those who come
to him. He must identify himself with his consultants, sharing their
sorrows and their tears, and he must be a good listener who guards their
secrets and, where the conscience is unduly disturbed, is not censorious.
Above all, he "must not be dismayed by small results after long effort." [61]

A perennial problem was to get some of those who most needed help
to come to the minister for counsel. "The minister is seldom sent for,"
Henry Scougal complained, "till the physician has given the patient
over; and then they beg him to dress their souls for heaven, when their
winding sheet is preparing and their friends are almost ready to dress
the body for the funeral." It is rather difficult, he suggested, to deal
with their condition when they are "ready to leave the world and step
in upon eternity; when their souls do, as it were, hang upon their lips,
and they have one foot, as we used to say, already in the grave."
Physicians, when they "undertake the cure of bodily distempers," have
an advantage, for "they have the consent of the party; he is ready to
comply with their prescriptions."

> But our greatest difficulty is in dealing with the wills of men and making them
> consent to be cured. They hug the disease, and shun the medicines as poison, and
> have no desire to be well. Hence it is they do all they can to keep us strangers to
> their souls, and take as much pains to conceal their distempers as they ought to do
> in revealing them. . . . It is hard to do anything towards a cure when they will
> not let us know the disease.[62]

Thus Scougal was led to stress the importance of preaching to awaken contrition and to force people to acknowledge that they are proud, passionate, vengeful, covetous, and uncharitable, and thereby be led to inquire how these vices and distempers may be subdued.

Scougal was speaking to fledgling ministers and he overstated the situation for purposes of emphasis. Actually there were many who did come, and there were others who were held back only by reticence. These people, Baxter suggested, were "unacquainted with this office of the ministry and their own necessity and duty therein," and "it belongeth to us to acquaint them herewith, and to press them publicly to come to us for advice." [63] To encourage them, Baxter established in his home on Thursday evenings what today we might call a clinic for group therapy. Here people gathered to lay bare to one another their own "cases of conscience" and to seek their resolution. This served as a door to further consultation, for Baxter frankly informed them that they must have recourse to ministers "for the resolution of your weighty doubts, in private."

Make use of their help in private and not in public only. As the use of a physician is not only to read a lecture of physic to his patients but to be ready to direct every person according to their particular case . . . , so here it is not the least of the pastoral work to oversee the individuals and to give them personally such particular advice as their case requireth.[64]

John Dod's method was to use the church itself as a place for pastoral counseling that he might be easily accessible and "have room to walk in." There the perplexed would find him.

If he thought them bashful, he would meet them and say, "Would you speak with me?" And when he found them unable to state their question, he would help them out with it, taking care to find the sore, but would answer and deal so compassionately and tenderly as not to discourage the poorest soul from coming again to him.[65]

These were the major facets of the minister's pastoral duty—catechizing, visiting, disciplining, and counseling the members of his flock. As Richard Baxter remarked, it is evident that the pastoral office was much more than "those men have taken it to be, who think it consisteth in preaching and administering sacraments only." [66]

V

While the parish minister, with his broad responsibilities for preaching and pastoral care, was the typical clerical figure, there were other more specialized ministries. There is some question whether or not the parish clerk who set the Psalm and performed other incidental duties, including augmenting his income by the sale of "clerk ales," can properly be regarded as a cleric. The "reader," an office which was briefly and not altogether successfully revived, was an inferior kind of curate who was initially utilized to supplement the inadequate supply of properly beneficed clergy and was later employed in some parishes to read the service so that the preacher could conserve his energies for the sermon. The household or domestic chaplain, on the other hand, had a more definite clerical status and theoretically had the same duties and obligations to the household to which he was attached as a parson to his parish,[67] But more often his major responsibility was serving as tutor to the children of the family. He was often a young man who had taken his degree at the university, but had not as yet been able to secure a parish appointment. Other men frequently found in a chaplaincy a welcome means of escape from the necessity of conforming to the prescribed worship.

In addition to these offices, the parish clergy themselves often displayed diverse talents and developed a specialized ministry of their own. Jeremy Taylor, for example, remarked that the art of counseling "is not every man's trade," and he insisted that "it requires more wisdom and ability to take care of souls than those men, who now-a-days run under the formidable burden of the preacher's office, can bring from the places of their education and first employment." Consequently, there are many "who do what they ought not, and undertake what they cannot perform, and . . . do more hurt to themselves and others than possibly they imagine."[68] Fortunately, the reverse was equally true, and those who did display marked ability in dealing with troubled consciences soon gained a reputation and began to minister to people who lived far beyond their parish. Of a vicar of Newcastle, it is reported that "his known abilities in resolving cases of conscience drew after him a great many good people, not only of his own flock but from remoter distances, who resorted to him as to a common oracle, and commonly went away from him entirely satisfied in his wise and judicious resolutions."[69] Individuals, at the suggestion of their own pastors, frequently traveled great distances to consult the more famous casuists, such as Richard Greenham, John Dod, John Downame, and William Gouge.

An equally obvious specialization was that of preaching, and in connection with preaching a definite office or position developed. This was the lectureship which was usually established in connection with a parish church. The congregation as a whole, or some member or members of it, would undertake to provide the necessary support for a lectureship and would proceed on their own to select the lecturer. The duty of a lecturer was to "lecture" on the Bible—that is, preach—at times other than those set aside for the regular services.

One great advantage of a lectureship was that it allowed men whose consciences were troubled by portions of the Prayer Book to escape the requirement that the prescribed services be read, for the ordinary worship was conducted by the parson and not by the lecturer. There was also a corresponding advantage to the cause which the lecturers had embraced, for dependence upon voluntary support compelled the lecturers to put into plain English for plain people the message of redemption. "If they wished to survive, [they] had to find means to stir imaginations, induce emotional excitement, wring the hearts of sinners, win souls to the Lord, in other words, make themselves heard and felt." [70] So marked was the utility of these preaching posts that a permanently endowed foundation was set up for the planting of preachers at key points throughout the kingdom.

In essence, the lecturers constituted an order of preachers not unlike the older preaching orders of friars, and they presented a similar problem to those in authority. The objective of those establishing lectureships, William Laud complained, was "to make those ministers they preferred independent of the bishops and dependent wholly on them," while John Selden commented that the "lecturers do in a parish church what the friars did heretofore, get away not only the affections but the bounty that should be bestowed upon the minister." [71] In the end, Laud did succeed in dissolving the endowed lectureship foundation, and in 1629 it was ordered that all lecturers should read the service before their lecture and should not be allowed to preach unless they professed their willingness to accept a parish appointment as soon as it could be procured for them. But lectures were not easily suppressed, and they continued to be a prominent feature of church life.

The other clerical offices were mostly those associated with the episcopal staff. The fact that a time had arrived when at least one man was to "prefer a popular lectureship even to a bishopric" [72] was quite as

much a commentary on the decline of the episcopal office in public
esteem at is was an indication of the prestige and influence associated
with an important preaching post. The reason for the diminished
episcopal prestige is not difficult to ascertain. The bishops, while retain-
ing many of their responsibilities, had been stripped of most of their
powers by the Elizabethan settlement, and what was true of the bishops
was equally true of the other members of the diocesan staff. As early as
1558, Thomas Sampson had written to Peter Martyr, saying that he
did not believe he should accept a bishopric "because, through want of
church discipline, the bishop . . . is unable properly to discharge his
office." [73]

R. G. Usher has pointed out that the bishops did not possess the right
to appoint the men they were expected to govern, the prerogative of
determining what sort of men they should be, or the power to discipline
them once they had been inducted.[74] The decision as to qualifications
for ordination had been taken from the bishops by the State, while the
right of nomination to a parish post, after ordination, was largely controlled by lay patrons, and the bishops were forced to induct the
nominee if he met the most meager requirements. About the only test
of the fitness of the man to be inducted that the bishop was permitted
to impose was political. He was directed to admit men who would take
the oath of supremacy and agree to read the service book, and he was
instructed not to make too close an inquiry at other points. Once
installed in his parish, the minister was subject to very little control
by the bishop, and could usually make a successful defense in the
common law courts if the bishop attempted to deprive him of his
"living." The bishop, to be sure, did possess the power of visitation, but
this was a cumbersome procedure and was actually no more than an
inquiry into the conditions which prevailed in the parish. There was
no means by which compliance with ecclesiastical regulations could be
enforced, and the bishop was dependent almost wholly upon voluntary
obedience for the correction of any irregularities which a visitation might
disclose. To put the matter succinctly, it may be said that in practice,
whatever his principles, the Elizabethan parson was an Independent,
and that the Elizabethan situation was later to be roughly approximated
under the voluntary national establishment of the Commonwealth.

The situation did begin to change under Archbishop Whitgift, and
markedly so under Archbishop Bancroft, but it was not due to any new
increment of episcopal power. The new disciplinary authority was
secured by making use of the nonecclesiastical powers of the Court of

High Commission, an arm of the Privy Council, representing the residual powers of the crown to deal with extraordinary situations. Even with the growing stringency resulting from this intervention by the state, the individual parson was still able to maintain a considerable degree of independence. George Herbert commented that his model parson "carries himself very respectfully, as to all the fathers of the church, so especially to his diocesan, honoring him both in word and behavior, and resorting unto him in any difficulty, either in his studies or in his parish," [75] but there is no way of knowing how typical he was in this respect. On the whole, the attempt to exercise supervisory responsibilities remained a frustrating experience for the bishops and the members of their staff.

VI

There was little disposition on the part of anyone prior to the middle of the seventeenth century to minimize the importance of education as a qualification for the ministerial office. Indeed, the emphasis was in quite the contrary direction, for there was a strong insistence upon the necessity for a learned ministry. The person who would teach the mysteries of God, Richard Baxter was to declare, "must not be himself a babe in knowledge," and he must take heed that he "be not unfit for the great employments" which he would undertake.

What qualifications are necessary for that man that hath such a charge upon him as we have! How many difficulties in divinity to to be opened! . . . How many obscure texts of Scripture to be expounded! How many duties to be done, wherein ourselves and others may miscarry, if in the matter . . . they be not well informed! . . . How many weighty and yet intricate cases of conscience have we almost daily to resolve! Can so much work and such work as this be done by raw, unqualified men?[76]

Thus, as Henry Scougal was to explain, it was necessary for a minister to spend "his time and much of his fortune in the schools of the prophets to fit himself" for his calling.[77]

The universities had always been regarded as the seedbed of the clergy and, as the sixteenth century moved to its close, it became increasingly the normal expectation that a minister should possess a university degree. Indicative of the concern for a more adequate supply of properly educated clergy was the founding of two new colleges specifically for the training of ministers as well as the establishment of newly endowed scholarships and lectureships with a similar purpose in mind at the older colleges. Basically, it was the old medieval program of instruction to which they were subjected. Rhetoric, logic, metaphysics, Latin, and some Greek were the major disciplines to be mastered for the bachelor of arts degree; and in the study of these disciplines, even in colleges dominated by Puritan influence, Aristotle, Cicero, Ovid, Demosthenes, and Homer occupied a conspicuous place. Lectures in Biblical theology had been introduced into the universities early in the sixteenth century, but the study of theology was officially restricted to those who were pursuing advanced degrees. The deficiencies of the formal course of study, so far as preparation for the ministry was concerned, were partially remedied by the tutors who directed their scholars into wider fields of reading, especially of the Bible and theological treatises. It became customary for the student to compile from his reading "a body of divinity," which would serve as "the storehouse of his sermons" and from which he would preach and teach "all his life." [78] In addition, he was constantly exposed to able preaching and was usually directed by his tutor to model his own pulpit discourse after the pattern provided by these exemplars of the homiletical art.

The greatest deficiency in the program of study was generally held to be the failure to provide instruction in the field of pastoral counseling, and it was not until late in the seventeenth century that professorships of moral theology or casuistry began to be established to meet this need. Even before the beginning of the seventeenth century, however, this deficiency was being remedied in two different ways. One method was to provide ministers with manuals or directories which they might keep close at hand for guidance in resolving the cases of conscience which were brought to them. The other method was for older ministers who were especially skilled in the art of counseling and who were keenly aware of its importance to establish a kind of post graduate seminar in their homes for the instruction of young men in this area of pastoral care prior to the beginning of their ministry. Thus Richard Greenham opened his home at Dry Drayton to recent graduates of the university "that thereby he might train up some younger men to this end and communicate his experience to them." [79] This practice seems to have been fairly extensive during the first half of the seventeenth century, and it appears that the tutors developed working arrangements with particular ministers to whom they directed their students.

The ideal of an educated ministry did not come into question in any serious way prior to the outbreak of the Civil War, and even then the "mechanick preachers" did not find too many defenders. The opposition to an insistence upon the necessity for an educated ministry was the product of several factors. In part, it stemmed from a rising lay spirit in the church.[80] For almost a century, the constitution of the church as well as the exigencies of politics had conspired to thrust the laity forward into positions of leadership in religious affairs. Furthermore, the laity had been constantly reminded of their priestly role and had been urged to read the Bible for themselves rather than meekly to accept the word of their preachers. If the simplest man was able to apprehend for himself all that was necessary to salvation, the question might properly arise, what need was there for that teaching which could be found only in the schools?

Another current which led in this direction was the insistence upon the necessity for a converted ministry. George Herbert had suggested that the aim and labor of students preparing for the ministry must be not only to get knowledge

but to subdue and mortify all lusts and affections, and not to think that, when they have read the fathers or schoolmen, a minister is made and the thing is done. The greatest and hardest preparation is within.[81]

In similar vein, William Perkins declared: "He must first be godly affected himself who would stir up godly affections in other men." [82] From the insistence that the minister must be godly, it was but a short step to an insistence that godliness is more important than intellectual competence; and from this some drew the illogical conclusion that education was not necessary.

Still another tendency which led in an anti-intellectual direction had its ultimate roots in the doctrine that every vocation is a divine "calling." Thus John Milton said that it is "the inward calling of God that makes a minister." [83] Milton went on to insist that "the ministerial gifts" need to be "manured" and improved by "painful study," but there were others who were to suggest that the inward call itself was sufficient. To those who insisted that knowledge of Greek and Hebrew were indispensable for the interpretation of Scripture, John Goodwin and Samuel Richardson could reply that this might be granted if the original copies of Scripture were extant, but since they were not and since the existing texts could not be certified as free from the errors of the copyists, the scholars were as dependent as the ordinary man upon the gift of the Spirit for the proper interpretation of the Biblical text. Finally, an appeal could always be made to the eminent gifts of a John Bunyan as justification for not insisting unduly that education was indispensable in the ministry.

Basically, however, it was the religious excitement of the Civil War period coupled with the collapse of the established religious structure that thrust forward for a brief time the "mechanick preacher" as a conspicuous figure in English religious life. If this lay preacher tradition was perpetuated to a degree in the dissenting churches, it was partly the consequence of the exclusion of the dissenters from the universities. This much is evident: as soon as a measure of freedom was recovered by the dissenting churches, they busied themselves with the founding of academies which were to play a not insignificant role in the training of ministers for the established church as well as for their own churches.

The lay preacher, then, was a minor figure who was not to come into his own in any significant fashion until the evangelical revivals of the eighteenth century. On the whole, throughout the period we have been considering, it was recognized that while "religion is every man's general calling," "it hath pleased the divine wisdom to call forth a select number of men who, being delivered from those entanglements [of worldly affairs] and having their minds more highly purified and more peculiarly fitted for the offices of religion, may attend continually on that very thing." [84] The task these ministers set before themselves, as they readily admitted, was far beyond their own competency to perform and it demanded not only the most earnest efforts to improve their gifts and the most rigorous budgeting of their time but a constant dependence upon God for success. A consistent feature of all the manuals dealing with the ministerial function was the recurrent reminder that the minister must never forget his high calling, and must never "study the gentleman so much" that he "forgets the clergyman." [85]

FOR FURTHER READING

Richard Baxter, *Gildas Salvianus: The Reformed Pastor*, 2nd ed. by John T. Williams (Chicago, 1950).

George Herbert, *The Country Parson*.

William Haller, *The Rise of Puritanism* (New York, 1938).

————, *Liberty and Reformation in the Puritan Revolution* (New York, 1955).

James Maclear, "The Making of the Lay Tradition," *Journal of Religion*, XXXIII, No. 2, 1953.

J. T. McNeill, "Casuistry in the Puritan Age," *Religion in Life*, 1943, XII.

Norman Sykes, *Old Priest and New Presbyter* (Cambridge, 1956).

VIII

The Rise of the Evangelical Conception of the Ministry in America (1607-1850)

SIDNEY E. MEAD

The whole history of the Church confirms the sentiment taught expressly in many passages of Scripture, and by implication, on every page of the New Testament, that the great agency appointed and employed of God in the work of instructing and saving men, is the living ministry of Christianity.[1]

The intent of this chapter is to discuss what the conception of the ministry and the practice of the ministers tended to become in America—and why—during the two hundred and fifty years from the planting of the first permanent English colony in 1607 to the stabilization of the new nation on the verge of the Civil War. It is designed primarily to help to provide a historical background and context for the discussions of the problems of the ministry today. In the mind of the author, it is one of his "essays to do good" by making a contribution to the kind of self-understanding that is the peculiar province of historical interpretations to provide. Such an approach demands the sketching in of a broad historical setting for the developments which are the immediate concern of the work. This will help to explain why the essay begins with matters apparently far off from the ministry itself, although the intention is to include nothing that does not contribute to a direct answer to the question stated in the first sentence.

I

The most obvious characteristic of organized Christianity in America is its diversity and fragmentation into many independent bodies, which makes it almost impossible for the historian to generalize about it with any assurance. It is a commonplace that the explanation of most of this striking diversity is transplantation through immigration. By the decade of 1850-60 America had become the repository of offshoots of almost all the religious groups of mother Europe, had added a few of her own, and all were luxuriating under the warm and vivifying sun of religious freedom and stimulated by the fertile opportunities for life and expansion offered by practically unlimited social and geographical space.

But just as the "American," as Crevecoeur noted, while first of all a transplanted European had nevertheless become a new creature, so these many transplanted European religious groups, although bearing enough family resemblance to their Old World progenitors to be recognized as of direct descent, yet had all been changed by the subtle magic of the new land and were different from any previous churches in Christendom. Hence the common descriptive categories of "church" and "sect"; of "right-wing" and "left-wing" Protestantism which make sense in distinguishing the divisions of Old World Christianity, are not applicable without confusion and distortion to the American scene. For there by around 1850 "churches" and "sects" as known in Europe had disappeared, while characteristics of both had been merged with others improvised to meet new situations to make the "denomination" and the "society"—two distinctively American organizational forms. Unlike traditional churches, the definitive nature of these forms was neither confessional nor territorial, and they were neither Erastian nor Theocratic in relation to civil government, but "free." And since there were no longer "churches," neither were any appropriately called "sects" in the traditional sense. Rather the denominations and their arms for co-operative endeavors, the Societies, were primarily purposive, voluntary associations engaged in the free society in the propagandization of the Gospel—each according to its own light, understanding, and ingenuity. Meanwhile, in the great bulk of American Protestantism an "evangelical" understanding of the faith had gradually supplanted the traditional sacramental outlook. With these great shifts extending over two centuries and a half and culminating in America in the decade of the 1850s, both the conception of the ministry and the practical life of the minister were metamorphosed into ways of thinking and doing that were different from anything previously known in Christendom.

II

The principle of adaptation . . . is certainly the life and virtue of the voluntary system.[2]

At the time when Englishmen first set their feet on America's eastern seaboard with the purpose of remaining as settlers, the prevailing intention was colonization—the projection of the empire into outposts where loyal citizens might reap profits from virgin land, unmined hills, unfished seas, and uncut forests. This called for the planting of small replicas of English towns with all their accepted customs, manners, and forms based on and cemented together with the true Christian religion as "now professed and established within our realm of England." England of course was passionately Protestant—at least as passionately so as the phlegmatic reserve of the English made possible and respectable. From the glorious days of their virgin Queen, after whom the first permanent colony was named, Protestantism had of necessity been synonymous with patriotism, and the clergyman-chaplain who accompanied the first expedition was recognized as the emissary of the "supreme Governor" of the *English* Church as well as of Christ, and as such was accorded the deference due his doubly representative office. The first charters and laws reveal the assumption that such position and deference would be maintained—with authority backed by coercive power if necessary—so that the Establishment would be perpetuated.

But the English Establishment itself was a majestic and dignified breezeway between Catholicism and Protestantism, firmly attached to both, but too open either to obstruct the passing zephyr or be permanently injured by offering too rigid a resistance to the hurricane. It was a magnificent exemplificaiton of the English genius for compromise and adaptation—qualities giving those who possessed them a high survival value in the emerging new world of rapid change bordering on turmoil. These people, even in their darkest hours, could say with almost irritating nonchalance, "There will always be an England"—but without meaning thereby that it must necessarily be exactly like the England I know. John Robinson spoke as much as an Englishmen as a Christian when he reminded his Pilgrim flock on the eve of their departure that there might be yet more light to break forth from the Word of God. Even the angular-minded New England Puritan Biblicist recognized that "it is the way of Christ in the Gospel to set up the practice of his Institutions as the necessities of the people call for them." [3] In 1767 the arch-Anglican, Dr. Thomas Chandler of New Jersey, reflected the same sentiment by insisting that while Episcopacy was of divine right and as obligatory as "baptism or the holy eucharist," yet "bishops according to the belief of the church of England, are necessary only where they can be had!" [4] Thus, foreshadowing what we have come to regard as something typical of the American mentality, when "all of Europe's logic" found itself arrayed against "all of New England's experience," it was the experience that won and became decisive.[5]

One may say that the trait here suggested indicates a genius for improvisation—or a somewhat stupid dependence on "muddling through"—or a tenacious belief in general revelation—but recognized it must be. And historically it sets the English empire apart from the Catholic Spanish and French empires, which were born with a kind of institutional rigor mortis that confused forms with godliness and made adaptation next to impossible. We may contrast this rigorism with Nathaniel Ward's dictum as the self-appointed spokesman for the most rigid of the English—the Bay Puritans—that while Scriptural injunctions make it impossible for the State "to give an Affirmative Toleration to any false Religion, or Opinion whatsoever" on the basis of concession as a right, yet it "must connive in some Cases." [6]

"Connive" the colonists did all up and down the coast, and for so many reasons, and with such a motley host of dissenters, that finally the nice distinction between concession of principle and connivance in practice was itself lost in the intricate web of argumentation necessary for its maintenance. Step by step they "adapted" themselves into a positive defense of religious diversity which spelled out religious freedom. Indeed, religious freedom was in a real sense the elevation of "connivance" forced by necessity to the eminence of a principle of action.

Adaptation was thrust upon the ministers from the beginning. Typical was the Rev. Jonas Michaëlius of New Amsterdam who, in explaining to his brethren back home in 1628 some of the irregularities attending the formation of his church and why he departed from its accepted forms in administering the Lord's Supper to the French "in the French language, and according to the French mode," noted simply that "one cannot observe strictly all the usual formalities in making a beginning under such circumstances." [7] Willingly or not, graciously or grudgingly, all the ministers who came had to recognize this bare fact or die with their churches. It is the combined experience of such people in all the churches that spells out the overall motif of adaptation.

III

But the English while showing a genius for adaptation have commonly appeared to be backing into the future by supporting even their revolutions by appeal to the past—to Magna Carta and the traditional rights of Englishmen—thus in their way showing "a decent respect to the [accepted] opinions of mankind." In this regard, for example, the American Revolution was no exception, and while Ezra Stiles applauded Jefferson in 1783 because he had "poured the soul of the continent into the monumental act of independence," yet he could not forbear exclaiming: "O *England!* how did I once love thee? how did I once glory in thee!" until "some demon whispered folly into the present reign." [8]

In religious affairs this is paralleled by the tendency chronic in Christendom but perhaps more acute among Englishmen, to support every contemporary innovation by an appeal to "primitive Christianity." Thus John Wesley in 1784, after vainly trying to get the Anglican bishops to ordain his Methodist preachers for America, proceeded to a kind of Presbyterian ordination—explaining that he had remembered or discovered precedent therefor in the practice of the ancient church at Alexandria. In this act of his evangelical contemporary Benjamin Franklin might have seen another illustration of what a "convenient thing it is to be a *reasonable Creature,* since it enables one to find or make a Reason for everything one has a mind to do." [9] Actually, however, he and his fellow Deists were not too different from the clerical innovators, for they rested their attack against contemporary ecclesiastical institutions on the pure religion and morals of Jesus—whom they saw as the first great Deist!

It should not surprise us to note that throughout the whole period of rapid adaptation to the exigencies of the "frontier" through the change of old and the proliferation of new forms, most of the ministerial leaders continued to insist, and apparently to believe, that there was really nothing new but only the repristination of the apostolic and hence normative ways. In 1783 Ezra Stiles was "not simply satisfied, but sure, from a thorough perlustration of all ecclesiastical history, that they [Congregational churches] are nearly apostolical as to *doctrine* and *polity."* Indeed, he added, there is "no *doctrine* no *ordinance* or institution of the primitive church, but may be found in general reception and observance among us." [10] This tendency helps to explain the somewhat puzzling fact that although the ministers of America have been the most pragmatic of all, and have been inclined to agree with Thomas Jefferson that "if we are Protestants we reject all tradition," nevertheless, they have in profession been the most extensively and woodenly Biblicistic.

IV

The times in which we live, as also the state of our American churches, have each their peculiarities, tending to modify very considerably the duties of pastors.[11]

Throughout the complicated process of adaptation to the exigencies of the new situation faced in America, one institutional development stands out as having tremendous influence on the conception and practice of the ministry, namely, the tendency in all the transplanted churches of whatever polity to gravitate toward an actual "congregationalism" or localism. Leonard Bacon, long-time pastor of Center Church in New Haven and perhaps more to be remembered for substance than for wit, noted in May, 1852, that "parochial and self-governed churches . . . is the distinctively American method of religious organization." [12] This was not just an exhibition of New England provincialism or Congregational bias, but an essentially correct historical observation.

During the early planting days of small things all the churches, whatever their polity and however rigidly it was insisted upon, had to begin as local, particular congregations whose ministers only later could be drawn together into Presbyteries, Ministeriums, Conventions, Conferences, or whatever their traditional polity called for. Meanwhile, the minister was likely to be completely isolated from the sustaining power and status-giving context of his church, and, thrown into intimate face-to-face contact with his lay people, made dependent upon his own character and something as intangible to most colonists as "the Spirit" for whatever of prestige he could gain and leadership he could give. Henry M. Muhlenberg, sent from Germany via England in 1742 to set the disordered Lutheran house in order and save it from Count Zinzendorf's brand of unification, discovered on the eve of his arrival in the Philadelphia area that

A preacher must fight his way through with the Sword of the Spirit alone and depend upon faith in the living God and His promises, if he wants to be a preacher and proclaim the truth [in America].[13]

In this situation the laity, in the absence of any visible and present reminders of ecclesiastical ubiquity and power to awe or influence them, tasted and relished the possibilities of control to such an extent that later they only grudgingly could be induced to surrender a part—and among Protestants they never surrendered all of it.

This development is most strikingly illustrated in the history of the Church of England in the colonies, which in the South was established from the beginning by the Charters, rather consistently supported by successive laws, and generally nurtured by the civil rulers. But with real Episcopal control as far away as London and tangibly represented only by relatively ineffective Commissaries, overall supervision of the scattered parishes theoretically devolved upon the Governor and Assembly while in practice actual control fell into the hands of lay Vestries. Thus the Vestries in America soon gained effective control of the spirituals as well as the temporals of the churches, largely through assuming power to hire and set the salary of the clergyman, plus a studied neglect of presenting him to the Governor for permanent induction into the "living" until forced to do so.[14] "In 1697 the Archbishop of Canterbury expressed surprise that the clergymen might 'be removed like domestic servants by a vote of the Vestry,'"[15] but obviously neither he nor anyone could do anything about it.

Further, because of the scarcity of regular clergymen the custom of hiring lay readers became common, and in some places these congregationally appointed officers were the backbone of the church.[16] Hence it is not surprising that from an early date the greatest coolness toward and open opposition to completion of the Anglican Church in the colonies with an Episcopate came precisely from those areas where that Church was ostensibly established. William White declared in 1782 that

there cannot be produced an instance of lay-men in America, unless in the very infancy of the settlements, soliciting the introduction of a bishop; it was probably by a great majority of them thought an hazardous experiment.[17]

Even the Venerable Society with all its resources, prestige, power, and numerous dedicated missionaries was unable during the eighteenth century to make effective headway toward an Episcopate, and for the want thereof, the missionaries spearheaded the calling of "conventions" of the clergy in the 1760's. One or another of these conventions asserted the "right to interfere in parochial affairs," recommended men for missions, effectively protested the settlement of others, and ruled that every priest "should consider himself obliged to attend the stated meetings."[18] It is obvious that these conventions greatly resembled the New

England Congregationalists' ministerial associations, although they actually wielded much less power because it was only assumed. However, they were effective enough to alarm some church authorities in England at this show of "Independency" on the part of their daughter in the colonies.

Small wonder that the Anglican missionaries began sadly to report that Dissenters were saying that "they saw no advantage in conforming, because there was 'no material Difference between ye Church & Themselves," and Dr. Chandler in 1771 expressed the prophetic fear that

possibly in Time we may come to think that ye Unity of Christ's Body is a chimerical Doctrine—that Schism is an Ecclesiastical Scarecrow—& that Episcopal is no better than ye leathern Mitten Ordination.[19]

After the achievement of independence when the Episcopal Church of its own volition got an Episcopate, and in spite of the pompous pretensions and sober protestations of such High-churchmen as Connecticut's Samuel Seabury, the new American church in order to attain organization on a national scale had to make the lay voice in its councils an essential part of its being.

This had been anticipated by the Rev. William White who had warned in August, 1782, that the outcome of the Revolution had broken both the civil and ecclesiastical chains that heretofore had held the Episcopal churches together, and hence "their future continuance can be provided for only by voluntary associations [of discrete churches] for union and good government," for in America there "will be an equality of the churches; and not, as in England, the subjection of all parish churches to their respective cathedrals." And this, he thought, will make it "necessary to deviate from the practice (though not from the principles) of that Church, by convening the clergy and laity in one body." The former, he predicted, will "have an influence proportional to the opinion entertained of their piety and learning," and he hoped they would never "wish to usurp an exclusive right of regulation." [20]

Later developments attested to White's prophetic ability. By the 1850's it was a commonplace observation that in America the Episcopalians "have allowed the laity a share in ecclesiastical legislation and administration, such as the high church in England never granted" and that as a matter of fact even a bishop "maintains his authority for the most part only by his personal character and judicious counsel." [21] In this respect they were hardly distinguishable from, and certainly no more securely authoritarian than, the clergy of the congregationally organized denominations. In fact in 1836 Calvin Colton, erstwhile Presbyterian minister and journalist who had recently been converted to the Episcopal Church, argued with convincing cogency that in the government of the Church of his present choice constitutional provisions provided for more lay power than in the other denominations. No one, he thought, could deny that the Secretary of the America Home Missionary Society actually wielded more uncontrolled power than "the whole college of Bishops presiding over the Episcopal Church of the United States" since "the clergy Employed" and "the congregations assisted" and "the kind of doctrine [permitted] to its beneficiaries" was "under the absolute control of the society." [22]

But of course by this time the acceptance of religious freedom and separation had changed all the one-time churches and sects into voluntary associations and had shorn their ministers of all but persuasive or political power.

As might be expected the most radical congregational development—which somewhere along the line assumed that eloquently descriptive title of "local autonomy"—took place in the churches of the Bay. It is not commonly noted that this *was* something evolved in the process of adaptation and not the original intention. One cannot here retell the extremely complex story pictured in exquisite detail in Perry Miller's *From Colony to Province*. Sufficient to note that the original overall conception was that of "a speaking aristocracy in the face of a silent democracy"—the former being in the local church a kind of ministerial presbytery "not one among the membership, but a separate power [ordained by Christ], holding a veto upon the people," and in the community at large the General Court in its civil-ecclesiastical capacity plus the Synod which alone had the power to declare the truth which bound the consciences of all men. [23] But in the tumultuous days of the "Half-Way Covenant" discussions when a faction of the First Church in Boston withdrew to form the Third (or Old South) Church and called for a council, the loyal members under the aged John Davenport "defied the entire polity by saying 'that to grant a Council tends to overthrow the Congregational way'" and Davenport urged the Court not to "further 'men's opinions' even though these be 'consented to by the major part of a Topical Synod.'" Meanwhile, as the local churches were revolting against overall control, there was widespread revolt against the power of the ministers in the local churches until "after the Reforming Synod [of 1697], the clergy found themselves shorn of every weapon except moral persuasion, and their threat of [Divine] vengeance." And already, as Urian Oakes had declared in 1673 "in many churches 'a few Pragmatical and Loquacious men' are . . . exercising real power, while the constituted authority is helpless." [24]

Connecticut Congregationalism did not move as far or as fast in this direction. There the essence of the "Proposals" which had failed in Massachusetts were incorporated into civil-ecclesiastical law through the Saybrook Platform of 1708 which so effectively "Presbyterianized" the Congregationalism of this self-styled land of "sober-habits" that its leaders commonly made no distinction between the two polities. Indeed, Lyman Beecher thought that "a Presbytery made up of New England men, raised Congregationalists, is the nearest the Bible of anything there is." [25] That such "Presbyteries" were effective is made clear by the short and efficient way in which the Associations and Consociations of Connecticut eliminated the budding Arian and Socinian ministers from their midst at the opening of the nineteenth century. But soon thereafter Connecticut Congregationalism in the midst of theological and ecclesiastical controversy "trotted after the Bay horse" as the die-hards said, along the road to "local autonomy"—a trend that was augmented by the revolt against supposed Presbyterian encroachments under the Plan of Union in the New England diaspora.

Washington Gladden, that eminent representative man of nineteenth-century Congregationalism, while advocating a modified socialism in political and economic affairs, as ardently advocated anarchy in ecclesiastical matters. By "the primary Congregational principle," he concluded, each church had "the right to make its own creed." And since the old creeds "had become utterly antiquated" his own personal theology within the vague limits of "a brief confession of the 'evangelical faith'" "had to be hammered out on the anvil for daily use in the pulpit. The pragmatic test was the only one that could be applied to it: 'Will it work?'" [26]

Similar developments took place among the Presbysterians and have been precisely delineated by Professor Trinterud in his excellent reappraisal of their colonial period. [27] Within that Church the course of the controversies over the revivals tended to demonstrate the impossibility in the long run of any effective ecclesiastical control according to traditional standards over those considered to be innovators, heretics, or schismatics if they had the support of a local church and a group of like-minded cohorts—and if their efforts were "successful" in producing tangible results.

However, the Presbyterians so far as the clergy were concerned did not move even as far as the Episcopalians toward congregational control. This was partly because of their form of government and their long experience in running their own affairs both as an Established Church and as dissenters. But the struggle for dominance between Synod and Presbytery in which the latter won at least the crucial right of control over examinations for ordination, permitted thereafter within the overall context of the denomination a kind of "localism"—that is, for example, one presbytery might emphasize Christian experience judged by one's "walk," and another correctness of doctrine judged by subscription to the accepted standards.

Henceforth this kind of "localism" has been an essential characteristic of the free-churches, and a barrier to any tendencies toward overall uniformity imposed from above. Its development, and the more radical congregationalism described, meant that the minister in whatever church was from an early date placed in an intimate relationship with the lay people, and was maintained and if necessary judged by them or by his neighboring peers in the ministry. Not all of the laity were as crudely assertive as Crevecoeur's "Low Dutchman" who, that "American farmer" said,

conceives no other idea of a clergyman than that of a hired man; if he does his work well he will pay him the stipulated sum; if not he will dismiss him, and do without his sermons, and let his church be shut up for years.[28]

But the laity were in a position to wield decisive power in every denomination.

And this did a great deal to prepare the ministers for separation by training them in dependence upon persuasion unbacked by even a possibility of coercive power, and teaching them reliance upon political sagacity and the necessity for very down-to-earth political activity at least in ecclesiastical affairs. Under freedom and separation such action was no longer optional, but necessary, and de Tocqueville should not have been as surprised as he apparently was to discover that in America everywhere "you meet with a politician where you expected to find a priest." [29] Horace Bushnell in 1854 uttered the fervent prayer in a letter to a friend:

May God in his mercy deliver me . . . from all this ecclesiastical brewing of scandals and heresies, the wire-pulling, the schemes to get power or to keep it, the factions got up to ventilate wounded pride and get compensation for the chagrin of defeat. . . . Lord save me from it![30]

But the very vehemence of his utterance betrays his awareness of the real situation—that there was no balm for the politically allergic in the American denominational Gilead.

Lyman Beecher described the true situation.

No minister can be forced upon his people, without their suffrage and voluntary support. Each pastor stands upon his own character and deeds, without anything to break the force of his responsibility to his people.[31]

This kind of political relationship, because of overt and immediate dependence upon the local congregation, tended to make the American minister—unless of more than average abilities or wealth—very sensitive to the peculiar provincialisms of his parish and often subservient to and the spokesman for them. And this often created within him a strong tension between the universality of the Christian Gospel and the limits imposed by a parochial layman's apprehension of it, thus many times in effect imposing upon him the hard choice between applying his professed standards of Christian love and justice to the local scene and securing food, clothing, and shelter for himself and family. When this situation is recognized one is in a position to realize that the remarkable thing is not that ministers were sometimes timid, evasive, and time-serving, but that as a whole they displayed such a degree of efficiently applied dedication, intelligence, and courage that the sober foreign visitor was led to declare in 1845 that "in the active discharge of the duties of their office they perhaps surpass all" ministers in other countries.[32] This is a tribute both to their adherence to the Christian faith—wherein they might appear to be as harmless as doves—and to their political sagacity—wherein they had to be as wise as serpents.

V

. . . a grand truth of revelation [is] the divine unity of the Church. We have all, who love our Lord Jesus Christ in sincerity, substantially *one Lord, one faith, and one baptism.* We are all *called in one hope of our calling,* and in one body, and that the body of Christ. We have all one Saviour, one Gospel, one Bible, one Heaven, one destination, one and the same eternal home; by whatever name we may here be called.[33]

Throughout the long hard process of institutional adaptation to the exigencies of a new world during which traditional churches and sects were metamorphosed into denominations and a kind of congregationalism came to prevail in every group as lay influence burgeoned, the spiritual and ideological apprehension of the faith itself was being transformed from one primarily ritualistic and sacerdotal to one primarily evangelical—a change that greatly affected the whole conception of the ministry.

It is extremely difficult to trace this change and give it historical structure amidst all the diversity and contending claims of the American denominations, since what happened was due more to a subtle change of emphasis than to the introduction of new elements. It was merely that something which had always been represented in Christianity by a minority voice gained the dominant voice in America by around 1850 —but perhaps in the perspective of history only temporarily so.

As Dr. Hudson notes, this subtle change began during the Reformation in England with the gradual fading of emphasis on the sacerdotal aspect of the ministry, and it is further complicated by being inextricably bound up with the corresponding change that took place in the conception of society and its ·government. Both were carried to their logical and perhaps "enthusiastic" extreme in the United States.

At the dawn of England's colonial thrust into the American continent, the prevailing view did not distinguish between the ends of State and Church—the two being conceived indeed as "personally one Society, which society . . . [is] termed a Commonwealth as it liveth under whatsoever form of secular law and regiment, a Church as it hath the spiritual law of Jesus Christ." [34] Thus the whole venture in Virginia was premised upon the view that the King's "principall care" in all his "Realmes" was "true Religion, and reverence to God," defined, as in the first Charter, "according to the doctrine, rights, and religion now professed and established within our realme of England." Hence, as declared in 1610, "our primarie end is to plant religion, our secondarie and subalternate ends are for the honour and profit of our nation."[35] Therefore all laws and regulations were designed in order that "all his [the King's] forces wheresoever" might "let their waies be like his ends, for the glorie of God" from whom "we must alone expect our success." Hence there were elaborately detailed laws "declared against what Crimes soeurer, whether against the diuine Maiesty of God, or our soueraigne, and Liege Lord, King *Iames*" with the threat of death for anyone who "shall willingly absent himselfe, when hee is summoned to take the oath of Supremacy."[36]

Within this context, in many areas the representative of the king was interchangeable with that of the archbishop. For exmple, the clergymen, in the absence of bishops, were subject to being "censured for their negligence by the Governor" and even threatened with "losing their Entertainment."[37] The minister's duties as emissary of both Christ and King were defined in detail by law. He was to preach every Sabbath morning 'after diuine Seruice," to "catechise in the afternoon," to "say the diuine seruice twice euery-day," morning and evening, to "preach euery Wednesday," and to "keepe a faithful and true Record . . . of all Christnings, Marriages, and deaths" within this parish. He was to "chuse vnto him, foure of the most religious and better disposed" men to inform him of "the abuses and neglects of the people in their duties, and seruice to God" and to help him oversee the upkeep of Church property.[38]

The *Lavves Diuine, Morall and Martiall &c,* codified and published in 1612 in order that all residents might "take survey of their duties, and carrying away the tenour of the same, meditate & bethinke how safe, quiet, and comely it is to be honest, just, and ciuill,"[39] make two things clear—that the savage punishments threatened would guarantee that the offender's life would be neither safe nor quiet, and that the "duties" were primarily what we should call religious observances. The Laws of 1619 which passed the newly formed representative House of Burgessès, while mitigating the punishments threatened, defined the duties of the clergyman almost word for word as did the earlier laws. And they emphasize the official oneness of Church and State by stipulating that a Church member for "enormous sinnes" might be suspended "by the minister," but that excommunication required the approval of a regular

Quarterly meeting of "all the ministers" *and* the consent of the Governor
—wherewith the offender was subject to seizure of person and confisca-
tion of goods.[40]

That from the beginning the routine observances of the Church in
the worship of God were deemed an essential aspect of the being and
well-being of the Commonwealth is made abundantly clear from the
early records. John Smith in 1630, in answering criticisms of the colony
current in England, recalled that

> When I first went to *Virginia,* I well remember wee did hang an awning
> (which is an old saile) to three or foure trees to shadow us from the Sunne, our
> walles were rales of wood, our seats unhewed trees till we cut plankes, our Pulpit
> a bar of wood nailed to two neighboring trees. In foule weather we shifted into
> an old rotten tent; for we had few better. . . . This was our Church, till wee
> built a homely thing like a barne, set upon Cratchets, covered with rafts, sedge,
> and earth; so was also the walles . . . that could neither well defend [from] wind
> nor raine.
>
> Yet wee had daily Common Prayer morning and evening, every Sunday two
> Sermons, and every three moneths the holy Communion, till our Minister died:
> but our Prayers daily, with an Homily on Sundaies, we continued two or three
> yeares after, till more Preachers came: and surely God did most mercifully heare
> us. . . .[41]

The overall conception, then, was that of the sacramental efficacy of
the regular observances of the Church in relationship to the State, in
which the work of the priest-clergy was to direct all the individuals
composing the dual Society into the daily walk defined by the Church,
for the sanctifying of the whole. This it was that assured that "their
waies . . . like his [the King's] ends" were all "for the glory of God."

This overall conception—defined with varying degrees of clarity and
insisted upon with varying degrees of rigor in particular times and places
—together with the consequent priestly conception of the nature and
work of the ministry—remained the predominant one in the Church of
England in the colonies. In spite of all colonial vicissitudes the formal
definition of the work of the ministry remained as stated in the Virginia
laws of 1619: "duely [to] read divine service, and exercise their ministerial function according to the Ecclesiastical laws and orders of the
Churche of Englande. . . ."[42] Thus the goal and the determination of
the generations of dedicated ministers who served the English Church

throughout this period might be expressed in the words of that early governor of Virginia, Sir Thomas Dale. The chief end, he suggested, is "to build God a Church," and in order to do this "I am bound in conscience" to leave "all contenting pleasures and mundall delights, to reside here [Virginia] with much turmoile, which I will rather doe than see God's glory diminished, my King and Country dishonoured, and these poore soules I haue in charge reuined." [43]

But meanwhile the complex movements of history had pushed concern for the individual "poore soules" into the foreground of service for "God's glory," while the communal concern suggested by the words for "King and Country" tended to fade into the misty background of consciousness. William White recognized in 1782 that the future of the Episcopal Church in America, where the distinction between "Church" and "Dissenters" would not be known, depended on *not* "confounding english episcopacy, with the subject at large." But, he noted,

unhappily there are some, in whose ideas the existence of their church is so connected with that of the civil government of Britain, as to preclude their concurrence in any system, formed on a presumed final separation of the two countries.[44]

The old conception was long in dying in the Episcopal Church—and perhaps it never really died at all—as witness the repeated suggestion that the name be changed to The National Church of America, not to mention the continuing deference paid to Canterbury.

But when White wrote in 1782 Methodist preachers had already been welcomed by the Rev. Devereaux Jarrett into the bosom of the Church of England in Virginia. Two years later they would go their separate way—with John Wesley's reluctant blessing, and with his injunction uppermost in their minds: "You have nothing to do but save souls." Here was suggested the very center of the evangelical conception of the ministry—something quite different from the English episcopal view.

On the graph of the history of Christianity in America the great curve of "evangelical" Protestantism turns upward from the beginning of the revivals which swept the colonies from the 1720's, moves sharply upward with freedom and separation, and reaches its highest point sometime in the 1840's. The Rev. Albert Barnes—that distinguished Presbyterian minister and careful scholar whose *Commentaries* sold over a million copies—stood very near the peak in 1840 when he wrote:

We [evangelicals] regard the prevailing spirit of Episcopacy, in all aspects, high and low, as at variance with the spirit of the age and of this land. This is an age of freedom, and man *will* be free. The religion of forms is the stereotyped wisdom or folly of the past, and does not adapt itself to the free movements, the enlarged views, the varying plans of this age. The spirit of this age demands that there shall be freedom in religion; that it shall not be fettered or suppressed; that it shall go forth to the conquest of the world. It is opposed to all bigotry and uncharitableness; to all attempts to "unchurch" others; to teaching that they worship in conventicles, that they are dissenters, or that they are left to the uncovenanted mercies of God. All such language did better in the days of Laud and Bonner than now. . . . The spirit of this land is, that the church of Christ is not under the Episcopal form, or the Baptist, the Methodist, the Presbyterian, or the Congregational form exclusively; all are, to all intents and purposes, to be recognized as parts of the one holy catholic church. . . . There is a spirit in this land which requires that the gospel shall depend for its success not on solemn processions and imposing rites; not on the idea of superior sanctity in the priesthood in virtue of their office; not on genuflections and ablutions; not on any virtue conveyed by the imposition of holy hands, and not on union with any particular church, but on solemn appeals to the reason, the conscience, the immortal hopes and fear of men, attended by the holy influences of the Spirit of God. . . . [45]

During that decade the Rev. Robert Baird, in his treatise on *Religion in America,* reflected current acceptation by dividing all the Protestant denominations into "evangelical" and "unevangelical." The former, he said, were characterized by adherence to the great doctrines that Christians had always deemed essential for salvation, plus (although he did not use this terminology) explicit individual apprehension of the faith through a conversion experience. Church polity, he intimated, whether Episcopal, Presbyterian, or Congregational, was a matter of human preference, perhaps largely determined by tradition.

Baird's contemporary exponent of "American Lutheranism," Samuel Simon Schmucker (1799-1873), agreed that there are fundamental "unchangeable . . . points of doctrine, experience, and duty in the Christian religion . . . which, in the judgment of the great mass of the Protestant churches, are clearly revealed in God's Word." But, he thought, "whilst each denomination must naturally prefer its own peculiarities"—as we *"Lutherans* . . . prefer the doctrines, the organization and usages of the American Lutheran Church"—it would be a "dangerous error" to regard "these peculiarities as equal in importance with the great fundamentals of our holy religion, held in common by all." In summary he quoted with approval Professor Samuel Miller of Princeton (where he had received his seminary training), that "it would never occur to us to place the peculiarities of our creed among the fundamentals of our common Christianity." [46]

Concurrent with the development of this sense of common evangelical Protestant doctrines during the two hundred years of fragmentation into denominations in America, had come the increasing emphasis on a personal conversion experience which had spawned the "revival system" as a means of reaching individuals gathered in groups for such personal decisions. Meanwhile, the conception of the church under the impact first of "toleration" and then of complete freedom and separation had largely lost the sacramental dimension which traditionally had sanctified her regular observances under Episcopal direction by making them intrinsically meaningful, and had become that of a voluntary association of explicitly convinced Christians for the purpose of mutual edification in the worship of God and the propagandization of the Christian faith as the group defined it.

Necessarily during this long process the conception of the relationship of the church to the society and its government was also transformed. The sense of organic unity of Church and State which had drawn such a vague line between the duties of the representatives of each, while not completely forgotten, tended to fade under the evangelical impact. This development is most strikingly seen in the history of the Methodists. During the famous Christmas Conference in Baltimore in 1784, the assemblage asked the question, "What may we reasonably believe to be God's Design in raising up the Preachers called Methodists?" and recorded as answer, "To reform the continent, and to spread scriptural Holiness over these lands."

Whatever was meant by the two phrases, it seems clear that some distinction was intended between reforming the nation *and* spreading "scriptural Holiness." But thirty-two years later such distinction had so faded that Bishop McKendree could answer that "God's design in raising up the preachers called Methodists in America was to reform the continent by spreading scriptural holiness over the land." By that time the basic conviction was that "if the man's soul was saved fundamental social change would inevitably follow." [47] In brief, the securing of "conversions" plus, it should be added, "the perfecting of the saints," was equated with, or took the place of, responsibility for the society.

Hence "to reform the nation" had come to mean "to convert the nation" in the Methodist way.

Those of the Reformed or Puritan tradition—whose most influential spokesmen were Congregationalists and Presbyterians—never assumed so much. In the first place, in keeping with their more churchly tradition, no matter how evangelical they became they never totally lost sight of pastoral care. However actual practice might deviate from the ideal, they continued to stress the dual character of the minister's work. "The great end for which the gospel is preached . . . is, the conversion of sinners, and the spiritual advancement of believers" was the motto. And J. A. James who declared that "the salvation of souls [is] the great object of the ministerial office" immediately explained that

this is a generic phrase, including as its species the awakening of the unconcerned; the guidance of the inquiring; the instruction of the uninformed; and the sanctification, comfort, and progress of those who through grace have believed—in short, the whole work of grace in the soul.[48]

In the second place, they never lost their strong sense of the church's direct responsibility for the being and well-being of the commonwealth. But they soon learned that under religious freedom in the Republic this had to be instrumented through the indirect influence on the general population of voluntary associations of what Lyman Beecher called "the wise and the good." In 1829 he declared:

These voluntary associations concentrate the best hearts, the most willing hands, and the most vigorous and untiring enterprise. And being united by affinities of character, they move with less impediment and more vigor than any other bodies can move, and constitute, no doubt, that form of the sacramental host by which Jesus Christ intends to give freedom to the world.[49]

Such sentiments lay back of the numerous Societies organized between 1800 and 1850 to work for the reformation of individual morals or social betterment. Together they constituted what a contemporary participant described as "a gigantic religious power, systematized, compact in its organization, with a polity and a government entirely its own, and independent of all control." [50] So pervasive were these Societies that in 1850 a Unitarian minister, but by no means an enemy to evangelical sentiments, complained that "the minister is often expected to be, for the most part, a manager of social utilities, a wire-puller of beneficent agencies," and his character is often judged "by the amount of visible grinding that it can accomplish in the mill of social reform. . . ." [51]

Such widespread co-operation in Societies demanded, of course, that the individuals engaged should meet on common ground—and while for the committed Christians who provided the central impetus the ground was that of evangelical Christianity, the more inclusive ground of the community at large was belief in the necessity for good morals. Hence de Tocqueville, acute observer that he was, perhaps pointed to the true state of affairs when he noted that

> The sects which exist in the United States are innumerable. They all differ in respect to the worship which is due from man to his Creator; but they all agree in respect to the duties which are due from man to man. Each sect adores the Deity in its own peculiar manner; but all the sects preach the same moral law in the name of God. [52]

But since evangelicals generally assumed that Christianity was the only sound basis for good morals and hence of American liberties, and that a Christian life began with a conversion experience, the sense of Christian responsibility for the society itself tended to reinforce the evangelical emphasis on revivals.

More subtly, the evangelicals' zeal for the conversion of sinners adumbrated the view that the revivals themselves had a kind of sacramental quality, since their conduct was the outward evidence of the inward desire to sanctify the whole Society unto God, and indeed did so. In America, Albert Barnes wrote for *The Christian Spectator* in 1832, one seldom sees

> a city, or town, or peaceful hamlet, that has not been hallowed by revivals of religion; and in this fact we mark the evidence, at once, that a God of mercy presides over the destinies of this people. . . . [53]

Meanwhile, the long line of handbooks or lectures on revivals of religion that marched forth from the American presses indicate that the conduct of revivals tended to become as self-conscious, formalized, and ritualistic as the Episcopal "forms" which the evangelicals so vehemently rejected. The Rev. Calvin Colton, writing in the early 1830's to inform "British Christians," began by noting that "American revivals . . . may properly be divided into two classes: one, when the instruments are not apparent; the other when the instruments are obvious." [54] Until recently, he thought, the former were the rule. "Christians waited for them, as men are wont to wait for showers of rain, without even imagining, that any duty was incumbent on them, as instruments." But now "the promotion of revivals by human instrumentality has, . . . been made a subject of study, and an object of systematic effort." "The first class of revivals," Colton thought, was merely

a school of Divine Providence, in which God was training the American church for action—and raising up a corps of disciplined men, . . . who should begin to see and feel, more practically, that . . . men are ordained to be the *instruments* of converting and saving souls—and the instruments of Revivals of Religion.[55]

Therefore, revivals are now regarded as "the Divine blessing upon measures concerted and executed by man, where the instruments are obvious." Indeed, said Enoch Pond of Bangor Seminary in his *Young Pastor's Guide* published in 1844, while there should be at all times "a feeling of entire *dependence* on the aids and influences of the Holy Spirit," nevertheless, "in laboring to promote a revival of religion, or the conversion of a soul," one should adapt and use means "as though no special Divine influences were needed or expected in the case." [56]

Meanwhile, all seemed to be elated to note that the revival system was snowballing in the churches. "Every fresh revival, of any considerable extent," Colton had added,

multiplies candidates for the ministry, who, . . . after a suitable training and culture, themselves enter the field, and become active and efficient revival men. The spirit of revivals is born into them [in their second birth], and bred with them, and makes their character.[57]

During the period since 1800, wrote Robert Baird in 1843, revivals "have become . . . a constituent part of the religious system of our country" to such an extent that "he who should oppose himself to revivals, *as such,* would be regarded by most of our evangelical Christians as, *ipso facto,* an enemy to spiritual religion itself." [58]

It is worth noting in passing that Horace Bushnell, who is often regarded as an enemy of revivals, actually wrote in 1838 "to establish a higher and more solid confidence in revivals." [59] Nor did he shy away from the excitement they commonly generated. "Nothing was ever achieved, in the way of a great and radical change in men or communities," he said

without some degree of excitement; and if any one expects to carry on the cause of salvation, by a steady rolling on the same dead level, and fears continually lest the axles wax hot and kindle into a flame, he is too timorous to hold the reins in the Lord's chariot.

All he wished to "complain and resist" was "the artificial firework, the extraordinary, combined jump and stir" which some suppose "to be requisite when anything is to be done." What he pleaded for was a little less self-conscious and officious management—a slightly more subtle approach. In the "jump and stir" context, he argued, making "conversions . . . the measure of all good" can have "a very injurious influence" by concentrating the attention of the church on "the beginning of the work" of the gospel, which is "to form men to God," and to depreciate the substantial and necessary work that takes place during "times of non-revival." [60] But aside from this mild warning, which even Charles G. Finney might agree with after 1835, Bushnell was an evangelical of the evangelicals.

No wonder, then, that Theodore Parker—whose passion for social justice led him to suppose that the revivals did not reach the right people —grumpily suggested that "the revival machinery" which was set in motion in 1857-58 was "as well known as McCormick's reaper" and used about as mechanically.[61]

It is obvious that within this broad context the conception of the minister practically lost its priestly dimension as traditionally conceived, and became that of a consecrated functionary, called of God, who directed the purposive activities of the visible church. The "visible church" included of course the denomination and the Societies as well as the local congregation. Already in 1828 the "Bible Societies, Sunday Schools, Tract Societies, Concerts of Prayer, and Missionary and Education Societies" had become so important that the president of Washington College in Virginia thought that

when they become fully known, they must, and will, in some measure, form a test of Christian character. They have so much of the Christian spirit, that all who love the gospel will love them, and every true Christian will do something for their advancement.[62]

Twenty-four years later President Heman Humphrey of Amherst, advising his son on the duties of the ministry, after dwelling upon the work of the local parish, urged him not to neglect the denomination and the societies. "There is," he said, "a general as well as a particular oversight of the churches, which devolves upon the pastors, or upon the pastors and delegates," and "it may be necessary also, that you should devote a good deal of time to the direct management of Missionary, Bible and other benevolent societies." Indeed, "somebody must do it, or they cannot be kept up," [63] and it was to him unthinkable that they should not be.

This suggests the evangelical conception of the kinds of ministries possible. Parish ministers, missionaries, secretaries of societies, teachers and professors, and in some cases, evangelists or revivalists as well as other functionaries, were all looked upon as equally engaged in the legitimate ministry of the one church.

Chief among the activities of the church which defined the common ground of the ministry was the conversion of souls. Albert Barnes spoke for all the evangelicals when he said,

the grand, the leading object of an evangelical ministry everywhere—[is] the conversion of the soul to God by the truth, the quickening of a spirit dead in sin by the preached gospel, the conversion and salvation of the lost by the mighty power of the Holy Spirit.[64]

Consequently, the work of the minister tended increasingly to be judged by his success in this one area. J. A. James argued that "if souls are not saved, whatever other designs are accomplished, the great purpose of the ministry is defeated." [65] And Heman Humphrey went even further in advising his son:

I do not suppose that the exact degree of a minister's fidelity, or skill in dividing the word of truth, can be measured by the number of conversions in his parish, nor even that uncommon success in "winning souls to Christ" is a *certain* evidence of his personal piety. But I think it is an evidence that he preaches the truth.[66]

Meanwhile, long experience had provided a convincing demonstration that such success depended upon the religious state of the preacher. The Rev. Gilbert Tennent in 1740, presuming to warn against "The Dangers of an Unconverted Ministry," bowed in passing to accepted Presbyterian doctrine by asserting that of course, "God, as an absolute Sovereign, may use what means he pleases to accomplish his work by." But he added as a good pragmatic empiricist, "We only assert this, that Success by unconverted Ministers' Preaching is very improbable, and very seldom happens, so far as we can gather." And why should it—"since they themselves know nothing of the struggle of soul through which earnest seekers after God must go, they are but little help to those who are seeking God." [67]

A hundred years later sober evangelicals argued that "our own personal religion is the mainspring of all our power in the pulpit" and "whatever other deficiencies we have, the chief of all lies in the heart" that "fount of eloquence." Therefore,

an unrenewed man, or one with a lukewarm piety, may preach elaborate sermons upon orthodox doctrines, but what are they for power and efficiency, when compared with those of the preacher, who feels as well as glories in the cross, but as the splendid coruscations of the aurora borealis to the warm and vivifying rays of the sun? [68]

In this sense the evangelical conception was that the institutional ministry should be charismatic, and not formal. Hence the reiterated assertion of the rejection of all forms as inimical to the gospel—for which the Episcopal Church was an ever-present and welcome whipping boy. "The Saviour," argued Albert Barnes, "originated the evangelical system and detached it at once, wholly and forever, from the Jewish forms." And all historical experience shows that "It has never been possible permanently to connect the religion of forms with evangelical religion"—"the religion of forms has never been permanently blended with the gospel." Hence, for example, while there are clergymen of undoubted evangelical sentiments in the Episcopal Church, *"they are compelled to use a liturgy which counteracts the effect of their teaching."* [69]

It was this evangelical conception of the sole efficacy of a converted ministry, plus the stress placed upon the conversion of sinners, that was the source of all the familiar disagreements over the nature and amount (if any) of formal training and education necessary for the minister. To this we shall recur in the next section.

VI

I know a minister who pulls his own teeth, and manufactures artificial teeth to be inserted in their place. But all ministers cannot do this. Some ministers can be mechanics, husbandmen, artisans, teachers; but all are not adapted to such employ-ments. There is a *diversity of gifts,* "even where there is the same good spirit."[70]

In keeping with the general theme of this chapter and within the context developed above, our discussion may now be rounded out by a more particular attention to certain aspects of the ministry during our period.

Calling to the Ministry, "License," and Ordination

In no major denomination was there any radical departure from the traditional view of Christians that the ministry is a vocation to which individuals are "called" of God, but always in the context of a church which guards entrance upon the duties of the office with regulations deemed Scriptural, and defines the minister's role. All evangelicals were agreed that basic piety was essential in the individual called—that "he whose business it is to convert men to Christ should himself be con-verted; he who is to guide believers should himself be a man of faith" [71] —and that "for the lack of this, no talents, however brilliant or attractive, can compensate." [72]

They differed primarily on the "orders" of the ministry, and the nature and efficacy of the traditionally accepted forms of ordination— items that mark the dividing line between the "Catholic" and Episcopal groups and all others. By and large the latter from their beginnings in America were consciously under the necessity to steer the middle course between belief in the efficacy of the forms (which they imputed to the English Episcopal Church), and the immediacy of the "enthusiasts" and Quakers who seemed to eliminate the role of the church entirely and lead to antinomianism and anarchy. Throughout the colonial period these groups traveled the middle road to the evangelical conception of which they had arrived by around 1850—not without controversy, of course.

In guarding the office, all the evangelical churches recognized the necessity somehow to take cognizance of five things in the examination of the candidate: the authenticity of his religious experience, the acceptability of his moral character, the genuineness of his call, the correctness of his doctrine, and the adequacy of his preparation. The differences, not only between denominations, but also between factions within each group, came over the relative emphasis to be placed on each of these five, and in what individual group within the church the power of examination and judgment lay. All five might be, and increasingly were, subsumed under the evangelicals' conception of "the call" and the evidence therefore. The "call," wrote the Rev. H. Harvey, a Baptist, has three aspects: the internal call, the call of the church, and the call of providence. The evidence of the first is "a fixed and earnest desire for the work," "an abiding impression of duty to preach the gospel," and "a sense of personal weakness and unworthiness and a heartfelt reliance on divine power." The church bases its call upon evidence of the candidate's "sound conversion," "superior order of piety," "soundness in the faith," "adequate mental capacity and training, scriptural knowledge," "aptness to teach," "practical wisdom and executive ability," and "a good report of them which are without" (i.e., general reputation). These qualifications may be present either "in their germ and promise" or "in their fully-developed form." And since

the individual himself is not the proper judge as to his possession of these qualifications, the church is the natural medium of the call, and its decision ought ordinarily to be accepted as final.

Third is "the call of providence" which comes "to the man of prayer . . . in the events of his life"—or in other words, what Lincoln called the "plain physical facts of the case." Hence, for example, if circumstances "absolutely forbid" the candidate's "entering the ministry," the presumption is that he is not called to do so.[73]

Evangelicals generally practiced a form of probation by granting a candidate deemed worthy, a license "for the trial and improvement of [his] gifts." This meant that he would be "received by the churches as an accredited and regular preacher" although he could not "administer the sacraments."[74] Among Congregationalists and Presbyterians licensure was the prerogative of Associations and Presbyteries, among Methodists of the Quarterly Conference, and among Baptists of the local church —which might as in the case of William Miller of Adventist fame, most eloquently state that

We are satisfied Br. Miller has a gift to improve in Public and are willing he should improve the same wherever his lots may be cast in the Zion of God.[75]

The licentiate was under the scrutiny both of lay people in local congregations and the ordained men whose fraternity he aspired to enter—

and subject to the approbation or censure of either or both. Hence in effect during the period of probation, the candidate was under constant examination by the church regarding the genuineness of his "call."

Commonly ordination took place when he received a call from and was settled over a local congregation, or as among Methodists, when he was sent to a church or a circuit by the bishop, in whom the power of ordination lay. In other groups the power of ordination was by 1850 settled in what even the Baptists on the frontier commonly called "a presbytery of ministers."[76] The evangelicals generally would agree with Thomas Smyth to "include under the term presbyterian, all denominations which are governed by ministers who are recognized as of one order, and who, as well as their other officers, are chosen, are removable, and are supported by the people." This included the Baptists, Lutherans, Reformed, "the Protestant Methodist church," and "the whole body of the New England Puritans" as well as the Presbyterian churches.[77]

Social Sources and Social Status of the Ministers

The descendants of Europe's "right-wing" State churches maintained a position of prestige, power, and dominance in America throughout the colonial period. All of these bodies shared with Massachusetts Bay Puritans the dread of leaving "an illiterate ministry to the Churches, when our present ministers shall lie in the Dust." And even though this was the twilight period of aristocracy, still the conception of learning verged on the ideal of universal knowledge, and was almost the exclusive privilege of the upper classes, automatically conferring prestige and social status on the educated man.

This meant that not only were the ministers of these churches largely recruited from "good" families, but that whatever their origin, entering the ministry itself conferred a measure of prestige in a community. Not unnaturally the clergy of the two legally established churches were most conscious of their position. An English visitor to the Bay in 1671— not entirely unprejudiced of course—found the rulers so "inexplicably covetous and proud" that "they receive your gifts but as an homage or tribute due to their transcendancy, which is a fault their clergie are also guilty of. . . ."[78] And Burr concludes that the missionaries of the Society for the Propagation of the Gospel in New Jersey "generally regarded the Church as an island of refinement and rational piety in a

restless sea of ignorance, 'Enthusiasm,' skepticism, and open infidelity"—
a regard that reflects the relatively high opinion they held of themselves.[79]

The social status of the minister, then, down through the eighteenth
century, in practically all the groups derived from his belonging to, or
being elevated to, a class, plus a kind of imputation of charismatic
power to the clergy by the general population. This was true even of
Baptists and Quakers. The former maintained an educated leadership
in the line of Roger Williams and John Clarke that founded Brown
University in 1765. To be sure, many of the Quakers who so shocked
the colonists in the seventeenth century were practically without formal
education or family position. But during the eighteenth century Friends
combined the gains of the Counting House with the quiet piety of the
Meeting House and found themselves in the possession of material
prosperity, social prestige, and political power that at least equaled that
of Anglicans, Presbyterians and Congregationalists.[80]

After 1800 as the nation moved rapidly through "the era of good
feelings" into the era of Jacksonian equality, ministers were recruited
more and more from the lower social and economic strata of the society.
This change is reflected, for example, in the formation of Education
Societies to help worthy and pious but indigent young men along the
road to theological training. And the observation of Frederick von
Raumer in 1846 that in America there were proportionately more
clergymen and on the average they were better paid[81] is probably a
comment on his estimation of the low pay of European ministers rather
than a suggestion that their American brethren were affluent. Certainly
the most common complaint of the ministers of all denominations was
insufficient salaries.

Meanwhile, the relatively high status of ministers in the society
perhaps was due primarily to the generally prevailing and sometimes
almost superstitious regard for "the Book" and "the cloth." Baird
explained that most Americans "have been taught from childhood that
the preaching of the Gospel is the great instrumentality appointed by
God for the salvation of men,"[82] and hence, even though not church
members, they quite generally respected the churches and clergy. For
example, General Andrew Jackson—not particularly famous for evenness
of temper and sweetness of disposition—apparently did not resent Peter
Cartwright's shouting in his face when he entered the church, "Who
is General Jackson? If he don't get his soul converted God will damn
him as quick as he would a Guinea Negro."[83] The Governor of Ohio

and his wife would entertain "Brother Axley" of the Scioto Circuit at dinner, even though "he knew nothing about polished life" (says Cartwright of all people), ate his chicken after the manner we have come to know as "in the rough," and "threw the bone down on the carpet . . . for the little lap dog." [84] And the incorruptibly English Frances Trollope who thought that "strong, indeed, must be the love of equality in an English breast, if it can survive a tour through the Union," was surprised and shocked to note the high position and regard accorded by the people of Cincinnati to itinerant preachers who, to her, seemed "as empty as wind" which they resembled in that "they blow where they list, and no man knoweth whence they come, nor whither they go." [85]

The obverse side of the prevalence of this kind of sentiment throughout the population is that what anticlericalism there was in the United States was "sectarian" rather than "secular." In fact, if one means by secular "not religious in character," it would be difficult to find any genuinely secular anticlericalism or antiecclesiasticism anywhere during our whole period. Almost without exception, the outstanding political leaders of the Revolutionary epoch were Deists, who like Thomas Paine opposed atheism with even greater vehemence than they did clericalism. Commonly, as did Thomas Jefferson, they based their attack against existing ecclesiastical institutions on the pure religion and morals of Jesus—and hence were insofar "sectarian."

No doubt there were some genuine atheists, at least according to their own unsophisticated estimation, especially, for example, on the early Kentucky frontier. But one cannot always trust the testimony to this provided by the frontier preachers. Probably the majority so called were at most "infidels" in the Paine sense, but preachers commonly were not precise in their definitions. Hence, when Cartwright notes that among the Germans "many who were Catholics, Lutherans, rationalists and infidels, were happily converted to God," [86] it does not appear that his distinctions were particularly clear.

Sectarian anticlericalism was of course almost universal in America. If all the Protestant groups are seen on a continuum with say Quakers on the left and "catholic" Episcopalians on the right, one can say that each group tended to criticize the "clericalism" of all the groups to its right. Indeed such criticism was an essential element in each group's definition of itself.

Aside from this prevailing climate of sentiment, the status of the minister depended in part upon the general cultural level and attainments of the denomination to which he belonged. Voluntaryism which encouraged mobility between groups tended to give each denomination a drawing power related to its social and cultural reputation and class structure, so that a minister on first sight would probably be judged by his group.

Obversely, the general reputation of the group naturally exerted a kind of power over the minister, impelling him to acquit himself as became its representative. For example, the Rev. Heman Humphrey, president of Amherst College, obviously felt that the Presbyterian minister could not "be excused from fostering schools and colleges," and to that end should use all available means, even "if need be, unite with others in memorializing the city government and the legislature." [87] But Peter Cartwright, who actually during his lifetime did a tremendous amount for education by the distribution of literature and the support of schools, had such a conception of Methodism and the "Western world" as seems at times to have made him compulsively boorish.

But finally the ministers who, as Lyman Beecher said, were "chosen by the people who have been educated as free men," and were "dependent on them for patronage and support," [88] achieved such status as their reputation for personal piety, character, and ability made possible in the society in which they lived. What Timothy Dwight said of the clergy of Connecticut might be applied to the clergy generally. They have, he said,

no power [officially], but they have much influence . . . the influence of wisdom and virtue . . . which every sober man must feel to be altogether desirable in every community. Clergymen, here, are respected for what they are, and for what they do, and not for anything adventitious to themselves, or their office.[89]

And the distinguished professor of history in the University of Berlin concluded in 1846 after his tour of the United States that "the absence of an elevated wealthy hierarchy and of a direct worldly influence, has not diminished but rather increased the respect paid to the American preachers." [90] Such judgments, of course, constitute a high and not undeserved tribute to the exemplary personal lives and good character of these men, and to the effectiveness of their ministry.

Training of Ministers and the Relation of Theological to Secular Learning

No Protestant group of any consequence has ever officially denied the necessity for some kind of special preparation for its ministers. They have differed over the content of such education, its form, and the most desirable and efficient ways and means of instrumenting it.

The great watershed in ministerial education is the period of the Enlightenment, or, in America, the Revolutionary epoch (roughly 1775-1800).[91] Before that time learning as such was all of a piece. With that period came the beginnings of the general estrangement of Protestant Christianity from the dominant intellectual currents of the modern age, during which the churches relinquished the control of education, which previously had been their prerogative. Consequently, from the beginning of the nineteenth century the education sponsored directly by the denominations has been on the defensive. Meanwhile, the fragmentation into denominations meant that not only were all the groups thrown in common on the defensive against the rising "secular" learning, but each was in effect thrown on the defensive against the education sponsored by all the others. Donald C. Tewkesbury's classical study of *The Founding of American Colleges and Universities before the Civil War* [92] is convincing evidence for this.

It is a commonplace that down through the eighteenth century it was assumed that ministers should be intellectual leaders in their communities. Cotton Mather, who himself had no small reputation for learning in all areas, obviously assumed this in his "Directions for a Candidate of the Ministry" in 1726.[93] His minister was first to cultivate "PIETY"—which is "CHRIST" *formed in you;* and Christ *Living in you*"—and fill his life with "Essays To Do Good"; second, to cultivate "that Learning and those *Ingenuous* and *Mollifying Arts,* which may distinguish you from the more Uncultivated Part of Mankind." What he suggests is a very broad general education, plus, of course, particular learning in church history, theology, and systems of divinity.

Seventy years later a Boston minister writing fatherly open *Letters to a Student in the University of Cambridge, Massachusetts* [94] noted that "by design" he had refrained from asking "whether it is your intention to be a lawyer, a physician, or a minister;—whether study is to be the employment of your life, or the pleasing entertainment of a leisure hour," because even "if I could predict your future employment, it would produce no change in the tenor of my counsels" as it should "have no influence in the choice of your studies." And, he added,

general knowledge is the object contemplated by a publick education. And . . . your acquisitions should be as various as the branches of science cultivated at the university; and as extensive as the transient tenor of four years will allow.

But in Mather's comment on "the almost Epidemical Extinction of true Christianity . . . in the Nations" is revealed his sense of living in the twilight of an era. That he had perhaps unwittingly set his face toward the good time coming is revealed in his injunction that "the END of all your studies" must be the "SERVICE OF GOD" and "the MOTTO upon your whole ministry . . . CHRIST IS ALL." Avoid, he said, that "Fashionable Divinity" which "says nothing of a conversion to God" and in all "your Preaching" aim to *"Save them that hear you"* by spreading *"the Nets of Salvation* for them . . . with all possible Dexterity."[95] Already as he wrote revivals were under way in the Dutch Reformed and Presbyterian churches to the south, and Mather unknowingly was fanning the spark in New England that eight years later would burst into flames in Jonathan Edwards' Northampton church—flames which would consume much of the world he looked back upon, and from which the new world would emerge.

It now seems fairly obvious that Mather's suggestion that all preaching be directed toward the conversion of sinners to God contained within it an emphasis that—granted the American situation—would in the long run tend to undermine his view of the kind of general education necessary for the minister. By 1831 all the evangelicals of whatever denomination and wherever located on the variegated cultural map of America would agree with Albert Barnes' formal statement that the chief end of the ministry was "the conversion of souls"—*"to save souls,* and to labour for revivals of religion,"[96] and hence that "this . . . is the starting point from which we are to contemplate the kind of preparation [necessary] for the ministry." Inherent in this view was the conception that the minister's formal education was instrumental to this end, and therefore its content would be determined by the situation he was expected to face.

Hence scholar that he was, of Presbyterian tradition, and laboring in the relatively high-level cultural context of Philadelphia, he concluded that effective work in the conversion of souls and the conduct of revivals "demands in the ministry *all* the culture which can find mind to conflict with mind." Since "the gospel is such a system . . . [as] supposes a decided *act* of the mind in its reception, or its rejection," ministers must be prepared to present it to men's minds, although this means "a comparatively long and tedious training, involving often an apparently great waste of time."

Every preacher, he continued, "stands there professing his ability to explain, defend, and illustrate the book of God" and since "there are henceforth to be no trammels on the freedom of the mind, but such as reason, and conscience, and thought can fasten there," the minister must be prepared through education to meet and conquer the prevailing "infidelity" and superstition of the age. Indeed,

Unless you can train your ministers to meet them in the field where the freedom of mind is *contemplated,* and let argument meet argument, and thought conflict with thought, and sober sense and learning overcome the day-dreams and dotage of infidelity . . . you may abandon the hope that religion will set up its empire over the thinking men of this age.[97]

It is obvious that Barnes, unlike Mather, attempted to justify the broadest possible education for the minister, not on the ground that he might be the intellectual leader of his community and set the educational standards and patterns for all, but that he might be prepared to meet the learned skeptics and infidels in that community.

But Methodist circuit riders on the rough frontier who were fighting the battle for the conversion of souls in a different cultural context, while—or rather because—they held essentially the same instrumental view of education as did Barnes, could see no need for "fancy" learning.

Peter Cartwright, who knew the West as well as Barnes new Philadelphia, thought that

the great mass of our Western people wanted a preacher that could mount a stump, a block, or old log, or stand in the bed of a wagon, and without note or manuscript, quote, expound, and apply the word of God to the hearts and consciences of the people.

Hence he ridiculed the "many young missionaries sent out . . . to civilize and Christianize the poor heathen of the West." These men who "had regularly studied theology in some of the Eastern states, where they manufactured young preachers like they do lettuce in hot houses" did not understand the Western world, and of course "they produced no good effect among the people" there.

In contrast to them,

A Methodist preacher in those days, when he felt that God had called him to preach, instead of hunting up a college or Biblical institute, hunted up a hardy pony of a horse, and some travelling apparatus, and with his library always at hand, namely, Bible, Hymn Book, and Discipline, he started, and with a text that never wore out nor grew stale, he cried, "Behold the Lamb of God, that taketh away the sin of the world."

Of course Cartwright himself knew it was not quite as simple as that. He recalled that he had started on a circuit in 1803 under the guidance and instruction of an older brother in the ministry and that "William M'Kendree," his presiding elder,

directed me to a proper course of reading and study. He selected books for me, both literary and theological; and every quarterly visit he made, he examined into my progress, and corrected my errors, if I had fallen into any. He delighted to instruct me in English grammar.

And this way of training while already in the ministry, wherein men "could [both] learn and practice every day . . . would be more advantageous than all the colleges and Biblical institutes in the land." [98]

It is in this sense that theological education for ministers during the heyday of evangelicalism tended to become more and more instrumental. It was determined primarily by the felt need to train men to become effective revivalists. Its intellectual content as such was more and more geared to training men to fight a rearguard action against the hosts of "secularism" that had seized the initiative in education. Hence the theological schools were increasingly laid open to the full sweep of whatever movements or fads originated in the "secular" schools.

How this came about is the long and complicated story of the "secularization" of our civilization in modern times, which increasingly has placed theological education on the defensive. It is important to realize that Pietism, which emerged in the second half of the seventeenth century and swept throughout Protestantism during the eighteenth, bore within itself a strong tendency to relinquish the intellectual battle with the "world"—a tendency which seemed so striking to A. N. Whitehead. "It was a notable event in the history of ideas," he said, "when the clergy of the western races began to waver in their appeal to constructive reason." [99]

What Professor John T. McNeill says of John Arndt, might be said of Pietism in general: its

aim was to induce theologians and lay people to turn from controversy to fellowship and charity, and from the confessions of faith to faith itself. He held it essential to add holiness of life to purity of doctrine. [100]

Philipp Jacob Spener (1635-1705), the apostle of Pietism, held that the aim of preaching should be to "awaken faith and [to] urge the fruits of faith," and hence that the aim of ministerial training should be "not only to impart knowledge but to have truth penetrate the soul." This led him to argue strongly for "practical studies" and "nonpolemical and edifying books" to "replace controversial theology."[101]

Pietism flowed into the American colonies through many channels. The basic sentiment was latent in much of seventeenth-century Anglicanism and, more obviously, in all of New England Puritanism, ready to be cultivated by such ministers as Cotton Mather at the beginning of the eighteenth century, and Devereaux Jarrett at its end. It was carried directly from Europe by such leaders as Count Zinzendorf, Henry M. Muhlenberg, and Theodore Freylinghuysen, and—crossed with English evangelicalism or Methodist—it blossomed with several mutations and sports in the hothouse atmosphere of the Great Awakenings. But whereas on the continent and in Britain Pietism and Evangelicalism spawned movements that were largely held within the saving forms of the dominant churches, in America where the church forms were already greatly weakened, Pietistic sentiments tended through revivalism to become so dominant that denominations were formed on this basis alone.

This tendency inherent in Pietism was augmented by the fact that all the ideological lines of the eighteenth century came to focus on the idea of uncoerced, individual consent as the basis for all man's organizations —with a consequent depreciation of all inherited forms and traditional formulations.

Pietists, with their emphasis on personal religious experience, were prepared to rebuild the church on this basis alone. At the same time, the climate in which the intellectuals moved—those who were leading the social and political revolutions of the age—was rationalistic. Inherent in both Pietistic and Rationalistic sentiment regarding religion was a basis for religious freedom and separation of Church and State in practice. In the accomplishment of this practical goal these movements complemented each other to the end of the eighteenth century, and there was very little controversy between their representatives in America.

The achievement of separation dissolved this bond between Pietistic revivalists and Rationalists. At the same time the events of the French Revolution made plausible in religious circles the view that rationalistic "infidelity" was inimical to all order and government as well as to

Christianity itself. Consequently came the widespread reaction against the whole ethos of the eighteenth century, during which the churches tended to turn back to the dogmatic formulations of classical Protestantism for theological structure. At the same time the basic sentiments of the Enlightenment continued to inform the emerging modern world. Insofar, then, learning and intelligence came increasingly to be defined in terms of the burgeoning scientific movement—the afterglow of the Enlightenment—while religion was generally defined in the terms of traditional dogmatic theology seen through the somewhat foggy sentiments of American revivalistic evangelicalism. Through this fog the evangelicals generally fumbled for an educational program that would be both intellectually respectable and dogmatically sound.

It is within this context that the generally familiar ways and means of training ministers must be seen. So long as the culture sustained—as it did on the whole through the eighteenth century—a conception of "general education" for all learned men, prospective ministers were exposed to the same basic training as others. The nine colleges founded by the several denominations during the colonial period were of this nature, but since they were dominated and staffed by clergymen, ministerial training was a central aspect of their work. In 1754, for example, President Thomas Clap of Yale declared that "Colleges are Societies of Ministers for training up Persons for the Work of the Ministry." [102]

Meanwhile, from early in the eighteenth century, specifically theological training was commonly acquired through study under the supervision of established clergymen, either parish ministers or ministerial professors. Such training combined advanced study with practice in the regular duties of the parish. Several of the outstanding ministers of New England thus conducted theological schools in their homes—their wives providing and supervising food and lodging for the students. [103] William Tennent's famous "log college" merely combined features of both established colleges and such personal instruction and direction, and provided more emphasis upon personal religious experience and revivalism than was customary. To apply a distinction that became common in the nineteenth century, the colleges provided training *for* the ministry, settled clergymen provided training *in* the ministry.

But in the period of very rapid growth and expansion following independence, it soon became evident that a system of theological education must be developed to meet the greatly increased demand for ministers and to give candidates training more adequate than could be provided by one man. The establishment of professional schools especially in law and medicine (an indication of the rise of professional self-consciousness) was an added stimulus. Finally, competition between denominations, and even between factions within denominations, in which each sought to assure its perpetuity by providing schools where future leaders might be well indoctrinated in the peculiar tenets of the group, played no small part. Once begun, the founding of seminaries proceeded rapidly, and between 1807 and 1827 no less than seventeen permanent institutions had their beginnings.[104]

Meanwhile, during the Revolutionary epoch and immediately following, "there arose an active sentiment in favor of state-controlled institutions of higher education and an equally active sentiment against sectarian colleges." During this period generally successful efforts were made by the states either to take over all the colleges or at least to secure strong representation on their boards. Five of the twelve permanent colleges founded between 1800 and 1819 were state institutions,[105] and until the Dartmouth College decision in the latter year the future of denominational colleges was problematical. That decision guaranteed the perpetuity of private institutions by indicating that they could not be taken over by the states—and the golden day of denominational colleges followed (1830-60).

But while denominational schools thus gained legal security, no legal decision could return to the churches the initiative in setting the patterns for education in the culture. Further, several factors in the situation militated against their doing so. Outstanding was the rivalry and competition between denominations, which one leader recognized in 1858 as "contagious, as well as debilitating." [106] F. A. P. Bernard of the University of Mississippi noted in 1856 that nearly all our colleges are

the creations of the different religious denominations which divide our people. They are regarded as important instrumentalities, through which the peculiarities of doctrine which distinguish their founders are to be maintained, propagated, or defended.[107]

Hence, being as Tewkesbury said an integral part of "the larger strategy of the campaign of evangelism," they were self-consciously defensive—against the rising "secular" learning, against Roman Catholic learning, and finally, against the "sectarian" learning of the other Protestant groups. The intensity of the defensive rivalry between groups is suggested by the fact that the mortality rate of colleges founded before the

Civil War in sixteen of the states was 81 per cent.[108] Hence it is not unfair to say, as above, that a primary controlling motif of the education provided was instrumental—not learning for learning's sake, but for the sake of the peculiarities of the founding sect.

This situation tended to sharpen the distinction between theological and secular learning. However, since the evangelical-revivalistic mind was not particularly keen when it came to making sharp and precise distinctions, this dichotomy did not become a problem during our period. But already in 1853 an outstanding clergyman noted sadly "an impression, somewhat general, that an intellectual clergyman is deficient in piety, and that an eminently pious minister is deficient in intellect." [109]

Sermons and Preaching

While the church is considered as the pillar and ground of the truth, preaching must, beyond all question, be regarded as its most important duty. . . . The preaching of the gospel by the living voice . . . has, in all ages, been the principle instrument in the hand of God, by which the church has been sustained and advanced.[110]

The preceding chapters of this book make clear that the great traditional doctrines of Christianity have provided the substance of what was preached in every age. The peculiar form and content of sermons in particular times and places have been determined by three factors. The first is the prevailing conception of the chief end of the ministry, which has been illustrated above in discussing the evangelicals. Second is the status and role accorded to the minister by the society in which he is placed. Third is the immediate cultural context, since the minister in preaching has always, willy-nilly, felt the necessity to adapt himself somehow to the general level of interest and understanding of the people who sat in the pews.

As noted above, when pietistic sentiments and revivalistic techniques swept to the crest of evangelicalism in America, the conversion of souls tended to crowd out other aspects of the minister's work. This greatly affected preaching. In the Preface to the 1828-29 volume of *The American National Preacher,* the editor said he noted among some ministers "a strong temptation to preach more frequently to saints, than is consistent with the rule of *giving to every one his portion in due season.*" Hence, he declared his intention as editor thereafter "to insert a greater proportion of such Sermons, as are designed, by divine help, to have an immediate and permanent effect on *sinners.*" Indeed, he thought, the preacher "surely may even *forget* those already gained, if so doing, he can *persuade others* to turn, ere they reach the impassable gulf." A decade later Robert Baird explained that in America preaching was designed primarily "to bring men to a *decision,* and to make them decide *right* on the subject of religion." And, sober Presbyterian though he was, he thought "we ought not to be too timid or fastidious as to the means employed in awakening them to the extremity of their danger." [111]

Here Baird stood in line with Jonathan Edwards who, when criticized for frightening people in hell-fire sermons, replied that he thought it not amiss to try to frighten them out of hell. Baird's contemporary advocate of "an earnest ministry" noted that the Sunday School, the cheap tract, and the religious periodical had become "competitors" with the pulpit "for the public mind," and concluded that the ministers would have to turn on more heat.[112] Charles G. Finney, always more blunt in saying what many of his Congregational and Presbyterian brethren really thought, openly advocated the creation of excitement in order to attract the attention of the unconverted—a view with which, as we have noted, Horace Bushnell was inclined to agree.

The real danger, thought J. A. James in 1848, lies in "dull uniformity, and not enthusiasm," and he advocated as ideal a middle course in preaching between "the contortions of an epileptic zeal" and "the numbness of a paralytic one." [113] The writer who introduced James to his American readers summed it up by saying that America demanded a ministry that was learned, scriptural, spiritual, and practical. But among these qualifications, evangelicalism—conditioned by the American situation—tended to bring the stress down on the "practical." "American preaching," declared Robert Baird, "is eminently *practical.*" [114] James emphasized that from the earnest minister, people "do not look for the flowers of rhetoric, but for the fruit of the tree of life" which establishes "his character as a *useful* preacher." [115]

This emphasis on the "useful," "practical," and immediate results of preaching, in the context of voluntaryism, pressed ministers to adapt their preaching to the prevailing cultural level about them. Hence Baird was no doubt right in supposing that in the United States preaching varied more "in manner than in substance," for while all preach the same gospel, "much depends on the kind of people" the minister "has to do with." [116]

Thus as in the context of evangelicalism, learning for the minister was increasingly conceived as instrumental, the conversion of sinners became the real test of effectiveness, and preaching tended to become almost exclusively persuasive. Exposition of the Word tended to be supplemented by application of the Word to the consciences of men for immediate decision. Of the three parts of the usual sermon in the previous period—exegesis of a text, laying down of the doctrine, and application—the third almost crowded out the other two. Even as learned and sober an adviser to ministers as J. A. James by implication belittled the first as "a meatless, marrowless bone of criticism," the second as "a dry crust of philosophy," and extolled the third as "the bread which cometh down from heaven." [117]

This kind of emphasis, plus the felt necessity to adapt to the cultural level of the people addressed, meant that the traditional "plain style" which educated preachers of all ages had consciously striven for was in America always in eminent danger of being leveled into plain vulgarity —as witness the succession of revivalists from Buchard and Finney to Billy Sunday.

For the same reasons, the preaching of such earnest evangelicals tended increasingly to become anecdotal, thus making sometimes dubious application of the principle of the parables. This was perhaps particularly the case among the pietistic Methodists. Certainly the circuit riders became consummate storytellers, as witness Peter Cartwright's *Autobiography*—the bulk of which appears to be made up of stories he had told hundreds of times in the more than fourteen thousand sermons he is alleged to have preached. These stories are obviously worn smooth from long usage, and every one is a clever illustration of a sermonic point—sometimes, indeed, more clever than fair or discerning.

For example, he did not demolish the "proselyting Baptist" preachers' arguments for immersion by amassing Scriptural and logical opposition, but said that

they made so much ado about baptism by immersion, that the uninformed would suppose that heaven was an island, and there was no way to get there but by *diving* or *swimming*.[118]

And on another occasion—on a bet involving "a new suit of clothes"— he overcame the arguments of "a Baptist minister, who was tolerably smart" by laying down the premise that "that Church which has no children in it [is] more like hell than heaven." Therefore, he concluded triumphantly, "there being no children in the Baptist Church, it . . .

[is]more like hell than heaven." This was practical preaching, adapted to the listeners, and it was immediately effective. "I was listened to for three hours," Cartwright gloats, "and it was the opinion of hundreds that this discussion [with the defeated Baptist] did a vast amount of good." [119] At least it was such preaching that enabled these Methodist "shock troops" of Christendom—as Bushnell called them—to set the whole "western world" on fire with the gospel, and to become by 1850 the largest Protestant denomination in America.

The rivalry between religious groups inherent in the free-church system in America where around 90 per cent of the people were unchurched in 1790, also greatly affected the form and content of sermons —as is suggested, for example, by Cartwright's relationships with Baptists, Presbyterians, and others. The minister's self-conscious definition of himself as a leader of his group demanded constant definition and defense of its peculiar tenets, and by the same token, attack on the tenets of all other groups.

This, to be sure, had its bad features and was always in danger of being carried to extremes. But the constant controversies were by no means merely battles in a war of attrition between the growing evangelical groups. All, of course, opposed "unevangelical" groups—ranging from Roman Catholics through Unitarians and Universalists to infidels and atheists. This was the war from which there was no release. But evangelicals thought of their "churches" as "denominations" where "the word 'denomination' implies that the group referred to is but one member of a larger group, called or denominated by a particular name." [120] Professor Hudson has documented how "the denominational theory of the church" took form in the minds and practices of some "seventeenth century Independent divines within the Church of England." Central to this theory was the view that

God hath a hand in these divisions to bring forth further light. Sparks are beaten out by the flints striking together. Many sparks of light, many truths, are beaten out by the beatings of men's spirits one against another.

Hence, in the context of a common Christianity and always conscious of "our own frailty," each sought, as Thomas Hooker put it, merely "to lay down . . . the grounds of our practice according to that measure of light I have received," accepting always the possibility of more light to come through earnest discussion of differences.[121]

The eighteenth-century rationalists played a primary part in giving constitutional and legal structure to the practice of separation of Church and State. And their conception of religious freedom, on which such separation rested, clearly made the controversy between those of different religious "opinions" a positive good as the way by which error is eliminated and truth approximated.

The relationship between these views of seventeenth-century English Independents and eighteenth-century American rationalists has not yet been made clear by historians. But certainly both views—if they *are* separable—lay back of the "denominationalism" that gave organizational shape to Christianity in the United States between 1787 and 1850.[122] Already in 1828 George A. Baxter, president of Washington College in Virginia, was defending the necessity of "the controversies which must arise between different denominations in the church." The "two great principles which ought to direct all the intercourse of the church," he argued, are "the love of peace, and the love of truth." But "truth" should not be sacrificed for "peace," and indeed the Reformation was founded upon the conviction that "not only peace, but life itself, should be hazarded for the cause of truth." Hence in America, while we must love peace and abhor "the spirit of party" with all its dangers, nevertheless the discussion even with intent to proselytize must go on.[123]

It is this view and spirit which lies back of most of the controversial preaching and the great debates between leaders of different denominations during the first half of the nineteenth century. It helps to explain the zest with which ministers entered the fray as champions of the views of their particular group, supposing as they did that this was one road to truth. And their supposition was apparently borne out by their experience. Alexander Campbell is somewhat typical. His own position was hammered out and hence the Disciples' position made clear in the series of public debates he held between 1820 and 1843 with outstanding Baptist, Presbyterian, and Roman Catholic representatives, and with the infidel Robert Owen.

The latter debate, held in Cincinnati in 1829 in fifteen successive meetings, puzzled and shocked the impeccable Mrs. Trollope. Day after day, she noted, the Methodist meeting house which would seat about a thousand people was crowded with eager listeners. No one's mind seemed to be changed by the debate, but the thinking of both sides was clarified. Meanwhile, the disputants, she noted, never "appeared to lose their temper," spent much time together, and "on all occasions expressed most cordially their mutual esteem." And little as she understood the genius of American "denominationalism," she sensed its power and paid it a high tribute in concluding that while she was "not quite sure that it was very desirable" that such a debate "should have happened any where" she was sure that "all this . . . could only have happened in America." [124]

VII

The dependence of our ministers upon their flocks for their salaries seems not to affect in the least their faithfulness in preaching "their repentance towards God," and "repentance towards our Lord Jesus Christ." [125]

The story here told is indeed that of a "living ministry of Christianity" which grew in and with the changing scenes in America from the first feeble plantings to the stabilization of a great new nation. It is the story of adaptation to the exigencies of a world that was new both geographically and culturally, in which faithful ministers guided the churches through sweeping institutional changes, and through the rough ideological waters of these troubled centuries. At the center of the story stands religious freedom and separation of Church and State, which posed problems undreamed of during the previous centuries of Christendom, and the sweep of "evangelicalism" which enabled the denominations to triumph in a world of regnant individualism.

By around 1850 they had demonstrated that armed only with persuasive power, they could "Christianize" the nation—set the accepted mores and moral patterns, and provide the foundation of commonly shared religious beliefs which were so essential for the being and well-being of the Republic. And withal, they had built for themselves and their churches a position of dignity, respect, and high regard. Lord Bryce's tribute published in 1894 is as applicable to the pre-Civil War period:

No political party, no class in the community, has any hostility either to Christianity or to any particular Christian body. The churches are as thoroughly popular, in the best sense of the word, as any of the other institutions of the country.[126]

Who can deny to the overwhelming majority of these ministers the appellation of good and faithful servants who not only kept the faith, but also fought a good fight, and one by one finished the hard course set before them in and by this terrifying but magnificent new world of America?

IX

The Protestant Ministry in America: 1850–1950

ROBERT S. MICHAELSEN

Henry Adams demonstrated his awareness of the revolutionary character of his age when he wrote:

> My country in 1900 is something totally different from my own country of 1860. I am wholly a stranger in it. Neither I, nor anyone else, understands it. The turning of a nebula into a star may somewhat resemble the change. All I can see is that it is one of compression, concentration, and consequent development of terrific energy, represented not by souls, but by coal and iron and steam.[1]

Revolutionary change, compression, and concentration which prepared the way for even greater change, industrialization, urbanization, ascension in world power, tremendous growth in population—these were the predominant characteristics of those forty years. And what was begun then has accelerated at an ever-increasing rate since 1900.

Adams was impressed by the industrial revolution that had occurred in America during his lifetime, but perhaps he experienced even greater awe in contemplating the intellectual revolution. In appraising his formal education after fifty years he came to the conclusion that

> In essentials like religion, ethics, philosophy; in history, literature, art; in the concepts of all science, except perhaps mathematics, the American boy of 1854 stood nearer the year 1 than to the year 1900.[2]

Between 1850 and 1900 there had been a new Copernican revolution. Chief among the artificers of this revolution were Charles Darwin and Karl Marx. As Copernicus had initiated a fundamental change in the view of the place of the earth in the solar system so these men, and others, were helping to bring about a change in man's views of himself,

250

his origin and ancestry, and his relations to his fellow men. They were aided by minor revolutionaries in such fields as astronomy, geology, physics, historical criticism and comparative religion.

The goal of millions of immigrants, America has become since 1850 the land of expanding geographic, economic, and scientific frontiers, under the influence of at least two revolutions with all the factors that caused, accompanied, and were produced by them. Adams was aware of both the change and the complexity, and in the early 1900's he realized that the pattern started in the nineteenth century would accelerate in the twentieth. "The child born in 1900," he recognized, "would . . . be born into a new world which would not be a unity but a multiple." [3]

Protestantism, and the Protestant ministry, has been profoundly affected by the revolutions and the increasing complexity of the last century. Protestant thought suffered severe shocks under the impact of intellectual revolution. The essential unity of the evangelical orthodoxy of mid-century became a multiplicity under the influence of this impact and other factors. The changes which fostered, accompanied, and were produced by the industrial revolution—such as urbanism and all that it implied—put to stringent test the practices and institutional patterns of a Protestantism which had been closely identified with rural society and culture. The increase of the number of Americans with non-Protestant orientations created for the first time a condition in which Protestantism's domination of American culture could be challenged. Religious and cultural pluralism became a reality, and this affected the status of the Protestant minister in the American community.

Along with the nation Protestantism in America has become more complex in the course of the period. This is due in part to the nature of Protestantism, a movement which has been fissiparous from its beginnings. But this characteristic has been enhanced by those factors which have made American culture itself increasingly complex. Class, cultural, ethnic and intellectual differences brought on by such factors as industrialism, sectionalism and immigration, have had a marked influence on Protestantism.

One can, however, all too easily become caught up in change and complexity to the point where he loses sight of the elements of continuity between this century and former centuries, where he fails to realize that ministers today face essentially the same kinds of problems and deal essentially with the same types of people as their forebears did a century or two ago. Their basic questions remain: How can we best declare the Word of God's saving grace in Jesus Christ? How can we most adequately minister to the needs of His people? Men give differing answers as they vary in their interpretations of the Gospel and of the needs of their time. The questions are the constants, the answers the variants. Today as in the first century minister implies servant. *How* one serves will depend on his understanding of the will and way of the Master and his appraisal of the most effective approach to his age.

Protestantism in America has experienced the tension between gospel and world as acutely as most other forms of Christianity in other ages and other lands. The Protestant ministry in America has faced as difficult a challenge in communicating the gospel to the world and ministering to the needs of people as the Christian ministry has in most other situations. The contrast between world and gospel has not always been as clear-cut in America as it has sometimes been in the history of Christianity. Situations calling for the sacrifice of the martyr have not always been as obvious as in some other times and civilizations. If anything, the American world has been too attractive and seductive and Protestantism has had a constant struggle to keep from capitulating to it entirely. Separation of Church and State has compelled religious groups in America to rely on their own initiative. This has made especially strong the temptation to formulate and present the gospel almost entirely in terms of the language and practices of the world. On the other hand, competition between religious groups and life in a constantly changing and rapidly expanding new world have stimulated an extraordinary amount of ministerial resourcefulness in devising ways of communicating the gospel relevantly but without undue compromise.

I

Various types of ministry and ministers have emerged during the last hundred years, some more in continuity with earlier Protestantism than others, many reflecting clearly the influence of the events of the period, and all dealing in their own separate ways with the tension between gospel and world. Typology is always somewhat artificial; one cannot pour the volatile fluids of history into static molds. Yet it can help us see the large patterns—especially if we are aware of the exceptions and of the frequent overlapping of types. This method is followed here in an effort to discern some pattern in exceedingly complex developments almost too close to the mind's eye to be viewed in proper focus.

The Ministry of Cultural Protestantism

One of the striking things about this period is the extent to which the Protestant ministry has reflected new cultural patterns and ideals. The culture-accommodating ministry is a common type.

John C. Calhoun observed in 1850 that one of the strongest of the ties holding the nation together, the spiritual and ecclesiastical, was the first to give way under the pressures of the slavery issue.[4] The reactions of Protestantism to the sectionalism that precipated the Civil War, to the War itself and to Reconstruction, tell us much about its nature in America. In the mid-nineteenth century (and continuing until recently) Protestantism was in a sense America's national religion. The nation's causes became its causes. It was a religion of the people, close to the people. As a result it became too closely identified with the causes of the moment, but at the same time it ministered valiantly to the needs of the people at times of great national peril.

The churches were intensely active on both sides during the Civil War. The words of one minister describe what was probably typical of many: "I . . . wrote, printed, stumped, talked, prayed and voted in favor of my government and . . . fought on the same side."[5] President Lincoln pointed out that he had had "great cause of gratitude for the support so unanimously given by all Christian denominations of the country."[6] Hundreds of chaplains from all major groups extended the ministry of the church to the opposing armies. A lay as well as an ordained ministry carried on extensive educational and humanitarian activities. Countless acts of mercy by both layman and minister gave comfort to those who suffered under the impact of the War.

Unfortunately many of the words and acts of churchmen during and after the Civil War were far from the spirit of a ministry of reconciliation. Instead hostility and resentment frequently motivated the ministry, especially in the denominations that had split over the slavery issue. Perhaps those who did most to heed the call to reconciliation were the great political leaders, Lincoln and Lee. They had the sense of tragedy and of the inscrutable majesty of providence lacking to many Protestant ministers.

Following the War clerical carpetbaggers preceded political carpetbaggers. Ministers of the North looked upon the South as mission territory, and regarded all Southerners—including their ministerial brothers—as unregenerated sinners who needed to be converted. In "that sinful and unrepentant region . . . the very conscience of the professedly religious portion . . . was debauched . . ." and the ministry was "guilty beyond the power of language to describe in that they were debauchers, and . . . both preachers and people were backslidden into a depth out of which even the mercy of God might fail to lift them."[7] This spirit could not but provoke an equally strong reaction on the part of Southern ministers. As they had called on their religion to justify slavery before the War and to assure the righteousness of the "cause" during the War, so once again they summoned it to build up their defenses again the outrageous onslaught of the Yankee—who became the "infidel Yankee."

The church was one of the few institutions in the South to which the defeated and despairing people could turn in an effort to recoup some sense of purpose and hope. During the period of Reconstruction the Protestant ministry played an important role in developing Southern defenses—emotional and spiritual—against Yankee encroachment. Gradually it helped paint a picture in which "Yankeeism" was portrayed as synonymous with infidelity and atheism, and the South as the true home of virtue and the Christian religion. Because the ministry was identified frequently with a supposedly happier and purer past, because it had lent strong theological sanction to slavery and the cultural patterns of the pre-Civil War period, and because it remained one of the few intact professions after the War, it was held in high esteem in Southern eyes and its power was great.[8]

Fanatical support of one side or the other during the War and clerical carpetbagging—and its obverse—after the War are examples of a type of ministerial activity that has plagued Protestantism in America periodically over the last one hundred—and more—years. Many times during this period large segments of the Protestant ministry committed themselves wholeheartedly to a single cause or movement, or to the mores of a segment of society, with the apparent certainty that this was what the ministry required of them. Henry F. May has called the period from 1861 to 1876 "The Summit of Complacency," and has shown how the majority of leading Protestant clergymen in the North supported the optimism of the "gilded age" while overlooking the easy morality or amorality of the "robber barons." The battle against "demon rum" became increasingly intense as the century progressed and many a Protestant minister came to believe that the chief test of a man's character was to be found in whether or not he drank spirituous liquors and that the cause of Christianity rose or fell with the fortunes of the temperance movement. With the coming of World War I many preachers "presented arms" in defense of nation, democracy, virtue, and God. They little doubted which side the Lord took. Protestant ministers were among the leading promoters of the crusading spirit which characterized America's approach to the War.[9] Afterwards, as disillusionment set in many turned to pacifism (frequently tinged with isolationism) or to the social gospel or both as the best way toward realization of the Kingdom of God on earth. Today many a would-be popular preacher is being seduced by the attractive "cult of reassurance" which has been so successfully proclaimed as the way to happiness here and hereafter, and which has so many characteristics of a cultural religion.

The ministry becomes a cultural ministry or a ministry of cultural Protestantism whenever it tends to identify the gospel or the Kingdom of God with a culture or with a movement or cause in this world.

The Evangelical Minister

Other types of ministry have appeared in America in the interactions of gospel and world and in response to the challenge of the rapidly changing, complex American society. One which shows the greatest continuity with the period before 1850 and which has been a constant since then is what we may call the Evangelical type.

The greatest evangelist of the latter half of the nineteenth century, Dwight L. Moody, was little affected by the revolutions going on about him. He very successfully adapted revival techniques to the urban community, but made little attempt to speak directly to the problems created by burgeoning urbanism and industrialism or to examine their causes critically. The adaptation was accomplished in order to preach effectively in cities the same gospel early nineteenth-century revivalists had preached in the backwoods of Kentucky. Moody refused to become directly involved in the controversies created by the intellectual revolution of his day; he chose to ignore these as much as possible and to stand fast by the evangelical Protestantism of his forebears, yet his influence was as widespread as that of any Protestant in his time. In his period he was the outstanding representative of one type of evangelical ministry which has deep roots in America and which is still the norm for many Protestants.

Moody was never ordained, yet few who heard him ever doubted the validity of his "call." He had powers which enabled him to command the attention of millions and to sway the lives of thousands. But this power did not come from any ecclesiastical body, or through control of the sacraments, or by virtue of an academic degree or training, or by a majority vote of a church assembly. Those who came under his influence were convinced it came directly from God. Before and since Moody the chief standard of success as an evangelist (and a minister) in American Protestantism has been evidence of such charisma, of power not possessed by ordinary folk—the ability to manifest in a convincing way that one represents more than himself, in short, that one is a man of God. Authenticity is not easily measured and there have been charlatans and border-line cases, but there has also been a host of sincere and effective ministers called of God, servants of the Lord.

Moody preached a gospel with but one center, God's saving act in Jesus Christ, and one goal, the conversion and salvation of the sinner. All other ends were secondary. His technique and his message were dominated by this interest. Public morality was to be improved through saving individuals. The church was a voluntary association of the saved.

Moody's orientation was substantially that of eighteenth- and nineteenth-century evangelical or pietist Protestantism with its special emphases and interpretations of sin and judgment, conversion, salvation, redemption, heaven and hell, literalistic use of the Bible, its suspicion of the wisdom and ways of this world, its moralism and individualism. Essentially the same gospel was preached by thousands of evangelical ministers in Moody's time and has been followed by a multitude since.

The career of the present-day evangelist, Billy Graham, seems to indicate that the evangelical minister still occupies an important place in America Protestantism. There have been many changes in the last century, but if one symbol of the ministry stands out above all others it is that of the simple, unassuming "unadorned" man of God, standing with Bible in hand, expounding the gospel of salvation in and through Jesus Christ.

The Liberal Minister

There were others in Moody's time who could not avoid being caught up in the currents and crosscurrents of intellectual strife which blew across the period with such force that the whole structure of evangelical Protestantism was threatened with collapse. Some endeavored to strip the structure down to the "fundamentals" and presumed to plant the footings deeper so as to preserve the building intact no matter what took place around it. Others attempted to meet the crisis by adding modern, up-to-date features here and there, and rearranging floor plan and structural supports.

The Darwinian theory of evolution was the blast which appeared to threaten evangelical Protestantism most seriously. Together with other developments in the "new science" it caused a series of reactions among Protestants which by the early twentieth century had resulted in a sharp cleavage between liberalism and fundamentalism.

Henry Ward Beecher, an early liberal, introduced evolutionary thought into his sermons in the 1870's. He identified evolution with God's way of doing things, overlooking some of the less pleasant aspects of the theory. His example was followed by others until by the end of the century many Protestant ministers found little difficulty in adjusting to the theory which appeared radically unchristian to many others.

Beecher spent much of his energy in reaction against the doctrines and influence of his famous father. He was thoroughly grounded in the evangelical Protestantism of Lyman Beecher but it became evident very early in his ministry that he was not wedded to it. On the contrary, he developed a freedom which enabled him to embrace most of the ideas that were suggested by the advancing science of his time. Without scientific training, he embraced only the simplest ideas of the new science, those which could most easily be marketed in popular form. He showed an extraordinary ability to adjust and adapt the thought forms of a previous generation to the temper of his own. He displayed an unusual sensitivity to the currents and crosscurrents of his time and a remarkable ability to shift with the prevailing winds. He built on the foundations of evangelical Protestantism, but he looked to current ideas and needs for the material out of which to form the superstructure.

Beecher's outlook on the role of the ministry was clearly set forth in the first series of Lyman Beecher lectures delivered at Yale in 1871. "The providence of God is rolling forward a spirit of investigation that Christian ministers must meet and join," he asserted.

There is no class of people upon earth who can less afford to let the development of truth run ahead of them than they. You cannot wrap yourselves in professional mystery, for the glory of the Lord is such that it is preached with power throughout all the length and breadth of the world, by these investigators of his wondrous creation. You cannot go back and become apostles of the dead past, drivelling after ceremonies, and letting the world do the thinking and studying. There must be a new spirit infused into the ministry.

To those afraid that such freedom might destroy the whole structure of Christianity Beecher recommended:

> You take care of yourselves and of men, and *learn the truth as God shows it to to you all the time,* and you need not be afraid of Christianity. . . . We must be more industrious in investigation, more honest in deduction, and more willing to take the truth in its new fullness. . . .[10]

Openness to new discoveries of truth and willingness to adjust one's beliefs and practices to them—this became the standard of the liberal minister. He was not a Biblical literalist. The Bible remained a source of authority but authority was also to be found in the discoveries of the scientist and the insights of the poet. If he was regarded by his congregation as speaking with authority it was because he spoke for a modern God or God in modern guise. He was not a creedalist; creeds restricted him too much. If he used one it was likely to be of his own making. He shied away from the use of the traditional theological language, preferring instead new words and often new concepts. He never became so free, however, as to discard entirely the concepts of historical Christianity but rather endeavored to reinterpret them. Usually well-educated, he could use the new terms of the intellectuals though he might not always have understood them fully. He was permissive in his attitude toward his congregation, allowing them a good deal of freedom in matters of belief and, to a lesser extent, in practice. In most instances he was identified with the middle or upper classes in American society.

The liberal minister has become a common figure in most of the major Protestant denominations. When, a short time ago, *Life* magazine chose twelve of America's "Great Preachers" nine of those selected were Protestants. The majority of these nine could be classified as liberals or as men whose early ministry at least was shaped by the patterns of liberalism.

The Fundamentalist Minister

The liberal minister attempted to adjust the essentials of evangelical Protestantism to the intellectual trends of the time; the fundamentalist minister attempted to maintain his version of evangelical Protestantism intact, to shut it off from "alien" influences and preserve it from change. The one was open to new discoveries in science, believing that more truth was to be disclosed; the other either closed his mind to all discoveries that seemed to contradict the truth that he knew, or sought to keep science and theology wholly separate. The liberal minister left some questions undecided and attempted to imbue a spirit of investigation in his congregation whereas the fundamentalist minister declared and expounded the truth he already possessed.

The fundamentalist minister possessed a clear-cut sense of call, usually defined in terms of a single identifiable experience. Education tended to be of little importance save for the purpose of a better understanding of Biblical revelation. Understanding of recent trends in learning was of little or no concern to him; it might even be a hindrance since all that was necessary for salvation had been once and for all revealed. Preaching was the most important way of communicating the truth. The preacher was God's messenger. His approach tended to be emotional and directed toward individual conversion. Pastoral work tended to follow a stereotyped pattern. The minister was expected, when he called at the home or on the sick and the bereaved, to offer prayers that followed a pattern—though appearing to be impromptu—and to bring assurances based on an otherworldly orientation. He was expected to inquire after the morality of his people and to denounce any irregularities. Religious education was not a particularly important aspect of his work since conversion was far more important than nurture.

Fundamentalism has been characterized by (1) vigorous resistance to developments in the world of science that appeared to contradict the Biblical text; (2) Biblical literalism; (3) individualism; (4) moralism; and (5) insistence on belief in certain "fundamentals" such as the inerrancy of the Scriptures, the virgin birth of Jesus Christ, and his second coming. It developed out of the evangelical Protestantism of the early nineteenth century, gaining a stronghold especially in the South where the majority of Protestants regarded themselves as the true defenders of the faith while the liberal Yankees were stultifying it. Fundamentalism is in many ways similar to evangelical Protestantism; the chief difference between them is one of mood and spirit. Fundamentalism is evangelical Protestantism on the defensive and thus in its more rigid and ossified form. To be sure, liberals could become dogmatic about their liberalism, and fundamentalists could be fair-minded about their convictions.

The Minister as Social Reformer

The revolutionary social, economic, and intellectual developments in post-Civil War America stimulated within Protestantism attempts to develop a new prophetic ministry which would exercise critical judgment on the injustices which accompanied the radical changes of the period and would point the way to a new application of the gospel to the social needs of the time. A segment of the Protestant ministry became impressed with the need for a systematic approach to those factors which are most fundamental in bringing about social change for good or ill. Many men who had begun a conventional pastoral ministry sometime in the latter half of the century found themselves so deeply involved in the forces of social change that they felt compelled to alter radically their concept of the ministry. Involvement in the multitudinous problems of a rapidly expanding urban area or exposure to the increasingly bitter struggle between labor and management or entanglement in the luxuriant and rank growth so abundantly fostered by the new wealth of the "gilded age": these and other factors caused many men to re-examine their roles as ministers and to seek more effective ways of ministering to the needs of their time.[11] Perhaps the most important thing that happened to such men was that they became aware of the many factors bearing on human welfare and thus of importance to the Christian gospel. As it was once put in homely fashion, they found out that the gospel had something to do with the plumbing.[12]

Seeing an urban slum, being exposed to the vice, crime, disease, and poverty of the city, becoming aware of the plight of an underpaid or unemployed worker, the wideawake minister felt that something was wrong and expressed his feeling in moral protest. He plunged into a renewed examination of the Bible in an effort to find there the foundation for a Christian approach to these evils. Many men turned to the literature of social protest and reform to find additional assistance in their search for an effective approach to the ills of their work. Societies were formed for "the advancement of the interests of labor," for the promotion of the ideals of the Kingdom, and for other such causes. Like-minded individuals banded together to make their protest more effective. Meetings were held, resolutions passed, journals published— all in the interest of reform. A few ministers actively engaged in politics and a very small minority joined such essentially protest groups as the Socialist party.

Many ministerial reformers were concerned to be as scientific as possible in their reform activities. Hopkins says that "clergymen were among the leading diagnosticians of the industrial maladjustments of the late 'seventies,"[13] and their work became more thorough in later decades. For assistance in diagnosis of social ills and in finding remedies, many clergymen turned avidly to the new field of social science. "We are beginning to see that the divine methods are scientific," Josiah Strong asserted, "and that if we are to be effective 'laborers together with God,' our methods must also be scientific." [14] Ministers were active in the founding and promoting of organizations formed to advance the study of society. Many ministers occupied early academic chairs in sociology and other related fields. Outstanding pioneer social scientists strongly urged the clergy to train themselves adequately in this new and promising field. John R. Commons requested them to study sociology and to "give one-half their pulpit time to expounding it. . . ." [15] Richard Ely "proposed that half of theological students' time be devoted to social science and that the divinity schools be the chief intellectual centers for sociology." [16] Many seminaries took the advice seriously and instituted courses in Christian Sociology and Social Ethics.

Thus the concept of and approach to the ministry was definitely broadened under the impact of the Social Gospel Movement. In the minds of many a successful ministry now entailed a study of society and of the social forces involved in the shaping of the life of the individual, an awareness of social evils as well as personal sins, and some knowledge of the means of "social salvation" as well as of individual redemption. The minister was to identify himself with an advancing Kingdom of God which reached far beyond the confines of the church; he was to engage in service to the community as a whole and not to the church alone. He was to

become a vital factor in his city, a man to be reckoned with in every great movement, a man to be consulted upon all important questions affecting the life of the people, a dominant force in the making and the molding of the democratic order.

In some way he was to become *the* minister of the great social order which was developing. [17]

There were some who were apprehensive that the minister might go so far as a social reformer that he would neglect the other aspects of his ministry. Edward Judson declared:

Social problems are so difficult and so fascinating that they easily absorb all a minister's time and energy. He neglects his study and the care of his flock. He loses his priestly character and becomes a mere social functionary. [18]

Nevertheless, one of the most profound changes which has taken place among certain segments of the Protestant ministry in the last century has been the growth of concern for analysis of society and the reform of social ills. The trend which began with the Social Gospel Movement in the late nineteenth century has continued as an important aspect of Protestantism since. The minister as social reformer has most frequently also been a liberal. But not all liberal ministers have been concerned with social reform and not all ministerial social reformers have been liberals.

The Urban Minister

Urbanization, asserts H. Paul Douglass, has brought about in the church "the greatest inner revolution it has ever known. . . ." [19] This may be an exaggeration, but there is truth in it. Urbanization has brought a highly mobile population. It has created an increasingly complex society in which the individual has found himself as part of a multiplicity rather than a unity, associated with many different groups and institutions of which the church is merely one. In America it has also involved an increased religious and cultural pluralism. These and other factors have created problems of adjustment for church and ministry.

Urbanization has called forth two types of reaction in Protestantism: first, the church and the ministry have devised numerous means of reaching out to all kinds of people and groups in the cities; and second, attempts have been made to strengthen the inner fellowship of the local church, to bring about a genuine community in which each individual has a sense of being a member of the one body. These two approaches have gone on simultaneously, but the extensive outreach was more characteristic of the late years of the nineteenth and the early years of the twentieth centuries whereas the intensive cultivation has become more common in recent years.

The chief methods of the church's outreach in the cities remained preaching and evangelism. Moody, Beecher, and Brooks made far greater impact on the cities of the late nineteenth century than any other three ministers of that period, and Moody was chiefly noted for his evangelistic techniques and abilities; Beecher and Brooks for their preaching. But these methods were supplemented by a host of activities and organizations of educational, humanitarian, and recreational nature. These included the Sunday School Movement, the Y. M. C. A., the

Y. W. C. A., various other young people's organizations; the establishment of the parish house, the institutional church, the settlement house, and deaconess institutions of various types; the provision of athletics, public baths, savings banks, and trained nurses; the use of house-to-house visitation, and open-air services; and the support of special work with workingmen and recent immigrants; tenement-house reform, organized charity, fresh-air funds, holiday houses, et cetera.

One of the outstanding products of such efforts to meet the needs of the growing and changing city was the development of the institutional church. Many a church had been left stranded as the old residents moved out and was quite useless to the incoming tidal wave of new settlers. It faced the alternative of moving with the ebb or adjusting to the flow. If it did neither it died. The institutional church developed out of an effort to adjust to the incoming groups. As many of the old members as possible were held. But a new program was developed to appeal to the changing community, a program which went far beyond the traditional methods of ministration.

The ideal of the institutional church, as expressed by The Open or Institutional Church League, was one of "ministration to all men and to all of the man." It stood for "open church doors every day and all day, free seats, a plurality of Christian workers, the personal activity of all church members, [and] a ministry to all the community through educational, reformatory and philanthropic channels. . . ." [20]

One minister presided over the multifarious activities of the institutional church. Success in this position required real administrative ability. The staff under his authority might include associate and assistant ministers, deaconesses, social workers, numerous lay volunteer workers, secretarial and custodial help. Each member of the staff had his own special duties and area of operation assigned to him by the chief or by staff consultation. The institutional church adopted techniques of efficiency and organization from the industrial and business world. It was one of Protestantism's most effective weapons in meeting the problems created by advancing urbanism.

Somewhat related to this type of institution but even more strictly organized and more specialized was the Salvation Army. The Army was founded in 1878 by William Booth as a result of his conviction that the churches were not doing their work adequately. Booth developed a strict plan of military discipline under which men and women devoted themselves to a ministry to the down-and-outers of industrial society. Dressed in quasi-military garb and under military command these ministers of the gospel attempted to appeal to the publicans and sinners by means of street-corner preaching, instrumental music, and hymns sung to catchy and popular tunes. Rather soon after coming to America the Army developed a system of social service. The "leaders began to realize that the pauper poor needed a thoroughgoing reformation in which physical, as well as spiritual and moral, improvement must play a part." [21]

Protestantism's struggle to minister adequately to the needs created by increasing urbanization continues. Much of the heart of the city has been lost to it, but constant efforts are being made to devise adequate ways of ministering to urban areas. In recent years frequently effective endeavors have been made through such means as group ministries in parishes in critical neighborhoods of large cities and various types of co-operative work in newly created housing areas.

Urbanization has also had the effect of causing Protestantism to seek methods of strengthening its inner life. Pastoral calling has assumed a new importance as the urban church has sought to develop a sense of community among its members. Henry Sloane Coffin is reported to have made as many as one thousand pastoral calls a year during his ministry at the Madison Avenue Presbyterian Church in New York City. Activities have been developed to appeal to specific age and interest groups—the young married couples, families, professional women, et cetera. Protestant churches have sought to build a sense of unity and wholeness among church members. This can prepare them to engage in the church's ministry to the world, to operate from a position of inner strength in appealing to those on the "outside."

The Rural Minister

With the increasing impact of urbanization and industrialization on America distintegration began to take place in rural communities. The rural ministry gradually became a stepping stone for young men on their way to more prosperous city churches or a final resting place for the man who had given his most vigorous years to urban centers. Rural churches were becoming poor country relations. Some religious leaders, being convinced that Protestantism had a special responsibility for rural communities and that it would benefit from a strong rural America, became concerned to develop a specialized rural ministry.

President Theodore Roosevelt appointed a special Commision on Country Life to investigate what was happening to the rural areas and determine what was needed to maintain their vitality. The report of this

Commission, issued in 1911, had a great impact on the development of a specialized rural ministry. It called for the recruiting and training of country pastors who knew rural problems, loved the country, and had sympathy with rural ideals and aspirations. It pointed to the need for specialized training to be provided by "ministerial colleges and theological seminaries" in co-operation with the argicultural colleges of the nation.[22] Many institutions responded to the needs pointed up by the Commission and by others, by developing such specialized training. Something approaching missionary zeal for the rural ministry has developed in this century as an increasing number of young men have decided to devote themselves to it.

The Lay Minister

Laymen were called on to help meet the challenges thrown before Protestantism by the industrialism and urbanism of the late nineteenth century. Graham Taylor, speaking in 1889 before the Evangelical Alliance's General Christian Conference in Boston, called attention to the need for "Arousing and Training the Activity of the Laity." Recalling Protestant emphasis on the "priesthood of the people," Taylor called for a lay ministry which would include: (1) a "Sunday-school army," (2) Christian associations, (3) the utilization of the "great multitude of women who publish the Word in home and school, mission-bands and temperance unions, and the thousand forms of woman's work for women and for the church," and (4) the use of the "600,000 youth from Christian Endeavor Societies." [23] An empire of lay activity grew up among the organizations suggested by Taylor and many others. Many institutions for the training of lay workers sprang into existence.

An example of a laymen's movement which reflected the spirit of the period was The Men and Religion Forward Movement. Formed in 1911 primarily by businessmen, its object was declared to be

an effort to secure the personal acceptance of Jesus Christ by the individual manhood and boyhood of our times, and their permanent enlistment in the program of Jesus Christ as the world program of daily affairs.[24]

Displaying the enthusiasm of a time committed to the evangelization of the world in one generation the Movement engaged in a highly organized form of evangelism, carrying out a planned campaign by outstanding businessmen in several major cities. Effective during the period of initial enthusiasm, by 1914 the energy of the Movement had been spent.[25]

Probably the most effective laymen's organizations during the latter part of the nineteenth and the early twentieth centuries were the Y. M. C. A. and the Y. W. C. A. In their beginnings both regarded themselves as arms of the church, specialized organizations designed to carry on a ministry not provided by ordinary local churches nor by denominations. In its convention of 1856 the Y. M. C. A. declared:

> We do not intend that this institution shall take the highest place in our affections, or the largest share of our labors, but, that we hold this organization as auxiliary to the divinely appointed means of grace, the CHURCH *and the preaching of the Gospel.*[26]

The Y's engaged in many activities including social service and humanitarian work, evangelism of an interdenominational sort, the training of laymen for such work, and activities designed to appeal especially to young men and women. They were among the first organizations to carry on an effective ministry in American universities and colleges.

Many of the lay organizations formed in the late nineteenth or the early twentieth centuries have now ceased to exist or their work has been greatly modified—as in the case with the Y's, for example. Denominations have become increasingly conscious of the importance of making use of the energies of laymen and have established organizations of their own to do this. Possibly we are experiencing a renewed awareness of the nature of the church as a ministering institution, a body which ministers to the needs of the world through all its members. The minister may function as a leader, a source of inspiration, an organizer, an administrator, but he cannot singlehandedly, or even with a staff, carry on the service which is the church's vocation. The complex and pressing demands made upon Protestantism by the rising industrial and urban society have brought with them a renewed awareness of the role of the church as a ministering body in which both lay and ordained ministers are called as servants of the gospel, not only in the church but also in the world.

Women Ministers

The needs of the period prompted many denominations to give serious consideration—some for the first time—to the use of women in specialized ministries. Protestantism has never been fully clear in its own mind about the role of women in the ministry. Some denominations have granted the same ordination status to them as to men. Others have refused. In most denominations women have been commissioned to carry on special humanitarian and educational services. In the latter part of the nineteenth century the Protestant Episcopal, Lutheran, and Methodist denominations in particular called upon women in comparatively large numbers to serve as deaconesses. Abell reports that nearly "a hundred and fifty well-equipped deaconess institutions arose between 1885 and 1900. Under the circumstances," he continues, "this was amazing progress, reflecting as nothing else did the impact of the social crisis upon conventional modes of religious behavior." [27]

Social crisis or no social crisis, however, many denominations still refuse women ordination and even in those that grant it women do not play the same role as men. The issue has been a topic for debate in many ecclesiastical bodies. In 1947 the Presbyterian General Assembly refused ordination on the grounds that this privilege would likely "mean scandal in the church." The 1955 Assembly reversed this decision, perhaps because it was more scandalous not to allow ordination than to permit it. Seldom are ordained women placed in full charge of a local church, save in some small town and rural congregations that cannot afford or find a man. Any female minister must overcome a tremendous prejudice. The church is probably the most conservative of all institutions in this regard. Women have gained far more status in most other professions than in the ministry. Most women ministers find their places as directors of religious education or in other special capacities on the staffs of large city churches, or as ministers to students and directors of student work, or as wives of ordained men.

The Negro Minister

There would be little point in singling the Negro out for special attention were it not for the fact that following the Civil War and until recently the minister has occupied a unique role in the Negro community. His status in it was unsurpassed by any other profession and unsurpassed also by the status of ministers in any other Protestant group in America. The one institution which the Negro was able to run for himself after the Civil War was the church. This then became the institution through which the greatest personal prestige could be obtained, and we should add, through which the most immediate service to the people could be rendered. The one man in the Negro community who usually owed his position to no one outside that community was the minister. Because of this and because of his unique position of authority as a religious leader he could frequently do and say things that no one else in the community could do or say. In many cases during the post-War period he was the only man in the community with any semblance of an education. He performed many functions beyond the normal work of the ministry, being on occasion teacher, lawyer, doctor, and statesman. The social pattern of the Negro community in the post-War period might be described as theocratic with the minister occupying the role of chief, prophet, educator, and political leader. He was, Woodson says, "the walking encyclopedia, the counselor of the unwise, the friend of the unfortunate, the social welfare organizer, and the interpreter of the times." No man, continues Woodson, was "properly introduced to the Negro community unless he [came] through the minister, and no movement [could] expect success there unless it [had] his cooperation or endorsement." [28]

But more recently the status of the minister in the Negro community has been on the decline while other professions have grown in power. The ministry has become less and less attractive to vigorous and promising young men because of its identification with a rejected older order, the stereotypes which have developed, and probably most important of all because the "old time religion" no longer appeals to many of the young.

The educational level of the Negro minister has never been high nor even adequate in most instances. Fortunately, in recent times this level has risen slightly, but the gains are small. The Negro community continues to experience a serious, if not critical, shortage of well-trained ministers. This condition does not augur well for the future of Protestantism in the Negro communities. Efforts, however, are being made to correct it by encouraging the development of a kind of ministry which will overcome some of the common defects, by improving the caliber of professional education available to Negroes and by enrolling an increasing number of Negroes in interracial seminaries. [29]

The Immigrant Minister

For more than a century after the establishment of the United States immigrants poured on to American shores by the millions. Rarely has such a mass migration occurred or have so many religious groups been transplanted. The problems of effecting a satisfactory settlement were large. For the churches the fundamental problem was to distinguish between those cultural forms which were extraneous to the gospel, or mere vessels for its transmission, and those beliefs and practices which had to be preserved if the faith was to stand. The tension between gospel and world was as strong in the immigrant church as in any native group, if not stronger.

The immigrant minister faced the task of maintaining sufficient contact with the old ways so as to preserve the roots of faith while also adapting his ministry to the new environment. Frequently the church proved to be one of the strongest ties with the mother country and its ministers among the slowest to adapt themselves to the new culture. They clung tenaciously to the language and forms of the home church and all too often came to be—especially for the young people—a resented symbol of the peculiar ways of the "old country" which the young rejected in their consuming desire to identify themselves with the new world. On the other hand, many an immigrant pastor became an important leader in holding a people together during the difficult period of adjustment which these first-generation Americans faced. The position of the pastor in the immigrant community was similar to the place of the minister in the Negro community. He often played the role of community leader.

Such men frequently found it necessary to develop new methods of ministration and to occupy unaccustomed roles. A man trained to be a parish pastor in the established Church of Sweden and accustomed to the prerogatives of such a position was not too well prepared to carry on an effective ministry among struggling immigrants in a strange land and surrounded by an alien people. Nevertheless, many responded vigorously to the challenge and came to prefer the new country to the old.[30]

No immigrant minister could long remain entirely free from the influence of the ministerial patterns of the new world. The voluntaryism of American denominationalism forced new practices upon him. Laymen assumed an important role, and most immigrant churches tended toward congregationalism in America no matter what the form of church government had been in the native land. Sermons had to be made interesting and understandable if the congregation was to be held. Pastoral calling assumed a new importance in maintaining contact with the flock, many of whom were tempted to pursue the false gods of the new world or merely become indifferent toward the old faiths. The education of the young became crucial, for among the second generation the ties with the old ways were usually weak and the pressures to adjust to the new world were especially strong. If the young could not be held the cause was lost.

The Missionary

In his monumental *A History of the Expansion of Christianity* Kenneth Scott Latourette refers to the period between 1800 and 1914 as "The Great Century." He devotes three volumes of a seven-volume work to this period. During this time Christianity expanded on a far greater scale than during any preceding period and Protestantism played a greater role in this expansion than did the other branches of the Christian movement.[31] From within Protestantism came a surge of missionary endeavor unparalleled in strength and magnitude of goal in previous Protestant history, and perhaps unparalleled in the history of Christianity. This movement had its origins chiefly in the Protestantism of the British Isles and the United States, whence also it derived its main support. It was "from the United States that the majority of the missionaries and more than half of the funds of the Protestant missionary enterprise eventually came." [32] The end of the nineteenth century was to witness a Protestant people in America bent upon evangelizing the world in one generation and hurriedly devising the methods and providing the means by which this might be done.

Thus during our period the missionary calling was one of the most important types of the ministry within American Protestantism. It was somewhat distinct from those ministries carried on among a people the majority of whom already professed to be Christians. Furthermore, the missionary ministry came to imply a greater awareness of calling or a more urgent sense of need and purpose. It came to play a role somewhat similar to that of the monastic calling in Catholicism, demanding a special measure of singleness of purpose and devotion.

The missionary "call" led to more than one type of ministry. Techniques somewhat different from those in use among "Christian people" had to be developed. Chief among the ministries was that of evangelization, but ministries of teaching and healing also assumed an important role. Students and lay men and women entered the lists in unprecedented numbers. Missionary societies were formed locally and nationally to facilitate the church's ministry.

The call to missionary activity remains strong in Protestantism. Denominations have their recruiting agencies and seminaries provide specialized training which in many instances utilizes the techniques and knowledge supplied by relevant sciences. An interesting development is the program which sends recent college graduates to mission fields for periods of three years or more. This is both a recruiting device and a way of staffing mission stations. Its success demonstrates the dramatic appeal of the missionary call and the efficiency of denominational missionary organizations.

Ministry to Institutions

In the last century an increasing specialization of ministries has developed as the churches have continued to follow the historical practice of seeking people out wherever they are. As American society has become increasingly institutionalized, the churches have sent more and more ministers into institutions of various types.

Chaplains have served in the armed forces in ever-increasing numbers, many for a short period of time—especially during war—others for the entire length of their ministries. Men are also turning in greater numbers to ministries in hospitals, prisons, schools, and colleges, and other institutions. Some seminaries now provide a form of specialized training designed to prepare men for service in particular kinds of institutions. Professional organizations of institutional chaplains have come into existence on denominational and interdenominational levels. Standards of training have been established in certain cases by these organizations. In some instances special journals deal with the peculiar problems of such a ministry.

II

Calling, Education, and Ordination

What qualifies a man for the ministry? It has been generally characteristic of evangelical Protestantism in America to single out a special call as fundamental. This call has been conceived as a summons from God made known to the individual through an identifiable and distinctive personal experience. It has been assumed that usually prior to this experience the individual has responded positively to a similar call to become a Christian. After these experiences professional training might be added, although it has not always been regarded as necessary. Some denominations have engaged in family quarrels while weighing the relative merits of inner call and professional training.

Emphasis on the professional character of the ministry has increased during the last hundred years. Vigorous attempts have been made to raise the standards of ministerial education and training. An increasing number of seminaries has come into existence, and seminary education has become more professionalized—by emphasizing more specialized and practical training than a minister received a century ago.

Nevertheless, most denominations still regard an authentic call— usually understood as a personal experience or series of experiences—as fundamental for entrance to the ministry. In some groups this inner call may be all that is necessary to ordination. In others in which summons by an ecclesiastical body is as important as an inner call the latter must be supplemented or tested by a period spent under the supervision of a bishop, a conference, a presbytery, or some other official body. The inner call must also be deepened and enlarged by a long process of education and training. Preaching is not permitted until after ordination by some denominations.

Methods and standards by which the authenticity of the call is determined vary widely. In the strictest form of congregationalism the local church is the sole judge. More frequently conferences, dioceses and associations of churches, bishops and other supervisors exercise the right.

Standards may be heavily doctrinal in character or more experiential. In many cases the test of authenticity is formulated in terms of certain theological statements and standards to which the individual is expected to give assent. In others he is closely questioned on the nature of his experience of an inner call, the manner in which he received it, and the effect it has had on his life. During the last century there has been some tendency in certain groups toward relaxation of doctrinal standards, while efforts have been made to raise the educational standards.

The trends in education and training described in the preceding chapter continued in the period after 1850. In many instances theological education was on the defensive against the increasing power and influence of secular education. For the most part, theological schools did not occupy a very important role in the educational world. Their denominational character tended to widen the breach between theological and other types of education and to isolate the seminary from the prevailing intellectual currents.

However, certain institutions did attempt to bridge the growing gap between the theology of evangelical Protestantism and the intellectual issues of the late nineteenth and early twentieth centuries. Many of the teachers in these seminaries were trained in Germany, the center of advanced Protestant theology. Others received their training in one of the new sciences in an American university, and were thus better prepared to adjust theologically to trends in the world of science. Seminary administrations—especially in the university schools—were frequently motivated by a desire to bring theological education in line with the highest standards of secular education.[33]

The constant danger existed that these seminaries might go so far in adaptation to recent developments in theology and in other academic areas that they would lose touch with the churches. Churches oriented in evangelical theology were little prepared to cope with the findings of Biblical criticism and comparative religion, or to adjust their outlook to the recommendations of the social ethics professor. Sometimes a difficult situation was created for many graduates of these schools when they attempted to gain the approval of their denominations and to adjust to the theological orientation of their congregations.

The university schools such as Yale, Harvard, Chicago, and Union in New York, have frequently been at the growing edge of Protestantism in the last half century. Most of them have become interdenominational in character. They have influenced denominational seminaries toward a greater adjustment to intellectual trends, have offered advanced training for their graduates, and have been an important source of their teachers. They have prepared many college teachers, leaders of the ecumenical and other interdenominational enterprises, and have trained men and women for other special types of ministry which do not fit readily into the traditional pattern of theological education.

Meanwhile, the number of denominational seminaries has greatly increased during the past century. Such denominations as the Methodists, Baptists, and Disciples have shown an increasing interest in graduate theological education, and various denominational splits and new movements have apparently created the need for more institutions. Denominationalism has in some instances become intensified in theological education. Efforts to bring together seminaries of various denominations have met with difficulty, although they have been fairly successful in cases where great care was exercised. Many denominational schools have performed valuable service in aiding their churches both to maintain their traditional orientations and to adjust themselves enough to social and intellectual developments so as not to lose contact with the ongoing world. At this point the denominational seminary has certain advantages over the interdenominational because of its close contact with denominational practices and traditions.

The tendency for theological education to become increasingly pragmatic was noted in the previous chapter. This tendency has increased in our period. Ministerial education, like education in general, has moved away from the classical pattern toward a greater emphasis on practical arts and vocational training. An obvious evidence of this shift is seen in the gradual de-emphasis of classical language study. Some seminaries have dropped requirements in Hebrew, Latin, and Greek. Some still cling to one or two of these but many demand no great proficiency in any language except English and sometimes even that is lacking.

There has been an enormous increase in the number and variety of courses offered, an increasing provision of electives, increasing opportunity to prepare for various forms of specialized ministry, and an extension of the seminary's responsibility to include on-the-field operations. Certain trends in the content of courses are also evident. Robert L. Kelly in his study *Theological Education in America,* published in 1924, found in the seminary curricula of 1872 an emphasis on exegetical theology and the study of the original Biblical languages. By 1895 there was less emphasis on exegetical theology and more on historical and practical theology. New kinds of courses were being introduced into the curricula, including missions, sociology, and ethics, and more time was being allotted to elocution or "sacred oratory." By 1921 the curricula provided for more specialization and a more practical emphasis. Requirements in original languages had declined. The increase of courses in practical theology, sociology, religious education, psychology of religion, rural and urban church, demonstrated both the specialized and practical emphases. Kelly's summary of the trends in the curriculum of Oberlin Seminary applies to many others as well: "The program of study was changing from the dogmatic to the practical, from the ecclesiocentric to the socio-centric. . . ." [34] More recent examinations show the continuation of these emphases in our time though they also show a revival of interest in systematic and exegetical theology and in the Biblical languages.

A discussion of the education and training of the ministry would not be complete without some reference to the large number of ministers who have received little or no professional training. An analysis of the 1926 Religious Census figures for seventeen of the largest white

Protestant denominations in the United States showed that over 40 per cent of all the ministers of these denominations were graduates neither of college nor of theological seminary, while only 33 per cent were graduates of both. Actually these figures are high since the census bureau was very liberal in its interpretation of the meaning of college or seminary.[35]

Reliable and comprehensive statistics are not available for the periods previous to or since 1926. On the basis of what evidence is at hand one can conclude that while there has been a gradual rise in the level of theological education in the last half century the training of a significant number of Protestant ministers is very inadequate, if adequacy is measured in terms of college and seminary training.

It is an extremely difficult and slow process to raise the educational level because of a lack of qualified candidates, a strong tradition of lay control, and suspicion of education in many quarters. It is the general impression that not enough men of first-class ability are being attracted to the ministry to meet the existing needs. Competition from other professions and occupations has become more acute over the last century. At one time the ministry was at the top of the professions in terms of status and prestige. This is no longer the case, and the churches face a difficult and constant task in recruiting and training men.

Protestantism in America, as indicated in the preceding chapter, has been almost from the first strongly lay-centered and lay-controlled. In many instances the tradition of a lay ministry has militated against ministerial education. If a conscientious and consecrated layman does the work of preaching the gospel why bother to send a man to college or seminary for training? This attitude is not as prevalent as it once was, but it still crops up—especially in the form of lay apathy toward standards of training.

There has also been in certain branches of Protestantism a long-standing suspicion of education. Perry Miller once said that Protestantism has always had difficulty in preventing the doctrine of justification by faith from being interpreted as meaning justification by ignorance. This suspicion of learning became especially strong among some Protestants in the face of the intellectual revolution of the late nineteenth century. It ranged from a deliberate cultivation of an attitude of ignorance and an obscurantism that reveled in the "old time religion," to a mistrust of certain "modern" universities and seminaries. Many denominations went through a period of strenuous self-examination and discussion of the merits or lack of merits of a ministerial education and on the matter of what kind of education—if any—should be approved.

Typical of the attitude of many churchmen was the sentiment expressed by Bishop Pierce of the Southern Methodist Church in 1872. "The best preacher I ever heard," averred the Bishop, "had never been to college at all—hardly to school." This statement was made in the course of a controversy over the establishment by the church of a university. The Bishop was especially suspicious of the theological training that might be offered. "It is my opinion," he affirmed, "that every dollar invested in a theological school will be a damage to Methodism. Had I a million, I would not give a dime for such an object." [36]

A very strong minority of the officials of the Southern Methodist Church sided with the Bishop in his suspicion of theological education. An attempt was made in the Conference of 1870 to secure a central theological school for the church. Although a majority of a special committee on theological education supported the proposal, the minority was able to rally Conference support to its position. The minority report gives a clear indication of an attitude which continued to play an important role in many church circles and is present even today. The history of theological schools, asserted the report,

has little that is favorable to Methodism, and much that is adverse. They have been fruitful sources of heresies innumerable, of a manner of preaching not generally desirable and rarely effectual among us, and of that formalism that never favors experiential religion. . . .

The report called for the support of existing colleges and of local Bible schools which had sprung up in profusion.[37]

Such mistrust of any education tinged with "modern" influences resulted in the creation of scores of Bible colleges and training schools for ministers. In many instances the level of training in these institutions has been of rather doubtful quality. On the other hand leaders of the Bible school movement have been developing a theory of liberal arts education with the Bible at its center, and through an accrediting association have moved toward standardization and steady improvement of a program which seeks to synthesize conservative evangelical Christianity with a valid educational ideal.

In some groups the attempt to raise the level of theological education still goes on against strong opposition despite the rise in the level of general education in the nation. Successful efforts have been made to raise and maintain standards through the formation of the American Association of Theological Schools and its system of accreditation.

III

Social Sources and Status

After 1800, as has been pointed out, Protestant ministers in America came in increasing numbers from the lower social and economic strata. This trend continued throughout the nineteenth century and well into the twentieth. Douglass and Brunner found that

responses to the call of the ministry are strongly skewed in favor of candidates from small communities, from relatively humble antecedents, both educationally and economically, and from the less well-established racial elements of the population.[38]

During the early part of the nineteenth century this fact of less privileged social and economic origin did not appear to affect adversely the status of the minister. His remained a privileged position. Whether there has been a decline in social status since 1850 is very difficult to judge. If such a decline has occurred it has probably taken place in two areas—influence on the practical affairs of the community and standing in intellectual circles.

The famous observer of the American scene, Lord Bryce, testified that the position of minister carried with it a good deal of prestige. "It gives a man a certain advantage in the society . . . to which he naturally belongs in respect of his family connections, his means, and his education," he asserted.

In the great cities the leading ministers . . . are among the first citizens, and exercise an influence often wider and more powerful than that of any layman. . . . In cities of the second order, the clergymen . . . move in the best society of the place. Similarly in country places the pastor is better educated and more enlightened than the average members of his flock, and becomes a leader in works of beneficence.

Although he felt that the standing of clergymen remained high in the United States after the Civil War, Bryce did note a change in the character of ministerial influence on communtiy affairs. Ministers no longer had as much political influence as in an earlier period. They "must not now interfere in politics."

It is only on platforms or in conventions where some moral cause is to be advocated, such as Abolitionism was before the war years . . . or temperance is now, that clergymen can with impunity appear.[39]

These observations would appear to continue to hold true for the later period. Ministers of the more established denominations do move in the higher social circles in most communities. But for the most part their influence is small in the organizations—political parties, labor unions, manufacturers' associations, farm groups—which are most effective in determining the direction of community affairs. The minister can be counted on for support of the obvious moral issues, but when the issues become complex and ambiguous his support probably will not be sought. Samuel Gompers expressed the trade unionist's lack of confidence in ministers accusing them of being apologists and defenders of the *status quo* and of using "their exalted positions to discourage and discountenance all practical efforts of the toilers to lift themselves out of the slough of despondency and despair."[40] Heywood Broun declared in 1929, "If I were promoting some cause which seemed to be right and true I would rather have the help of one able editor than of a dozen preachers."[41] Doubtless this was an extreme position but it was tacitly assented to by many.

It is quite possible that the depression years and after have seen a slight reversal of this tendency to undervalue the influence of ministers in the practical affairs of the community. At the same time there has developed in certain theological circles what appears to be a more realistic approach to politics and economics.

A clear indication of a change in intellectual status can be gained by a glance at the place of ministers in the world of education. Ninety per cent of the presidents of colleges before the Civil War were ordained ministers.[42] In the post-War period these men were rapidly replaced, especially in the larger and more influential institutions, by members of other professions. Today it is extremely rare to find an ordained minister occupying the presidency of a large and influential state or private university.

Andrew White, one-time president of Cornell University, expressed one common sentiment in university circles of the late nineteenth century when he quoted with approval "an eminent member of the . . . British government" to the effect that "'a candidate for high university position is handicapped by holy orders.'" White was careful to indicate that no one honored the "proper work" of the clergy more than he did.

"My belief is," he affirmed, "that in the field left to them . . . the clergy will more and more . . . do work even nobler and more beautiful than anything they have heretofore done." It was clear to White that this field was not in the university.[43] President Eliot of Harvard asserted that "multitudes of educated men" had come to be suspicious of the intellectual abilities of the clergy, and he saw this as a "potent cause of the decline of the ministry during the past forty years."[44]

As a profession the ministry was not attracting as large a number of graduates of the outstanding universities as it had before 1850. More and more seminary recruits came from small denominational colleges. "From 1850 to 1895 Yale's total number of graduates doubled, and in the same period the number of Yale graduates who entered the ministry decreased more than sixty per cent."[45] Furthermore, the percentage of all college graduates entering the ministry has declined over the last century.[46]

However, our generation may be witnessing a gradual reversal of these tendencies. There are indications that an increasing number of seminary students are coming from larger private and state institutions of higher learning and also that the ministry is attracting a growing number of high caliber students. Another important development may be seen in the entry into the ministry of a significant number of well-qualified men who had been training for, or actively engaged in, other professions or vocations.

If there were circles where anticlericalism was in vogue in the past century it was among certain sophisticated intellectuals, among whom Sinclair Lewis' *Elmer Gantry* achieved a degree of popularity. Yet in the minds of perhaps the great majority of the people the minister remained a pillar in the community.

Protestants in America have looked to their ministers as the defenders of morality and the representatives of spirituality. They have expected them to stand out as examples of what people ought to be morally and spiritually, "It makes no difference what the minister wears," said Woodrow Wilson when he was president of Princeton. "But one thing matters supremely. He should never be in any company of men for a single instant without making them realize that they are in the company of a minister of religion."[47]

As one who fills this role in the community the minister has received many special privileges. Sometimes these have been granted out of genuine respect for the office; sometimes as a means of gaining the benefits that come from supporting a good thing. Clergy passes and special clergy rates have been granted by the nation's railroads. Many stores give clergy discounts; physicians and other professional men frequently have extended professional courtesy by refusing or reducing fees. Ministers' children have been granted special tuition rates or charged no tuition at all in many institutions of higher learning. Congregations continue to supplement salaries by provision of parsonages, sometimes cars, occasionally food.

Legally also the minister occupies a privileged position. The Supreme Court of the United States has recognized a clergyman as a professional man not "a laboring man," and as such "entitled to respect, veneration, and confidence." By statute clergymen have been exempted from such common public duties as jury and military service. The latter exemption has also applied to theological students.[48]

Salaries of ministers, however, have rarely reflected a privileged status in the American community. A survey of standing based on income alone would probably place the minister close to the public school teacher and the semiskilled wage earner. In 1928, for example, the average salary for all ministers was $1,407. In the same year the average for elementary school teachers was $1,788 and that for wage workers in iron and steel was $1,619.[49] Of course ministerial status is determined by many other factors besides salary.

IV

The Minister's Roles in the Church

The pulpit has stood at the front and center of the Protestant church in America—both in practice and in theory; preaching has been by all odds the most important aspect of the minister's work. Melville detected well the spirit of evangelical Protestantism when he wrote:

For the pulpit is ever this earth's foremost part; all the rest comes in its rear; the pulpit leads the world. From thence it is the storm of God' quick wrath is first descried, and the bow must bear the earliest brunt. From thence it is that the God of breezes fair or foul is first invoked for favorable winds. Yes, the world's a ship on its passage out, and not a voyage complete; and the pulpit is its prow.[50]

The post-Civil War period was the era of the reign of the great "princes of the pulpit." There had been popular preachers before 1865 but no one of them [51] ever matched the national popularity of such men as Henry Ward Beecher, Phillips Brooks, T. DeWitt Talmadge, and Russell Conwell. The nation hung on their words and doted on their persons. Sermons "were not infrequently front-page news, and those of some of the more prominent of the clergy were regularly syndicated nationally in their entirety." [52]

The combination of disestablishment with the Protestant tradition of emphasis on preaching the Word created the right conditions in the churches for a major emphasis on the sermon and the personality of the preacher. Ministry meant pre-eminently preaching. As preacher the minister conveyed the word of the gospel; as preacher he built up his congregation; as preacher he educated his people; and as preacher he ministered to their needs. He was called to the pulpit and it was expected that in the pulpit he would put forth his greatest effort.

Post-Civil War conditions also favored the preacher. The population was growing rapidly and was becoming more concentrated in the cities. The spoken word was the chief means of entertainment and education. Any man who could speak well at the popular level was assured of an audience.

A marked characteristic of the preaching of the time was its awareness of the popular mind. "More humanity, less divinity" was the cry of the day. "*Man* was the thing," said Henry Ward Beecher.

Henceforth our business was to work upon man; to study him, to stimulate and educate him. A sermon was good that had power on the heart, and was good for nothing no matter how good that had no moral power on man.[53]

This sensitivity to man and his problems had a definite effect on both the content and the form of preaching. It came to be centered in human situations, concerned with problems that were agitating the congregation. Expository preaching on Biblical texts gave way to topical preaching on "living" issues. Beecher led the way in speaking on current topics in the language of the day. "It is the duty of the minister of the gospel," he asserted in 1862, "to preach on every side of political life." And thereafter, as Hudson points out,

the practice of relating religious truth to every "topic of the times" which involved "the welfare of men" was a characteristic feature of his ministry. In sermons and addresses he discussed the problems of emancipation, Reconstruction, immigration, the currency, taxes, a standing army, women's rights, Civil Service, reform, local party politics, municipal corruption, free trade, pacifism, presidential candidates. . . .[54]

The effect of Beecher's preaching, says John Burroughs, "was to secularize the pulpit, yea, to secularize religion itself and make it as common and universal as the air we breathe." [55]

Preaching became more informal. The extensive use of dramatic illustration; the change of pace from oratory to the chatty style; the minimizing of liturgical elements in the service; the use of architecture and furnishings to center attention on the preacher: these were characteristic of the late nineteenth century, and have continued into the twentieth. When Beecher accepted the call to Plymouth Church in Brooklyn his first step was to clear away the pulpit and to replace it with a platform which extended out into the midst of the congregation. He wanted to be free to move about, to dramatize, and above all to be as close to his congregation as possible.

The popular pulpit personality found a normal nonecclesiastical outlet for his oratorical talents on the public lecture platform. Preachers were the leaders among the desired Chatauqua and Lyceum speakers. Probably the most famous of these was the Baptist preacher Russell Conwell who, it is said, delivered his "Acres of Diamonds" over 6,000 times.

Because of his power in the pulpit the preacher was not only in demand as a popular lecturer but was also regarded as an authority on a wide variety of subjects. An interesting case in point is Joseph Cook, Congregational minister, who is most famous for his Boston Monday lectures. Lecturing on a wide variety of subjects—"everything from Asia to biology" [56]—Cook reached an immense audience. Twice after beginning his regular lectures in 1875 he had to move to larger auditoriums. It has been estimated that in 1880 his lectures "published in newspapers both in America and in England, were reaching a million readers weekly." During the winter of 1877-78 Cook delivered outside of Boston "over one hundred and fifty addresses that involved more than ten thousand miles of travel. . . ." [57] Yet his popularity as a lecturer hardly matched that of such men as Talmadge, Conwell, and Beecher.

Although public speaking and rhetoric were common subjects in the theological curriculum prior to this period, "homiletics" now received particular attention as a result of the outstanding place of the preacher. The world-famous Lyman Beecher lectures on preaching were started at Yale in 1871. Henry Ward Beecher, Lyman's son, delivered the first three series. He was followed by Phillips Brooks. An examination of the early lectures on this foundation discloses the centrality of preaching in the lecturers' conception of the ministry. It seems generally to have been accepted that, in the words of one of the lecturers, "the most critical and influential event in the religious week is the sermon," or, as another put it, that the minister "must focus his whole heart and life upon the pulpit. . . ."[58]

The personality of the preacher was as important as his words, if not more so. In some cases the preacher became the idol of the crowd. Drummond reports that

When Thomas K. Beecher preached on one occasion at Plymouth Church there was an unseemly rush for the doors, on the part of the sight-seers, as he entered the pulpit instead of the popular idol. Raising his hand he announced: "All those who came here to worship Henry Ward Beecher may now withdraw—all who came to worship God may remain!"[59]

"Truth through Personality is our description of real preaching," said Phillips Brooks.[60] "The priest has no great demand for personality," writes Baxter in summarizing the Yale series; "with the preacher, however, such is not the case. More important than almost anything else is the man himself." William Jewett Tucker affirmed in 1898 that "the law is, the greater the personality of the preacher, the larger the use of his personality, the wider and deeper the response of men to truth."[61]

Only one of the early Lyman Beecher lecturers objected to the common notion that preaching and personality are the most important elements in the minister's equipment. P. T. Forsyth, speaking in 1907, declared:

You hear it said, with a great air of religious common sense, that it is the man that the modern age demands in the pulpit, and not his doctrine. It is the man that counts, and not his creed. But this is one of those shallow and plausible half-truths which have the success that always follows when the easy, obvious underpart is blandly offered for the arduous whole. No man has any right in the pulpit in virtue of his personality or manhood in itself, but only in virtue of the sacramental value of his personality for his message. We have no business to worship the elements, which means, in this case, to idolise the preacher. . . . To be ready to accept any kind of message from a magnetic man is to lose the Gospel in mere impressionism. It is to sacrifice the moral in religion to the aesthetic. And it is fatal to the authority either of the pulpit or the Gospel. The Church does not live by its preachers, but by its Word.[62]

But many a local church in America since the Civil War has lived by its preacher. For many Protestants the ministry is very nearly the whole church, and the minister is the "preacher." Such an overemphasis on preaching and the personality of the preacher has frequently entailed neglect of other aspects of the ministry and other phases of the work of the church. Foreseeing in 1859 some of the dangers which were to overtake Protestantism in the latter part of the nineteenth century a conservative Unitarian, Henry W. Bellows, urged upon his fellows a rediscovery of the *ecclesia* of the Scriptures. Pointing out that the "Protestant principle" is the way to anarchy if it loses sight of the historic Church, he called for a

"new Catholic Church" to thunder into the deaf ear of humanity the saving lesson of the Gospel. "No lecture room can do this; no thin, ghostly individualism or meagre congregationalism can do this. It calls for the organic, instituted, ritualized, impersonal, steady, patient work of the Church."[63]

In this task some of the Protestantism of the latter half of the nineteenth century failed. And yet we should not overlook the fact that the "princes of the pulpit" unquestionably conveyed the gospel to very many people. Their preaching, and that of many others, played a central role in the life of Protestantism. Their influence continues to be felt. Although preaching may have been overemphasized in the Post-Civil War period still the "princes" did much to make vital this important part of the church's ministry. What they said and how they said it was a joy to hear in comparison with some of the dry doctrinal fare of the late eighteenth and early nineteenth centuries. They also made it mandatory on later generations to preach relevantly.

Preaching has continued to be a central element in the Protestantism of the twentieth century. Possibly no individuals of this period can compare with the "princes" of the nineteenth century but America still has its noted and influential preachers. And many a young minister in the twentieth century has modeled his preaching after the great masters, Beecher and Brooks. Books on preaching continue to be popular, and the role of the preacher continues to be elevated. Writing in 1921 Arthur S. Hoyt, professor of homiletics and sociology in Auburn Seminary, claimed that "since Plymouth Rock, preaching has never been a greater element than now."[64] And in 1930 Joseph Fort Newton stanchly maintained that "preaching . . . is the noblest vocation on earth."[65] Presumably speaking of ministerial attitudes in the twentieth century, Bishop Gerald Kennedy once defined the sermon as something "a minister will not go across the street to hear but will go across the country to deliver." [66]

Yet a change of emphasis becomes apparent in the twentieth century. Preaching remains perhaps the most dramatic, most effective, and most used means of communicating the gospel in Protestantism and will always be central in a tradition that stresses the primacy of the Word of God. However, an increasing number of Protestant ministers in this century have complemented attention to the sermon with concern for meaningful worship, pastoral care, religious education, and other avenues of ministry.

An examination of such factors as church architecture, the organization of the service, the curricula of the seminaries, and the books read by the minister would indicate some of the changes taking place in the conception and practice of the Protestant ministry in this century. Very few churches are building mammoth auditoriums with pulpits at the center of the chancel. The chancel is likely to be divided with pulpit on one side, lectern on the other, and altar in the center. Sermons are shorter than they were a generation or two ago. More of the service is given over to prayers, confessions, responsive readings, Scripture readings, and singing. Efforts have been made to reconstruct a meaningful liturgy based on historical patterns and contemporary needs. The seminaries are giving increasing attention to preparing men to lead worship. Although few Protestant ministers would care to be assigned the role of priest, as this role is generally understood, still there are many indications of a growing seriousness about the minister's function as an instrument or vessel for the communication of God's grace through worship as well as in other ways.

The new church building is also likely to have a large area for Christian education. In many cases this may be the first wing put up by a church lacking sufficient funds to finance a complete structure at one time. This is an indication of the increasing emphasis placed on education as the church constantly prepares itself for its ministry to a stormy and complex world. The minister is expected to function as a religious educator. If he has had seminary training it will have included courses in religious education. He may not regard this role with the same seriousness he gives to preaching or pastoral care, but there are indications of an increasing sense of responsibility for this function. If he is fortunate and his church is rich enough he will be provided with a director of religious education—usually a woman—who has received a specialized seminary training.

Comfortable rooms are likely to be available in the new church building for the pastor's use in counseling. Protestant ministers have carried
on a quietly effective work over the years as pastors, as comforters of
the sick, the distressed and the bereaved, as counselors of the perplexed,
as guides and guardians to those seeking spiritual light and moral
rectitude. But we have seen in the last half century an increasing awareness of the importance of the role of the minister as pastor. Discoveries
and advances in the field of mental hygiene have stimulated an increasing concern for proficiency in this work. Psychology of religion has
encouraged in the church an increasing scientific concern for the
individual. Developments in psychoanalysis, psychotherapy, and psy-
chiatry have been followed closely by certain forward-looking men in
Protestantism, and they have attempted to increase the skill of the
pastor by exposing him to some of the elemental principles and practices
of these fields.

Protestant seminaries have given in the twentieth century increasing
attention to the development of a systematic training in pastoral care—
or pastoral theology or psychology as it is sometimes called. Courses in
the area are frequently required. The practice of requiring students to
spend some time in apprenticeship or clinical training in pastoral care
of the sick is being extended.[67] A new literature has sprung up in this
field, and it is likely that an examination of the content of the reading
of a group of representative ministers would disclose a high frequency
of materials on pastoral care and related areas.

If the modern church is affluent enough ministerial specialists will be
employed not only in religious education but also in pastoral care and
other areas while the chief minister concerns himself primarily with
preaching and the administration of the sizable institution and staff.
The local church today is larger, more complex, and more highly
organized than a century ago. The minister must have administrative
ability. The danger exists that ministers become so specialized and so
involved in administrative detail that they lose contact with the people.
This is the experience of business, industry, and education as they
become more complex. However, at the same time a counterbalance to
this tendency is appearing in the increasing awareness of the reality of
the church as a close-knit fellowship and in the growing concern for
its role as a ministering institution.

Whether the minister has been leader or follower in this process is
difficult to say. He has probably been both. At any rate he has been
forced to become much more than a preacher addressing an audience.

He is called upon to be the shepherd of the flock, the symbol of its unity in fellowship and purpose, and the leader in its ministry. He is called to show forth in all possible ways the grace of God in Jesus Christ, through his preaching, yes, but also through conducting a service of worship which directs attention beyond himself to God, through ministering to those in need, and through the intelligent use of the best-known techniques of education.

"The minister is nothing apart from the Church," declared Henry Sloane Coffin in his Lyman Beecher lectures in 1917. "It is not his ministry that is of first importance but the Church's ministry in which he leads," [68] Looking at this statement a generation after it was uttered one is impressed not only with its truth but also with the remarkable extent to which this truth has been taken seriously by recent Protestantism.

Who is the minister and what is he doing? In recent years many in the ministry have been put in a quandary as they have been confronted by these questions. But questioning has led to a seeking for answers, a deeper searching perhaps than that of any former period in American history. Two things appear to be taking place in this search. One is the desire to understand the gospel and the historic Christian tradition as fully as possible, to grasp the objective foundation of the ministry and the church. As there has developed in the past generation an increased awareness of the richness and depth of the church's ministry through the ages, the meaning of the ministry of today has been enhanced.

At the same time we are witnessing the emergence of an intensive desire to understand the contemporary world more fully so as to make the gospel relevant without compromising it. The social sciences which have developed so rapidly in the last fifty years have put new resources at the disposal of the alert and conscientious theological student and minister of the mid-twentieth century.

Both of these trends appear to augur for good. We reflect again upon the tension between gospel and world, a tension which is as strong as ever. The mood of the present is based on an awareness of this tension, perhaps more acute than for some time. The spirit in the ministry today appears to be to achieve as full a grasp of gospel and world as possible and to achieve the most effective available application of the one to the other.

FOR FURTHER READING

Ray Hamilton Abrams, *Preachers Present Arms* (New York, 1933). A study of ministerial attitudes toward World War I.

William Adams Brown, Mark A. May, and others, *The Education of American Ministers*, IV vols, (New York, 1934). Helpful more as a source than a secondary work. Reflects an approach to the ministry in the early 1930's.

Hunter Dickinson Farish, *The Circuit Rider Dismounts; A Social History of Southern Methodism, 1865-1900* (Richmond, Va., 1938). Especially good for developments in the post-Civil War South.

Harry Emerson Fosdick, *The Living of These Days* (New York, 1956).

George Hodges and John Reichert, *The Administration of an Institutional Church; A Detailed Account of the Operation of St. George's Parish in the City of New York,* (New York, 1906).

Robert L. Kelly, *Theological Education in America* (New York, 1924). Helpful for some early developments in the seminaries.

Charles Stedman Macfarland, ed., *The Christian Ministry and the Social Order; Lectures Delivered in the Course in Pastoral Functions at Yale Divinity School, 1908-1909* (New Haven, 1909).

H. Richard Niebuhr, *The Purpose of the Church and Its Ministry* (New York, 1956).

Ernest Trice Thompson, *Changing Emphases in American Preaching* (Philadelphia, 1943).

George Huntston Williams, ed., *The Harvard Divinity School: Its Place in Harvard University and in American Culture* (Boston, 1954).

Carter G. Woodson, *The History of the Negro Church* (Washington, D.C., 1921).

X

The Ministry from the Placid Decade to the Present: 1950–1980

SYDNEY E. AHLSTROM

When Robert Michaelsen concluded his many-faceted account of American Protestantism in 1956, he was dealing with a relatively stable religious situation. With his chapter Michaelsen could assume that Protestantism and its ministers were among the best-known institutions on the American scene. What he did not and could not know was that the so-called Placid Decade in which he worked and thought would soon be seen as the beginning of a revolutionary period, and that in the decades to follow, both the Protestant and the Catholic traditions would be profoundly disrupted.

Most surprising would be the ways in which youth would play a major role in the religious change and the fact that similar upheavals would occur in France, Germany, and even Japan.

A historical account of the ministry in this stormy period would be almost meaningless if it did not at almost every point seek to show and explain the close correlation between religious and political, social, economic, intellectual, and cultural dimensions of the national experience. Even though the political aspects of life are often crucial, what ministers have done or not done at certain times in the country's past has also had significant consequences. By the same token, there have been many times in the nation's history when the opposite situation has obtained, especially when secular developments have forced ministers into unaccustomed activities and even into large-scale demissions from their callings.

Readers of this book who have lived through these years may remember the extensive literature of the late 1950s and 1960s on the problems of ministry: Peter Berger on *The Noise of Solemn Assemblies*, Gibson Winter on *The Suburban Captivity of the Churches*, Will Herberg's *Protestant–Catholic–Jew*, and many others, all of whom insisted that a new era in ministry was at hand, an era when social pressures were drastically altering what Michaelsen had so well described.

But one must recognize, of course, that in many regions of the country and in many sects and denominations, there were sheltered areas where ministers and church leaders ignored the seething discontent and manifest problems of the republic. As one decade yielded to the next, a great many young people began to widen the generation gap that became a major feature of the period. Indeed, David Riesman suggested in his introduction to Edgar Z. Friedenberg's book on *The Vanishing Adolescent* this new and possibly enduring aspect of American life.

With these introductory observations on the fact that there were manifold ways in which the ideals and practices of the ministry have been challenged and transformed during the years since Professor Michaelsen defined the situation, it now becomes the difficult and perhaps impossible task of the historian to organize and explain the turbulent currents that have characterized the intervening years.

Most difficult is the fact that throughout the period many important events and developments were happening at the same time. Only in an approximate way can this history be regarded as chronological. Somewhat in the manner of Michaelsen, therefore, it is advisable to structure this chapter on the issues even though the overall result will be broadly historical. We begin where the previous chapter left off—in the middle of the Eisenhower administration in the 1950s, when a social and demographic revolution was in progress.

The So-Called Placid Decade

As the years and decades have gone by, the Eisenhower period has been fondly remembered as a halcyon time when peace and peacefulness prevailed. Whether or not this image is credible, we should still consider some of the events that had a great deal to do with developments in the field of ministry.

The euphoria that followed the great military victories of World War II and the new social ethics that arose with the coming of peace and the rapidly opening vistas of prosperity led to an age of affluence in a peaceful world. The Great Depression and its sacrifices and fears were fading from memory. The cold war was a stimulus to patriotism, and Americans were enjoying access to long-denied goods and pleasures. The election and then reelection of General Eisenhower added a new dimension to a growing confidence in the American future. Nor was it only confidence that he conveyed. From the first he became a religious figure, who was privately baptized early in his administration. In one of his informal talks with the press he contributed to the strength of the old American civil religion with the now-famous observation: "Our government makes no sense unless it is founded on a deeply felt religious faith—and I don't care what it is."

Because of this and various other testimonies and confessions, as well as by his own behavior, one can even speak of an Eisenhower Revival. Prayer breakfasts came to be held by major members of his administration, and reporters were soon speaking of a new "Piety on the Potomac."

There were other manifestations of religion. The American Legion organized a Back to God movement; Billy Graham launched his radio and television campaigns in these early years of the fifties. However, the new aspects of religion in this period were usually not confessional or fervid. For many young people as well as for many parents, religion was merely a generic stance. Just to be religious was deemed to be salvific.

For others the emphasis was on the utility of being religious, and in this realm it was Norman Vincent Peale who became the greatest practitioner, with his slogan on the power of positive thinking. Though his background was Methodist, in New York he became the pastor of the old Marble Collegiate Church in the Dutch Reformed tradition. His theology, however, was far removed from the Belgic Confession. Peale's message was well summed up in the title of his most important book, *The Power of Positive Thinking*. Emphasis fell on the need for confident living; sin and salvation had little place in his theology. Nevertheless, he won an enormous audience and made himself a veritable institution. There was hardly a medium that he did not use. His success was so great that he put a permanent stamp on the practice of ministry and soul care in Protestant America. It can also be said that he established a tradition that reached from his own time to the 1979 construction of Robert Schuller's Crystal Cathedral in California.

In quite another vein he, together with his associate Dr. Smiley Blanton, made a significant contribution to the increasing interest in Freudian approaches to the practice of pastoral counseling. It is well to recall in this connection that Dale Carnegie had played a similar role and was remembered by his admirers with almost religious esteem, and before him, Ralph Waldo Trine made a lasting contribution to this harmonial tradition, though behind them all stands the awesome example of Ralph Waldo Emerson. Yet the fact remains that Peale is a landmark in the tradition. It might be said that he in no little way conduced to the religious radicalism of the next decade. There can also be no doubt that he had an important impact on ministry. He certainly helped account for the rise in church affiliation during these years. Why all of this came to pass, however, is very complicated.

There were powerful forces of change at work in the social, cultural, and political realms, and most of them were related to the rapidly growing gross national product. In the public sphere, the passage of the Interstate Highway Act led almost immediately to the rapid growth of the suburbs which, in turn, conduced to the shattering of old personal and family relationships. Contributing to the same result was the Federal Housing Administration with its low-interest loans that made it possible for many to move—to change their place and mode of living. These vast changes created a great deal of loneliness and disorientation; one of the major results was the *Lonely Crowd* that David Riesman diagnosed. Uprooted Americans stood in need of togetherness, and the churches were the most natural resort. At the very least it was an important era in American ministry, but whether it was a boom or a bane can be argued. This is not the whole story, for there was another movement of people from the rural regions of the South to the crowded slums of the North. In many cities a vast population, mostly white, moved out of the city while another population, mostly black, but later Hispanic, moved in. The poor bought at bargain prices the fine churches that had been hemmed in by slums and, in this new situation, also turned to the tasks of ministry.

But in the lonely crowds of suburbia, in an alien environment and in varying degrees of status anxiety, there was a great need for personal counseling beyond the suggestions that Pealism produced. Fortunately, however, there were works by several very insightful writers who spoke appropriately to the problems that the times created. One of the most effective of these was the book *Peace of Mind* by Joshua Loth Liebman, a young Reform rabbi with deep psychological insights who understood the problems of the many displaced persons who peopled the new suburban wilderness. Most important were his cautious but wise interpretations of Sigmund Freud.

Liebman's book was not the only one that challenged the Christian ministers. Anne Morrow Lindbergh's *Gift from the Sea* was almost immediately recognized as a minor classic. She was a woman who had had her portion of woe, and in this little book she addressed herself to other women who inhabited the new society. She knew the situation in which they lived, and she spoke of the *zerrissenheit*, or "torn-to-pieces-hood" that made their lives frantic but spiritually empty. Her beautifully written message drew on many sources, including Plotinus and other mystics. Her chief aim seems to have been that her readers should, above all, look to their inner selves and understand the values and uses of solitude and introspection. In this book she also anticipated some of the issues that later feminists would be voicing. Given the enormous readership the book received, she deserves remembrance as a major religious voice.

There were, of course, many other books that strove to provide an understanding of the many dilemmas that people were facing. One remembers especially Harry Overstreet's *The Mature Mind* and Joseph Sittler's address at Yale University on "The Maceration of the Ministry." But it was probably Martin Marty's many thoughtful books and essays that addressed most directly the actual problems of ministers. Perhaps the most important of these works was his fine analysis *The New Shape of American Religion* because, better than any other book at the time, it made clear that a turning point of enduring significance had been reached. For the campaign and election of John F. Kennedy gave rise to a minor crisis whose origins can be traced to the earliest times of the country.

Puritanism can be defined as systematic anti-Catholicism, and down through the centuries it had always been assumed that the United States was a Puritan-Protestant nation. In 1960 it soon became clear that a great many evangelical Protestants were still of that persuasion. Billy Graham, Norman Vincent Peale, and many others organized a public conference in New York in order to prevent a Catholic victory. Almost immediately Republican leaders recognized that this opening of the religious question was a serious mistake. Peale even resigned from his church, only to be exonerated by his parishioners quite soon afterward.

In the campaign that followed, Kennedy was often quizzed on his relationship to the pope, and on one occasion when he was asked what he would do if he had to put the Vatican's view before his country's, he said he would resign. There were also anonymous critics who republished the scurrilous anti-Catholic propaganda that had been published in the previous century's antebellum period. Nevertheless, after the American people came to see, and in a sense, to know the young family in the White House and, even more, when they beheld the concert grief of the whole world after the President's assassination, anti-Catholic sentiments almost disappeared from the American scene.

Although the subject will be treated later, there should be noted at this juncture the almost simultaneous election of Pope John XXIII who, due to his gracious and ecumenical disposition, contributed strongly to the same reduction of anti-Catholicism. It almost seemed that the counter-reformation was a thing of the past.

Though brief, the Kennedy years were to be momentous for the Christian ministry. Before considering these years, however, we should call attention to the simultaneous Evangelical renaissance that became such a powerful factor. Just why this flowering arose at this time is an almost unanswerable question, but there is no doubt about its reality for the fourteen or fifteen million people who were and are of that persuasion. Certainly the new and irenic Evangelism of Billy Graham was one major factor. In addition, the Supreme Court's shocking decision that religious ceremonies and Bible reading were inappropriate in the public schools provided more grounds for renewed activity. The new status of Catholicism might also have had some effect. But by far the most important reason was the recognition among Evangelicals of the necessity to update their tradition and make it more palatable for the new social order that American affluence was creating. There was great need to be able to address the rapidly growing middle class with something better than the old tired arguments of fundamentalists.

The scholars, seminaries, and publishing houses that contributed to this renewal are far too numerous to be listed here. But much that was done was stimulated by C. F. H. Henry, a New Testament professor from Northern Baptist Seminary in Chicago, and Harold J. Ockenga, a pastor of the State Street Church in Boston and later President of Gordon-Conwell College and Seminary. Both these men had high standards of scholarship and strong gifts of organization. At this point, two very important developments took place. In 1956, Henry founded and became the first editor of *Christianity Today*, a national fortnightly journal that almost immediately became a very important Evangelical voice. At about the same time the National Association of Evangelicals was coming into its own with over one and a half million members making themselves heard over against the more liberal, socially concerned National Council of Churches of Christ in America. It was not surprising that the National Association became a major supporter of Senator McCarthy and McCarthyism.

The Kennedy Years—The Early Sixties

From their beginning, the Kennedy years had an ethos of their own, even in the realm of religion, but it was in no way due to the President's religious views, which in any case he only rarely expressed. It was rather that his general openness inspired others to express their own views. There were events that were inescapably of great importance to ministers as well as to the general public.

What happened at this time was truly remarkable. Most important was the need to bolster the commitment to civil rights and to respond to the determined demands of black power. Immediately in the train of these demands came others that produced much reordering during the sixties, namely, the call for the recognition of women's rights from Betty Friedan and others—then a movement threatening that most conservative bastion, the clergy, with a call for the ordination of women and an accompanying request for acceptance of inclusive language—and at almost the same time, Rachel Carson's concern for the environment and natural resources.

THE RISE OF BLACK POWER AND THE CIVIL RIGHTS MOVEMENT

Before we go any farther in this history of the issues and crises that have inevitably shaped the calling of the ministry, we must confront the single greatest tragedy in the American experience, which is, of course, the failure of western Christendom, and America in particular, to resist the lure of the slave trade.

In the antebellum period in the midst of the Second Great Awakening, Charles Grandison Finney, the founder of modern revivalism, sounded the tocsin for reform. A vast and determined host of Evangelicals organized an antislavery juggernaut that led to the end of slavery once and for all. In the years that followed the Civil War, however, the reforming impetus was marked mostly by the noise of dragging feet. Then in 1954 came the great unanimous ruling of the Warren Court that made segregation illegal in the public schools. It was a milestone in the history of civil rights. To his everlasting credit, President Eisenhower handled the first confrontation with dispatch by calling out the National Guard when Governor Faubus of Arkansas denied entrance of a black child to Central High School in Little Rock. Though this was the first event, there were many, many more to follow; indeed they became widespread and innumerable.

The most climactic event was probably James Meredith's application for admission to the University of Mississippi in the fall of 1962. He was not admitted, whereupon the Justice Department brought suit, which in turn led to serious violence and rioting. Nor was this the only crisis that Meredith precipitated. For in 1966 he decided to walk from Memphis to Jackson. He was shot and wounded by a sniper, a deed that led all blacks who regarded themselves as leaders of anything to get down to that road. The march very soon became a perambulating conference of black leaders. In a few days Americans came to hear of black power. It was a sign that blacks were taking charge of their own liberation just as the Jews had done years before with their antidefamation league. One also heard in this new situation, "Black is beautiful." Adam Clayton Powell had used the term "black power" from time to time, and in the book *Malcolm X Speaks*, published in 1965, the substance of the idea was forcefully stated. It cannot be denied that traditional civil rights people were shocked and belittled by these declarations of black independence. In the years that followed many of the older civil rights organizations lost their significance.

Surely though, the most important result of the entire history of the movement was the emergence of Martin Luther King, Jr., in Montgomery, Alabama. Here it was that Rosa Parks decided not to go to the back of the bus, and here it was that King organized a bus boycott that in turn led to his founding of the Southern Christian Leadership Conference in 1957. From that time to his assassination in 1968, he did more to preserve the ethical dignity of the American people than any other person in the country.

But aside from the activities of many young Freedom Riders in the South, there was no great public demonstration until the famous civil rights March on Washington, August 28, 1963, when King delivered his "I Have a Dream" oration. It was this demonstration more than any other that awakened the American people to the seriousness of the civil rights issue, and it is from this time that American Protestant ministers along with other clerics began to realize their potential as an extremely powerful force in the life of the country. This clerical response, however, was in no sense unanimous.

Evangelicals, for instance, in no way repeated the example of their antebellum forebears who had led the antislavery movement, and there were many other denominations that avoided these social and political activities. As one might have expected, moreover, the laity tended to object to the activism of their pastors. Thus, the tendency was strong, especially among liberals, simply to leave the ministry as it was exemplified in its traditional parish context. Throughout the country, ecclesiastical authorities, both Catholic and Protestant, were being besieged. We should pay tribute to the countless ministers who continued to support the civil rights movement and who continued to demonstrate their commitment in both small and large confrontations, all the way down to the end of American military action in Vietnam in 1976. Selma and Little Rock and Jackson State and Birmingham and Ole' Miss and, finally, Kent State are occasions that deserve remembrance just as much as Gettysburg and Shiloh.

One should especially note the role of chaplains in the colleges and universities at this time. It was the chaplains who first discovered the rapidly changing attitudes and mores of their constituency. They were capable of turning the increasing social concerns of the times into constructive channels. Much too little attention has been given to the significance of these chaplains by the public or reporters of the period.

THE WOMEN'S RIGHTS MOVEMENT

There seems to be a consensus among feminist historians that Betty Friedan provided the crucial statement in her book *The Feminine Mystique*, published in 1962. Its aim was to declare that women were an oppressed race in America. Her proposals were relatively moderate, but they were remarkably adapted to the times. The consequences of women's liberation, as everyone knows, have had a marked effect on all women everywhere.

The issue of women's rights, to be sure, has had a long prehistory, but the movement begun in the sixties has had a far more decisive result than earlier battles in this cause. Not only has it changed our use of the language, but it has changed the entire awareness of women's place in the life of the nation. Furthermore, it precipitated a veritable sexual revolution, which forced almost every denomination in the country, and even the Vatican, to reevaluate traditional views. Very soon it led to a reconsideration of laws and practices in the fields of divorce, birth control, and abortion. As a result, divorces have increased in number and cohabitation arrangements have become the choice of millions of Americans. That this situation has had a huge impact on the ministry is obvious. Yet there is a special result of the women's movement that has had an even greater and more specific impact on the ministry, and this has to do with the roles of women in that most conservative of all traditions, namely, the Christian church.

WOMEN AND THE MINISTRY

There have been times in the history of religion when God was a woman, and in the Roman Catholic tradition the Virgin Mary has been venerated as a mediatrix of salvation. The priesthood was the exclusive domain of men, though. In the Roman tradition women have held many important positions of authority, that is, as heads of schools and hospitals and even as managers of large convents that included the rule of principalities. But in post-Reformation times, the religious roles of women have, for the most part, been limited to their own auxiliary organizations.

In the 1960s and 1970s, however, this ancient wall was breached at times by the ordination of a married couple and then, more frequently, of individual women. For several years these victories were few, and even then women were relegated to academic chaplaincies and other peripheral positions. One important breakthrough came when a group of Episcopal bishops, without official permission, ordained several women. From that time on the practice proliferated, with the result that ordination in most denominations has been accepted as a matter of course.

This development had another important effect in that it led to the further demand that Americans recognize the need for inclusive language and that they relinquish the sovereignty of the traditional masculine gender in their speech and writing. Among radical feminists there were even problems as to the proper words for addressing the deity. These language problems were not, of course, limited to the ministry, but it was in this realm that much of the new crusading was carried out.

NATURE'S RIGHTS

Another major social concern that gained a startling amount of interest in these years was that raised by Rachel Carson in her book entitled *Silent Spring*. Rarely has a book met social, religious, and ethical questions so powerfully as has hers. Indeed, Americans had shown almost no interest in the problems of pollution, contamination, or conservation since the days of Theodore Roosevelt's presidency. The degree to which her warning to the nation—and to the world—has been heeded is now a well-known fact, with much ecological legislation on the books and many agencies and departments overseeing the current use of resources. It remains to be seen, however, whether other pressures will reverse this concern for the national patrimony. From earliest Colonial times most Americans have regarded Mother Nature as something to be raped, so it does not behoove us to take recent progress for granted.

Though many of these concerns arose during the Kennedy years—the early sixties—for a history of ministry the most revolutionary event of this period was the astounding change in the Roman Catholic church.

The Roman Catholic Church in America

When Columbus delivered his first report to Queen Isabella, he exulted in the fact that he had opened a vast new realm for the expansion of the Catholic faith at a time when the Protestant Reformation had only recently ended the universal sway of the Church in the West. But even in his most ecstatic dreams how could he foresee the consequences of the Columbian exchange for the whole world? Least of all how could he foresee that the first and most powerful Protestant country would arise in North America? And almost nothing in the history of American Catholicism is more fateful than the fact that this new colonial power was belligerently anti-Catholic. Nevertheless, due to the early pluralism of the nation, Catholics soon became a vital factor in the new republic. From the beginning, storm-tossed, poor, and persecuted peoples from every part of the world have made their way to America, and in almost every wave, Catholics have come in the greatest numbers, whether from Ireland, Germany, Poland, Portugal, Italy, or as most recently, from Spanish-speaking areas. One can safely say, therefore, that the Catholic Church in America has faced a larger and more complex challenge to ministry than any other denomination.

Ministry is, of course, a generic term, and John McNeill in his *History of the Cure of Souls* sees Socrates and even Confucius as early practitioners in this vital human need. The term *ministry*, however, is not widely used in Catholic parlance, and that is due to the centuries-long process that finally led to the confessional and the sacrament of penance. It was this institution and practice that provided most of the spiritual guidance for the millions of Catholics who migrated to America. This time-honored solution conduced to increasing legalism, undue scrupulosity, and triviality, all of these becoming routine both in Europe and in America. Adding to this situation in the minds of many theologians was Rome's structure and the view that Rome never changes and has nothing new to say. These attitudes led John Tracy Ellis to an outburst on anti-intellectualism in 1955, in his *The Catholic Church in America*.

A surprising break in this situation occurred in the pontificate of Pope Pius XII, who was usually regarded as very conservative, when he promulgated in 1943 the encyclical *Divino Afflante Spiritu*, which for the first time allowed Catholic scholars to interpret the history of the Church in its cultural setting rather than in terms of the ideal setting. It is amazing that this unusually conservative and ascetic pope who had spent much of his time in political manipulation would now open the way for the discussion of many thorny and controversial issues. But this he did, and it is very probable that his stance had something to do with the decisions and deeds of the next pope, who was, of course, the epoch-making John XXIII.

When John XXIII became the Pope of Rome, the world soon came to discover that he was a most remarkable man. His gentleness, kindness, geniality, and openness, even his sense of humor, were in sharp contrast to the formality of his predecessor. Far more important, however, were the speed and decisiveness with which he acted on his ideals, the most important of which was his conviction that modernization was the first need of the Church. To this end he duly decided to call for an ecumenical council, and on January 25, 1959, he publicly issued such a call, despite the very strong objections of the Papal Curia, whose members tried in every possible way, first, to stop the meeting, and later, to make the results as innocuous as possible. Pope John outflanked these men and put matters to a vote of the assembled bishops of the whole Church, thus opening the way for debate and vote on a full range of reform issues.

What made this council especially important was that the first Vatican Council of 1890 had been heavily directed by the very conservative Pope Pius IX, who had promulgated the doctrine of papal infallibility at a time when the papacy was under severe duress. But in 1959 Pope John, in his call, was striving for a modern stance.

As is now widely known, the result was an immensely long and revolutionary agenda for the bishops to consider. Indeed, it was so complex that they could not possibly foresee all of the implications of their decisions for the future. For very much the same reasons it is impossible in this chapter to describe all of the ways in which the lives of Catholics have so drastically been changed. Nevertheless, some of the major reforms resulting from the Second Vatican Council are: renewal; a new vision of the Church's secular responsibilities; a fundamental transformation in the liturgy—in both the celebration and the theological understanding of the Holy Eucharist—and in the physical church building; and finally, a decree on ecumenism—an enlarged and more vital search for Christian unity, which includes a gradual emergence of something like a consensus that the full understanding of the Word of God is an eschatological category. These points are discussed more fully in George Lindbeck's *The Future of Roman Catholic Theology*.

The first issue, renewal, was a revival of the old Greek vision of a world renewed, that is, a Christian understanding of the great apocatastasis—the notion of a restoration of all things. Not since the earliest years of the Church have Catholics spoken so realistically of the coming of the Kingdom of God. Commentaries on renewal flowed from such disparate theologians as the Communist Ernst Bloch and the priest Teilhard de Chardin.

The second major issue to be taken up followed almost ineluctably from the first, namely, that Catholics in all walks of life and with all degrees of piety must be awakened to a concern for social justice and thus accept fully the secular mission of the Church in a new and more complex world. Such an awareness was new for the Catholic tradition, but the time was ripe for change, and the response was widespread and enthusiasm high. Although Catholics had long been quietistic in the face of social problems, they now began to play a very strong role, almost as if to make up for lost time. One sign of this awakening was the decision made by the Jesuit order to remove their seminary Woodstock from the open country near Baltimore to New York City, where the greatest needs were felt to be. Many of the younger people, whether clergy or laity, were inspired to take up the radical views of Dorothy Day and the *Catholic Worker*. It was her 1930s slogan, "Those who stand with the poor and work for peace will never go far wrong," that came to be the call for these new activists. It is doubtful that until this time anyone had accomplished so much for the secular mission of the Church as she had. However, most sensational and activistic of the post-Council workers for peace and social justice were the Berrigan brothers, both Jesuits, and their associates, some of them nuns.

Third, and certainly the most visible issue dealt with by the Second Vatican Council, was the Divine Liturgy, which is regarded at once as the summit and the source of Catholic life. Thus, right worship is a central concern for both clergy and laity. It is not surprising, therefore, that it is in this realm that faithful Catholics have found most wrenching the abandonment of so many ingrained aspects of their religious life. And of these changes, most disorienting has been the discontinuance of Latin as the normal liturgical language and its replacement by various vernacular tongues. Not only the language but the very form of the liturgy has changed, most notably with the adoption of certain aspects of Protestant modes of worship. The clergy were instructed to place a larger emphasis on the office of preaching, with more concern for the interpretation of biblical texts. Additionally, there has been an effort to involve the laity more directly in parish affairs.

But these reforms were made even more upsetting by the many structural changes in traditional church interiors. Deep chancels were left unused in favor of a fully visible altar closer to the people. Always popular side altars were closed to emphasize the importance of the main altar, and churches were cleared of distracting shrines.

Finally, there are the changes that the decree on ecumenism has produced. Truly important among Catholic Americans has been the overwhelming joy and sense of liberation in relationships with other denominations. The results have touched the smallest towns as well as the largest cities. In all of these places there has been a strong impulse to make ecumenism an active reality, and to this end, many interfaith activities have been organized. On countless occasions this sharing has been extended even to the Eucharist itself. It must also be noted, though, that this sense of freedom has allowed many in the Church to leave it altogether: numerous lay persons and hundreds of nuns, priests, and even some bishops. Because of these many demissions from religious vocations and the reduction in number of new candidates for the priesthood and other orders, many seminaries and other institutions have closed or been sold.

The reform in ecumenism has also dealt with amity and cooperation among the world's churches—the dream and hope for reunion of the world's almost numberless Christian churches. From the earliest days of his pontificate, John XXIII lamented the fragmentation of Christianity and hoped for ways in which it could be healed. Progress in this realm was very limited, but one of these limited deeds was the effort to improve Rome's relations with the Orthodox Church of the East. There was also a recognition of the unity of the Church in a general way, and such cooperation has become more evident. In the last analysis, though, ecumenism is an eschatological category, and we cannot imagine the fulfillment of these hopes on this side of paradise.

The Council took place during a time of ferment both within and without the Church and thus allowed other changes to occur in the American Catholic Church. One surprising development in the restructuring of Catholic piety and worship in the post-Council years has been the widespread rise of a charismatic movement within the Church, and in due time this has even led to the founding of communes, with attending clergy. Pentecostalism is of course as old as the New Testament, and ecstatic religion was well known to Saint Paul, but these manifestations had rarely if ever appeared in the Catholic Church in America. Until this time Pentecostalism had been chiefly confined to Protestant churches in the Methodist and later the Holiness denominations. Again one becomes aware of the influence of an important Protestant tendency. What the final effects of all these changes will be may not be known for many years, but Catholic church attendance has by and large declined. (Overall Protestant attendance, it must be said, has also declined.)

The Rise of Radical Theology

At the same time that the Roman Catholic Church was rethinking its theology, Protestant thought was flowering. Because theology is an esoteric discipline, there has probably never been a time when Christian churches have not been in a state of contention. The 1960s were an extreme demonstration of this fact: the rifts were so wide that it was a desolating time for ministers and theologians.

It is important to see how the radical movement developed. Over the long term, its origins were chiefly in German philosophy and biblical scholarship. Most immediate was the immense following of Paul Tillich. Most startling was the publication of Dietrich Bonhoeffer's *Letters and Papers from Prison*, in which he commended Rudolf Bultmann's call to demythologize Scripture. He also on his own account advocated that preachers develop the secular meaning of the Gospel, rather than preach only the Law as was their wont.

The most nearly classic statement of the radical position by an American thinker was that of H. Richard Niebuhr. He had broached his basic ideas in a critique of his brother Reinhold's activism in 1931, and he now enlarged on those views in a small but arresting book, *Radical Monotheism*, in 1960. It served as an inaugural address to the decade. The book is an austere summons to the ministry and the churches. He calls them to the God beyond the gods and to avoid the heresy of henotheism, which he defines as the worship of collective entities such as the nation or the church. In 1931 he had dramatized his position with Hegel's famous dictum: The history of the world is the judgment of the world. But he now enforced his determinism by defining True Virtue in the same terms as Jonathan Edwards had: True Virtue is consent to being in general, or love of the whole system of the universe. The final paragraphs of his book suggest that he had been reading Spinoza.

This was the last book that Niebuhr would see through the press. To be sure, he was at some remove from the neoorthodoxy that had arisen in the forties and fifties, but on the other hand, it was for this reason that he was closer to the views of Calvin and Augustine, and in the years since this book appeared, scholars have been paying much more attention to his work.

At almost the same time, Gabriel Vahanian put forth the ambiguous concept of the death of God in his *The Death of God; The Culture of Our Post-Christian Era*, and during the entire decade of the sixties similar works appeared, all of them being far removed from the old agnosticism of Robert Ingersoll or the legendary village atheist. To the contrary, most of the authors were erudite and disciplined theologians with positions in prominent institutions—in seminaries or universities. For the most part they hoped to carry out the programs of Bultmann and Bonhoeffer and to demagicalize the Christian faith. In these efforts they had something in common with John Calvin himself, but they were almost always misunderstood, and still are.

One of the most surprising aspects of the so-called death of God movement was the fact that nearly all of the leaders had been strong admirers of the great Swiss theologian Karl Barth. This provides us with an important insight into the time. Barth had in the years after World War I rejuvenated Protestant theology in a most striking way through his commentary on Paul's Letter to the Romans, and Americans of the 1960s were much moved by his social and theological teachings. His message had lost some of its power with the passing years, however, and Rudolf Bultmann, who had been a major figure in the confessing church under Hitler, seemed to be much more relevant. He was also more liberal in his theology. Given the upheaval in religion that ensued in the years after Eisenhower, radicalism found many supporters. Indeed, new kinds of ministry had come into existence, and in most denominations various "tent-making" ministries had become common.

In the seventies, for reasons that are not easily diagnosed, creative theology virtually passed from the scene, though one can surmise that this dearth can be attributed to the swirling social events that agitated the nation as a whole. That lack of theological concern—whatever its cause—can only be regarded as a tragedy.

The Late Sixties and Seventies

THE JOHNSON YEARS

Lyndon Johnson could have been one of America's greatest presidents. The Great Society that he hoped for was the work of an idealist; his ambitions for the country were laudatory. Yet he threw the country into a state of turmoil unprecedented in the nation's history when, almost immediately after his inauguration, he escalated the war in Vietnam. The result was catastrophic. A huge communication gap about his intentions opened up, which led to an equally wide generation gap between parents and their children. Violence broke out first in the universities—most tumultuously in those of California, then with equal fury in New York at Columbia—and finally almost everywhere. The draft was widely excoriated, and a vast counterculture of the young and not-so-young developed. Theodore Roszak, and others more radical, pronounced our technological society bankrupt. The best students in the best universities and colleges sought new life-styles, and a new culture did in fact arise. Joan Baez, Bob Dylan, and above all, the Beatles provided a new ideological hymnody. Those who had the good fortune to experience Woodstock looked back on the occasion as a mount of transfiguration. For many parents and pastors the world seemed upside down. Never before had there been such a challenge to the churches and the ministry. Never was there greater failure. The most significant effect in the religious realm was the serious search of many of these young people and others for alternative religions. Many indeed were found—from Sufi to Zen, from the wildest and most esoteric cults to the most disciplined forms of Yoga. Thus, in addition to Vietnam the rise of cults was a major concern of the Johnson years.

THE PROBLEM OF CULTS

The first problem of cults is one of definition, for in popular usage the term refers to almost any and every religious movement of any type or size. To the Jews, early Christianity was a cult or perhaps a sect. The Roman Catholic church speaks of its cult—by that referring to its liturgy or rites. In American parlance a cult is a unique religious group that is headed by a powerful and dictatorial leader whose doctrines depart drastically from the Judeo-Christian tradition. Elijah Muhammad, whom Malcolm X followed for a time, was such a cultic leader, and there have been many others in America.

The most famous and successful of all in this American tradition was Joseph Smith, who published the Book of Mormon in 1830. Americans persecuted the Mormons mercilessly for many years. One can in fact generalize that all three of the great biblical traditions—Hebrew, Christian, and Islamic—have been extremely intolerant of other religious movements.

Due to its pluralistic and ideological heritage, the United States is the most tolerant nation in the West, but even here the role of cults has created serious problems for both pastors and parents, especially since the 1960s, and there can be little doubt that the Unification Church has grown the most and has created the greatest stir. Since President Reagan took office, there have been several proposals to deport the Reverend Sun Myung Moon, but no action has been taken, and there are grounds for saying that such a move would be unconstitutional. Under the same scrutiny and resentment has been the intensely evangelical New Testament Fellowship and many other such organizations, large and small.

A new profession has been born out of this problem, that of the deprogrammer, but here again a question of ethics and law enters in, since people who are of age have the right to lead their own lives. For many ministers and their parishioners, the parents, these issues have been a difficult concern. So common are these problems of cults that the Graduate Theological Union in Berkeley, California, has made them an object of intense study.

THE ORDEAL OF VIETNAM

After the assassination of President Kennedy and more especially after Lyndon Johnson was sworn in as his successor, Americans began to experience the most fracturing series of events since the Civil War. When Johnson decided to enlarge the American military presence in Vietnam, he almost immediately encountered the wrath of the peacemakers. Not only had he departed from the position that President Kennedy had taken, but he had violated his own pledge to be a peacemaker. Contention and violence were the immediate results. Indeed, toward the end of his term President Johnson found it almost impossible to address an outdoor audience unless he was at a military installation or on a battleship. Facing this situation, and proud as he was, he decided to announce that he would not seek further political office.

By this time, however, the peace movement had grown much larger and more radical. It had also turned toward other social problems. But both the war and social concerns continued to be important during Richard Nixon's presidency. The carnage in Vietnam was still going on. It was with this background that the great March on Washington was planned.

November 15, 1969, beheld the greatest demonstration up to that time. From all over the nation clergy, chaplains, students, and laity were rallied. Churches arranged for buses. There were some who said that if the demonstration had been much larger, the country would have been on the verge of a revolution. No one made an accurate count, but the number of ministers may have exceeded the number that marched for civil rights at Selma and Birmingham. They were the people who awakened sleeping souls in the pews and brought them to the social and ideological concerns that led to the march itself. In the minds of the planners, like William Sloane Coffin, the chaplain at Yale University, the March on Washington was an immense success. In this instance, as in many other encounters, the police overreacted and created a situation where civil rights were violated. As a result, the march was followed by numerous lawsuits from people who had been mistreated.

The conflicts of these years contributed to a considerable extent to the near impeachment of Richard Nixon and led Gerald Ford to the White House. As fate would have it, it was while Ford was celebrating the opening of the Bicentennial observance of the American Revolution at Lexington and Concord that he received the news that the American-supported regime in Vietnam had fallen into disarray and chaos, thus ending the long and bitter legacy of conflict that President Johnson had created.

THE CARTER YEARS

With the inauguration of President Carter, the nation had for the first time a Bible-reading, born-again Evangelical in the White House. Before taking office he even confessed his sins in *Playboy* magazine. He also expressed his faith on many occasions, most controversially when he applied his millennial interpretations to the ultimate return of the Jews to the Holy Land. It was the fate of his turbulent administration that oil and energy were in one way or another at the base of his problems, both domestic and foreign.

The great dramas of the Carter administration were to a large extent religious, involving clashes of biblical religions in which Israel, the Arab nations, and Iran were the participants. The ending to one encounter, the Camp David accord, seemed a victory, but Carter's last ordeal had its beginnings in the putsch in the 1950s that sent Iran's Ayatollah Khomeini into exile and installed a modernizing shah to rule the country. In 1979 retribution was visited on the United States with the seizing of the embassy staff as hostages. It is uncertain what effect this incident has had on people in general and on the ministry in particular, though there is quite real evidence that many felt the country was becoming impotent and that this belief has had something to do with the rise of the Moral Majority and many other manifestations of social paranoia. It has certainly led to a political revival among Evangelicals.

The Eighties

PRESIDENT REAGAN AND THE MORAL MAJORITY

A final episode in this history of the ministry is concerned with President Reagan and the Moral Majority. This movement achieved national prominence on October 3, 1980, when the President, then a candidate for office, addressed a conference of religious broadcasters in Lynchburg, Virginia, at the invitation of Jerry Falwell. In his address Reagan spoke warmly of some of the aims of the Moral Majority. This, though, was a campaign speech and in no way a commitment to all the tenets of this new movement that had suddenly come to the attention of the American people. But the rise of the Moral Majority, of which Falwell is the incorporated president, is a significant event in American religious history, and its character deserves close scrutiny. Its importance should be neither exaggerated nor minimized. In the minds of many it is a menace to both science and the humanities, though others see the movement as harmless and in accord with traditional American values.

Jerry Falwell was born in 1933 as the nation slid deeper into the Great Depression. He was educated in the Lynchburg schools and was generally a good student. After various business ventures, he decided to enter the Baptist ministry and organized the independent Thomas Road Baptist Church. His talents soon became obvious and led to the building of an enlarged church that seats thousands in multiple services. The most striking characteristic of his ministry is his understanding of God's chain of command that makes the pastor the ruler of the congregation. This same attitude is carried into his notions of family discipline.

The primary fact to remember about Falwell's Moral Majority is that it is an intensification of the conservative beliefs of the huge Southern Baptist Convention. Piety of this kind is almost endemic in most Southern denominations; there is no other large region of the country in which concern for the Church is given such serious commitment. Rosalyn Carter on one occasion summed this up in her remark that she knew some people who did not put the Church first in their lives, but that she could not imagine what kind of a life that would be. It is this attitude that one must understand if the Moral Majority is to be understood.

However, the Moral Majority is difficult to categorize. It can with justice be deemed a unique and independent religious movement. On the other hand, in the taxonomic theory of Ernst Troeltsch it can be described as a sect in that it is separate from the Southern Baptist Convention and it is so on the grounds that the Convention has lost its earlier zeal and, even worse, is wasting its energies and is developing a large bureaucracy. The Convention's methods in the field of Christian education have also been sharply criticized. Inevitably, there have been accusations of creeping liberalism in some of the Convention's seminaries.

In the Convention itself there is constant rivalry about who is taking the most conservative position. For instance, Harold Lindsell has intensified the controversy through creating an additional goad to ultra-orthodoxy by raising the question of scriptural infallibility as opposed to inerrancy, even though the two terms would seem to be synonymous. Lindsell, however, manages to make inerrancy the stricter view for absolute fundamentalists. One of the entailments of his principles is an extreme form of legalism that leads to an almost rabbinic interpretation of the New Testament.

The effect of competing conservatisms has had relatively little to do with the actual degree of willingness to accept every word of Holy Scripture. True conservatives assert that anything less than absolute acceptance would make them pariahs and heretics. It is in this light that we should view the slogan of the Moral Majority, "Fundamentalism is alive and well." The fact that this slogan is actively supported by millions of Americans is a most serious challenge for Protestant ministers, and politicians as well.

THE RISE OF NEO-PENTECOSTALISM

In the crisscrossing of religious beliefs in the last three decades, and while the Moral Majority has been shaping itself, another disrupting movement has developed: the rise of Neo-Pentecostalism and the supposed baptism of the spirit. From April 23, 1960 (when an Episcopalian priest in California had to resign for having spoken in tongues), the movement has spread to almost all denominations, including Roman Catholics, producing constant controversy and dissension. In the seventies and eighties, these tendencies have been weakened by widespread privatism, self-realization, and other narcissistic attitudes that tend to undermine all kinds of religious concerns —and civil concerns as well. Indeed during this time the once-vaunted civil religion has fallen into ideological disarray. In a country like America, which thinks of itself as God's New Israel, social attitudes take on religious implications.

Retrospect and Prospect

To bring this history of ministry in America to a close, we must emphasize again the astounding changes that we have noted since 1956. In the process old solutions have had to yield to new problems. Ministers have had to grapple with the unaccustomed issues of civil rights, women's rights, the war in Vietnam, the ordination of women, the changes in the Roman Catholic church, radical theology, the rising interest in new religions, and above all, the seething dislocations of the social order as a whole.

For Protestant ministers, however, it may be that the most difficult change to accept has been the movement into the field of soul care, a movement that has disrupted, or at least challenged, the ancient understanding of pastoral counseling. We are speaking here of the rising insistence that the care of souls should involve clinical training and a certain amount of study in the field of depth psychology—in effect, an understanding of Freudian theory. Wayne E. Oates, a professor at the University of Louisville, is one major figure in this field. He early on played a role in convincing Protestant churches of its usefulness. Anton Boisen, who was a professor of pastoral care at the University of Chicago, is another. He was a leader in this new approach to pastoral theology, but before long there were many others. Religion and health became a major movement, with many prominent men and women showing strong interest in its possibilities; among them were Paul Tillich, Rollo May, and Seward Hiltner. Boisen went on to organize a system of clinical training, to place the movement on a sound academic basis. Such training is now a prerequisite for ordination in many churches, and in 1967 the Association for Pastoral Education was founded.

As we come down to the more recent past, a significant contribution to the ongoing life of the Protestant ministry has been the enormously important book that is helping ministers to evaluate their work—namely, *Ministry in America*, edited by David Schuller, Merton Strommen, and Milo Brekke. The volume scientifically and statistically studies the performance of the ministry. It deserves the closest examination by all concerned with this chapter, for there has never been so responsible an analysis of the ministry. One of the great ironies of the present, however, appears in their definition of the minister as the "wounded healer" (a term borrowed from the book by Henri J. M. Nouwen). It comes as no surprise that Schuller and his associates have discovered a prevailing uncertainty among ministers, both as to their purpose and their capability in a rapidly changing world. These are not optimistic points to end on; nevertheless they are the challenge for the coming years.

Notes

Chapter I. The Ministry in the Primitive Church

[1] I am indebted here to an illuminating suggestion by C. F. D. Moule, "Deacons in the New Testament," *Theology*, LVIII, 1950, 405 ff.

[2] I Cor. 15:5. But some regard this reference to "the Twelve" as of doubtful authenticity.

[3] So A. Fridrichsen in "The Apostle and His Message," Uppsala Universitets Arsskrift, 1947.

[4] *Kirchliches Amt und Geistliche Vollmacht in den ersten drei Jahrhunderten* (Tübingen, 1953), esp. 32 ff.

[5] The text of the Revised Standard Version is followed here except that with the majority of translators we have understood *proistamenos* as meaning "presiding" rather than "giving aid."

[6] See the highly instructive article by F. V. Filson, "The Christian Teacher in the First Century," *Journal of Biblical Literature*, LX (1941), 371 ff.

[7] See his *The Apostolic Preaching* (New York, 1937) and *Gospel and Law* (New York, 1951).

[8] The identification of "bishops" with "pastors" is also suggested by Acts 20:28 and I Pet. 2:25.

[9] See B. S. Easton, "Jewish and Early Christian Ordination," *Anglican Theological Review*, V (1922-23), 308 ff. and VI (1923-24), 285 ff.

[10] See here the very suggestive article, "Zur altchristlichen Verfassungsgeschichte" by H. Lietzmann in *Zeitschrift fur wissenschaftliche Theologie*, LV (1914), 97 ff. This article has been especially helpful to the writer of this chapter.

[11] See B. S. Easton, *The Pastoral Epistles*, 212-14.

[12] One is bound to think here of the office of "superintendent" in the Qumran community which is mentiond in both the *Manual of Discipline* and the *Damascus Document*. Any discussion as to whether a connection should be seen between this office and the most primitive "episcopacy" in Jerusalem must wait upon the achievement of a clearer picture of the relations of the community of the Dead Sea Scrolls with the beginnings of Christianity.

[13] See A. Ehrhardt, *The Apostolic Succession in the First Two Centuries of the Church* (London, 1953).

[14] *The Mission and Expansion of Christianity in the First Three Centuries,* (New York, 1908), 445 ff.

[15] "The Development of the Early Ministry," *Anglican Theological Review,* XXVI, (1944), esp. 148 f. Shepherd, following Sohm and Lowrie, regards the presbyters of an earlier time as only the older or more honored men in the congregation. He sees the origin of the presbyterate *as an order of the ministry* in the authority which the monarchical bishops delegated to their representatives in the various house churches under their care.

Chapter II. The Ministry of the Ante-Nicene Church
(c. 125-325)

1 The term "charismatic" has been used to designate this triad of what Adolf von Harnack called the "universal" as distinguished from the "local" ministry. The term became prominent in the writings of Karl Holl and Max Weber, who stressed the distinction between inspired and institutional leadership. The occasional employment in the present chapter of the term "charismatic" to designate the triad of ministries which Harnack and Holl, each in his own way, had in mind does not necesarily imply an acceptance of their theories for classifying the ministries of the ancient church.

2 This view has been put forward with freshness by Friedrich Gerke (with special reference to Clement of Rome) in his contribution to The Ministry and the Sacraments, Roderic Dunkerley, ed. (New York and London, 1937), 343 ff.

3 An excellent survey chapter of the Jewish influence in the organization of the ancient Church is that of T. G. Jalland, The Origin and Evolution of the Christian Church (London, 1948), chaps. 1-5. For a quite recent study, see E. Stauffer, "Jüdisches Erbe im urchristlichen Kirchenrecht," Theologische Literaturzeitung, LXXVII (1952), 4.

4 This has been especially clearly seen by Arnold Erhardt, "The Beginnings of Monepiscopacy," Church Quarterly Review, CXL (1945), 113 ff.

5 Henri Grégoire has recently argued that Polycarp died in 177, Analecta Bollandiana, (1951), 1-38.

6 Martin Werner has given prominence to the eschatological motif of co-rule with Christ as the authentically apostolic element in the rise of monepiscopacy. The bishop's throne is the symbol of his future role in the Kingdom. Die Entstehung des christlichen Dogmas (Bern, 1941), 636-66.

7 Though this ideal renews that of the pastoral epistles, it should also be observed that the concern for widows, orphans, and the poor is a characteristic motif of the ancient mirrors of princes.

8 Eusebius, Ecclesiastical History, v, 20, 5-8.

9 Ibid., 24, 17.

10 Ep. to Polycarp, 1, 2.

11 Martyrdom of Polycarp (c. 156), xvi, 2.

12 The view of F. F. Vokes, The Riddle of the Didache (London, 1938).

13 The Epistle of Clement has been subject to exhaustive scrutiny, as it is of capital importance, both for those who prefer to stress the institutional ministry with its historic sanctions and those who favor the "charismatic" ministry. A noteworthy analysis of the legitimist tradition is that of Gregory Dix, The Apostolic Ministry, Kenneth Kirk, ed. (New York and London, 1946), 253-62; another, in the spiritualist tradition, is that of F. Gerke, loc. cit., 357-63.

14 On the influence of the Jerusalemite Sanhedrin on the theory and practices of both the ecclesiastical and the synagogal presbytery, see Arnold Ehrhardt, "Jewish and Christian Ordination," Journal of Ecclesiastical History, V (1954), 125.

15 Our principal sources are Jerome (behind whom perhaps we can identify Origen), Ambrosiaster, the two Severi, and Eutychius. It is Patriarch Eutychius (933-940) who belatedly supplies us with the figure twelve. See the classical discussion of the peculiarities in J. B. Lightfoot, "The Christian Ministry,"

Philippians (rev. ed.; London, 1881), esp. 230 ff. For a recent reconstruction of the obscure period in Alexandrian Christian history, see W. Telfer, "Episcopal Succession in Egypt," *Journal of Ecclesistical History*, III (1952), 1 ff. and *idem*, "Meletius of Lycopolis and Episcopal Succession in Egypt," *The Harvard Theological Review*, XLVIII (1955), 227.

[16] *Dialogue with Trypho*, 19, 116, 117. On the place of Melchizedek in cult and polemic, see Georges Bardy, "Melchisédech dans la tradition patristique," *Revue biblique*, XXXV (1926), 496; XXXVI (1927), 25; Marcel Simon, "M. dans la polemique entre juifs et chrétiens," *Revue d'histoire et de la philosophie religieuses*, XVII (1937), 58.

[17] The detail about very early morning is derived from the roughly contemporary Letter of Pliny to Trajan (112). The description is compounded of *The First Apology*, 67 and 66; the translation is that of Edward Hardy, *Early Christian Writers*, Christian Classics, I, edited by Cyril Richardson (Philadelphia, 1953), 286 ff. (italics mine).

[18] *Apud* Eusebius, *H. E.*, iv, 23, 10.

[19] *Ibid.*

[20] *Didascalia*, ii, 20; cf. the prayer in the so-called Clementine Liturgy:

"Look upon him now being admitted to ready thy Holy Scriptures to thy people, and give him a holy spirit, a prophetic spirit; thou who didst make wise thy servant Esdras to read thy laws to thy people, now also in answer to our prayers make wise thy servant. . . ." (*Apostolic Constitutions*, viii, 22.)

[21] Others claim that it evolved from the diaconate. Cf. Adolf von Harnack, "On the Origin of the Readership and the Other Lower Orders," *Sources of the Apostolic Canons*, tr. by L. A. Wheatley (London, 1895). In an introductory essay John Owen, seeing the readership enhanced with the rising culture of the ancient Church, goes so far in interpreting the excursus by Harnack as to construe the whole history of Church orders as a continuing conflict between Reader and Priest, that is, between instruction and liturgy. A solid Catholic consideration of the readership, taking Harnack into account, is that of Franz Wieland, *Die genetische Entwicklung der sogenannten Ordines minores*, Römische Quartalschrift, Supplementheft 7 (Rome, 1897).

[22] *Dialogue with Trypho the Jew*, ii, 8.

[23] *Ibid*, 49, 82.

[24] *Letter to Flora*, c. 160; preserved by Epiphanius, *Panarion*, xxxiii, 7. This is the first appearance in extant Christian literature of the terms. The succession in this case appears to have been Ptolemy, Valentinus, Theodas—in his youth a hearer of Paul.

[25] The act of the laying on of hands had diverse meaning in the ancient Church. It was also used in solemn benediction, in the exorcism of healing, at baptism, in confirmation, and ordination. Five important studies here are Johannes Behm, *Die Handauflegung im Urchristentum* (Leipzig, 1911), Joseph Coppens, *L'imposition des mains* (Louvain, 1925), Pieter Elderenbosch, *De Oplegging der Handen* (The Hague, 1953), Arnold Ehrhardt, *The Apostolic Succession* (London, 1953), and *idem*, "Jewish and Christian Ordination," *Journal of Eccleesiastical History*, V (1954).

[26] This asseveration would indicate that in considerable measure Justin, in his description of the Eucharistic service in *The Apology*, had in mind not the

bishop's service but that of one of the presbyters in his own house and that the reason for giving two largely repetitive descriptions of the Eucharist is that one is the postbaptismal Eucharist at which the bisop of the Roman community would have been present and the second was the more intimate local gathering without the bishop.

[27] *Martyrdom of Justin,* as translated by Robert Grant, *Second Century Christianity* (London, 1946), 110.

[28] *Against Heresies,* iv, xxvi, 2. Recent works on the ministry in Irenaeus are John Lawson, *The Biblical Theology of Saint Irenaeus* (London, 1946), chap. 13; Einar Molland, "Irenaeus of Lugdunum and the Apostolic Succession," *Journal of Ecclesiastical History,* I (1950), 12; L. Spikowski, *La doctrine de l'Eglise chez S. Irénée* (Strasbourg, 1926).

[29] *Ibid,* iii, 3, 1.

[30] *Ibid,* iv, xxvi, 2.

[31] *Ibid,* v, xxxiv, 3.

[32] *Ibid,* iv, xviii, 4 f.; v, ii, 3.

[33] *Ibid,* iii, xvi, 7.

[34] The apologetic motif is stressed by B. LeRoy Burkhart in "The Rise of the Christian Priesthood," *Journal of Religion,* XXII (1942), 187: ". . . under the necessity of meeting pagan criticism Christian leaders brought back into use the ancient terminology of religion."

[35] *Against Heresies,* iv, 18, 4-6.

[36] Rather than being the New Testament *counterpart* of the Old Covenantal priest, as, for example, in Clement and the *Didache,* 13.

[37] Polycrates to Victor of Rome (189-98), *apud* Eusebius, *H. E.,* v, 24, 3.

[38] That the *Tradition* was the work of Hippolytus was denied by J. Vernon Bartlet, *Church Life and Church Order during the First Four Centuries* (London, 1941) and held open to question by A. Hamel, *Die Kirche bei Hippolyt* (Gütersloh, 1951). The basic work of each was done (respectively, 1922 and 1929) before Gregory Dix completed his masterful reconstruction (the original Greek being largely lost) from the various Oriental and Latin versions, *The Apostolic Tradition* (London, 1937). Most scholars agree with Dix and his fore-runners, B. E. Easton and notably R. H. Connolly, in assigning it to Hippolytus and differ only in the details of the reconstruction and preferred readings. Cyril Richardson has found reasons to date the *Tradition* as a tract for the times on the death of Victor in 197, *Anglican Theological Review,* III (1948), 38. Perhaps the most recent vindication of the Hippolytan authorship is that of Odo Casel, "Die Kirchenordnung Hippolyts von Rom," *Archiv für Liturgiewissenschaft,* II (1952), 115. Casel agrees with H. Elfers against R. Lorentz that despite the Alexandrian elements in the *Tradition* it is the work of Hippolytus. The long review deals especially with the Eucharist. Besides the critical English (Greek and Latin) text of Dix, there are the Coptic-German text, edited by Walter Till and Johannes Leipoldt, and the Ethiopic-German text by Hugo Duensing (1946).

[39] The Greek and Latin nominatives in the various versions and reconstructions are *nominatio, electio, eklesis.*

[40] From the *Tradition* and other church orders sources we know that the act of witnessing to the faith in time of persecution qualified one to be cleric and also that a distinction was made among confessors between slaves and freemen.

Hippolytus wished to make the distinction absolute and disqualify his rival, the former slave, Callistus.

[41] In Latin *consentio,* in Greek *syneudokeo;* the latter is used also of the act of the whole Church in I Clement 44:3.

[42] So, the Coptic *Canons of Hippolytus,* can. 2, Wilhelm Riedel, ed., *Die Kirchenrechtsquellen des Patriarchats Alexandrien* (Leipzig, 1900), 201.

[43] The Syrian of Palestinian apocryphal *Acts of Peter,* chap. x (c. 190), representing the Lord as laying his hands on the apostles, may reflect this usage for bishops at a slightly earlier date than the *Tradition.*

[44] *Tradition,* ii, Dix, ed., 2-5. It is possible that the much later Coptic *Canons of Hippolytus* preserves an authentic reading where the ordaining prayer is extended to beseech the episcopal gift of "dissolving all the shackles of the iniquity of the demons and of healing all sicknesses." W. Riedel, *op. cit.,* 202. In the pseudonymous Epistle of Clement to James, ii, which prefaces the *Clementine Homilies,* binding and loosing are interpreted in terms both of the physician's and the teacher's art.

[45] Hippolytus refers to a decree of indulgence by Callistus, *Philosophoumena,* ix, 12, and this decree has commonly been identified with the "peremptory edict" referred to by Tertullian in *De pudicitia,* 1. Herein he attacks one whom he calls sarcastically *pontifex maximus, episcopus episcoporum.* Much of recent scholarship is inclined to identify the object of Tertullian's wrath with Bishop Agrippinus of Carthage, whom Cyprian also mentions adversely, *Ep.* 71, 4.

[46] *Philosophoumena,* ix, 12. See Albert Koeniger, "Prima sedes a nemine judicatur," *Beiträge zur Geschichte des Altertums* (Bonn and Leipzig, 1922) and Werner, *op cit.,* 60 (660).

[47] *Op. cit.,* i, *praefatio,* 6.

[48] *Epistola apostolorum,* 41; M. R. James, *The Apocryphal New Testament* (Oxford, 1924), 500; with reference to the Greek text behind the Coptic and Ethiopic, C. Schmidt, *Texte und Untersuchungen,* 43, 132 f.

[49] This exclusiveness may be related to the fact that a crown of lilies was associated with virgins, while martyrs carried crowns of roses to their execution.

[50] Following C. H. Turner, as does Gregory Dix, who separates the preface common to the ordaining prayers of each from the prayers proper to bishop and presbyter, respectively, *op. cit.,* 80.

[51] To simplify a complicated and shifting nomenclature, it should be noted that originally *martyr* meant a witness of Christ's resurrection. *Confessor* was the Latin equivalent. In due course both terms were used in Latin and Greek forms, and a distinction was sometimes made between those who had physically suffered under torture (martyrs) and those who had valorously but without hurt witnessed the faith (confessors), The most important recent study of the place of the confessor and martyr is that of Hans von Campenhausen, *Die Idee des Martyrium in der alten Kirche* (Göttingen, 1936), replete with the earlier literature.

[52] The installation (*katastasis*) of a confessor as a bishop, however, does require the imposition of hands.

[53] Nevertheless, *Philosophoumena,* ix, 12, 22, does include deacons among the clergy, which, of course, is not the same as the presbyterate or the later priesthood. A very full account of the ante-Nicene diaconate is that of Adam Otterbein, *The Diaconate according to the Apostolic Tradition of Hippolytus and Derived*

Documents, Catholic University of America Studies in Sacred Theology, No. 95 (Washington, 1945).

54 Didascalia apostolorum, ii, 44; R. H. Connolly, ed. (Oxford, 1929), 109.

55 Loc. cit., ii, 28; Connolly, op. cit., 80.

56 Not, however, in the Tradition, xxxiv, where a watchman maintained by the bishop at the cemetery is mentioned. Originally doorkeepers and gravediggers were one with the subdeacons. Eventually, with the extension of the catacombs, these functions were differentiated and fully clericalized.

57 Op. cit., i, 17, 8.

58 Libanius, for example, thus refers to teachers. Cf. G. R. Sievers, Das Leben des Libanius (Berlin, 1868), 41, with notes. I am indebted to my colleague Professor Glanville Downey of Dumbarton Oaks for this reference.

59 That he was a presbyter of the church in Carthage we have solely from Jerome.

60 On Baptism, 17.

61 On Penitence, 9. In the Epistola canonica, c. 254, of Gregory the Wonder-worker, wherein the system of stational penitence is described, the bishop rather than the presbyters is the administrator of the acts of forgiveness.

62 De praescriptione, 41.

63 On Exhortation to Chastity, 7.

64 On the Soul, 9.

65 The best overall account of Clement's place in the history of the ministry is that of R. B. Tollinton, Clement of Alexandria (London, 1914), II, chap. 15.

66 Such is the fascinating conjecture of the already cited article of W. Telfer, "Episcopal Succession."

67 Armenia, which had also received Christianity very early, had only one bishop as late as around 250.

68 Serapion was bishop from c. 339 to c. 350. The simple prayers suggest greater antiquity than the fourth century, as does the mention of only three orders in a unique sequence. On the antiquity of the formularies both Gregory Dix, who projected a new edition, and J. Vernon Bartlet agreed. Cf. Dix in The Apostolic Ministry, 214, n. 1, and Bartlet, op. cit., 27. The text is available in English, John Wordsworth, ed., 2nd ed. (London, 1923).

69 Who is the Rich Man that shall be Saved? xiii; A.N.F., II, 603 f.

70 Stromata, vi, 13; A.N.F., II, 504.

71 Ibid., vii, 1, 3.

72 Ibid., vi, 13. Observe how gnostic spirituality, Pauline spirituality, and the apostolic expectation that the saints would judge and co-rule with Christ here coalesce in fascinating substantiation of M. Werner's thesis. See above, n. 6.

73 The idea has been suggested by Karl Holl, Enthusiasmus und Bussgewalt (Leipzig, 1898); cf. Gesammelte Aufsätze, II (Tübingen, 1928), 256 ff.; Walter Völker, Das Volkommenheitsideal des Origenes (Tübingen (1931), esp. 187-92; idem, "Die Vollkommenheitslehre des Klemens," Theologische Zeitschrift, III (1947), 15; von Campenhausen, op cit.

74 As such, Origen was the effective founder of the School of Alexandria. Gustave Bardy, "Aux origines de l'École d'Alexandrie," Recherches de science religieuse, XXVII (1937), 65.

75 The texts have been gathered by W. Völker, Das Vollkommenheitsideal, 180

ff. Origen seems to have distinguished between an Aaronic and a Melchizedekian high-priesthood.

[76] *Apud* Cyprian, *Ep.* lxxiv, 2.

[77] Translated by Henry Chadwick in *Alexandrian Christianity*, Christian Classics, II (Philadelphia and Edinburgh, 1954).

[78] Eusebius, *H. E.*, vii, 29.

[79] *Op. cit., praem.*, xiii.

[80] See E. G. Weltin, "Origen's .'Church'", *Studies Presented to David M. Robinson*, George E. Mylonas and Doris Raymond, eds. (St. Louis, 1953), II, 1015 ff. I have not been able to see Carl V. Harris, "Origen of Alexandria's Interpretation of the Teacher's Function in the Early Hierarchy and Community," doctoral dissertation, Duke University, 1952. R. B. Tollinton has assembled several beautiful passages on "The Task of the Teacher," *Selections from the Commentaries and Homilies of Origen* (London, 1929), 156-93.

[81] W. Metcalfe, ed., *Gregory Thaumaturgus: Address to Origen* (London, 1920), 62 ff.

[82] *In Lucam*, xxxviii; Tollinton, *op. cit.*, 164.

[83] *In Leviticum, Hom.* v, 8; Tollinton, *op. cit.*, 178.

[84] *In Johannem*, vi, 1 f.; Tollinton, *op. cit.*, 160.

[85] The Catholic scholars: Yves Congar and Abbé Long-Hasselmans point out, significantly, that Cyprian limited his use of the priestly designations like *sacerdos* to bishops and presbyters when actually engaged in priestly functions, reserving the older usage to refer to them as officers of the Church. Both these Catholics feel that Cyprian's usage indicates the survival of a strong sense of the clergy as priests in their representative capacity as spokesmen of the whole royal-priestly people of God. "Sur la sacerdoce," *Revue des sciences religieuses*, XXV (1951), 187; 270.

[86] *Epistle LXII*, (63, 17).

[87] Martin Werner is very illuminating in analyzing the problem of Cyprian and the confessors in eschatological terms, *op. cit.*, 636-66, esp. 659; see also H. Koch, *Cyprianische Untersuchungen, Arbeiten zur Kirchengeschichte*, IV (1926), 79-131; 211-64.

[88] *Epistle XXIII*.

[89] The Numidian confessors spoke of him thus, *Epistle LXXVIII*, 2. Cf. Harnack, "Cyprian als Enthusiast," *Zeitschrift für neutestamentliche Wissenschaft*, III (1902).

[90] *Epistle LXVIII* 4; 9.

[91] *Ibid.*, 8.

[92] *Epistle LI*, 20.

[93] *Epistles LXIII, LXVIII*.

[94] *Epistle LXVII*, 5.

[95] *Ibid*, 3; 5.

[96] *Epistle LXV; De lapsis*, 6.

[97] In the much later *Testament of Our Lord*, i, 23, the laity are not merely *prospherentes* (*offerentes*) but they in a sense concelebrate with the bishops in repeating the eucharistic prayer aloud.

[98] This is particularly prominent in the stenographically preserved account of Origen's synodal interview with Heraclides, after which "the people must give solemn consent."

99 See E. E. Kemp, *Canonization in the Western Church* (Oxford, 1948), chap. 1.

100 *The Liberian Catalogue.*

101 The description purports to be the words of Peter as embodied in a letter by Clement of Rome to James of Jerusalem. The whole letter to James, "bishop of bishops," introduces the Pseudo-Clementine *Homilies.*

102 The popularity of the Clementine literature and the frequent allusion to this particular image vouch for its accuracy as a poetic transcript of the corporate ministry in the period of its composition. The crucial text is that of Bernard Rehm, *Die griechischen christlichen Schriftsteller,* XLII (Berlin and Leipzig, 1953), 16; the English translation is that of Thomas Smith, *A.N.F.,* VIII, 220 f.

103 Cf. the elaboration of this marine image in the later *Apostolic Constitutions,* lv, ii.

104 Preserved by Eusebius, *H. E.* vi, 43, 11.

105 This is the view of F. Wieland, *op. cit.*

106 Cyprian, *Epistle VII,* 4, 5.

107 *Op, cit., xvi;* the same is true in the fourth-century *Apostolic Constitution,* viii, 26.

108 See further Evelyn Frost, *Christian Healing . . . in the Light of the Doctrine and Practice of the Ante-Nicene Church* (London, 1949).

109 *The Apostolic Church Order* in its present form dates from the end of the third century, but Bartlet, among others, would date parts of it as early as 200, *op. cit.,* 102. For the whole of the evidence on the female diaconate, see the well-documented but insufficiently integrated Report to the Archbishop of Canterbury entitled *The Ministry of Women* (London, 1919); also G. Huls, *De dienstder vrouw in de Kerk* (Wageningen, 1951).

110 The distribution of the *fermentum* in Rome is documented as late as the episcopate of Innocent I (402-17), *Epistle XXV,* 5. The distribution of the episcopally eucharized bread to the presbyters is roughly analogous to the reservation of confirmation as the episcopal prerogative in the compound action of baptism-confirmation. Both represent efforts to preserve something of the older unity of the church embodied in the pastoral actions of their bishop in accommodation to an ever-growing membership.

111 *Didascalia,* ix; *Apostolic Church Order,* can. 11.

112 *Apostolic Church Order,* can. 2.

113 *Testament of our Lord,* i, 34, 12 which in its present form dates from the fifth century but which may well preserve ancient material. The *Testament* must surely preserve ante-Nicene usage when in the ordaining prayer it beseeches the Lord not to "take away from the (corporate) presbyterate the Spirit of presbyterate." *Op. cit.,* i, 35; cf. *Apostolic Constitutions,* viii, 28; 46, 1. Also primitive may be the gift of healing in presbyters, *Testament,* 1, 47; 29; *Apostolic Constitutions,* viii, 16.

114 *Op. cit.,* viii-ix. The *food,* literally *salt,* must refer to fellowship meals (*agapes*).

115 *Didascalia,* ii, 27. The translation is that of R. H. Connolly, *op. cit.* At this point our text goes on echoing the phrases of Ignatius, likening the deacons to Christ and the deaconesses to the Holy Spirit. Elsewhere, the deacon is likened also to the prophet, ii, 29.

The other references in the following paragraphs to the *Didascalia* are, ii, 2; ii, 26; 32 f.; ii, 5; 45-53.

[116] Bo Reicke, "A Synopsis of Early Preaching," *The Root of the Vine*, Anton Fridrichsen, ed. (New York, 1953).

[117] The characterization is J. Leclercq's in "Chorévêques," *Dictionnaire d'archéologie chrétiennes et de Liturgie*, III (Paris, 1913); of the same view is Jacques le Clef, "Chorévêques," *Dictionnaire de droit canonique*, III (Paris, 1942).

[118] For the probable early date, see above, n. 109.

[119] Theodor Schermann, ed., *Die Allegemeine Kirchenordnung*, I (Paderborn, 1914), 24 f.

[120] For the reconstruction of the canons, see R. B. Rackham, "The Text of the Canons of Ancyra," *Studia Biblica et Ecclesiastica* (Oxford, 1891), III, 139-216, esp. 192.

[121] But cf. the seventy elders of Israel, Num. 6:16 f.

[122] The usual version of this canon indicates that the structure applied to the country priest in a city church, but the reading of the version edited by G. B. Howard gives what seems to me the more probable meaning. *The Canons of the Primitive Church* (from a Syrian MS London, 1897), 25.

[123] *Apud* Eusebius, *H. E.*, vii, 24, 6.

[124] Text adapted from that of H. J. Schroeder, *Disciplinary Decrees of the General Councils: Text, Translation, and Commentary* (St. Louis and London, 1937), 49.

[125] Tertullian was the first to use *concilium* ecclesiastically; Dionysius of Alexandria the first to use *synodos*. The most recent study of the councils is that of Monald Goemans, *Het algemeen concilie in de vierde eeuw* (Nijmegen, 1945).

Chapter III. The Ministry in the Later Patristic Period
(314-451)

[1] *Paroikia* was originally the community of strangers or immigrant sojourners in any city, a term which was appropriated by Christians in view of their primary citizenship in heaven. "Diocese," originally a major subdivision of the Empire, larger than a province, was not used until much later as the designation for the bishop's "parish."

[2] Canon 9: ". . . for the majority have affirmed that ordination blots out other kinds of sins." The majority might well have appealed to the purifactory and healing efficacy immemorially associated with the laying on of hands in baptism, exorcism, etc.

[3] The Council *in Encaeniis* was Arianizing. It condemned Athanasius. E. Schwartz holds that the canons of such a council would never have been declared authoritative in Orthodox canon law and therefore argues for an earlier date (329) and an Orthodox assembly as their source, "Zur Geschichte des Athanasius, VIII," *Nachrichten*, IV (Göttingen, 1911), 395 f.

[4] At Chalcedon the canons of Nicaea, Gangra (later also Laodicea), and two already cited ante-Nicene synods, Ancyra and Neocaesarea, constituted the basic corpus of canon law.

[5] A convenient English translation of the canons of the ecumenical councils and

several of the lesser synods is that of the *Nicene and Post-Nicene Fathers,* XIV. The already cited work of Schroeder is especially useful with its much more recent bibliographical notes.

6 Canon 18 of Encyra had decreed the same.

7 On the tendency of the Arianizing bishops to be more responsive to the urgency of bringing policy into line with politics and the correspondingly greater constitutional conservatism of the Nicene bishops, I have written in "Christology and Church-State Relations in the Fourth Century," *Church History* XX (1951), Nos. 3 and 4. On the concern of the Nicenes to insist on the authority of metropolitans over their provincials and of the Arians to defend the parity of all bishops under the emperor, see K. Lübeck, *Reichseinteilung und kirchliche Hierarchie,* Kirchengeschichtliche Studien, V: 4 (1901), 193. Cf. F. Hatch, *Organization,* 169. That these canons of Antioch belong to an earlier and orthodox synod of 329, see E. Schwartz, *op. cit.,* 395 f.

8 The fact that the word "mob" (*tois ochlois*) is used may mean that orderly election (*ekloge*) by the properly constituted *laos* is not expressly excluded, but this was a marked tendency from the beginning in the East with the metropolitan appointing or the emperor nominating as chief layman. Popular suffrage survives much longer in the West. Even Pope Leo could exclaim: "He who is to preside over all must be elected by all." *Ep.* X; similarly, *Ep.* xiv.

9 *Op. cit.* viii, 4. The Scriptural basis for the threefold assent would be Matt. 18:16.

10 *Op. cit.,* 21.

11 *Op. cit.,* ii, 4, 28; A.N.F., VII, 411; 45.

12 *Op. cit.,* viii, 46. This is, of course, an echo of I Pet. 2:25, which with related passages in Hebrews had long been influential in fixing the image of Christ and the bishop as one.

13 For an invaluable account of the partial assimilation of the episcopate and presbyterate but with a different emphasis in view of the narrower definition of "ministry," see T. G. Jalland, *Apostolic Ministry,* chap. 5, "The Parity of Ministers."

14 The imperial administrative term was first taken over in the Latin West for ecclesiastical purposes in the fourth century. See W. K. Boyd, *The Ecclesiastic Edicts of the Theodosian Code* (New York, 1905). On the bishop's judicial functions, see further, "Audientia episcopales," *Reallexikon für Antike und Christentum,* I (Stuttgart, 1950), Col. 1915.

15 Not documented, however, until *c.* 500. See Jalland, "Parity," Additional Note: The Decline of the Diaconate, *loc. cit.,* 347.

16 It is embedded in his *Quaestiones Veteris et Novi Testamenti.*

17 *Op. cit.,* viii, 28.

18 Paul from whom this group stemmed was bishop of Samosata and viceroy under Queen Zenobia of Palmyra; he was condemned for heresy by two synods (264, 269); and one of the incidental charges brought against him was that he trained women to sing in the church choir. Eusebius, *H. E.,* vii, 30.

19 VIII, 20; A.N.F., VII, 392.

20 The prominence of widows in the *Testament,* communicating, for example, before the readers and subdeacons, may be due to Montanist competition. The

most recent study here is that of Linus Bopp, *Das Witwentum als organische Gliedschaft im Gemeinschaftsleben der alten Kirche* (Mannheim, 1950).

[21] Hugo Koch, *Virgines Christi, Texte und Untersuchungen*, 31 (Leipzig, 1907), 91 f. Their public vow was taken as marriage to Christ.

[22] Pseudo-Jerome, *De septem ordinibus ecclesiae* (c. 420), Athanasius W. Kalff, ed., inaugural dissertation (Würzburg, 1935). See also J. Lungkofler, "Die Vorstufen zu den höheren Wiehen nach dem *Liber pontificalis*," *Zeitschrift für katholische Theologie*, LXVI, (1942), 1.19.

[23] Cf. Julian the Apostate, *Ep.* 87, 6, Bidez, ed.

[24] H. U. Instinsky, *Bischofsstuhl und Kaiserthron* (Munich, 1955). F. Loofs had long ago shown how Paul of Samosata had anticipated the later evolution of the *cathedra* into a throne when he built in his cathedral a high throne comparable to his in his role of chief minister of Queen Zenobia. Paulus von Samosata, *Texte und Uuntersuchungen*, 44/5, 34; 33 ff. See also Theodor Klauser, *Die Kathedra im Totenkult* (Münster, 1927), 179 ff.

[25] Theodor Klauser, *Der Ursprung der bischölichen Insignien und Ehrenrechte*, Bonner Akademische Reden, I (Bonn, 1948).

[26] Philippe Gobillot, "Sur la tonsure chrétienne," *Revue d'histoire ecclésiastique*, XXI (1925), esp. 411. The tonsure was understood as a kind of self-sacrifice; the tonsure in the form of a crown may have betokened spiritual royalty.

[27] *On the Priesthood*, vi, viii, 550; translated by T. Allen Moxon (London, 1907); 153. Although the later Greek Church came to recruit its bishops largely from the monastery, Crysostom warned that when monks entered the conflicts for which they had never practiced, they were often "perplexed, and dazed, and helpless."

[28] These dangers refer especially to the charge of widows and the management of finance.

[29] *On the Priesthood*, i, xvi, 291.

[30] *Ibid*, iii, xii, 241.

[31] *Ibid*, 244.

[32] *Ibid*, iii, xv.

[33] The contrast between the Antiochene East and the West in this respect has been pointed out by Johannes Quasten, "Mysterium Tremendum: Eucharistische Frömmigkeitsauffassungen des vierten Jahrhunderts," *Vom christlichen Mysterium* (Düsseldorf, 1951).

[34] *On the Priesthood*, iii, iv, 178-80. The contemporaneous Syrian *Apostolic Constitutions*, ii, lvii, 21, echoes this sense of the awesome majesty: ". . . let every rank by itself partake of the Lord's body and precious blood in order, and approach with reverence and holy fear, as to the body of their king."

[35] *On the Priesthood*, vi, iv, 520.

[36] *Ibid.*, iii, iv, 175.

[37] *Ibid.*, iii, v, 182-89.

[38] For the important place of Chrysostom, see Oscar D. Watkins, *A History of Penance* (London, 1920), I, 328-48; on excommunication, see Werner Elert, *Abendmahl und Kirchengemeinschaft in der alten Kirche* (Berlin, 1954).

[39] *On the Priesthood*, ii, iv, 110; iii, 107.

[40] *On Penitence*, Homily II.

[41] So, Bernard Botte, ed. *Sources chrétiennes*, XXV (Paris, 1949), 23

[42] In contrast to Chrysostom, however, the action at the Christian altar suggests to Ambrose, not the shudder before a lightning bolt, but the ecstasy of the bride and the bridegroom.

[43] In *De dignitate sacerdotali*. I have shown elsewhere that this anonymous work, a very revealing *concio ad clerum*, should be reassigned to Ambrose: "The Golden Priesthood and the Leaden State," *Harvard Theological Review*, XLIX (1956).

[44] An English translation of the exemplary and contemporary biography is that of Herbert Weiskotten, *Vita* (Princeton, 1919).

[45] Possidius, *loc. cit.*, 121; the remaining quotations are from 135, 131, and 123.

[46] First formulated by Augustine in *De baptismo contra Donatistas* (400), i, i, 2: "Just as he who is baptized, even if he separates himself from the unity of Church, does not lose the sacrament of baptism; so likewise he who is ordained, if he depart from the unity, does not lose the sacrament which confers the power to give baptism." Cf. *De bono conjugale*, xxiv, 32; *Contra Epistolam Parmeniani*, ii, 28 f.

[47] The most recent study is that of Plato Kornyljak, *De efficacitate sacramentorum* (Vatican City, 1953).

[48] See Albert Schebler, *Die Reordinationen in der "altkatholischen" Kirche* (Bonn, 1936).

[49] *On the Baptism of Christ*, N.P.N.F., 2nd series V, 519, Migne, P.G., XLVI, col. 581.

[50] *Op. cit.*, viii, 28, 46. See K. Hofmann, "Absetzung," *Reallexikon für Antike und Christentum*, I (1950), col. 38.

[51] This process has been well characterized by Dix in *The Apostolic Ministry*, 286 f.

[52] See Edward E. Malone, *The Monk and the Martyr*, Studies in Christian Antiquity, XII (Washington, 1950).

[53] In the West the monks were eventually distinguished from the secular clergy (in the world) as the regular clergy (living by a rule).

[54] For example, a monk appropriately called Demophilus in Pseudo-Dionysius, *Ep.* VIII. See Holl, Bussegewalt.

[55] Odo Casel, "Die Mönchsweihe," *Jahrbuch für Liturgie-wissenschaft* V (1926), 23, and the article "Abbas," *Beiträge zur Geschichte des alten Mönchtums*, Supplement, 1.

[56] *Commentary on the Lord's Prayer and on the Sacraments of the Baptism and the Eucharist*, A Mingana, Woodbrooke Studies, VI (Cambridge, 1933), 82, 83.

[57] *Ibid*, 91 f.

[58] *The Liturgical Homilies*, R. H. Connolly, ed., *Texts and Studies*, VIII, No. 1 (Cambridge, 1909), 7 ff.

[59] *Ibid.*, 45.

[60] *Ibid.*, 7, 67.

[61] *Ibid.*, 63.

[62] *Ibid.*, 64 f.

[63] *Ibid.*, 21.

[64] I cannot refrain from mentioning at this point that in a decretal ascribed to Bishop Callistus of Rome the conscientious and self-disciplined teacher of the Church is vigorously defended from defamation by the people and pupils from rebuke and from control of his instruction by bishop and ruler. The decretal

belongs to the Pseudo-Isidorian forgery of the ninth century but undoubtedly preserves material perhaps of the period of the Pseudo-Clementine:

"Teachers (*Doctores*) . . . , who are called fathers are rather to be borne with than reprehended, unless they err from the true faith. . . . For as the Catholic teacher (*doctor*) and especially the priest of the Lord, ought to be involved in no error, so ought he to be wronged by no machination or passion. . . . Consequently an unjust judgment, or an unjust decision instituted or enforced by judges under the fear or the command of a prince, or any bishop or person of influence, cannot be valid." *Decretales Pseudo-Isidorianae*, P. Hinschius, ed., 136 f.; translated in *A.N.F.*, VIII, 614.

65 Significantly, in contrast, the Emperor Marcian had been acclaimed by the fathers of Chalcedon as, like Christ, at once king, priest, and prophet, i.e., doctor of the faith. The competence to formulate doctrine made the emperor the last and most effective of the ancient order of teachers. 176. *Ep.* XIV, 1. 177. *Ep.* LXV, 2.

66 *Ep.* XIV, 1.

67 *Ep.* LXV, 2.

Chapter IV.   The Ministry in the Middle Ages

1 Chrysostom, "On the Priesthood," *Nicene and Post-Nicene Fathers*, IX.

2 Shotwell and Loomis, *See of Peter*, (New York, 1927), 577-80.

3 Theodoret, "Ecclesiastical History," 17, *Post-Nicene Fathers*, Ser. 2, III, 143-45.

4 Maude Aline Huttmann, "The Establishment of Christianity and the Proscription of Paganism," Columbia University, *Studies in History, Economics and Public Law*, LX, 2 (1914), 149-57 and 62-63.

5 Letter 52, *The Nicene and Post-Nicene Fathers*, Ser. 2, VI, 91.

6 Eusebius, *Historia Ecclesiastica*, VII, 30.

7 F. Holmes Dudden, *The Life and Times of St. Ambrose* (Oxford, 1935), 66.

8 The code of the just war is elaborated in the *De Officiis*. Exhortations to the emperor to fight the Arian Goths appear in the *De Fide*.

9 Letter 77, *op. cit.*, 160.

10 Hans von Schubert, *Geschichte der christlichen Kirche im frühmittelalter* (Tübingen, 1921).

11 Henri Pirenne, *Economic and Social History of Medieval Europe* (New York, 1937).

12 James Westfall Thompson, *An Economic and Social History of the Middle Ages 300-1300* (New York, 1928), 614-15.

13 Evelyn Mary Spearing, *The Patrimony of the Roman Church in the Time of Gregory the Great* (Cambridge, 1918).

14 Émile Lesne, *Histoire de la Propiété ecclésiastique en France*, 8 vols. (Lille, 1910-43).

15 George Gordon Coulton, *Five Centuries of Religion*, 4 vols. (1923-50) especially III.

16 James Westphal Thompson, *History of the Middle Ages* (New York, 1931), 172.

[17] Carl Erdmann, *Die Entstehung des Kreuzzugsgedankens* (Stuttgart, 1935).

[18] Anna Comnena, *The Alexiad*, tr. Elizabeth A. S. Dawes (London, 1928), 255-56.

[19] Leona C. Gabel, "Benefit of Clergy in England in the Later Middle Ages," *Smith College Studies in History*, XIV, Nos. 1-4 (Oct., 1928-July, 1929).

[20] Ernest Harold Davenport, *The False Decretals*, (Oxford, 1916).

[21] Edwin Hatch, *The Growth of Church Institutions* (New York, 1887), chap. 12.

[22] Henry C. Lea, *An Historical Sketch of Sacerdotal Celibacy* (Boston, 1884), 152.

[23] Edward L. Cutts, *Parish Priests and Their People in the Middle Ages in England* (London, 1898), 164, 166-67, 183.

[24] H. Maynard Smith, *Pre-Reformation England* (London, 1938), 138.

[25] *Bede's Ecclesiastical History*, II, xiii, tr. L. Gidley, (Oxford, 1870), 150.

[26] *Ibid.*, III, XXV, 254.

[27] Norman Boggs, *The Christian Saga*, 2 vols. (New York, 1931), 329.

[28] *De Gradibus Humilitatis*, XIV, G. B. Burch, ed. and tr. (Cambridge, Mass., 1940).

[29] R. S. Arrow-Smith, *The Prelude to the Reformation* (London, 1923), 14-15.

[30] Cutts, *op. cit.*, 97.

[31] R. A. R. Hartridge, *A History of Vicarages in the Middle Ages* (Cambridge, Eng., 1930), 163, 196.

[32] *Ibid.*, 14.

[33] Hatch. *op. cit.*, 55.

[34] Arrowsmith, *op. cit.*, 9.

[35] John R. H. Moorman, *Church Life in England in the Thirteenth Century* (Cambridge, Eng., 1945), 12.

[36] Smith, *op. cit.*, 60.

[37] Arrowsmith, *op. cit.*, 46.

[38] Moorman, *op. cit.*, 92-93.

[39] Bernard Lord Manning, *The People's Faith in the Time of Wyclif* (Cambridge, Eng., 1919), 13.

[40] Moorman, *op. cit.*, 87. Quotations modernized.

[41] Lecoy de la Marche, *Anecdotes historiques—Etienne de Bourbon* (Paris, 1877), 155.

[42] Smith, *op. cit.*, 133-34.

[43] *Post-Nicene Fathers*, 2d series, XII, 40-41 *passim*.

[44] *Materials from the Life of Jacopo da Varagine*, ed. Ernest Cushing Richardson (New York, 1935), 102-3.

[45] John Myrc, "Instructions for Parish Priests," *Early English Text Society*, 1868, 1-3, modernized.

[46] Moorman, *op. cit.*, 79.

[47] Smith, *op. cit.*, 106.

[48] G. R. Owst, *Preaching in Medieval England* (Cambridge, Eng., 1926), 175.

[49] G. R. Owst, *Literature and Pulpit in Medieval England* (Cambridge, Eng., 1933), 389-90.

[50] *Ibid.*, 342.

[51] Margaret Deanesley, *A History of the Medieval Church* (London, 1934), 203.

[52] Owst, *Literature and Pulpit*, 300-301.

[53] Ray C. Petry, *No Uncertain Sound* (Philadelphia, 1948), 132, 156-57, 108-9.

[54] G. G. Coulton, *From Saint Francis to Dante* (London, 1906), 21 and 29.

[55] Karl Hefele, *Der hl. Bernhardin von Siena und die franziskanishe Wander-predigt in Italien während des 15, Jahrhunderts* (Freiburg im Breisgau, 1912).

[56] Owst, *Preaching*, 169, modernized.

[57] Thompson, *op. cit.*, 672.

[58] Cutts, *op. cit.*, 120-21.

[59] Willibald, *The Life of Saint Boniface*, G. W. Robinson, tr. (Harvard translations, 1916).

[60] Ernst Benz, *Ecclesia Spiritualis* (Stuttgart, 1934).

[61] Palmer Throop, *Criticism of the Crusade* (Amsterdam, 1940).

[62] J. P. Whitney, *Hildebrandine Essays* (Cambridge, Eng., 1932), 16.

[63]. Moorman, *op. cit.*, 64.

[64] Smith, *op. cit.*, 46.

[65] Walter Map, "De Nugis Curialium," Dist. 1, cap. xxxi, in *Anecdota Oxoniensa* (Oxford, 1914), 61.

Chapter V.   The Ministry in the Time of the Continental
Reformation

[1] John Calvin, *Institutes of the Christian Religon*, 7th American ed. (Philadelphia, 1936), IV.1.10.

[2] "On the Ordering of the Divine Service in the Congregation." W. A. (=Weimar Edition of Luther's *Works*), Vol. 12, pp. 32 f.

[3] W. A. ; *Tischreden (Table Talk)*; Vol. 4, p. 62, l. 5.

[4] W. A. Vol. 6, p. 564.

[5] W. A. Vol. 11, p. 224.

[6] *De potestate papae*, 1523.

[7] *De institutione ministerii ecclesiae*, 1523.

[8] *Church Postil*, 1522.

[9] W. A. Vol. 10¹, Pt. 2, p. 48, l. 5.

[10] W. A. Vol. 34¹, p. 395, l. 14.

[11] W. A. Vol. 43, p. 381, l. 28.

[12] W. A. Vol. 28, p. 479, l. 31.

[13] W. A. Vol. 30², p. 533, l. 20.

[14] *Inst.* IV.3.2.

[15] *Ibid.*, IV.3.1.

[16] *Ibid.*, IV.1.5.

[17] *Pastorale. Das ist Von der waren Seelsorge und dem rechten Hirtendienst wie derselbige in der Kirchen Christi bestellet und verrichtet werden soll* (Strassburg, 1536). Reprinted frequently, also in a Latin translation included (under the title *De vera cura animarum*) in Bucer's *Scripta Anglicana*.

[18] Ulrich Zwingli, *Eine Auswahl aus seinen Schriften* (Zürich, 1918), 410.

[19] W. Koehler, *Züricher Ehegericht*, II (Zürich, 1951), 503. This work contains a very full discussion of all these issues.

[20] *Inst.*, IV.1,4,5.

[21] Quoted from G. Loesche, *Analecta Lutherana et Melanchthonia*, 1891, No. 290, by Hans Achelis, *Lehrbuch der Praktischen Theologie*, II (Leipzig, 1911), 268.

[22] W. A. *Tischr.* Vol. 3, p. 310, 1. 8; Vol. 6, p. 196, 1. 43.

[23] *Ibid.*, Vol. 4, p. 447, 1. 19.

[24] E.A. (Erlangen ed.), 59, 194.

[25] Hermann Werdermann, *Der evangelische Pfarrer in Geschichte und Gegenwart* (Leipzig, 1925), 21.

[26] *Ibid.*

[27] *Vix credibile est, quantus sit fructus consectus. Vita Joh. Calvini,* chap. 13.

[28] *Von der wahren Seelsorge,* 180.

[29] *Inst.,* IV.12.1.

[30] *Ibid.,* IV.12.2.

[31] *Inst.,* IV.12.10.

[32] This is an abbreviation containing all key terms and phrases of the article *De ministris ecclesiae ipsorumque institutione et officio.*

[33] *Inst.,* IV.12.14. (Italics mine.)

[34] *Inst.,* IV.3,16.

[35] *Ibid.,* IV.3.10.

[36] *Ibid.,* IV.3.11.

[37] *Ibid.,* IV.3.15.

[38] *Ibid.,* IV.3.7.

[39] Paul Drews, *Der evangelische Geistliche in der deutschen Vergangenheit,* 2nd ed. (Jena, 1924), 20.

[40] *Ibid.,* 16.

Chapter VI. Priestly Ministries in the Modern Church

[1] From exhortation in "The Form and Manner of Ordering Priests," *Book of Common Prayer* (in the American *Prayer Book,* 538-41); the arguments for ascribing this majestic exhortation to Cranmer (who here writes as Catholic Reformer) rather than to Martin Bucer advanced by W. K. Firminger ("The Ordinal" in W. K. L. Clarke, *Liturgy and Worship,* London, 1932, 671-72) seem to me conclusive—Bucer's *De ordinatione legitima* is not a source of the English Ordinal but a proposed revision of it—see Bucer's own statement in *Scripta Anglicana,* 1577, 504, and editors' note there.

[2] The clause in parentheses was added in 1662 for further clarity; the intention of the service, however, was throughout as noted below.

[3] *Wealth of Nations,* Book V. chap. i, part iii, Article 3.

[4] Sermon, *"A Distinction of Orders in the Church Defended upon Principles of Public Utility,"* William Paley, *Works,* Newport, 1811, IV, Sermon ii.

[5] R. H. Church, *The Oxford Movement,* 1891, chap. 1 (reprinted London, 1922, 4).

[6] John Keble, *The Christian Year,* "Evening" (the source of the hymn, "Sun of My Soul").

[7] H. J. Todd, *Some Account of the Deans of Canterbury,* Canterbury, 1793, 250-251 (quoted in R. D. Middleton, *Magdalen Studies* [London, 1936], xi).

8 J. H. Newman, "John Keble" (review of *Lyra Innocentium*, 1846), in *Essays Critical and Historical*, II, London, 1871, 443-44.

9 On Littlemore see R. D. Middleton, *Newman and Bloxam, the Story of an Oxford Friendship* (London, 1947), chap. 3, 31-50; and on church arrangements generally G. W. Addleshaw, *The Architectural Setting of Anglican Worship*, (London, 1948).

10 *Journal of the Proceedings of the 55th Convention of the Protestant Episcopal Church in the Diocese of New York, 1839*, 31, 33, 43-44; this was Bishop B. T. Onderdonk whose predecessor, the High Churchman John Henry Hobart, had promoted the arrangement of churches with the pulpit behind the Holy Table, as at least making the altar visible—it is occasionally found in the eighteenth century, as in the Wesley Chapel at Bristol, or Bishop Seabury's church at New London, built in 1784-86 (Robert A. Hallam, *Annals of St. James's Church* [New London, 1873], 89-90).

11 Told of Thomas F. Davies, later Bishop of Michigan, 1889-1905, in J. G. H. Barry, *Impressions and Opinions* (New York, 1931), 83-84.

12 Chap. IV; Herbert's Will in G. H. Palmer, ed., *The English Works of George Herbert*, III (Boston, 1905), 218.

13 Sermon, "A Distinction of Orders," *Works*, IV (Newport, 1811), 44.

14 In Roger de Coverly papers, *Spectator*, No. 112, July 9, 1711.

15 Samuel Seabury, *Discourses on Several Subjects*, no. I, part ii, "The Duty of Christ's Ministers," I (Hudson, 1815), 16-18.

16 *The Church of England leaves her Children Free to whom to Open their Griefs* (London, 1850), 3.

17 Thomas Ken, *Edmund*, Book IX, lines 129-30. Herbert's reference to "the temper of his Parish" indicates a circumstance which has affected Anglican as it has Eastern Orthodox practice—namely, that when the choice is open, the ordinary laity seem to prefer married pastors, not necessarily for reasons of suspicion.

18 The rule is therefore one that could be changed; cf. observations of J. Jorgenson, *St. Bridget of Sweden*, II (New York, 1954), 217.

19 Charles Smyth, *Simeon and Church Order* (Cambridge, 1940), 259.

20 Anne Ayres, *The Life and Work of William Augustus Muhlenberg*, 4th ed. (New York, 1889), 69, to which the biographer adds, "His visits had been those of an acquaintance only, and he was free to excuse himself." The episode is dated vaguely some years after Muhlenberg's ministry at Lancaster, 1821-26; the biographer further explains that "he believed, indeed, and inspired others with the belief, that in all ages and in all the parts of Christendom, there have been individuals who, from supreme love to God chose to forego the ordinary ties of earth, remembering our Lord's words, 'He that is able to receive it, let him receive it'; but he condemned entirely the imposition of rules to this end upon organizations or classes, either of men or women" (70). Phillips Brooks was also an unmarried preacher of the Word, though he probably belonged more to the class of clerical bachelors than to that of celibates.

21 Peter F. Anson, *The Call of the Cloister, Religious Communities and Kindred Bodies in the Anglican Communion* (London, 1955), 217-18, 542.

22 The apologist Joseph Butler, for instance, held the wealthy Deanery of St. Paul's along with the relatively poor bishopric of Bristol.

23 G. C. B. Davies, *Henry Phillpotts*, (London, 1954), 92-96, 117-21.

[24] In American exchange, $1400, but in internal purchasing power probably at least twice that sum (as of 1955). The American Missionary Society figure of $500 will be found in W. W. Manvoss, *The Episcopal Church in the United States, 1800-1840* (N. Y., 1938, 120-21).

[25] Oliver Goldsmith, *The Deserted Village,* line 124.

[26] William Oughtred, described in John Aubrey, *Brief Lives, s. v.*

[27] W. Ward, *The Life and Times of Cardinal Wiseman,* 2nd ed., I (London, 1897), 248.

[28] H. P. Liddon, *Clerical Life and Work* (London, 1894), 41. (From an article, "The Priest in His Inner Life," first published in 1856-57); since 1910 the *Breviarium Romanum* appoints this psalm for Sundays and greater Festivals.

[29] Quoted from *Charles Lowder, A Biography* by Maria Farrar (New York, 1883), 157-58.

[30] From Wilson's *Meditations on His Sacred Office (Sacra Privata),* reprinted in *Tracts for the Times,* No. 48: Devotions for Wednesday (in *Works,* 1860, V, 152-53).

[31] Liddon, *op. cit.,* p. 22

[32] As a sample I may quote the rule of Priest-Associates of the Society of St. John the Evangelist (American Congregation) known as the Cowley Fathers; to secure an hour daily for prayer and devotional reading, public or private—to say daily the offices of Morning and Evening Prayer, or the day hours of the Breviary —to celebrate the Holy Eucharist, if possible, every week and on the greater festivals, in all cases fasting from midnight; and if debarred from sacramental, then to make an act of spiritual Communion—to say daily the three Memorials of the Society, and, as opportunity offers, to make use of the missionary Memorials—to read daily a portion of Holy Scripture as God's voice to the soul—to observe the fasts and days of abstinence appointed by the Church—to make sacramental confession to a priest at least once a year, at Easter, and at other times when convenient—to dress as a priest unless especially dispensed. As a modern parallel to Liddon's essay cf. Francis Underhill, "The Priest of Today," in *Feed My Sheep,* F. Underhill, ed. (London, 1927).

[33] Izaak Walton, *Life of George Herbert,* at beginning; S. Jebb, "Life of Ferrar" in J.E.B. Mayor, *Nicholas Ferrar, Two Lives* (Cambridge, 1855), 11. John Evelyn, *Diary,* 1680, Oct. 31-Nov. 7.

[34] Walton, *op. cit.,* near end; Wilson, *Meditations,* Wednesday (*Works,* V, 158-59).

[35] Session XXIII, July 15, 1563, Canon 18.

[36] A rather similar program is provided by the Lutheran Missouri Synod and (although in one institution) by the Greek Orthodox Church of America.

[37] Cf. on this history generally the admirable book of Owen Chadwick, *The Founding of Cuddesdon* (Oxford, 1954), a model of institutional history.

[38] Law was in Deacon's Orders when he refused the oath of allegiance to George I in 1714, and soon after his ordination to the priesthood in 1732 retired from active participation in church affairs. (Henry Broxap, *The Later Nonjurors* (Cambridge, 1924), 313.

[39] Information from the late Professor G. P. Fedotov; see Macarius of Optino, ed. Iulia de Beausobre, *Russian Letters of Direction,* 1834-1850 (Westminster, 1944); Nicholas Arseniev, *Holy Moscow* (London, 1940), especially 89-91; Metropolitan Seraphim, *Die Ostkirche* (Stuttgart, 1950), 290-320.

40 H. L. M. Cary, s.s.j.e., "Revival of the Religious Life," in *Northern Catholicism*, 365.

41 *Church Times*, London, Jan. 16, 1953; Anson, *Call of the Cloister* (London, 1955), 214-17.

42 Henry G. J. Beck, *The Pastoral Care of Souls in South-East France during the Sixth Century* (*Analecta Gregoriana*, LI, series fac. hist. eccles., B., n. 8), (Rome 1950), xiv.

43 The Prayer Book uses it only of bishops; in monastic usage the title "Father" for abbots, or for older, professed, or ordained members of the monastic family, generally is ancient; in modern times it gradually spread, through the active missionary orders doubtless, to the Roman Catholic clergy of Ireland; the heroic ministry of Charles Lowder and other priests during the cholera epidemic of 1866 in London seems to have started the common use of "Father" for nonmonastic Anglicans. (See *Charles Lowder, A Biography*, 227.)

44 Seabury, *Discourses*, I, 37.

45 Biographies exist for most of the men mentioned in this paragraph; there is an interesting portrait of Dolling as "Father Rowley" in Compton Mackenzie, *The Altar Steps*.

46 Ronald Knox, "*Absalom and Abitofhell*," line 56 (*Essays in Satire* [New York, 1930], 83.

47 Address to Anglo-Catholic Congress of 1923, quoted in H. Maynard Smith, *Frank, Bishop of Zanzibar*, (London, 1926), 302.

48 I owe this item to a Belgian illustrated paper sent to me at the time of the Cardinal's death by the late James J. Lyons, S.J., of Santa Clara, then a student at Louvain.

49 Reply of the Archbishops, *Saepius officio*, March 29, 1897, in *Anglican Orders* (English and Latin versions), (London, 1943), XI. Though issued in the names of Archbishops Frederick Temple and William Maclagan, the Reply was mainly drafted by John Wordsworth, Bishop of Salisbury, in consultation with the previous Archbishop of Canterbury, E. F. Benson (see E. W. Watson, *Life of Bishop John Wordsworth* (London, 1915), 326-33).

50 *The Kingdom of Christ* (London, 1843), Pt. II, chap. 2, iv, 341.

51 Reply of the Archbishops, XIX, with footnote quotation from Peter Damian, *Dominus Vobiscum*, viii; Pius X in *Motu Proprio* on church music.

52 Cf. Abbé Michonneau, *Revolution in an Urban Parish*, Eng. tr. (Westminster, 1952); Joost de Blank, *The Parish in Action* (London, 1955); I venture to mention *This Holy Fellowship, The Ancient Faith in the Modern Parish*, Hardy and Pittenger, ed. (New York, 1939).

53 Among recent works cf. *Priesthood*, H. S. Box, ed., (London, 1937); L. Bouyer, *Liturgical Piety*, (South Bend, 1954); more conservatively E. G. Mascall, *Corpus Christi* (London, 1953); and the series of attractive books on the priesthood by Leo J. Trese, e.g. *Vessel of Clay* (New York, 1950).

54 John H. C. Wu, *Beyond East and West* (New York, 1951), 360.

55 *Apophthegmata Patrum*, Theophilus 5 (*Patrologia Graeca* LXV, col. 201).

56 C. Butler, *The Life and Times of Bishop Ullathorne*, II (London, 1926), 295.

57 H. M. Smith, *Frank, Bishop of Zanzibar*, 264, 317 (account of the funeral by an African deacon).

58 G. L. Prestige, *The Life of Charles Gore* (London, 1935), 532-33.

Chapter VII.   The Ministry in the Puritan Age

[1] H. H. Henson, *The Church of England* (London, 1939), 149.

[2] William Haller, *Liberty and Reformation in the Puritan Revolution* (New York, 1955), xi.

[3] George Herbert, *The Country Parson*, chaps. 21, 35; reprinted in *The Preacher and Pastor*, E. A. Park, ed. (New York, 1849), 193, 218.

[4] *Ibid.*, preface.

[5] *Ibid.*, chap. 8, 175.

[6] *Ibid.*, chap. 14, 185.

[7] *Ibid.*, chap. 11, 182.

[8] M. M. Knappen, *Tudor Puritanism* (Chicago, 1939), 469.

[9] *Ibid.*, 383.

[10] Richard Baxter, *The Reformed Pastor* (New York, 1860), 109.

[11] Henry Scougal, "The Importance and Difficulty of the Ministerial Function," reprinted in *Works* (New York, 1846), 206-7.

[12] Thomas Fuller, *The Church History of Britain, III* (London, 1868), Bk. ix, sec. vii, 21-23.

[13] Herbert, *op. cit.*, chap. 7, 174. Cartwright also suggested that preachers should "always endeavor to keep themselves within one hour." Horton Davies, *The Worship of the English Puritans* (London, 1948), 193. This seems to have been the general consensus of opinion.

[14] Fuller, *op. cit.*, III, Bk. ix, sec. v, 3-4.

[15] William Haller, *The Rise of Puritanism* (New York, 1938), 30.

[16] Herbert, *op. cit.*, chap. 7, 172.

[17] William Addison, *The English Country Parson* (London, 1947), 47.

[18] P. M. Dawley, *John Whitgift and the English Reformation* (New York, 1954), 198.

[19] *Ibid.*, 199-203.

[20] *Ibid.*, 205.

[21] Scougal, *op. cit.*, 210.

[22] Richard Baxter, *op cit.*, 75, 128.

[23] *Ibid.*, 170.

[24] *Ibid.*, 169, 170.

[25] Herbert, *op. cit.*, chap. 4, 168.

[26] *Ibid.*, chap. 7, 172. Scougal, *op. cit.*, 218.

[27] Haller, *Rise of Puritanism*, 134-35; Herbert, *op. cit.*, chap. 7, 172-74.

[28] S. C. Carpenter, *The Church in England*, (London, 1954), 330. As late as 1581, Aylmer declared that in the more than three hundred and fifty parishes in Essex, there were not more than seven where the service was performed in the same way. R. G. Usher, *The Reconstruction of the English Church* (New York, 1910), I, 212.

[29] *Ibid.*, 217, 218.

[30] Baxter, *op. cit.*, 130.

[31] *Ibid.*

[32] Horton Davies, *op. cit.*, 43.

[33] Scougal, *op. cit.*, 209-10.

[34] Baxter, *op. cit.*, 30.

[35] Herbert, *op. cit.*, chap. 21, 192-93.

[36] Haller, *Rise of Puritanism*, 63.
[37] Baxter, *op. cit.*, 22, 23, 27, 32, 131.
[38] *Ibid.*, 131, 138.
[39] Herbert, *op. cit.*, chap. 14, 185 f.
[40] Baxter, *op. cit.*, 133-36.
[41] Scougal, *op. cit.*, 208 f.
[42] Baxter, *op. cit.*, 200.
[43] *Ibid.*, 34, 41.
[44] *Ibid.*, 43.
[45] Scougal, *op. cit.*, 210.
[46] *Ibid.*, 218 f.
[47] *Ibid.*, 219.
[48] Baxter, *op. cit.*, 136.
[49] Haller, *Rise of Puritanism*, 92.
[50] Baxter, *op. cit.*, 131.
[51] J. T. McNeill, "Casuistry in the Puritan Age," *Religion in Life*, XII (1942-43), 76.
[52] Richard Baxter, *Works*, IV (London, 1845-47), 926; J. H. Overton, *Life in the English Church, 1660-1714* (London, 1885), 332 f.
[53] This is emphasized by McNeill: "It is not, I think, justifiable to attempt a clear separation . . . between Anglican and Puritan strains. To a large degree each writer uses his own judgment, and where the particular opinions of predecessors are evaluated there is little or no evidence of party alignment." *Op. cit.*, 83
[54] Baxter, *Reformed Pastor*, 131.
[55] Herbert, *op. cit.*, chap. 5, 170.
[56] Baxter, *Works*, I, 267; IV, 934.
[57] *Ibid.*, I, 781; IV, 933.
[58] *Ibid.*, I, 528.
[59] *Ibid.*, I, 267, 376; IV, 934.
[60] *Ibid.*, IV, 933..
[61] McNeill, *op. cit.*, 84.
[62] Scougal, *op. cit.*, 209, 211.
[63] Baxter, *Reformed Pastor*, 132.
[64] Baxter, *Works*, I, 583, 589.
[65] Haller, *Rise of Puritanism*, 58.
[66] Baxter, *Reformed Pastor*, 162 f.
[67] Herbert, *op. cit.*, chap. 2, 166.
[68] Jeremy Taylor, *Works*, IX (London, 1855), xxiii.
[69] Overton, *op. cit.*, 333.
[70] Haller, *Rise of Puritanism*, 23.
[71] *Ibid.*, 81; Carpenter, *op. cit.*, 395.
[72] Haller, *Rise of Puritanism*, 40, 74.
[73] Usher, *op. cit.*, I, 91.
[74] *Ibid.*, 95-99.
[75] Herbert, *op. cit.*, chap. 19, 190.
[76] Baxter, *Reformed Pastor*, 72 f.
[77] Scougal, *op. cit.*, 214.
[78] Herbert, *op. cit.*, chap. 5, 169.
[79] Haller, *Rise of Puritanism*, 28; Knappen, *op. cit.*, 386.

80 J. F. Maclear, "The Making of the Lay Tradition", *Journal of Religion*, XXXIII (1953), 113-36.

81 Herbert, *op. cit.*, chap. 2, 166.

82 Haller, *Rise of Puritanism*, 116.

83 *Ibid.*, 351.

84 Scougal, *op. cit.*, 201.

85 *Ibid.*, 222.

Chapter VIII.   The Rise of the Evangelical Conception of the
Ministry in America: 1607-1850

1 *Minutes of the General Assembly of the Presbyterian Church [Old School] in the U.S.A. with an Appendix.* XI (1846). (Philadelphia, 1846), 355.

2 Andrew Reed and James Matheson, *A Narrative of the Visit to the American Churches, by the Deputation from the Congregational Union of England and Wales,* II (New York, 1836), 194.

3 Quoted in Perry Miller, *The New England Mind from Colony to Province* (Cambridge, 1953), 97.

4 Quoted in William White, *The Case of the Episcopal Churches in the United States Considered,* Richard G. Salomon, ed. (Philadelphia, 1954 [first pub. 1782]), 40.

5 Miller, *From Colony to Province,* 97.

6 "The Simple Cobler of Aggawam" (1647), in Perry Miller and Thomas H. Johnson, *The Puritans* (New York, 1938), 231.

7 In J. Franklin Jameson, ed., *Narratives of New Netherland 1609-1664* (New York, 1909), 125.

8 *The United States Elevated to Glory and Honour. A Sermon Preached before His Excellency Jonathan Trumbull, Governor and Commander in Chief, and the Honorable the General Assembly, of the State of Connecticut, Convened at Hartford, at the Anniversary Election, May 8th, MDCCLXXXIII.* 2d ed. (Worcester, Mass., 1785), 79, 53, 52.

9 *Autobiography,* in Frank L. Mott and Chester E. Jorgenson, *Benjamin Franklin* (New York, 1936), 34.

10 *The United States Elevated to Glory and Honour,* 137, 101.

11 Enoch Pond, *The Young Pastor's Guide: or Lectures on Pastoral Duties* (Bangor, 1844), vi.

12 *The American Church. A Discourse in Behalf of the American Home Missionary Society, Preached in the Cities of New York and Brooklyn, May, 1852* New York, 1852), 19.

13 *The Journals of Henry Melchior Muhlenberg,* trans. Theodore G. Tappert and John W. Doberstein, I (Philadelphia, 1942), 67.

14 Note concise discussion of this point in "The Virginia Clergy; Gov. Gooch's Letters to the Bishop of London 1727-1749," *The Virginia Magazine of History,* XXXII (July, 1924), 214-16.

15 Elizabeth Davidson, *The Establishment of the English Church in Continental American Colonies* (Durham, 1936), 19.

16 Nelson R. Burr, *The Anglican Church in New Jersey* (Philadelphia, 1954), 217-8.

[17] *The Case.* . . , 29.

[18] Burr, *Anglican Church in New Jersey*, 292-94.

[19] *Ibid.*, 253.

[20] *The Case.* . . , 23, 22.

[21] Frederick von Raumer, *America, and the American People*, trans. William V. Turner (New York, 1846), 328, 329.

[22] *Thoughts on the Religious State of the Country with Reasons for Preferring Episcopacy* (New York, 1836), 90-91.

[23] See in Williston Walker, *The Creeds and Platforms of Congregationalism* (New York, 1893), "The Tentative Conclusions of 1646," 191-92; and chap. 17 of the Cambridge Platform, 324-37.

[24] The quotations in this paragraph are all from chap. 8 of Miller's *From Colony to Province*, in the following order, 110, 110, 107, 110, 142, 111.

[25] Charles Beecher, *Autobiography, Correspondence, etc., of Lyman Beecher, D.D.*, (in two vols., New York, 1864), I, 116.

[26] *Recollections* (Boston, 1909), 287, 163.

[27] Leonard J. Trinterud, *The Forming of an American Tradition: A Re-examination of Colonial Presbyterianism* (Philadelphia, 1949).

[28] J. Hector St. John Crevecoeur, *Letters from an American Farmer*. Reprinted from the original edition, with a prefatory note by W. P. Trent and an introduction by Ludwig Lewisohn (New York, 1894), 64.

[29] Alexis de Tocqueville, *Democracy in America*, trans. Henry Reeve, 4th ed., I (New York, 1841), 335.

[30] Mary Bushnell Cheney, *Life and Letters of Horace Bushnell* (New York, 1880), 324.

[31] *Works*, I (Boston, 1852), 14.

[32] F. von Raumer, *American, and the American People*, 338.

[33] *Minutes of the General Assembly of the Presbyterian Church* [New School] *in the U.S.A., at Their Adjourned Meeting in Cincinnati, Ohio; with an Appendix. A.D. 1847* (New York), 160.

[34] Quoted in Evarts B. Greene, *Religion and the State: The Making and Testing of an American Tradition* (New York, 1941), 12.

[35] *A True Declaration of the Estate of the Colonie in Virginia. . . . Published by Aduise and Direction of the Councell of Virginia* (London, 1610), 5. In Peter Force, *Tracts and Other Papers Relating . . . to the Origin, Settlement, and Progress of the Colonies in North America.* . . . . III (Washington, 1844, #1).

[36] *For the Colony in Virginia Britannia. Lavves Diuine, Morall and Martiall, &c.* (London, 1612). In Force, *Tracts*, III. #2, 9, 20.

[37] *Ibid.*, 11; Lyon Gardiner Tyler, ed., *Narratives of Early Virginia 1606-1625* (New York, 1907), 271.

[38] *Lavves Diuine, Morall and Martiall, &c.*, 11.

[39] *Ibid.*, 7.

[40] *Narratives of Early Virginia*, 272.

[41] "Advertisements for the unexperienced Planters of New-England, or any where . . . ," London, 1631. In Edward Arber, ed., *Travels and Works of Captain John Smith*, II (Edinburgh, 1910), 957-58.

[42] *Narratives of Early Virginia*, 271.

[43] Quoted in Arber, ed., *op. cit.*, II, 251.

[44] *The Case.* . . . , 31, 45-46.

45 "The Position of the Evangelical Party in the Episcopal Church," in *Miscellaneous Essays and Reviews*, I (Chicago, 1855), 371-72.

46 *The American Lutheran Church, Historically, Doctrinally, and Practically Delineated, in Several Occasional Discourses* (Springfield, 1852), 247; and *Church Development on Apostolic Principles. An Essay Addressed to the Friends of Biblical Christianity* (Gettysburg, 1850), 40. In keeping with the sentiment of the time, Schmucker held that the "fundamentals" were those enunciated by the Evangelical Alliance in 1846; see *Evangelical Alliance. Report of the Proceedings of the Conference, Held at Freemasons' Hall, London, . . .* 1846 (London, 1847).

47 Wade C. Barclay, *History of Methodist Missions*, II (New York, 1950), 8.

48 John A. James, *An Earnest Ministry the Want of the Times*, Introduction by J. B. Condit (New York, 1848), 40. And see, e.g., the discussion of the objectives of the ministry in *A Practical View of the Common Causes of Inefficiency in the Christian Ministry of the Congregational and Presbyterian Churches of the United States*. By a Baconian Biblist (Philadelphia, 1830), 3 ff.

49 "Propriety and Importance of Efforts to Evangelize the Nation," *The National Preacher*, III (March, 1829), 154.

50 Quoted in Gilbert H. Barnes, *The Anti-Slavery Impulse 1830-1844* (New York, 1933), 17.

51 Andrew P. Peabody, *The Work of the Ministry, A Sermon before the Graduating Class of the Meadville, Pennsylvania Theological School, June 26, 1850* (Boston, 1850), 7.

52 *Democracy in America*, I, 331.

53 *Miscellaneous Essays and Reviews*, II (Chicago, 1855), 106.

54 *History and Character of American Revivals of Religion*, 3d ed. (London, 1832), 2.

55 *Ibid.*, 4-5.

56 *The Young Pastor's Guide: or Lectures on Pastoral Duties* (Bangor, 1844), 187, 140. See also 138, 139.

57 *History and Character of American Revivals of Religion*, 9.

58 *Religion in America* (New York, 1845), 200, 202.

59 "Spiritual Economy of Revivals of Religion," *Quarterly Christian Spectator*, X (1838), 132.

60 *Ibid.*, 143, 144, 145.

61 *Works*, edited with notes by George Willis Cooke, IV (Boston, 1908), 385.

62 George A. Baxter, "Responsibilities of the Ministry and Church," *The American National Preacher*, III (Dec., 1828), 112.

63 *Twenty-four Letters to a Son in the Ministry* (Amherst, 1842), 256, 259. Enoch Pond of Bangor Seminary expressed similar sentiments; see *The Young Pastor's Guide*, 229, 234.

64 *Miscellaneous Essays and Reviews*, I, 355.

65 *An Earnest Ministry*, 39.

66 *Twenty-four Letters . . .* , 93.

67 Taken from Trinterud, *The Forming of an American Tradition*, 89-91.

68 James, *An Earnest Ministry*, 62.

69 *Miscellaneous Essays and Reviews*, I, 331, 332, 338, 339.

70 *The Young Pastor's Guide*, 233.

[71] James M. Hoppin, *The Office and Work of the Ministry* (New York, 1869), 423.

[72] Nicholas Murray, *Preachers and Preaching* (New York, 1860), 26.

[73] H. Harvey, *The Pastor: His Qualifications and Duties* (Philadelphia, 1879), 15-21.

[74] Humphrey, *Twenty-four Letters . . .* , 10-11.

[75] Miller's ministerial license is reproduced in L. E. Froom, *The Prophetic Faith of our Fathers*, IV (Washington, 1954), 495.

[76] See W. W. Sweet, *Religion on the American Frontier, The Baptists 1783-1830* (New York, 1931), 138, 139, etc.

[77] *Ecclesiastical Republicanism: or the Republicanism, Liberality, and Catholicity of Presbytery, in Contrast with Prelacy and Popery* (Boston, 1843), 52, 53.

[78] Letter of John Josselyn, as reproduced in Miller and Johnson, *The Puritans*, 379.

[79] Burr, *Anglican Church in New Jersey*, 180.

[80] See F. B. Tolles, *Meeting House and Counting House . . . 1682-1763* (Chapel Hill, 1948).

[81] *America and the American People*, 338.

[82] *Religion in America*, 189.

[83] W. P. Strickland, ed., *Autobiography of Peter Cartwright, the Backwoods Preacher,* (New York, 1856), 192.

[84] *Ibid.*, 94.

[85] *Domestic Manners of the Americans* (New York, 1904), 109, 113.

[86] *Autobiography*, 456.

[87] *Twenty-four Letters . . .* , 261.

[88] *Plea for the West*, 2d ed. (Cincinnati, 1835), 60-61.

[89] Quoted in Chauncey Fowler, *The Ministers of Connecticut in the Revolution* (Hartford, 1877), 5.

[90] F. von Raumer, *America and the American People*, 338-39.

[91] See S. E. Mead, "American Protestantism during the Revolutionary Epoch," *Church History*, XXII (Dec. 1953), 279-297.

[92] New York, 1932.

[93] *Manuductio ad Ministrium, Directions for a Candidate of the Ministry.* Reproduced from the original edition (Boston, 1726), with a bibliographical note by Thomas J. Holmes and Kenneth Murdock (New York, 1938).

[94] John Clarke, *Letters to a Student in the University of Cambridge, Massachusetts* (Boston, 42-44).

[95] *Manuductio ad Ministerium*; the quotations in this paragraph are from 94, 24, 93, 98, 104, in that order.

[96] *Miscellaneous Essays and Reviews*, I, 103.

[97] *Ibid.*, 104, 107, 110, 114-15, 116.

[98] *Autobiography*. The quotations in these two paragraphs are from 358, 307, 243, 63, and 78, in that order. As late as 1879 Alfred Brunson, one of Cartwright's younger contemporaries who had come to Wisconsin in the 1830's, was still not convinced that there was "anything superior to our old mode of training preachers *in* the work, instead of *for* the work." *A Western Pioneer . . .* , II (Cincinnati, 1879), 328.

[99] *Adventures of Ideas* (New York, 1933), 27-28.

[100] *Modern Religion Movements* (Philadelphia, 1954), 52.

[101] *Ibid.*, 57.

[102] Quoted in Tewkesbury, *Founding . . . .*, 55.

[103] See William O. Shewmaker, "The Training of the Protestant Ministry in the U.S. of America before the Establishment of Theological Seminaries," *Papers of the American Society of Church History*, 2d Series, VI (1921), 73-202; Mary Latimer Gambrell, *Ministerial Training in Eighteenth Century New England* (New York, 1937), Samuel Simpson, "Early Ministerial Training in America," *Papers of the American Society of Church History*, 2d Series, II, 117-29; B. Sadtler, "The Education of Ministers by Private Tutors, before the Establishment of Theological Seminaries," *The Lutheran Church Review*, XII (April, 1894), 167-83.

[104] See Leonard Woolsey Bacon, *A History of American Christianity* (New York, 1901), 251-52; W. W. Sweet, "The Rise of Theological Schools in America," *Church History*, VI (Sept., 1937), 260-73.

[105] Tewkesbury, *Founding . . . ,* 64, 70.

[106] *Ibid.*, 76.

[107] Quoted in *ibid.*, 4-5.

[108] *Ibid.*, 28.

[109] Bela Bates Edwards, "Influence of Eminent Piety on the Intellectual Powers," in *Writings* (Boston, 1853), II, 497-98.

[110] George A. Baxter, "Responsibilities of the Ministry and Church," *The American National Preacher*, III (1828-29), 106.

[111] *Religion in America*, 211, 209.

[112] J. A. James, *An Earnest Ministry*, 20-21.

[113] *An Earnest Ministry*, 52.

[114] *Religion in America*, 195.

[115] *An Earnest Ministry*, 49-50.

[116] *Religion in America*, 190, 124.

[117] *An Earnest Ministry*, 49.

[118] *Autobiography*, 134.

[119] *Ibid.*, 226, 228.

[120] "Denominationalism as a Basis for Ecumenicity; a Seventeenth Century Conception," *Church History*, XXIV (Mar., 1955), 32-50.

[121] *Ibid.*, the quotations are from 33, 40, 35.

[122] See S. E. Mead, "Denominationalism; the Shape of Protestantism in America," *Church History* XXIII (Dec., 1954), 291-320.

[123] "Responsibilities of the Ministry and Church," *The American National Preacher*, III (Dec., 1828), 110-12.

[124] *Domestic Manners of the Americans*, 132-33.

[125] *Religion in America*, 196.

[126] James Bryce, *The American Commonwealth*, 3d ed., II (New York, 1908), 711.

Chapter IX.   The Protestant Ministry in America: 1850 to
the Present

[1] *The Letters of Henry Adams* (1892-1918), Worthington Chauncey Ford, ed., II (Boston and New York, 1938), 279-280.

[2] *The Educaiton of Henry Adams* (Boston, 1927), 53.

[3] *Ibid.*, 457.

[4] Speech "On the Slavery Question," in the *Works of John C. Calhoun,* IV (New York, 1888), 557-58.

[5] Words of a Methodist clergyman as quoted by Ralph B. Morrow in "Northern Methodism in the South during Reconstruction," *Mississippi Valley Historical Review,* XLI, No. 2 (Sept., 1954), 197.

[6] Reply to a Baptist delegation (May 14, 1864); *Complete Works of Abraham Lincoln,* John G. Nicolay and John Hay eds., X (New York, 1894).

[7] Words of Bishop Davis W. Clark of the Methodist Episcopal Church as reported by Hunter Dickinson Farish, *The Circuit Rider Dismounts: A Social History of Southern Methodism, 1865-1900* (Richmond, 1938), 110. Clark's words appear to be typical of the views of many Northern Methodist leaders. Farish gives a detailed description of Northern Methodism's assault on the South.

[8] "There is no part of the world in which ministers of the Gospel are more respected than in the Southern States." A statement made in 1885 by "a distinguished Methodist minister and editor," as quoted by Farish, *ibid.,* 105. I am also drawing heavily on the thesis of W. J. Cash in his *The Mind of the South* (New York, 1941). Cash holds that the Protestant ministry played a significant role in creating the illusion of the idyllic cotton plantation South of the pre-war period.

[9] See Ray H. Abrams, *Preachers Present Arms: A Study of the War Time Attitudes and Activities of the Churches and the Clergy in the United States, 1914-1918* (Philadelphia, 1933).

[10] *Yale Lectures on Preaching* (New York, 1872), 88-90. (Italics added).

[11] This was essentially the experience of the two greatest leaders of the Social Gospel Movement, Washington Gladden and Walter Rauschenbusch.

[12] "Sanitation, and the administration of the city, and politics, and rent, and wages, and the conditions generally under which men work and live between Sundays, are of direct concern to the Christian religion," declared George Hodges. "Christianity has to do with the whole man, because all that enters into the life of man, all that affects his body or his mind, touches his soul, changes for better or worse the man himself, determines his character, and therefore his eternal destiny." (*Faith and Social Service.* Eight lectures delivered before the Lowell Institute, [New York, 1896], 8-9.)

[13] Charles Howard Hopkins, *The Rise of the Social Gospel in American Protestantism, 1865-1915* (New Haven, 1940), 67.

[14] *Religious Movements for Social Betterment* (New York, 1900), 17. The urge to be scientific was in danger of being carried to an extreme. George B. Foster asserted, for example, that "the dream is of a scientific ministry instead of the old religious ministry. . . . The church is not a temple but 'plant.'" *The American Journal of Theology,* XVI, 161.

[15] Henry F. May, *Protestant Churches and Industrial America* (New York, 1949), 139.

[16] Hopkins, *op. cit.*, 108.

[17] This "philosophy" was clearly expressed in a series of lectures delivered in the course in pastoral functions at Yale Divinity School in 1908-1909. "Apparently the minister is not simply to be sent out to shepherd a particular flock," declared Charles S. Macfarland. "He is to serve his community, and human society at large, in any and every way by which his personality may be brought to bear. He goes out into the kingdom of God rather than solely into a church." *The Christian Ministry and the Social Order*, Charles S. Macfarland, ed. (New Haven, 1909), 5 *et passim*.

[18] As quoted by Winthrop S. Hudson, *The Great Tradition of the American Churches* (New York, 1953), 205.

[19] In *America Now: An Inquiry into Civilization in the United States*, Harold E. Stearns, ed. (New York, 1938), 514.

[20] As quoted in Aaron Ignatius Abell, *The Urban Impact on American Protestantism, 1865-1900* (Cambridge, 1943), 162.

[21] *Ibid.*, 118.

[22] See the *Report of the Commission on Country Life* (New York, 1911).

[23] *National Needs and Remedies* (Boston, 1889), 264-65.

[24] Hopkins, *op. cit.*, 296.

[25] Hudson, *op. cit.*, 217.

[26] As quoted by Charles Howard Hopkins, *History of the YMCA in North America* (New York, 1951), 48.

[27] *Op. cit.*, 194.

[28] Carter G. Woodson, *The History of the Negro Church* (Washington, D.C., 1921), 281. W. E. B. Dubois writes: "The preacher is the most unique personality developed by the Negro on American soil. A leader, a politician, an orator, a 'boss,' an intriguer, an idealist—all these he is, and ever, too, the center of a group of men, now twenty, now a thousand in number." (*The Souls of Black Folk*, 190-91.) As quoted in Benjamin Elijah Mays and Joseph William Nicholson, *The Negro's Church* (New York, 1933), 38.

[29] *On the Theological Education of Negro Ministers* prepared by Theological Education in America. Bulletin #4. (Sept., 1955).

[30] See, e.g., George M. Stephenson's discussion of the "Augustana Pastor" in *The Religious Aspects of Swedish Immigration* (Minneapolis, 1932).

[31] See *A History of the Expansion of Christianity*, IV (New York, 1941), chaps. 1 and 2.

[32] *Ibid.*, 75.

[33] An extreme example was Harvard where President Eliot endeavored to put ministerial education in exactly the same category with education in other fields. Eliot believed that ministers, "as a class, and as a necessary consequence of the ordinary manner of their education . . . , are peculiarly liable to be deficient in intellectual candor. . . . No other profession is under such terrible stress of temptation to intellectual dishonesty. . . ." (As quoted by Henry W. James, *Charles W. Eliot*, I [Boston and New York, 1930], 378.)

[34] New York, 1924, 76.

[35] See C. Luther Fry, *The U.S. Looks at Its Churches*, (New York, 1930), 63, 144.

[36] Farish, *The Circuit Rider Dismounts*, 272-73. The Bishop would have found himself in agreement with the sentiments expressed by Archdeacon Mackay-Smith:

"A man mangled by a seminary is worse than one with no preparation, just as weeds in a neglected garden are ranker than those in the wilderness. . . ." "The Ministry and The Times," *Harper's New Magazine,* Vol. 78 (Jan., 1889), 208-9.

[37] *Ibid.,* 265-66.

[38] H. Paul Douglass and Edmund deS. Brunner, *The Protestant Church as a Social Institution,* (New York, 1935), 107. Cf. Kelly, *op. cit.,* 152.

[39] James Bryce, *The American Commonwealth,* II (New York, 1919), 775-77.

[40] As quoted by H. Francis Perry, "The Workingman's Alienation from the Church," *The American Journal of Sociology,* IV (1898-99), 622.

[41] Quoted in *The Churchman* 139:2 (Jan. 12, 1929), 25.

[42] Cf. George P. Schmidt, *The Old Time College President* (New York, 1930), 184.

[43] Andrew Dickson White, *A History of the Warfare of Science with Theology in Christendom,* I (New York, 1897), xi-xii.

[44] These words were written in 1883. James, *Charles W. Eliot,* II, 378.

[45] Everett T. Tomlinson, "The Decline of the Ministry," *World's Work,* IX (Dec., 1904), 5635.

[46] Mark A. May estimated in 1933 that "since 1870 the number of college-graduate men entering the ministry relative to the needs as measured by increasing population, churches, and clergymen has declined at least forty per cent and possibly as much as seventy per cent." (*The Profession of the Ministry,* Vol. II of *"The Education of American Ministers"* [New York, 1934], 25.) It is possible that Professor May's figures are more alarming than conditions actually warranted. No doubt the ministry has in a sense "suffered" as a result of competition with other professions and vocations over the last century. Thus the *percentage* of college graduates entering the ministry has declined. But whether the caliber of men entering this particular profession has declined is debatable.

[47] As quoted by W. A. Brown, *The Minister: His World and His Work* (Nashville, 1937), 26. One woman, responding to a survey conducted by Professor Muray Leiffer, gave a rather ingenuous argument for clerical dress. She supported it on the ground that "so many ministers don't look like anything in particular—not hard enough for businessmen, not unworldly-looking enough for professors, not sharp enough for lawyers, not glamorous enough for actors . . ." that they need something to make them stand out. (*The Layman Looks at the Minister* (N. Y., 1947), 124.

[48] Carl Zollman, *American Civil Church Law* (New York, 1917), 341 *et passim.*

[49] May, *The Education of American Ministers,* II 103-09.

[50] Herman Melville, *Moby Dick* (New York, 1930), 57.

[51] A possible exception is George Whitefield.

[52] Hudson, *op. cit.,* 158.

[53] In William C. Beecher and Samuel Scoville, *A Biography of Rev. Henry Ward Beecher,* 188. As quoted by Ernest Trice Thompson, *Changing Emphases in American Preaching* (Philadelphia, 1943), 69. Bushnell set the mood with two addresses, one delivered before the Porter Rhetorical Society of Andover Seminary in 1866 and the other to the Theological School of Chicago in 1858. The first he called "Pulpit Talent" and the second, significantly enough, "Training for the Pulpit Manward." In *Building Eras in Religion* (New York, 1903), 182-220 and 221-48.

[54] *Op. cit.*, 173.

[55] As quoted by Thompson, *op. cit.*, 75.

[56] May, *The Protestant Churches and Industrial America*, 164.

[57] Hopkins, *The Rise of the Social Gospel in American Protestantism*, 40-41.

[58] The first quotation is from John Watson's lectures delivered in 1896 and the second from William M. Taylor's delivered in 1876. See Batsell Barrett Baxter, *The Heart of the Yale Lectures* (New York, 1947), 5, 123.

[59] Andrew Landale Drummond, *Story of American Protestantism* (Boston, 1950), 375. T. K. Beecher is reported to have remarked on one occasion: "Being a son of Lyman Beecher and a brother of Henry Ward Beecher has been the greatest misfortune of my life." (*Ibid.*)

[60] *Lectures on Preaching* (New York, 1877), 8.

[61] Baxter, *op cit.*, 17-18. See his chapter on "Power of Personality" for many similar sentiments.

[62] *Positive Preaching and the Modern Mind* (New York, 1907), 60.

[63] Sydney E. Ahlstrom, "The Middle Period, 1840-1880," in *The Harvard Divinity School*, George Huntston Williams, ed. (Boston, 1954), 120 ff. Bellows' address was called *The Suspense of Faith: An Address to the Alumni of the Divinity School.*

[64] *The Pulpit and American Life* (New York, 1921), 226.

[65] *The New Preaching* (Nashville, 1930), 61.

[66] Edwin L. Becker, "Role of the Minister in Contemporary Culture," *The Drake University Bulletin on Religion*, XVI (Nov., 1953), 3.

[67] Seward Hiltner reports that since 1923 "several thousand clergy and students have . . . had such training, and its direct influence has been to underscore the importance of a dynamic pastoral psychology as one of the foundations for all the pastoral operations." It in turn has influenced the formal theological curriculum. "Pastoral Theology and Psychology" in *Protestant Thought in the Twentieth Century*, Arnold S. Nash, ed. (New York, 1951), 195.

[68] *In a Day of Social Rebuilding* (New Haven, 1918), 192-93.

Index

Abbots, 30, 77, 94
Abell, A. I., 267
Abortion, and women's movement, 297
Absolution, 158–159
Acadius, Emperor, 63
Achaicus, 8
Acolytes, 51, 52, 65
Acts and Martyrdom of Matthew, 52
Adams, Henry, 250, 251
Addison, 157
Agapes, 39
Ahlstrom, Sydney E., 289
Alexandria, church at, 33, 42–45
Ambrose, Bishop of Milan, 68, 70, 71–73, 78, 81, 83–84, 110
Ambrosiaster, 62, 64
America, colonial churches in, 154, 172; cultural pluralism in 251, 262; evangelicalism in, 207–249; modern Protestantism in, 250–287; religious pluralism in (*see* Denominationalism); salaries of ministers in, 163
American Legion, 291
American Revolution, 211
Ames, William, 196
Anabaptists, 119–120, 135
Anchorites, 30
Ancyra, Council of, 57, 58, 61
Andrewes, Bishop, 152, 157, 171
Angels, 43–44, 45, 69, 80
Anglicanism, adaptation of, in America, 209–210, 213, 219–222; Catholic tendencies in, 151–152; controversy of Puritanism and, 181–182; ministry in, 149–178
Anicetus, Bishop, 32
Ante-Nicene period, ministry in, 29, 30–59
Anticlericalism, 235, 279
Anti-intellectualism, 205
Antioch, church at, 13, 15, 23, 24, 25; Council of, 61, 66
Apollos, 17
Apostles, authority of, 7, 8, 19; division of responsibility among, 5–7; as "fathers and masters," 39; as first ministers,

4–9; as teachers, 17; work of, 7–9
Apostolic Church Order (Cephas), 51, 56–57
Apostolic Constitutions, 62, 64, 75, 77
Apostolic succession, 25, 36, 49, 62, 72, 76
Apostolic Tradition, 51
Archpriest, archdeacons, 66
Ardent, Raoul, 103
Arians, 85
Arles, Council of, 57, 59, 60; Synod of, 66
Arndt, John, 240
Asceticism, 168–169
Association for Pastoral Education, 309
Atheists, 235
Augsburg, Peace of, 117
Augsburg Confession, 110, 137
Augustine, Bishop of Hippo, 66, 68, 71, 73–76, 80, 81, 86, 110, 176, 303
Austen, Jane, 152

Bacon, Leonard, 212
Baez, Joan, 304
Baird, Robert, 223, 227, 234, 245
Bancroft, Archbishop, 186, 202
Baptism, 29, 38–39, 54, 57, 70, 96, 111; by deacons, 64; infant, 119; second, 41, 61; validity of, 74; of women, 52
Baptists, 232, 234, 246, 273
Barbarian invasions, 73, 85
Barnabas, 6, 13
Barnes, Albert, 222, 226, 229, 230, 238, 239
Barth, Karl, 303
Bartholomew, 64
Basil of Caesarea, 77, 110
Basileiad, 77
Baxter George A., 248, 283
Baxter, Richard, 184, 187, 188, 191, 193, 194, 195, 196, 197, 199, 203
Beatles, 304
Bede the Venerable, 103
Beecher, Henry Ward, 257–258, 262, 281, 282, 283, 284
Beecher, Lyman, 216, 218, 225, 236, 257
Beecher, Thomas K. 283
Belgic Confession, 291
Bellows, Henry W., 284
Benedict of Parma, 104

341